VIRGIL'S DOUBLE CROSS

Virgil's Double Cross

DESIGN AND MEANING IN THE *AENEID*

DAVID QUINT

PRINCETON UNIVERSITY PRESS
PRINCETON & OXFORD

Copyright © 2018 by Princeton University Press

Published by Princeton University Press,
41 William Street, Princeton, New Jersey 08540

In the United Kingdom: Princeton University Press,
6 Oxford Street, Woodstock, Oxfordshire OX20 1TR

press.princeton.edu

All Rights Reserved

ISBN 978-0-691-17937-7

ISBN (pbk.) 978-0-691-17938-4

Library of Congress Control Number: 2017949017

British Library Cataloging-in-Publication Data is available

This book has been composed in Arno Pro

Printed on acid-free paper. ∞

Printed in the United States of America

10 9 8 7 6 5 4 3 2 1

For Lina and for Ron and Susan

CONTENTS

Preface ix

Acknowledgments xxi

1 Virgil's Double Cross: Chiasmus
   and the *Aeneid* (Books 1 and 12)   1

2 *Aeacidae Pyrrhi:* Trojans, Romans,
   and Their Greek Doubles (Books 2–3 and 6)   28

3 The Doubleness of Dido (Books 1, 4, 6)   67

4 Sons of Gods in Book 6   82

5 Culture and Nature in Book 8 (Books 7–9)   114

6 The Brothers of Sarpedon:
   The Design of Book 10 (Books 9–11)   150

7 The Second Second Patroclus and the
   End of the *Aeneid* (Books 10 and 12)   180

Bibliography 191

Index 203

PREFACE

THE *AENEID* SECOND-GUESSES ITSELF. Through the actions of Aeneas, it celebrates the history—a history of warfare—that brought Rome to imperial dominance in the Mediterranean and beyond, and that raised Augustus Caesar to one-man rule over Rome. And yet, through its portrayal of those same actions, the poem takes back the celebration and the praise. The opposing readings that the *Aeneid* supports have divided its critics into two camps over the last sixty years. Both camps have found plenty of evidence to back up their views, even if defenders of a patriotic and imperial *Aeneid* play down the self-contradictions of the poem, while proponents of against-the-grain readings pay minimum lip service to its propaganda before launching into their "yes, but …" arguments. Virgil deliberately designed the *Aeneid* in order to produce the double effect that divides critics: it is not an either/or but a both/and. The poem performs its own immanent critique. The case studies in this book aim to flesh out that critique: I want to show how, and ask why, Virgil writes as he does.

This is not an entirely new proposition in itself. Still, it *is* a relatively new proposition after two millennia of reading the *Aeneid*.[1] How did we get here? Both modern critical camps had their origins after World War II and have continued under the Pax Americana. They are still going strong after the breakup

---

1. For a clear-eyed overview of the modern critical history that throws some cold water in advance over these remarks, see Schiesaro, 2006. See also Perkell, 1999, 16–22, for a survey very similar to my own. Thomas, 2001, arguing for the polysemy of the *Aeneid*, traces the history of the notion that the poem is a mouthpiece for Augustus and his regime and shows that it was very much a construction from its beginning. Ziolkowski and Putnam, 2008, provide an encyclopedic sourcebook of views on Virgil up to the beginning of the Renaissance. Ziolkowski, 1993, discusses opinions on Virgil in the twentieth century up to the end of World War II, some of which anticipate postwar developments. A critical view of Virgil as a courtier and propagandist for Augustus came into prominence in the eighteenth century; it anticipated the "Harvard school" by valuing the pathetic passages of the poem (see Harrison, 1967).

of America's only imperial rival. As W. R. Johnson acutely and wittily documents the story in *Darkness Visible* (1976), a European (mostly German) view of the *Aeneid* poem emerged in the 1950s and 1960s that sought to make the poem foundational once again, "one of the bibles of the Western world," as Viktor Pöschl put it in 1950.[2] This was an epic for a war-shattered continent in the course of rebuilding itself. Hitler had self-consciously emulated Augustus: the Third Reich institutionalized barbarity.[3] German scholars such as Pöschl, Vinzenz Buchheit (1963), and G. N. Knauer (1964) nevertheless turned to the *Aeneid* for the idea of a humane, rationally regulated, proto-Christian world order during a Cold War that, like Virgil's depiction of the battle of Actium, pitted West once more against East. They did so even if or especially because protection against barbarians now fell to American centurions. Virgilians in the United States were more uneasy. Publishing in roughly the same years, after the Cuban missile crisis of 1962 but before the escalation of the Vietnam War, scholars whom Johnson dubs "the Harvard School" emphasized what they saw as Virgil's second thoughts, the depictions in the *Aeneid* of individual sufferings and sorrow. Adam Parry (1963) wrote of two voices in the poem and concluded that "all the wonders of the most powerful institution the world has ever known are not necessarily of greater importance than the emptiness of human suffering"; Wendell Clausen (1964) wrote of Virgil's "perception of Roman history as a long Pyrrhic victory of the human spirit."[4] These sound like second thoughts, too, about America's newfound global authority. They also reflect the influence of the North American New Criticism (still widely influential in the mid-1960s), which valued irony and ambivalence, the peculiar power of literature to hold two ideas in balance in the same verbal structure.

More particularly, European and American commentators divided on an age-old controversy about the abrupt ending of the *Aeneid*.[5] Does Aeneas kill an embodiment of *furor* in the person of the suppliant Turnus? Or does Aeneas's own furious anger, as Michael Putnam (1965) argued, belie Anchises'

---

2. Pöschl, 1966, 12.

3. Scobie, 1990; Thomas, 2001, 226–235 on Goebbels and Virgil, 237–259 on the German Virgil scholars; Ziolkowski, 1993.

4. Parry, 1963, 80; Clausen, 1964, 146. Clausen in Horsfall, 1995, 313–314 dates his essay back to the late 1950s. But timing is all: his and Parry's essays had the resonance they had because of the world surrounding them.

5. Lactantius mounted a Christian critique of the end of the *Aeneid* in the *Divine Institutes* (5.10) in the early fourth century; see Lactantius, 1964, 352; see also the sixteenth-century disputes among Italian *letterati* discussed by Seem, 1990.

earlier promise of Roman forbearance to their subject peoples? In Italy, Gian Biagio Conte (1974) acknowledged that the perspectives and sufferings of the victims of Aeneas's mission revealed and relativized the *Aeneid*'s ideological bias but argued that generic expectations constrained Virgil to cling to that ideology and to a positive, constructive view of Rome if he wanted his poem to be an epic at all. For his part, Johnson (writing in the aftermath of the Vietnam War) sought a balance between the two critical schools that could offer an account of "the impartial interplay of opposites" in the *Aeneid*, of Virgil's "unique equilibrium of light and darkness." But as his title suggests, his own attention to the end of the *Aeneid* and to the fury-like Dira that Jupiter, not Juno, sends to finish off Turnus produced a metaphysical reading of the epic far more nihilistic than the mournful readings of the "Harvard School": "It is a terrifying poem."[6] The critical lines had thus been firmly drawn when, a decade later in Great Britain, Philip Hardie (1986) and Francis Cairns (1989) showed just how much an Augustan project informs the epic and, on the other side, R. O. A. M. Lyne (1987) extended Parry's second voice into "further voices" of doubts and sorrows. This was the British decade of Margaret Thatcher, who had enacted a miniature recovery of empire in the Falklands War of 1982, repeating history as deadly farce. In 1993 I wrote on the *Aeneid* in the wake of the first Gulf War (1990–1991), and I write now in 2017, after the second Gulf War and the interventions of the United States and its allies in Iraq and Afghanistan since September 11, 2001. The *Aeneid* has indeed become the Classic for our time, even if not in the way T. S. Eliot proclaimed in 1944; it urgently speaks to us now in the light and darkness of an American peace that is also a long order of wars.[7]

Hardie in 1993 sought, as Johnson had wished to do, to formulate a view of Virgil's epic that could encompass the divided critical opinions. He attributed the poetic power and richness of the poem, as well as its interpretative difficulty, to its setting out strict dualisms (e.g., Jupiter vs. Juno, heaven vs. hell) that turn out to be not so strict (the Dira).

> The whale-bone stiffenings of the epic plot with a rigidly dualistic scheme of the order of things might seem to lead only to an unwelcome simplification and abstraction of the genre. But Virgil's remarkable powers are

---

6. Johnson, 1976, 20, 15.

7. My colleague William Robins at Victoria University reports to me that reading the *Aeneid* has strong resonance for his Toronto students whose families are refugees or emigrants, displaced by recent global conflicts. They see themselves mirrored in Aeneas's exiled Trojans who rebuild versions of their lost homeland in a new country: *sunt lacrimae rerum*.

one step ahead of themselves. Virgil's dualistic scheme already contains its own contradictions and tensions of such a kind that final stability is never attained.[8]

This is very close to what I will argue in the chapters that follow. Johnson's terms, "impartial interplay" and "equilibrium," with their echoes of the New Criticism, have here been replaced by an instability that recalls the "undecidable" self-questioning valued by the deconstructive criticism of the 1980s. My finding of binaries in order to collapse them, and an emphasis, in particular, on chiastic structures of reversal, owe much to this critical turn and to my own relations to the "Yale School." But I am not trying to replace empire by irony-without-end, if that means a figure inescapably embedded in the structures of language itself. Virgil controls the ironies of the *Aeneid* in response to a particular historical situation: the emergence of a new princely regime and promised peace out of the series of civil wars that had torn apart the Roman Republic.[9] Even more than Hardie's description suggests, I believe, the second thoughts or second guesses of the poem about Aeneas, Rome, and Augustus are plotted out in advance: the doubts and fears are as much first thoughts as the affirmation and hopes.

The main claims of my study lie in the readings. They aim to show just how meticulously Virgil crafted the poetry of the *Aeneid*—both in its verbal surface and in its texture of allusions—to produce its opposing senses. This book is about a supreme poet's defining artistry and its uncanny effects. Its analyses expose the strategies of doubling and about-face built into the design of the *Aeneid*. Some principles informing these readings may need to be spelled out. I claim to be recovering authorial intention—with all due caveats about the limitations and (as I suggest below) advantages of my own historical situatedness as reader. It is not "close reading" of the sort recommended by the New Criticism, which rejected intentionality and assumed a minimally informed reader. My detection of verbal patterns presupposes them to have been put in place by Virgil in order to create deliberate effects. The same goes for my tracing of allusions, which I show, in cases like the battles of Book 10, to be systematic.[10] These are methodological presuppositions. If one does not look for a meaningful design intended by the author, one is not likely to find it. If one does not have a tolerance and patience for intricacy and detail,

---

8. Hardie, 1993, 58. See also Conte, 2007, 150–169.
9. Booth, 1974, 5–6 on the conditions of stable irony.
10. Hinds, 1998, distinguishes allusion, which the reader detects and treats as specific cases of authorial intention, from a broader intertextuality of tradition and convention.

one may miss out on the high aesthetic experience that a masterwork like the *Aeneid*—or any well-constructed literary text—has to offer. Part of that experience is the recognition and readerly acceptance—again it's a question of patience—of the contradictions and balance that Hardie describes. Parallels that a text reverses, oppositions that it collapses nonetheless remain in place as parallels and oppositions. The conflicting senses do not have to be resolved one way or the other. Instead, the conflict asks the reader to *think twice*. It challenges simplistic cultural categories and political essentialisms. These return us to the dialogue of the *Aeneid* with its historical context.

Virgil intentionally divides the poem's meanings against each other in a way that its overt Augustan ideology cannot contain. I argue, moreover, that Virgil exploits and makes discernible contradictions in the official ideology itself (a tactic of immanent critique) and at two points above all: the depiction of the last round of Rome's civil wars as a foreign war against Cleopatra and the uncertainty—expressed in the *Aeneid* in the contradictory genealogies of Romulus, from Trojan Iulus in Book 1 or from Italian Silvius in Book 6— about whether the history of the Roman people and the history of the Julian *gens* of Augustus coincided or were separate. These two contradictions go together. Did Augustus refound the state as a fresh beginning with a new if, in fact, age-old legitimacy going back to Iulus-Ascanius, the older Trojan son of Aeneas? Or was Augustus the continuator—he claimed legitimacy as the preserver of the republic and its institutions—of a history that, from Romulus's killing of his twin Remus onward, had led the state into civil strife?[11] In the lens of the *Aeneid*, Rome's civil wars appear at once to be the foundation, justification, and indictment of the Augustan principate. These are questions less about subjectivity and private sorrow than about political grand narratives and the ironies of history.

Virgil introduces doubleness as early as the first simile of the epic, which I analyze in chapter 1, an example of the use of chiastic structures that runs the length of the *Aeneid*. With its reversibility and implicit interchangeability of terms, chiasmus constitutes, I argue here and in subsequent chapters, a

---

11. I have made a similar claim and argument in Quint, 1993, 81–82. "The political contradictions of the *Aeneid* are those of an ideology that preached both forgiveness and revenge, that repetition of the past is disaster, that repetition is a way to overcome the past. The poem in this sense is never less than ideology." Jameson, 2009, 555–562 has redescribed this position in terms of a dialectic that allows "history"—the simultaneity of positive and negative, of success and failure—to appear. The two lineages, Romulan and Julian, were monumentalized in statuary and officially opposed—or united—to each other in the facing porticoes of the Forum of Augustus, begun shortly before Virgil's death and dedicated in 2 BCE; see Zanker, 1988, 113, 210–211.

master-trope of the poem and a symptomatic feature of Virgil's writing. It is a verbal form of the double cross to which my title refers. One such chiasmus is stagily plotted out in the twofold *aristeiai* (battlefield exploits) of Aeneas and Turnus in Book 12. Another frames the poem's last six books through the substitution, first of the fury Allecto, then of the Dira, for Homer's Athenas at the start of the *Iliad* and the end of the *Odyssey*. In chapter 2, I show how simile and narrative, carefully unified in Aeneas's first-person report of the fall of Troy in Book 2, make Aeneas a double and apparently unwitting accomplice of Pyrrhus, the degenerate son of Achilles, in bringing down the house of Priam. The subsequent visit by Aeneas in Book 3 to Buthrotum in Epirus connects this Pyrrhus to the fourth- and third-century BCE Epirote king Pyrrhus, a Greek nemesis to Rome who has been reborn in Cleopatra and defeated again at Actium. In both cases, and in the parade of heroes that Anchises points out to Aeneas in the underworld of Book 6, Rome's foreign enemies become difficult to distinguish from her internal ones. Chapter 3 examines how Virgil self-consciously layers his own invented story of Dido over the older "true" story of the founding queen of Carthage, a demonstration of how later history rewrites the past but also (here criticizing, on its own terms, the earlier story of a chaste Dido) an explanation of the demographic limitations that eventually doomed the Carthaginian empire. Chapter 4 returns to Book 6 and the episode of the underworld. Read as a complex reinterpretation of fame, the book turns inside out the Cumaean sibyl's declaration that it is easy to enter, hard to leave the realm of death. The masses of unremembered dead return to earth in new bodies and identities. The real task that the sibyl ascribes to a few is to live on in human memory and take up residence in Elysium, the afterlife created by the enduring verses of the *Aeneid* itself. The most famous are—or become—sons of gods, like Augustus, son of the deified Julius Caesar. Virgil, the self-conscious image-maker of the new regime, both promotes and debunks the ruler-god cult that the Julians brought to Rome by understanding it as a fiction of the poets.

Book 8, as I describe it in chapter 5, presents ambivalent accounts of the relationship of culture to nature as the Trojans bring wealth and Homeric epic, the high style, into the poor, rustic Italian world of Virgil's *Georgics* and *Eclogues*. The book culminates in the shield of Aeneas fashioned by Vulcan— the *Aeneid*'s emblem of itself as a work of art that is also a technological marvel, a god's-eye view of Roman history, and a weapon of war—measured against the timeless rhythms of a natural world indifferent to it. Chapter 6 documents the painstaking detail with which Virgil constructs and unifies the battle of Book 10 along the models of *Iliad* 16 and 22, so that from moment to moment within any individual duel, a combatant may play multiple, seemingly interchangeable, Homeric roles of victor and victim, now an Achilles, now a Hector, now a Patroclus, now a Sarpedon. The last of these—Sarpedon, the designated victim whom his father Zeus cannot save in the *Iliad*—provides a kind of key, not only to Book 10, but to episodes in the surrounding Books 9 and 11, that spells out the grim equality of war, even the expendability of the hero Aeneas himself. The duels of Book 10 are revisited in chapter 7, which argues for a further model superimposed on the ones I have just laid out for them. The slaying of Pallas by Turnus and the slaying of Lausus by Aeneas are twinned by their dependence on the same mythic model: the killing of Nestor's son Antilochus by Memnon the Ethiopian in the lost cyclical epic, the *Aithiopis*. The modeling of Pallas on Antilochus, the ephebic sexual beloved of Achilles who avenged Antilochus by killing Memnon in turn, goes some way to account for the passion with which Aeneas kills Turnus in the final lines of the *Aeneid*. The model contributes to a series of doublings between Aeneas and Turnus that have become vertiginous by the epic's close: Aeneas kills a series of versions of himself. The poem cannot shake off the specter of Roman civil war to which it seeks to declare an end.

I talk about textual balance, but I do not claim to be impartial. This book avowedly falls into the critical camp of dark readings of the *Aeneid*. It may do so simply by acknowledging that the *Aeneid* has another, dissonant side to it. But I emphasize the poem's reservations and questions, even downright negations, rather than its affirmations. Nevertheless, those affirmations do not go away, and those ayes may still have it: they have prevailed in much of the history of the *Aeneid*'s reception. The very structures of reversal I describe, the structure of irony itself, depend on there being something to reverse, on the positive that is to be negated.[12] They depend on the *Aeneid*'s proposal of a party line—on the epic's ostensible lack of impartiality. Virgil undeniably praises Augustus and Roman power, to the point of identifying them as the principle of cosmic order.[13] I bring twenty-first-century assessments of

---

12. Jameson, 2009, 60: "insofar as it is critical, the dialectic is also what must be called reactive thought."

13. Hardie, 1986. Conte, 1986 (1974), argues that the generic norms of epic, Roman patriotic epic (Naevius, Ennius) in particular, have a kind of *a priori* claim, too, on the interpreter just as they did on Virgil. The very fragmentary state in which Ennius and Naevius come down to us, however, means that we reconstruct them as normative according to our idea of what a Roman epic should be—on the basis of the *Aeneid*. The argument is circular, though it may still be

autocracy and imperialism to my reading of the poem, and it may not be surprising that I find them confirmed in its verses. Or, rather, such assessments have enabled myself and other critics to find unsuspected twists in Virgil's art and messages. For the reversals and contradictions, the negative meanings, *do* come as a surprise, like the last-minute appearance of the Dira at the end of the poem. The *Aeneid*'s veiled criticisms of what it more openly praises have the quality of a trick played on the poem's Roman reader as well as on the *princeps* himself. Because such subterranean meanings have to be excavated, because they produce the thrill of "A-ha!" moments, they may persuade the reader—I include myself—to regard them as deeper "truths" conveyed by the poem.[14] That is their uncanny literary power, but it has to be measured against Virgil's complicity with the real, coercive power of the Augustan state. The *Aeneid* provided for that regime an ideological message whose historical stakes were high and whose legacy has been long-term.

Where did Virgil stand behind the *Aeneid*? We cannot know.[15] The fourth-century *Vita* by Donatus (incorporating information from Suetonius) must be taken with a full shaker of salt.[16] It tells us that Virgil wanted the *Aeneid* to

---

valid. On epic norms, see Barchiesi, 1984 and 2015; Greene, 1963, 1–25, 74–100; Quint, 1993, 21–49.

14. Schiesaro, 2006, 510 drily comments: "In this way, professional critics can reap a handsome dividend. Not only do they succeed as the clever demiurges who hold a lamp to an immortal masterpiece only to reveals its deeper hidden colors; they are also, *eo ipso*, the privileged purveyors of humanistic values, the champions of peace against war, of truth against propaganda, of subversions against oppressive power." One might reply that somebody has to do it.

15. Compare the description by Albert Russell Ascoli of a similar interpretative crux in the case of Ariosto's *Orlando furioso*, a poem modeled on the *Aeneid* but consciously playing for smaller stakes in a minor principality in sixteenth-century Italy: "We might see Ariosto's recourse to oblique and allusive techniques of politico-social criticism as a cunningly subversive strategy calculated to undermine the powers that be—or we could see it instead as a failure of nerve, as an unwillingness to stand up for what one believes, combined with a courtier's readiness to be appropriated by a power structure whose vices he knows all too well ... we should not be too quick to opt for either pole in either of the two oppositions just sketched.... But even this 'open' reading is guided by personal preferences rather than by any ultimate certainty as to the poet's intentions." Ascoli, 2011, 234. Ascoli notes the additional complaint that Ariosto made about the inadequate patronage he received from his Este lords. Virgil appears to have been lavishly compensated.

16. Ziolkowski and Putnam, 2008, 181–198. Horsfall, 1995, 1–25 leaves little of the *Vita* left standing as fact; we read it more as ancient literary criticism.

be burnt, but the reason alleged was its unpolished state. It recounts that Augustus restored to him his Mantuan family farm after the poet had fled for his life when a sword-wielding centurion came to dispossess him. It states that Virgil acquired through patronage a fortune of ten million sesterces—perhaps an exaggeration (one million would have allowed him to enter senatorial rank)—a house on the Esquiline, and a villa in Campania. He was undeniably attached to the Augustan regime.

We might infer something about how Virgil viewed himself in two of the *Aeneid*'s poet-figures, but these, too, are dissimilar. The same ancient critic Donatus tells us that Virgil improvised during recitation a half line and subsequent verse (italicized below) to insert into his description of the trumpeter Misenus in Book 6.

> atque illi Misenum in litore sicco,
> ut uenere, uident indigna morte peremptum,
> Misenum Aeoliden, *quo non praestantior alter*
> *aere ciere uiros Martemque accendere cantu.*
> Hectoris hic magni fuerat comes, Hectora circum
> et lituo pugnas insignis obibat et hasta.
> postquam illum uita uictor spoliauit Achilles,
> Dardanio Aeneae sese fortissimus heros
> addiderat socium, non inferiora secutus. (6.162–170; emphasis added)[17]

> and as they came, they see Misenus on the dry shore, cut off by an unworthy death, Misenus, son of Aeolus, *than whom none was more outstanding in inciting men with his bronze and kindling war with his song.* He had been the companion of great Hector, and next to Hector had engaged in battle, famous for his trumpet and spear. After the victor Achilles had robbed Hector of life, this very brave hero had added himself to the company of Dardanian Aeneas, and followed no lesser arms.

The anecdote of improvisation recounted by Donatus may be improbable,[18] but it valuably draws attention—this was probably its intent—to a self-portrait of the poet of the *Aeneid*, and to what Virgil knew himself to be about. Misenus has transferred epic poetry—his trumpet ("*tubam*"; 6.233) that stirs men to

17. Citations of the *Aeneid* are taken from Mynors, 1969.
18. Conington and Nettleship, 1883–98, 2:446: "to the last degree unlikely."

fight wars[19]—from the *Iliad* of Hector and Achilles to the *Aeneid* itself. And Virgil claims, as Homer's successor, that there has been no falling off. But the long-winded trumpeter—Aeolus in introduced in Book 1 as lord of the winds (1.52)—who plays accompanist (*"comes"*) to the hero fares badly. Misenus madly, dementedly, places his resounding song in competition with the gods—"*personat aequora concha, / demens, et cantu uocat in certamina diuos*" (6.171–172)—and Triton casts him beneath the waves to his death.[20] He has a counterpart in Book 6 in the tyrant Salmoneus, condemned to Tartarus, who rode up and down on his chariot through Elis, also "*demens*" (590) and also the user of bronze, "*aere*" (591), to imitate the sound, "*sonitus*" (6.586), of Jove's thunder and to claim divine honors for himself: he is punished by Jupiter's real thunder.[21] Such are Virgil and his patron, the triumphator Augustus, on their bad days—and this Aeolides Misenus is also linked in the same Book 6 to the "*hortator scelerum Aeolides*" (6.529), the villainous Ulysses who, Deiphobus says, exhorts men to crimes—war crimes—as a "*comes*" (6.528) to the Greek chiefs of the *Iliad*. In this book of divine judgment, Virgil seems to come down hard on himself.

The connection between an "*Aeolides*" and a poet-figure reappears, however, in Book 9, where Turnus kills Clytius and Cretheus, his final victims, during his rampage inside the Trojan camp.[22]

> et Clytium Aeoliden et amicum Crethea Musis,
> Crethea Musarum comitem, cui carmina semper
> et citharae cordi numerosque intendere neruis,
> semper equos atque arma uirum pugnasque canebat. (9.774–777)

> and Clytius, son of Aeolus, and Cretheus friend to the Muses,
> Cretheus the companion of the Muses, whose heart was always in

---

19. Martial identifies Virgil with his war trumpet, the "*tuba*" (8.56.3–4), and does the same for Lucan (10.64.3–4).

20. On Misenus and poetic *hybris*, see Most, 1992, 1022. On Salmoneus, see chapter 4 below.

21. According to Diodorus Siculus (4.68.1–3), Salmoneus was also the son of an Aeolus, an "Aeolides."

22. See Hardie, 1994, 238, who points out that a Cretheus in *Odyssey* 11.237 bears the patronym of "Aeolides." This verse comes directly after the *Odyssey*'s only mention of Salmoneus (11.236): Tyro is the daughter of Salmoneus, wife of Cretheus. Poetic memory almost seems like free association here. But see the coupling of another Cretheus and another Aeolus as Turnus's victims in 12.538–547.

songs and lyres and to draw out numbers on the strings, and he always was singing of horses and arms and the battles of men.

In the dramatic action, Turnus almost kills off the poem itself in the person of this climactic, symbolic casualty, the poet Cretheus. It is a near thing for the Trojans, who now rally to drive Turnus out of their camp and preserve themselves and the rest of the *Aeneid*. "*Arma virum*," sang Cretheus, the opening words of the poem, and here, too, Virgil paints his self-portrait, this time as an epic poet overcome by the very wars that are his subject.[23] He is a "*comes*" first and foremost of the Muses, not to a captain in arms. His fall at the hands of Turnus suggests the fate of poetry before the violence of history, like the Chaonian dove before the eagle described in *Eclogue* 9 (11–13), a passage that possibly alludes to the centurion back home near Mantua.

Here, then, are two figures of the poet, linked to each other by the language of the poem. In Misenus, whose mobilizing war trumpet competes with divine power and who is punished for it, Virgil, whose epic equates Roman power with the voice and will of Jupiter, is self-lacerating. In Cretheus, the poet vulnerable to force, he is self-pitying. Perhaps self-justifying as well: Cretheus may stand up, if in vain, to the war-madness of Turnus. He and the poem are in need of the Augustus-like Aeneas, who is sailing to the rescue.

These linked, evidently personal vignettes afford us glimpses of Virgil in contrary moods about his writing of the *Aeneid*. Their doubleness carries over into the total design of his epic.

23. Hardie, 1994, 239, who also points out in his note to v. 775, that both the Misenus (6.162–165) and Cretheus passages share the figure of *epanelepsis*, a kind of chiastic repetition used here to bring out the pathos of the dying poet.

ACKNOWLEDGMENTS

I HAVE BEEN PRIVILEGED to have shared my work with some great scholars of Virgil. I admire them, and I take the occasion here to thank them for their care and criticism, and for their kindness and friendship. Gian Biagio Conte has been an inspiration and has encouraged my work on the *Aeneid*; the journal he edits, *Materiali e discussioni per l'analisi dei testi classici*, has published four of my essays on the poem. I want to thank him and Giuliana for their hospitality as well as for his help and critical insight. Alessandro Barchiesi has allowed me to present half-baked ideas and to pick his brains on numerous occasions. He also published an article of mine in the journal of which he is the general editor, *Studi italiani di filologia classica*. He read and commented on the entire manuscript of this book. So did Michèle Lowrie, who helped me with corrections and provided me with cues to think about it conceptually. Philip Hardie has read most of these chapters and criticized them with exceptional generosity and literary acumen, and with his encyclopedic knowledge of Virgil and Latin literature; he has furnished me with insights and saved me from some howlers I prefer not to remember. Michael Putnam has supported my work and read parts of this manuscript, which often seems to me to footnote his earlier findings. My debts to all these friends are more than intellectual.

Closer to home, I want to thank my Yale colleagues. Like my other books, this one grew out of teaching. At Yale I have been fortunate to co-teach the *Aeneid* with Christina Kraus on two occasions, and her voice is heard on many of these pages; it has been great fun and I have learned a lot from her. The first time around, Annabel Patterson sat in as an auditor but really as a third pedagogue who questioned all our assumptions about the poem. Annabel has read the manuscript of this book in the same spirit and helped me sharpen its arguments. I have also greatly benefited from conversations with my classicist colleagues, Kirk Freudenburg, Egbert Bakker, and Susanna Morton Braund. Beyond the Department of Classics, Larry Manley, Alexander Welsh, and

Ruth Yeazell have read parts of this book; I value their advice and their friendship. I owe a special debt to David Bromwich who, once again, read a preface of a book of mine and made it more elegant and reader-friendly.

I want to thank Richard Janko, Andreola Rossi, Brian Breed, Cynthia Damon, and Gareth Williams for invitations to speak on material related to this book. Christopher Celenza offered me hospitality at the American Academy in Rome during a brief fact-finding visit that shaped a section of the book. A conversation over dinner with James O'Hara gave me a series of important pointers. I have learned enormously from the studies of Sergio Casali. I also wish to express my gratitude to other interlocutors, Anthony Grafton, Lina Bolzoni, Joshua Scodel, Daniel Javitch, Glenn Most, Sarah Spence, James Nohrnberg, Beth Harper, Sergio Zatti, Ellen Oliensis, Froma Zeitlin, Michael Murrin, Pramit Chaudhuri, Charles Ross, Ayesha Ramachandran, Albert Ascoli, Timothy Hampton, Ronald Levao, Denis Feeney, Joseph Farrell, Elaine Fantham, and James Zetzel. My writing on the *Aeneid* was first encouraged by the late J. Arthur Hanson; I think of him when I read its verses.

I am grateful to Anne Savarese, my editor at Princeton University Press, as well as to my copyeditor, Daniel Simon. My thanks go to Ellen Foos, my production editor on this and my last book from Princeton.

An earlier version of chapter 1 appeared in the *American Journal of Philology* 132 (2011): 273–300 (reprinted with permission of The Johns Hopkins University Press). Part of chapter 2 appeared as a chapter in *Citizens of Discord: Rome and Its Civil Wars*, ed. Brian Breed, Cynthia Damon, and Andreola Rossi (Oxford: Oxford University Press, 2010), 133–144; it has been reproduced here by permission of the Oxford University Press. A version of chapter 3 appeared in *Studi italiani di filologia classica* XIV (2016), Annata CIX: 40–55. Earlier versions of chapters 5 and 6 appeared, respectively, in *Materiali e discussioni per l'analisi dei testi classici* 75 (2015): 9–47 and *Materiali e Discussioni per l'analisi dei testi classici* 47 (2001): 35–36. I am grateful for permission to republish them here. I am also grateful for all the help and suggestions I received from readers and editors.

Unless otherwise noted, English translations are my own.

VIRGIL'S DOUBLE CROSS

1

Virgil's Double Cross

CHIASMUS AND THE *AENEID*

"*FACILIS DESCENSUS*" (6.126), the sibyl of Cumae tells Virgil's Aeneas: it is easy to go down to the underworld, from A to B. The hard part is to get out again and retrace one's steps, "*reuocare gradum*," from B to A. The *Aeneid* is a poem of just such reversals, which can be generally grouped together under the modern term of chiasmus. Quintilian, the first-century CE Roman rhetorician, includes chiasmus, *antimetabole*, among the figures of speech (*figurae verborum*) that he lists in Book 9 of his *Institutio Oratoria*. It is constituted when an initial sequence of terms, *ab*, is subsequently inverted as *ba*. Quintilian defines it as a form of antithesis and gives the following example: "I do not live to eat, but eat to live" (9.3.85). In the same Book 9, Quintilian distinguished between such a figure of speech and a figure of thought (*figura sententiae*). If the first is a form of language or a patterning of words that in most cases departs from grammatical usage, the second concerns the sense or particular mental response the orator seeks to create. In Quintilian's three general categories, it can reinforce proof, rouse emotions, or give the general impression of good and elevated style. Quintilian's metaphor to explain figures of thought compares them to the side-strokes and feints of a skilled swordsman, surreptitious modes of attack that carry the day without one's adversary seeing them coming: they can be hidden persuaders. Figures of thought may contain one or more figures of speech, and the distinction between the two, Quintilian concedes, is not stable. Virgil repeatedly, almost obsessively, turns the figure of chiasmus into a figure of thought in the *Aeneid*. By so doing, he produces some of the epic's most characteristic effects, doubling or splitting its meanings.

Chiasmus gets its shape and name from the cross or X that can be drawn among its terms:

<pre>
        A   B
          x
        B   A
</pre>

If we understand this simple diagram initially to set up two columns or, as is inevitable in epic poetry whose subject is war, two adversarial sides, the operation of chiasmus is to move a term from one side to the other. In a perfect chiasmus the two sides exchange terms and may be themselves interchangeable. The reversal chiasmus effects is thus also a kind of *double cross:* it sets up a binary opposition only to break it down; it assigns one value to one side of an opposition only to load it with the value to which it had been initially opposed. The effect is irony, paradox, or the peculiar sense of saying two things at once: sometimes overtly, sometimes more surreptitiously, as Quintilian's account of figures of thought suggests. When spread over the course of a narrative, the pattern of chiasmus can partake in or resemble *ring composition—abccba*—a characteristic building block of Homeric poetry that became part of the inheritance of classical literary culture.[1] Virgil radicalizes the sense of reversibility of these concentric forms in the *Aeneid*, their potential inversion of meaning and collapse of distinction: A and B risk becoming identical.

Why did Virgil do so? He possessed a sympathetic imagination that perceived the two or more sides of human questions. He inherited this negative capability from Homer and bequeathed it in turn to Shakespeare and Cer-

---

1. Cole, 2008, 76 briefly discusses chiastic framing structures in ancient epic poetry. The appearance of the name of Achilles in the first line of the *Iliad*, Hector's in its last, could be one example, suggesting the epic's divided focus and sympathy with both Greeks and Trojans, and intimating that the funeral of Hector with which the poem ends is Achilles' funeral as well. On ring structure in Homeric epic, see Whitman, 1958. For studies in the figure of chiasmus in ancient literatures, see Welch, 1981. Welch's Virgilian example, 262, is drawn from *Georgics* 4. Martin, 1992, 34–36, discusses the figure of chiasmus in the arrangement of the poems of Virgil's predecessor Catullus and, 156–171, in the organization of Poem 64, the epyllion on the marriage of Peleus and Thetis. Chiasmus has occupied a privileged place in deconstructionist criticism; see the lucid essay of Rodolphe Gasché, 1987, 9–26. I treat chiasmus in the *Aeneid* as a response to a particular historical crisis, a poetic choice rather than as a figure inevitably embedded in the structures of thought and language.

vantes who learned from him.[2] But Virgil's use of chiasmus, the crossing figure that informs small units and episodes, as well as whole books and the larger structure of the *Aeneid*, also responded to a particular moment and crisis in Roman history. We might infer this context from Quintilian's final example of the figure of chiasmus, a grand flourish in Cicero's fourth *Philippic*:

> Si consul Antonius, Brutus hostis; si conservator rei publicae Brutus, hostis Antonius.
> (INST. OR. 9.3.86; PHIL. 4.3.8)[3]

> If Antonius is a consul, Brutus is an enemy; if Brutus is the preserver of the state, the enemy is Antonius.

The Brutus in question is Decimus Brutus, a trusted lieutenant of Julius Caesar, who had lured Caesar to his assassination at the hands of his kinsman Marcus Brutus and the other conspirators on the Ides of March in 44 BCE. Cicero's speech dates from December of the same year, when Decimus Brutus had taken up arms against the then-consul Mark Antony, the leader of the Caesarian cause and faction. With the support of the young Octavian (the future Augustus), Cicero attacked Antony as an enemy of the senate and, in this passage, praises the Bruti as the initial founders and now preservers of republican liberty. His rhetoric effectively strips Antony of his consulship. But the chiasmus already announce its reversibility, only reinforced by its "if" clauses. In the following year Octavian threw his own troops along with those of the senate to raise the siege to which Antony had subjected the army of Brutus at Mutina, where battles were fought in April 43 BCE. Then the adopted son of Caesar double-crossed his senatorial allies. He abruptly changed sides and joined the second triumvirate *with* Antony and Lepidus, abandoning Cicero to the murderous proscriptions that followed. By the end of the year, Cicero was dead and so was Decimus Brutus.

The historical irony that attached to his citation from the fourth *Philippic* could not have escaped Quintilian. Rome's civil wars changed today's friend and legal guardian of the state into tomorrow's enemy and outlaw. Mark Antony was Octavian's rival and enemy, then his partner and brother-in-law,

---

2. The expansive even-handedness of Virgil's imagination and the ambiguity to which it gives rise in his fictions has been much commented upon. See, with different inflections, Parry, 1962; Lyne, 1987; Conte, 1986; Fowler, 1990.

3. Quintilian, 1966, 3:496; Cicero, 2006, 242.

then—as the *Aeneid* itself portrays him—his rival and enemy once again. The struggle between republican constitutionality and Caesarian one-man-rule that Cicero's chiasmus describes was only papered over by the victory of Octavian and the title of Augustus conferred upon him by a senate he now controlled. He was *both* the preserver and enemy of the state. Virgil knew as much in the great epic poem that celebrates and questions the Augustan settlement and the history of civil strife that had led up to it.[4] That history shaped itself into forms of chiasmus, of identical Romans turning into adversaries, of adversaries disclosing their common identity. The propaganda for Augustus, including the *Aeneid*'s depiction of the battle of Actium on the shield of Aeneas in Book 8, declared his struggle with Antony to be a war against Cleopatra, of West against East, but Romans fought Romans nonetheless at Actium and in its aftermath. A central, repeated motif of the *Aeneid* is to collapse the distinction between foreign and civil conflict. Anchises, the father of the hero Aeneas, prophetically pairs Augustus with Romulus, portraying Augustus as a new founder of the Roman state, in the underworld scene of Book 6 (777–807). But Romulus had killed Remus, his *twin*. Virgil's humane instincts, his literary capacity both to see and to write double, were schooled in the fearful, shifting experience of civil war.

This introductory chapter examines instances that show how Virgil writes and thinks through chiastic reversal and doubling. These go back and forth from smaller units—a self-contained vignette of battle in Book 12 and the first simile of the poem in Book 1—to larger narrative structures, "big pictures," of the *Aeneid*. That it largely focuses on the epic's first and last books is not coincidental. Virgil uses chiasmus as a framing device, the container that makes—and simultaneously unmakes—those big pictures.

---

4. There is some critical agreement that the war between the Trojans of Aeneas and the Italians of Turnus, Mezentius, Latinus, and Camilla in Books 7–12 of the *Aeneid* reflects upon Rome's recent history of civil strife. On the relationship between Virgil's epic and the civil wars, see, *inter alia*, Syme, 1939, 304–306, 462–463; Camps, 1969, 95–104; Cairns, 1989, 86–108; Hardie, 1993, 19–32; Horsfall, 2000; Rossi, 2010. Marincola, 2010, and Barchiesi, 2012, suggest that the Social Wars, 91–88 BCE, as well as the civil wars are being recalled in the warfare in Italy in the second half of the epic. On the *Aeneid* and the project of forging national unity, see Toll, 1991, and Toll, 1997; Ando, 2002; Pogorzelski, 2009.

Exhibit X

Virgil programmatically maps out the form of chiasmus on the fighting of epic battle itself in an extended set piece in Book 12 (500–553). Coming late in the *Aeneid*, the fifty-line episode self-consciously epitomizes and comments retrospectively on the warfare of the poem's final four books. It exemplifies the kind of figure—of words and of thought—I seek to identify in the epic.

More than halfway through Book 12, Aeneas finds himself frustrated when the truce is broken that was to hold while he and the Italian hero Turnus fought a man-to-man duel. Their individual combat would have decided the war between Trojans and Latins and assigned to the winner the right to marry the Latin princess Lavinia. The frustration mounts as Juturna, the goddess sister of Turnus, disguised as his charioteer, carries Turnus over the battlefield but avoids a confrontation with Aeneas. The Trojan hero had already been wounded by an anonymous arrow and now has been nearly hit by an enemy spear that carries off the plumes from his helmet. Aeneas finally unleashes his rage, gives up on singling out Turnus, and begins a savage indiscriminate slaughter—"*saeuam nullo discrimine caedem*" (12.498). He starts a Homeric-style *aristeia*, a spree of enemy killing. Meanwhile, Turnus begins an *aristeia* of his own in a separate part of the battlefield. Virgil's verse switches back and forth between the two heroes and suggests how the violence of warfare renders them nearly the same: there is no more discrimination to be made between them than that which they make among their victims.[5] The resulting passage is a particularly intricate instance of a much repeated pattern of Virgilian composition.

> Quis mihi nunc tot acerba deus, quis carmine caedes
> diuersas obitumque ducum, quos aequore toto
> inque uicem nunc Turnus agit, nunc Troius heros,
> expediat? tanton placuit concurrere motu,
> Iuppiter, aeterna gentis in pace futuras?
> Aeneas Rutulum Sucronem (ea prima ruentis   505
> pugna loco statuit Teucros) haud multa morantem
> excipit in latus et, qua fata celerrima, crudum
> transadigit costas et cratis pectoris ensem.

---

5. For an extended reading of the episode, see Mazzocchini, 2010, 273–314.

Turnus equo deiectum Amycum fratremque Dioren,
congressus pedes, hunc uenientem cuspide longa, 510
hunc mucrone ferit, curruque abscisa duorum
suspendit capita et rorantia sanguine portat.
ille Talon Tanaimque neci fortemque Cethegum,
tris uno congressu, et maestum mittit Oniten,
nomen Echionium matrisque genus Peridiae; 515
hic fratres Lycia missos et Apollinis agris
et iuuenem exosum nequiquam bella Menoeten,
Arcada, piscosae cui circum flumina Lernae
ars fuerat pauperque domus nec nota potentum
munera, conductaque pater tellure serebat. 520
ac uelut immissi diuersis partibus ignes
arentem in siluam et uirgulta sonantia lauro,
aut ubi decursu rapido de montibus altis
dant sonitum spumosi amnes et in aequora currunt
quisque suum populatus iter: non segnius ambo 525
Aeneas Turnusque ruunt per proelia; nunc, nunc
fluctuat ira intus, rumpuntur nescia uinci
pectora, nunc totis in uulnera uiribus itur.
　Murranum *hic*, atauos et auorum antiqua sonantem
nomina per regesque actum genus omne Latinos, 530
praecipitem scopulo atque ingentis turbine saxi
excutit effunditque solo: hunc lora et iuga subter
prouoluere rotae, crebro super ungula pulsu
incita nec domini memorum proculcat equorum.
ille ruenti Hyllo animisque immane frementi 535
occurrit telumque aurata ad tempora torquet:
olli per galeam fixo stetit hasta cerebro.
dextera nec tua te, Graium fortissime Cretheu,
eripuit Turno, nec di texere Cupencum
Aenea ueniente sui: dedit obuia ferro 540
pectora, nec misero clipei mora profuit aerei.
te quoque Laurentes uiderunt, Aeole, campi
oppetere et late terram consternere tergo.
occidis, Argiuae quem non potuere phalanges
sternere nec Priami regnorum euersor Achilles; 545
hic tibi mortis erant metae, domus alta sub Ida,

Lyrnesi domus alta, solo Laurente sepulcrum.
totae adeo conuersae acies omnesque Latini,
omnes Dardanidae, Mnestheus acerque Serestus
et Messapus equum domitor et fortis Asilas 550
Tuscorumque phalanx Euandrique Arcades alae,
pro se quisque uiri summa nituntur opum ui;
nec mora nec requies, uasto certamine tendunt.
(12.500–553; emphases added)

What God can unfold for me so many horrors, who in song can tell such diverse slaughter and the death of captains, whom now Turnus, now the Trojan hero drives in turn over all the plain? Was it your will, O Jupiter, that in so great an onslaught should clash nations destined to live in everlasting peace in the future? Aeneas meets Rutulian Sucro (with that combat he started the Trojans' attack) and without much delay strikes him in the side and, where death comes speediest, drives the cruel blade through the ribs that fence the breast. Turnus throws down Amycus and his brother Diores from their horses, assailing them on foot, and strikes the one with the long spear as he advances, the other with his sword; then he hangs their two severed heads on his chariot and bears them away dripping with blood. The *former* ["*ille*"/Aeneas] kills Talon, Tanais, and brave Cethegus, three at one encounter, and dispatches sad Onites of Echionian name, whose mother was Peridia; the *latter* ["*hic*"/Turnus] kills the brothers sent from Lycia and Apollo's fields and Arcadian Menoetes who in youth hated warfare in vain, whose trade and modest house had been around the fish-laden river of Lerna, nor known to him were the gifts of the mighty, and his father sowed on hired soil. As fires driven from opposite sides upon a dry woodland and on crackling laurel thickets, or where, rapidly descending from high mountains, frothing rivers resound and rush to the sea, each laying waste to what stands in its path: with no less energy, Aeneas and Turnus race into battle; now, now wrath surges in them; their breasts that do not know how to yield are bursting, now with all their strength, they rush upon wounds.

With a stone and a huge whirling rock, the *former* ["*hic*"/Aeneas], strikes headlong and strews upon the ground Murranus, who boasts of grandsires and an ancient ancestral name and a whole lineage traced through Latin kings: beneath reins and yoke the chariot wheels rolled him along, and the hooves of his own horses, forgetting their master, trample over him with thick, rhythmic beat. The *latter* ["*ille*"/ Turnus] meets Hyllus who rushed forward, wildly shaking with fury, and whirls a spear at his gold-encircled brow: the weapon went through his helmet and stood fixed in his brain. Nor could your right hand, Cretheus, mightiest of the Greeks, save you from Turnus; nor did his gods protect Cupencus from the oncoming Aeneas; he placed his breast in the sword's path nor did the stay of his bronze shield avail the miserable man. You, too, Aeolus, the Laurentine fields saw perish and stretch your back across the ground: you die, whom the Argive phalanxes could not lay low, nor Achilles, the destroyer of Priam's kingdoms; here were your boundaries of death; yours was a stately house beneath Ida, at Lyrnesus a stately house, Laurentine soil your tomb. And now turned to the battle were all the Latin ranks, all the Trojan descendants of Dardanus, Mnestheus and fierce Serestus, and Messapus breaker of horses and brave Asilas, and the Etruscan phalanx and Evander's Arcadians on the wings, each doing his part, the men struggle with the utmost force of strength; no delay, no rest; they contend in a vast battle.

The symmetry between, indeed the interchangeability of, Aeneas and Turnus is indicated by the repeated use of the *hic* (this one, the *latter*) and *ille* (that one, the *former*) construction, reducing the heroes to pronouns, and by the reversal of these terms halfway through at verse 529 that effectively divides the narrative into two parts, themselves symmetrical. The first *ille/hic* construction, 12.513–520, refers to the sequence in 12.505–512, where first the *former* Aeneas, then the *latter* Turnus, dispatch their victims, a sequence that itself reverses verse 502, which names Turnus first, Aeneas second. The second construction, 12.529–537, refers back to verse 526, where now Aeneas is mentioned first, Turnus second. At this point the very grammatical construction is reversed, as Latin usage also permits, so that *hic* refers to the *former*, *ille* to the *latter*.[6] The pronouns themselves thus become interchangeable, and we can really only identify the heroes by the identities of their victims: in the first construction, *ille* refers to Aeneas, *hic* to Turnus; in the second, *hic* refers to Aeneas, *ille* to Turnus, and we note that the order of the construction is itself reversed: "*ille*...*hic*" in the first case, "*hic*...*ille*" in the second. (See list below.)

---

6. The *ille* of verse 512 and *hic* of 516 could refer back to the sequence of verse 502: "*nunc Turnus agit, nunc Troius heros.*" In this case Virgil would use *hic* and *ille* consistently throughout the passage to refer respectively to "the former" and "the latter." The chiastic structure of the whole passage is only reinforced, however, if the grammatical construction is itself turned inside out. See Mazzocchini, 290, who cites Gransden, 1984, 205.

This one, that one: the whole passage is built out of symmetries, alternations that reveal underlying identity. The simile (12.521–522) that evokes two interchangeable fires burning from opposite sides of a wood is itself doubled by the ensuing comparison (12.523–524) to two, similarly interchangeable, onrushing mountain streams, and the final phrase of the simile, "*quisque suum populatus iter*" (12.525), could refer to the fires as well as to the streams: whether it is a question of fighting fire with fire, or of contrasting fire to its enemy element of water, the violence of the two heroes is all the same. In each of the passage's two sections, Aeneas begins the killing, but the final victim belongs to Turnus and is given a backstory typical of the Homeric warrior killed in battle, a symmetry reinforced by the description of their house or home—"*domus*" (519; 547, 548)—the word itself repeated twice in the second passage.[7] This symmetry itself contains a contrast, the Greek Menoetes who hated war (12.517–520) and the Trojan Aeolus whom neither Greek arms nor Achilles could kill at Troy (12.542–547). The first is a Greek immigrant to Italy from Arcadia, whose modest house—"*pauperque domus*"—as well as the mention of his sharecropping father perhaps reminds us of the house of poor Evander—"*tecta subibant / pauperis Euandri*" (8.359–360)—the Arcadian king named at the very end of the passage (12.551) and of his son Pallas, Turnus's more distinguished Arcadian victim. It may point proleptically to the revenge that Aeneas will shortly take on Turnus for Pallas's death. The second comes from a lofty Trojan house, the twice-mentioned "*domus alta*," and it is intimated that Turnus may succeed where Achilles failed as the "*alius ... Achilles*" (6.89) predicted by the Cumaean sibyl back in Book 6, though the ensuing, long-deferred final duel with Aeneas will prove otherwise. In each case, we feel the pathos not only for the fallen warrior but also for what the process of history depicted in the *Aeneid* is sweeping away, a lost Arcadian pastoral of virtuous, peaceful poverty, a noble Trojan past and home to which there is no return and for which an Italian grave will be a final substitute. Humble and poor, noble and rich: death, in the form of Turnus, equalizes both men; their victims are as interchangeable as the two heroes. At the end of the passage, the heroes themselves are absorbed into the larger clash of the armies, described in the by now familiar pattern of alternation—Latins in 548, Trojans in 549, Latins in 550, Trojan allies, Etruscan and Arcadian, in 551— where the individual is reduced to the anonymous "*quisque*" of verse 552.

---

7. Schein, 1984, 73–76, analyzes such Homeric backstories, noting that they are usually ascribed to the defeated Trojans of the *Iliad*.

The reversal effected by the *hic* and *ille* construction, whereby what had been *ab* becomes *ba*, governs the entire disposition of Turnus and Aeneas in the passage, as the following table suggests:

502 Turnus, Aeneas
505 Aeneas kills Sucro
508 Turnus kills Amycus and Diores
513 (*ille*) Aeneas kills Talon, Tanais, Cethegus, Onites
516 (*hic*) Turnus kills Clarus, Thaemon, Menoetes
526 Aeneas, Turnus
529 (*hic*) Aeneas kills Murranus
535 (*ille*) Turnus kills Hyllus
539 Turnus kills Cretheus
540 Aeneas kills Cupencus
542 Turnus kills Aeolus

The double construction of *hic* and *ille* is itself placed within a set of killings on either side, where the two heroes are named, at or very near the beginning of the verse; the whole sequence begins and ends with Turnus. The resulting pattern is *abba* writ large, something like T-A-T-*ille*-*hic*-A-T-*hic*-*ille*-T-A-T.

XXXX. The larger structure of the passage contains several smaller instances of such chiasmus. In its second section the alternation between Aeneas and Turnus is briefly reversed at 12.539–541, where after Turnus (*ille*) has killed Hyllus, it is Cretheus, the victim of the now-named Turnus, who is mentioned before Cupencus, killed by Aeneas: A-T-T-A. There may be a corresponding pattern in the first section, 12.505–520, where the crescendo of killings in which Aeneas kills one enemy, Sucro, then Turnus kills two brothers, is reversed when Aeneas now kills four warriors—"*tris uno congressu*," the narration pointedly exclaims in awe, plus the unfortunate Onites—while Turnus can manage only three; 1-2-4-3. However interchangeable he seems here, Aeneas is still the top warrior. The verses that describe the new Italian dwelling-place of Aeolus are a near perfect example of the figure.[8]

> hic tibi mortis erant metae, domus alta sub Ida
> Lyrnesi domus alta, solo Laurente sepulcrum. (12.546–547)

> here were your boundaries of death: yours was a stately house beneath Ida, at Lyrnesus a stately house, Laurentine soil your tomb.

8. Mazzocchini, 2000, 298.

The lofty Trojan house of Aeolus, repeated in chiastic reversal (house Ida / Lyrnesus house) from one line to the next, is enclosed on either side by the boundaries of death and the Laurentine earth, which turn out to be synonymous: Aeolus's home reduced to the confines of the grave. The first of these verses is itself chiastic in structure: *"hic"* ("here in Italy") corresponds to *"sub Ida"* ("there at Troy"), *"metae"* to *"domus"*; chiasmus inside chiasmus inside chiasmus. Something similar occurs in the verses that directly follow which expand the poem's perspective from Aeneas and Turnus to the battle around them.

> totae adeo conuersae acies omnesque Latini,
> omnes Dardanidae, Mnestheus acerque Serestus
> et Messapus equum domitor et fortis Asilas
> Tuscorumque phalanx Euandrique Arcades alae. (12.548–551)

> And now turned to the battle were all the Latin ranks, all the Trojan descendants of Dardanus, Mnestheus and fierce Serestus, and Messapus breaker of horses and brave Asilas, and the Etruscan phalanx and the wing of Evander's Arcadians.

The first and fourth of these verses describe battle formations: *"acies"*; *"phalanx … alae."* The second names single Trojan heroes (Mnestheus, Serestus), the third Latin ones (Messapus, Asilas), although the *et* construction and enjambment of the three last lines confuses them together, not only with their named foes but with the massed troops that enclose them in the pattern of the verses. Much as the grave swallows up Aeolus and his noble house, here individual warriors are swallowed up into the nameless ranks of battle, where one combatant *is* in fact interchangeable with another. And, for a moment in the poem, Aeneas and Turnus have joined them.

With its structures of chiasmus within chiasmus and its multiple symmetries, the elaborately wrought passage is an example of Virgil's literary Alexandrianism, and it is almost too precious for the bloody matter it describes. The episode draws attention to itself, too, by its quality of anticlimax. It both holds off and contributes nothing to the real climax of the book and poem, the duel between Aeneas and Turnus. Aeneas gives up on finding Turnus on the battlefield, while Juturna, it will turn out with some kind of recognition on Turnus's part (12.632f.), has steered their chariot far clear of Aeneas. The episode and the killings it depicts are gratuitous and therefore the more symbolically marked. That it need not have taken place at all is picked up in the narrator's bewildered, opening question to Jupiter: how could peoples destined to live together in eternal peace have been permitted to clash so calamitously against one another? In other words, the scenario described by its chiastic parallels and reversals is potentially one of civil war, and the question contains a false naïveté as well as anguish coming from a Roman poet living in the last quarter of the first century BCE. What "eternal peace" could he be talking about, after a half century of internecine war had wracked Rome and destroyed its republic? His words apply not only to the battling Latins, Etruscans, and Trojans of the *Aeneid* who will be united into the Roman state to come, but also to the future crisis of that state and the civil strife that would tear it apart until it was destined to live again in another promised everlasting peace under Augustus, the state's refounder. The contending sides in civil war, already one people, become increasingly indistinguishable in its reciprocal violence. We might say that all warfare, insofar as its combatants all belong to the human family, is a form of civil warfare. That idea, too, underlies the collapse here of what appears to be a war of conquest by Trojan foreigners waged against Italian natives into civil conflict, for the opposition of Latins against the Trojan descendants of Dardanus near the end of the passage (12.548–549) breaks down when we remember that Virgil tells us that Dardanus himself came from Italy to found the Trojan line (3.167–168).[9] Warfare erases distinction—"*nullo discrimine*"—and civil warfare of like against like does so with a literal vengeance and ironic force.

Big Pictures

Virgil has used the figure of chiasmus here specifically to depict this civil-war-within war. But his lived historical experience of Rome's civil wars is never far from the chiastic reversal that becomes a habit of writing and mind throughout the *Aeneid*. The entire epic is structured by the turnaround of its Homeric models, where the *Odyssey* is a narrative "sequel" to the events of the *Iliad*. The *Aeneid*, by contrast, tells a version of the *Odyssey* in its first half, a version of the *Iliad* in its second.[10] The thematic chiasmus effected by this reordering

---

9. For the argument that the Italian ancestry of Dardanus is Virgil's invention, the source of Anchises' "*nouo ... errore*" (3.181), see Buchheit, 1963; Casali, 2007.

10. Even this succession of an Iliadic half on an Odyssean one may be more x-shaped than I describe. It is the contention of G. N. Knauer, 1964, that both halves of the poem equally and simultaneously imitate and allude to both Homeric poems; Cairns, 1989, 177–214 proposes, less convincingly to this writer, that the *Aeneid* as a whole conforms primarily to the model of

transforms Aeneas and his Trojan remnant from vanquished losers of the Trojan War, wandering in search of their Italian homeland in Books 1–6, to the eventually victorious invaders of Italy in Books 7–12, founders of what will eventually become the future Rome, victorious over the world.[11] It was easy, the sibyl tells Aeneas at the midway point, to descend into defeat and death; the hard part is winning one's way back up. In Italy, Aeneas and his followers fight a war that seems uncannily to replay the events at Troy—uncannily at least to these Trojans, less uncannily to the reader who watches Virgil imitating and inverting the *Iliad*. The second six books themselves enact this reversal and divide chiastically. In Books 7–9 the Italians under Turnus, their self-proclaimed new Achilles, seem to be playing the role of Greeks besieging the Trojans in their shoreside camp. In Books 10–12, the roles are exchanged: it becomes clear that Aeneas himself is the true new Achilles of the poem, and his forces take the parts of the *Iliad*'s Greeks while the Latins are forced back to defend their now Troy-like city of Laurentium. In retrospect, the Trojans' camp is now understood to have resembled the Greeks' fortifications by their ships in the *Iliad:* Turnus and the Italians have been playing the role of Homer's Trojans all along.[12]

Versions of chiasmus, or closely related patterns—ring composition, frame structures—govern individual sections, books, and units of the poem.[13] One instance, well known because of Bernard Knox's critical discussion, is the chain of imagery in Book 2 that couples tongue-licking serpents and tongues of flames (2.210–211), the agents first of Laocoon's and then of Troy's destruction, but transformed at the end of the book into the prodigious fire that encircles the brow of Ascanius, *"tactuque innoxia mollis / lambere flamma comas*

---

the *Odyssey*; Dekel, 2012, too, argues for the *Odyssey* as the overall shaping model for the *Aeneid* and as the work through which Virgil reads the *Iliad*.

11. In Quint, 1993, 21–96, I described this two-part structure of the *Aeneid* as a movement between two narrative models, the open-ended, repetitive, circular Odyssean "romance" of the defeated in history to the forward Iliadic teleological narrative of history's winners, those with the power of telling their story with beginning, middle, and end. The Trojan-Romans succeed in Italy in mastering a compulsion to repeat their traumatic loss at Troy by inflicting it on the Italians. Or so they seem to do. I have tried, like them, not to repeat myself in this book, but it is informed by the earlier study.

12. Anderson, 1957; Gransden, 1984.

13. Perhaps the closest critical discussion to the structures of chiasmus that interest me is von Albrecht, 1999, on mirroring. On framing and ring structures, see Harrison, 1976. If its thesis about Pythagorean proportions may not convince, there are still things to be learned from Duckworth, 1962.

et circum tempora pasci"—"and harmless to the touch, the flame licks his soft locks and feeds around his temples" (2.683–684)—the sign that history has now been reversed, a divinely ordained Roman future snatched from the jaws of defeat and disaster, and of the special dispensation given to the Julian line from which Augustus will descend.[14] It is easy enough to spot other examples framing each of the first six books of the epic. "*Pater Anchises*" gives the orders to set sail at the beginning of Book 3 (9), but the book ends with his death and his succession by "*Pater Aeneas*" (716), the father both of Iulus and of his country. In the opening verses of Book 4, Dido burns with love's hidden fire of love (2), and the face and words of Aeneas are fixed in her lovestruck breast—"*haerent infixi pectore uultus / uerbaque*" (4.4–5). At the book's conclusion she has fixed her breast with his sword—"*infixum stridit sub pectore uulnus*" (4.689)—on what will be her funeral pyre, a ghastly literalization of the wounds and fire of love. Book 5 begins with Palinurus unable to pilot the ships of Aeneas to Italy and asking what Neptune has in store (5.8–14); it ends with the death of Palinurus as the sacrifice demanded by Neptune (5.814–871) as the fleet reaches Italian shores.[15] The temple gates at Cumae and the death of Icarus depicted on them at the opening of Book 6 (13–32) correspond to the premature death of Marcellus and the gates of ivory and horn at its end.

Book 1 offers a particularly significant example of this framing device, because Virgil will frame Book 12 around the same terms, just as these opening and closing books frame the entire *Aeneid*. At the end of Book 1, Dido spurs Aeneas into recounting the fall of Troy and his wanderings by asking a series of questions:

> multa super Priamo rogitans, super Hectore multa;
> nunc quibus Aurorae uenisset filius armis,
> nunc quales Diomedis equi, nunc quantus Achilles. (1.750–752)

> asking much about Priam, much about Hector, now about the armor
> in which the son of Dawn had come to Troy, now about what the
> horses of Diomedes were like, now about how great was Achilles.

Dido's question about the armor of Memnon, son of Aurora, arms already mentioned earlier in the account of the reliefs on Dido's temple to Juno (1.489), announces a separate, important motif of the *Aeneid* that will be dis-

---

14. Knox, 1950.
15. Harrison, 1976, 102, 105.

cussed below in chapter 7. For the present argument, it is the last of these three verses that is of concern: Dido's two questions here are not so innocent, and they, too, announce a running, central motif of Virgil's poem. The reader who comes to the *Aeneid* from the *Iliad* will remember that the horses of Diomedes were once those of Aeneas himself, that the Greek hero won them at the same time that in *Iliad* 5 he wounded Aeneas in the thigh with a giant stone, brought him to his knees, and was closing in for the kill when Venus and Apollo intervened and carried Aeneas away.[16] The reader would also remember that Aeneas had to be saved from imminent death a second time when Neptune wrapped him in a cloud and flung him away from battle just as Aeneas was about to throw a giant stone of his own against the onrushing Achilles in *Iliad* 20. Homer used a rescued Aeneas and the motif of the stone as elements to link the *aristeiai* of Diomedes and Achilles in the *Iliad*, the first a rehearsal by a stand-in for the second by that epic's central hero.[17] Neither episode, however, does much credit for Aeneas.

Aeneas himself has remembered: his very first words in the poem, at the onset of the storm sent to his fleet by Juno and the winds of Aeolus, wish that Diomedes had done him in, and in those same words he recalls Achilles as well:

> o Danaum fortissime gentis
> Tydide! mene Iliacis occumbere campis
> non potuisse tuaque animam hanc effundere dextra,
> saeuus ubi Aeacidae telo iacet Hector? (1.96–99)
>
> O Diomede, strongest of the Greeks, why could I not have fallen on
> the fields of Ilium, my life blood spilled by your sword, where fierce
> Hector lies beneath the spear of Achilles?

This opening speech of Aeneas is thus matched at the end of Book 1 by Dido's embarrassing questions that dredge up again the twin defeats he suffered at Troy. Yet these questions may also remind us that Aeneas has survived, in spite of his wish that he had died on Trojan soil, while Achilles is dead and

---

16. Ahl, 1989, 26–27.

17. On the pairing of Diomedes and Achilles in the *Aeneid*, and on the subsequent reversal of the near-defeats of Aeneas at their hands in the final duel that Virgil's hero fights with Turnus, discussed below, see Quint, 1993, 65–83. See also Mackenzie, 1964; Lipking, 1981, 86–88. The Diomedes references are treated separately from their coupling with the figure of Achilles in Lyne, 1987, 133–135; Fletcher, 2006.

Diomedes, as we will subsequently learn in Book 11, has withdrawn from the heroic arena: he rejects (11.242–295) the Italians' invitation to fight against the Trojans once again. Aeneas has a future—the Roman future—still before him, though it will take the rest of the *Aeneid* for him to overcome his traumatic Trojan past.

This past is, in fact, reversed only in the last sixty lines of the poem, in Aeneas's final duel with Turnus. Turnus picks up a huge stone, hurls it at Aeneas, but fails to hit him; he thus fails to reenact the exploit of Diomedes and instead finds himself in the position of the Homeric *Aeneas* confronting Achilles. Aeneas, in turn, casts his spear, wounds Turnus in the thigh and forces *him* to his knees; Aeneas now plays Diomedes, a Diomedes *and* an Achilles, to a Turnus who, in his defeat, again assumes the part of the *Aeneas* of the *Iliad*. The perfect chiasmus formed by Virgil's imitation of Homer at the end of Book 12—Aeneas is saved twice from victorious Greek foes in the *Iliad* so that he can play their parts as victor, in turn, in a replay of the Trojan War in Italy—is only underscored by the book's opening simile comparing Turnus to a wounded lion.

> Poenorum qualis in aruis
> saucius ille graui uenantum uulnere pectus
> tum demum mouet arma leo, gaudetque comantis
> excutiens ceruice toros fixumque latronis
> impauidus frangit telum et fremit ore cruento: (12.4–8)

as in Punic fields a lion, gravely wounded in the breast by hunters, moves to attack, and exults, shaking its thick mane on its neck and fearless breaks the spear fixed in him by the thief, and roars with a bloody mouth.

Commentary on this famous simile has observed how the Punic home of this lion and its wound and adhering spear link Turnus to Dido, compared in pathetic simile back in Book 4 to a wounded doe with an arrow in her side (4.69–73) and bearing, as we have just observed, the wound of love fixed in her breast. Roaring with a bloody mouth, the lion also recalls the description of the Furor (of civil war) that the power of Augustus will conquer and bind in Jupiter's prophecy in Book 1: "*fremet horridus ore cruento*" (1.296). Less noted, but also of primary importance here, is the Homeric model and context that Virgil is imitating. *Both* Diomedes in *Iliad* 5 (136–142) and Achilles in *Iliad* 20 (164–173) are compared to wounded lions, and they are so just before they go out to meet Aeneas in battle. The lesser hero Diomedes is likened to a lion wounded by a single shepherd who goes after the sheep, the greater hero Achilles to a lion pursued by an entire village who, when wounded, seeks in his rage to kill his human hunters themselves. Like the huge stone and the wound in the thigh, like the rescued victim Aeneas, the lion simile is another shared element by which Homer couples the two passages, and once again, Virgil exploits this link: Turnus as lion begins Book 12 as a new Achilles and Diomedes.[18]

The pattern that is outlined in the table below thus creates a chiastic frame within each of Books 1 and 12 but also makes each of the books reflect upon each other as a frame to the entire *Aeneid*.

Book 1.96f. Aeneas remembers Diomedes and Achilles
Book 1.753 Dido asks about Diomedes and Achilles

Book 12.4–9 Turnus as lion: Diomedes and Achilles
Book 12.896f. Aeneas as Diomedes and Achilles

What may in Book 1 seem like Dido rubbing salt in the psychic wounds that Aeneas has acquired in his double defeats at Troy becomes in Book 12 a successful overcoming of the hero's career in the *Iliad*. In the vanquishing of Turnus, Aeneas avenges Homer's treatment of him in Homer's own terms, now

---

18. Incidentally, a related Homeric model explains why the Nisus who slays the sleeping and helpless soldiers in the Italian camp during his night exploit with Euryalus back in Book 9 is given the same tag, "*fremit ore cruento*" (9.341), when he, too, is compared to a hungry lion who creates mayhem in a sheepfold. For Nisus at this moment is repeating the actions of *Diomedes* when he and Ulysses entered by night into the Trojan ranks in the episode of the *Doloneia* in *Iliad* 10, an episode depicted on the walls of Dido's temple at Carthage (1.469–473). Homer's brief comparison of Diomedes to a hungry lion attacking sheep or goats (*Iliad* 10.485–486), which Virgil imitates here, and the carrying off of the horses of Rhesus link the *Doloneia* to the *aristeia* of Diomedes in *Iliad* 5, with its lion and sheep simile and the capture of the horses of Aeneas. It is a kind of seamy and underhanded parody of the hero's great moment of glory (sleeping men really are like sheep before a lion, as opposed to the fighters whom Diomedes kills in Book 5). Virgil picks up on the link by likening both Nisus and Turnus to roaring lions with bloody mouths, two apparent versions of Diomedes. Neither character manages to live up to his Homeric model. Nisus, out of love for Euryalus, runs on the swords of the Rutulians and thereby aborts this Virgilian version of the *Doloneia*. At this point in the *Aeneid*, the Trojans have not yet succeeded in taking on the role of the *Iliad*'s Greeks. They will have done so by Book 12, and so, as we have just observed, it is Aeneas, not Turnus, who will turn out to be the new Diomedes, as well as the new Achilles, in Virgil's second *Iliad* on the fields of Italy.

turned on their head in the new poem that bears the Trojan hero's name. In the person of Aeneas, Virgil traces the progress of his collective people from defeated Trojans to Roman victors, and the poet claims, no less than his hero, to overcome and supersede a Homeric past. This *abba* structure links Dido and Turnus, also linked by the similes of wounded animals: the two primary obstacles to, and victims of, Aeneas. The death wish that Aeneas, faced with the loss of country, wife, and father, expressed in his first words in the poem is transferred to the suicidal Dido, unable to bear the loss of her lover and good name.[19] Aeneas's experience of defeat and identity as victim are taken on by Turnus. It has been much noted that the poem's first sighting of Aeneas, chilled with fear and dismay before the oncoming storm,

> extemplo Aeneae soluuntur frigore membra (1.92)

is repeated and echoed in the chill of death that overtakes Turnus, his breast pierced by the avenging sword of Aeneas in the penultimate verse of the epic.

> ast illi soluuntur frigore membra. (12.951)

The reciprocity and structure of chiasmus could not be more clearly spelled out.

The First Simile

The exchange of identities between Aeneas and Turnus, the sense that Aeneas defeats and kills a version of himself, evokes Virgil's experience of a barely finished, *if* finished, civil war. The first simile of the *Aeneid* immediately announces this historical context. Both because of its position and because of its terms of comparison, the simile is a particularly emblematic instance of the way that Virgil frames his epic. It, too, contains a chiasmus. Thanks in part to an influential reading by Viktor Pöschl, however, the chiasmus has not been generally recognized, and the simile has been imperfectly understood.[20]

At the opening of the poem, Juno has persuaded Aeolus to let loose his imprisoned winds to raise the storm that threatens the fleet of Aeneas. Neptune raises his untroubled head—"*placidum caput*" (1.127)—above the waters, chides the winds, and restores calm to the sea. The god's intervention is then compared in simile to a statesman whose words placate the anger of a populace

---

19. I am grateful to Ruth Yeazell for pointing out this transfer to me.
20. Pöschl, 1962, 20–22.

that has already begun to fall into the violence—"*saeuitque animis*" (1.149)—of civil strife.

> ac ueluti magno in populo cum saepe coorta est
> seditio saeuitque animis ignobile uulgus,
> iamque faces et saxa uolant, furor arma ministrat;
> tum, pietate grauem ac meritis si forte uirum quem
> conspexere, silent arrectisque auribus astant;
> ille regit dictis animos et pectora mulcet:
> sic cunctus pelagi cecidit fragor, aequora postquam
> prospiciens genitor caeloque inuectus aperto
> flectit equos curruque uolans dat lora secundo. (1.148–156)

> As often happens when a great people has begun to riot, and the base mob grows passionately fierce, and now firebrands and stones fly through the air, for furor lends them arms; then if they should see some man eminent for piety and deserved honors, they grow quiet and stand about with attentive ears: he rules their passions with speech and soothes their breasts; just so all the roar of the sea subsided after the father, looking on the waves, driving beneath the clear sky, turns his steeds and, flying onward, gives reins to his responsive chariot.

The simile appears to establish fairly straightforward correspondences: Neptune speaks to the storming winds, the revered statesman speaks to the tumultuous crowd. It already suggests, as Pöschl and others have argued, a political reading of the epic to come.[21] The winds and the great people—and that must be the Roman people—are subject to angrily irrational and violent outbursts. The god and the great statesman—and that must surely be Augustus Caesar, the now-undisputed master of Rome celebrated by Virgil's epic—can reimpose reason and order. Philip Hardie has shown how the winds of Aeolus evoke and are part of the myth of the gigantomachy that runs through the *Aeneid*; in a pattern that was already employed by Hellenistic panegyrists, the political ruler's control is equated with that of the Olympian gods who put down the revolt of the giants that threatens the order of the cosmos itself.[22]

The simile does indeed support such a reading, at least at first glance, and it is a reading so familiar to us that we have become inured to it and perhaps

---

21. Pöschl, 1962, 20–22; G. Williams, 1983, 70–74; Cairns, 1989, 93–95.
22. Hardie, 1986, 90–110.

do not care to take a second look. It could be pointed out that Augustus was not much known as an orator, and Pöschl himself acknowledges that the scenario of the simile looks more like a story recounted by Plutarch about Cato the Younger, the enemy of Caesarism. We may already be alerted to some crossing of terms in the *ac ueluti ... sic* construction of the simile where it is the mutinous crowd that is watching ("*conspexere*") the statesman and Neptune who is looking out on ("*prospiciens*") the sea, a construction that in any event applies the simile to the aftermath of the action to which it is compared. But what is most salient is that the simile does not quite fit the facts of that action. Both Neptune and the statesman-orator bring about calm with their words: "*dicto ... dictis*" (142, 153). But while the statesman does so by soothing the crowd, Neptune's words are of a different kind, and he has something to back them up: his fierce trident.

> Tantane uos generis tenuit fiducia uestri?
> iam caelum terrramque meo sine numine, uenti,
> miscere et tantas audetis tollere moles?
> quos ego—sed motos praestat componere fluctus.
> post mihi non simili poena commissa luetis.
> maturate fugam regique haec dicite uestro:
> non illi imperium pelagi saeuumque tridentem,
> sed mihi sorte datum. (1.132–138)

> Do you have so much trust in your birth? Do you now dare, you winds, to mingle sky and earth without my orders and to raise up such great masses of waves? Whom I—but it is better first to calm the troubled sea. Next time you will not get off so easily for your crimes. Hasten your flight and say these things to your king: not to him, but to me, was given by lot the rule of the sea and the fierce trident.

Neptune may at first appear calm and unperturbed, as placid as the unarmed orator. But the god's anger can be heard to rise as he threatens the winds until he sputters the famous "*quos ego—.*" Words fail him. There had better not be a next time, he thunders, and he reminds them who holds the "*saeuumque tridentem*," the force to make the threat good. Now we should notice that this violence held in reserve allies Neptune verbally *not* with the eloquent statesman in the ensuing simile but with the violent crowd quelled by the statesman's words: the growing ferocity of the mob is described by the verb "*saeuit.*" The mob partakes of the fierce anger of Juno, the poem's frightening divine embodiment of the irrational and violence in the cosmos; she is described as *"saeuae"* in the fourth line of the poem, and again at verse 1.25 her grievances are described as *"saeuique dolores."*[23] But so partakes, it turns out, the power of Neptune, the restorer of order and calm. It is a power he forbears to use, it is true, but that fierce trident stands behind the menacing words that cow the winds. The implied chiastic figure created here looks as follows:

Neptune's words	Winds
Neptune's *"saeuum tridentem"*	
x	
Statesman's words	People *"saeuit"*

Augustus, to repeat, was not much known as an orator, but he did not need to be: he had the legions on his side, and people did as he said—or else. The disparity between the simile and the action of Neptune that it describes suggests that words by themselves may not be enough to quell the stormy passions of political life. Force will be a necessary part of the equation. While Virgil acknowledges the element of violence built into the settlement that Augustus imposed on the Roman political world, he may also be reflecting on the inefficacy of his own words, of the *Aeneid* itself, to bring order and peace to that world. Were we to complete the implied chiasmus, the statesman's words are not much more than blustering wind. The idea is not far-fetched or fetched no farther than from the *Aeneid* itself : *"uentosa in lingua"* (11.390), Turnus later comments on Drances, the poem's unflattering portrait of the unarmed politician. The way that this first simile of the *Aeneid* plots out its own reversal sets a pattern for Virgil's verbal art throughout the ensuing poem: it says two things at the same time.

A Big Picture in the Poem's Second Half

The episode of the sea storm and the ensuing simile opens the *Aeneid* as a whole and is particularly appropriate to its first half modeled on the tempest-tossed wanderings of Odysseus in the *Odyssey*. It also represents a chiastic use of allusion, a reversal of its Homeric model, when it depicts Neptune, the incensed deity who sends the storms that wreck Odysseus, here as the pacifier

---

23. On *"saeuus"* and Juno, see Murrin, 1980, 21–22; Oliensis, 2009, 135–136.

of the winds and waves. One further example of Virgil's chiastic imagination and poetic practice starts with an episode in Book 7 that begins the second half of the poem modeled on the *Iliad*. Summoned by Juno from the underworld, the fury Allecto visits the sleeping hero Turnus and sows discord in Italy: the civil strife to which the storm was compared in the poem's opening simile now becomes literalized.[24] Here, too, the full effect of the passage depends on our appreciation of how it inverts the terms of Homer's fiction. This episode, moreover, will itself be subjected to a reversal at the end of Book 12 with the descent of the Dira from Jupiter's throne, and the two passages provide a chiastic frame to the last six books of the poem.

Turnus is presumably the new and different Achilles—"*alius ... Achilles*" (*Aen.* 6.89)[25]—whom the Sibyl at Cumae predicts will rise in Italy to oppose Aeneas; Turnus at least claims to be such an Achilles himself (9.742). In the first book of the *Iliad* (*Il.* 1.188–222), Hera sends Athena to grab the hair of Achilles as the latter is about to draw his sword against Agamemnon, staying the wrath that Achilles declares is seething in his heart (*Il.* 1.217). The scene of divine intervention attracted ancient allegorists. In the *Homeric Allegories*, the first-century CE Greek writer Heraclitus, probably following earlier commentators, noted that Plato divides the soul into reason, located in the head, where Pallas Athena, the divine incarnation of wisdom sent down to earth by Hera, has seized Achilles, and into two irrational parts, anger or *thymos*, which resides in the heart, and lust nestled still further down in the liver.

> Achilles, full of anger, takes up his sword. He has let the reason in his head be darkened by the anger that is shaking his chest, but soon his reason has brought him to his senses, torn him away from this course of action, and led him into a better state. This conversion with the aid of reason is what the Homeric poems identify quite rightly with Athena. (19.5)[26]

This allegoresis of the opening of the *Iliad* provides a key to understanding its ensuing action in terms of the control of anger, an anger that finally relents in the reconciliation scene between Achilles and the suppliant Priam in Book 24, lending Homer's epic itself a kind of chiastic frame.

Virgil has this episode in mind as well as the allegorical tradition that surrounded it, and he characteristically turns them inside out. In the correspond-

---

24. Wofford, 1992, 120–135.
25. Traina, 1997, 78–79.
26. Heraclitus, 1962, 23.

ing scene in the book that begins Virgil's Italian *Iliad*, Juno, the Roman Hera, once more intervenes. In place of Homer's Athena, Juno sends Allecto—the embodiment of furor and civil discord rather than of reason—to incite Turnus to fight against Aeneas. When the Italian hero, in fact, seems reluctant to be prodded into action (7.435–444), the fury casts a firebrand into his chest, the seat of wrath; Turnus jumps up, crying for arms, and the ensuing simile that compares him to a cauldron overflowing above a heaped-up fire (7.462–466) recalls and may echo the seething sea in the storm in Book 1 (compare 7.464 to 1.107). In Virgil's rewriting of Homer's Athena taming Achilles, his second *Iliad* begins with the divine fomenting rather than the divine suppression of heroic anger. If Neptune can quickly quiet the storm sent by Juno in Book 1, Allecto ignites a firestorm that it will take all six books of the second half of the *Aeneid* to extinguish, and then only by transferring that anger in its final lines to Aeneas, the poem's true Achilles, kindled by the furies and terrible in his anger—"*furiis accensus et ira / terribilis*" (12.946–947)—as he overcomes his hesitation and kills the suppliant Turnus. Virgil's Juno may come to a settlement with Jupiter, but there is no final scene of human reconciliation in his Roman version of the *Iliad*.[27]

Instead, Jupiter sends down from Olympus one of the twin Dirae who sit beneath his throne. The presence of these chthonic furies among the heavenly deities is apparently Virgil's invention and is the clinching evidence for W. R. Johnson's bleak reading of the *Aeneid*'s theodicy.[28] As in the opening divine sequence of the poem, where Juno's epithet "*saeua*" was transferred to the trident of her brother Neptune, so is it now transferred to her brother and ruler, Jupiter, keeper of these Dirae: "*hae Iouis ad solium saeuique in limine regis / apparent*" ("they stand ready by throne of cruel Jupiter, on the threshold of the king"; 12.849–50). That "*saeui*" governs both "*Iouis*" and "*regis*" only

---

27. And perhaps for good reason. Critics normally see in the ending of the *Aeneid* the shortcoming of Aeneas measured against the magnanimity of Achilles in his acceptance of Priam's ransom for the body of Hector, a sublime moment of human solidarity between enemies. See Putnam, 1981; Putnam, 2011; Barchiesi, 1984, 106–122; Boyle, 1993. But the brutal final scene of the *Aeneid* may equally be understood as Virgil's criticism of a too easy Homeric ending that is only a temporary truce—and involves a less than sublime monetary transaction, as the reliefs on Dido's temple show (1.484)—before Achilles and the Greeks will destroy Priam and Troy. The poems may mutually criticize each other.

28. Johnson, 1976, 114–134; Putnam, 1965, 194–198. See also Hübner, 1970; Feeney, 1991, 163–173. On Allecto as a figure of civil discord, see Heinze, 1993, 148–150, developed by Fraenkel, 1945.

accentuates its centrality and the crossover that confuses the difference between Juno's savage rage and Jupiter's cosmic rulership. Like sister, like brother, the smiling Jupiter tells her (12.830–831). That the Dirae are the two sisters of the fury Megaera (12.845–847) seems to identify them with Tisiphone (see 6.555, 571; 10.761) and the same Allecto who has instigated the war in Italy in Book 7 and who, throwing off her disguise, introduces herself to Turnus as having come from the seat of the dread sisters, "*dirarum ab sede sororum*" (7.454). She echoes her introduction into the poem itself where Juno has summoned her from the seat of the dread goddesses, "*dirarum ab sede dearum*" (7.324). The second half of the *Aeneid* begins with the ascent from hell of a fury to Turnus, and Allecto is last seen diving back into the depths of Cocytus (7.563–571). It now ends with the descent from heaven of a fury to Turnus—the chances appear to be fifty-fifty that they are one and the same fury.[29] The beating of the wings of the Dira against the terrified hero's shield—"*sonans clipeumque euerberat alis*" (12.866)—echoes the cracking of Allecto's whip—"*uerberaque insonuit*" (7.451)—with which she made herself known to Turnus. Where Allecto roused Turnus from his slumber and apparent unwillingness to wage war, the Dira returns him to his first "*torpor*" (12.867), though this time to the numbness of fear, shortly to be succeeded by the sleep of death.[30] It turns him into a mirror image of the Aeneas who has experienced such moments of paralysis before divine portents three times earlier in the poem: "*arrectaeque horrore comae et uox faucibus haesit*" (12.868=2.773, 3.48, 4.280). Here, too, difference blurs between the two antagonists of the last six books of the poem.

What had begun this Iliadic half of the *Aeneid* as an infernal inversion of the heavenly descent of Athena in *Iliad* 1 to stay the anger and sword of Achilles and that rather saw Allecto inciting Turnus into arms now is itself inverted, a chiasmus of chiasmus, but this does not return us to the descent of Homer's Athena but to a still further distortion of it. No goddess descends from Virgil's heaven, but a fury in her place. Furthermore, this fury not only replaces the Athena of the opening the *Iliad* but, as Sarah Spence has pointed out, the

---

29. Hübner, 1970, 34–35; Pöschl, 1962, 133; Putnam, 1965, 198; and, on the confusion of heaven and hell, Hardie, 1993, 73–76. Lyne, 1987, 90–93, argues that the Dira may be Allecto herself; Hershkowitz, 1998, 114–124, upholds the difference between infernal and celestial furies. One might note the use of the epithet, "*sata Nocte*" ("offspring of Night"), applied to both Allecto (7.331) and the Dira (12.860).

30. See Putnam, 1965, 198, on the Dira and Somnus in Book 5.

Athena who also descends at the *end* of the *Odyssey* (24.487f.).[31] The goddess comes to earth to stop the fighting in Ithaca, after her colloquy with Zeus and after he has ordained an end to further civil war between Odysseus and the relatives of the suitors, a passage that Virgil has just recalled in the pact between Jupiter and Juno.[32] The Dira takes on the form of a little bird that Servius identifies as the *noctua*, the night owl sacred to Athena, but she puts no stop to the killing. "*Pallas te hoc uulnere, Pallas / immolat*" ("Pallas, Pallas sacrifices you with this wound"; 12.948–959), says Aeneas as he plunges his sword beneath the breast of Turnus and avenges Pallas, the last of the Arcadians. The goddess of the same name is not in sight. Virgil's double chiasmus writes her allegorical rationality and her pacifying roles at the beginning of the *Iliad* and at the end of the *Odyssey*—the frame of the two Homeric poems put together—out of the *Aeneid*.

Making and Unmaking

The crisscrossings of chiasmus constitute a figure of Virgil's thought in the *Aeneid*. In these examples of chiasmus, and in other cases of reversals and doublings that we shall encounter in subsequent chapters of this study, the epic stages the simultaneous assertion and negation of poetic figure and thought as they seek to make sense out of its subject: the violence and twists of history that have made the Rome of Virgil's time. Like warfare itself, chiasmus plots out distinctions and draws up sides, only to reveal an underlying reciprocity that undoes them or turns them into paradox. Such insistent, repeated formal patterns that contain their own reversal are a particular achievement of the *Aeneid*, rarely matched in other great works of literature. They aesthetically distance the poem from—and thus invite reflection upon—its own making of form and meaning.

Epic poetry takes the explanation of war as its generic task. The *Aeneid* specifically proposes to interpret Roman history for both patriotic and Augustan political purposes, a history that Virgil summarizes as a succession of wars—

---

31. Spence, 1999, 159–163.

32. For the reconciliation of Jupiter and Juno and the colloquy of Zeus and Athena at the end of the *Odyssey*, see Quint, 1993, 75–76. But perhaps the Dira also comes in place of the Athena of the *Iliad*, who descends in Book 22, first to urge Achilles on (213–224), then to take the form of Deiphobus and trick Hector into facing Achilles (225–247). Virgil may be recalling the *Iliad*'s own chiasmus built around the goddess, who restrains Achilles against his Greek commander, stirs him against his Trojan foe.

"*pugnataque in ordine bella*" (8.629)—at the opening of the ekphrastic description of the shield that the god Vulcan sculpts for Aeneas in Book 8. To give order to and explain such a history of violence, epic requires *both* its ascription to a divine plan *and* a poetic artistry that rivals the divine maker in striving for a unified wholeness of form. With its circular shape and cosmic associations, the shield is an emblem of such form, the poem's miniature version of itself.[33] Poetic totality and timeless, divine authority might each be taken to be the metaphor of the other, as if to say it all at once were the same as saying it once and for all. The shield's account alternates between foreign war (the Sabines, Alba, the Gauls, Veii) and civil war (Tarquin, Catiline, Cato) and in the case of Actium masks or fuses the latter with the former. We have to decide whether these are fought "in order," in some kind of meaningful form, like the *"longo ordine"* (8.722) into which the power of Rome and Augustus have arranged the foreign peoples they have conquered in the triumphal procession led before him at the close of the shield's description.[34] Have all these events been leading up to the endpoint of Actium, and have Augustus and the divine artist Vulcan retrospectively turned those chronologically ordered events into an order of meaning, a history, and a lasting one, *"longo"* in the sense of long-term: the empire without end and the peace, the closing of the gates of war, promised in Jupiter's prophecy to Venus in Book 1 (1.278–294)?[35] Or will that order itself collapse back into an unending sequence, one damned war after another, of a finally undifferentiated violence? The appearance of *"ordine"* at the beginning and end of the depiction of the shield is itself a small version of chiastic ring composition that self-consciously notes that its function, as rhetorical figure, is precisely to order the passage it contains. At the same time the figure reveals its inherent capacity to double-cross.

In his *Aesthetic Theory*, Theodor Adorno writes in response to Hegel that "works of art do not constitute at all that seamless unity or totality of form which aesthetic reflection always claims they have. In terms of their structure, they are not organisms; at least the finest products can be said to be hostile to the organic aspect in them which they expose as illusory and affirmative."[36] Adorno upholds a deliberate fragmentation and blockage of communication in modernist art. But something similar, he acknowledges, occurs in the art to

---

33. Hardie, 1986, 336–376.
34. See the remarks of Gransden, 1976, 162, and Barchiesi, 2005, 288–289.
35. Putnam, 1998, 152. On the question of justice and the shield's view of Rome's imperial history, see Zetzel, 1996; Rossi 2010.
36. Adorno, 1984, 132.

which the modernist aesthetic may seem to be most opposed: in unified classical forms—perhaps in epic above all—that nonetheless point to the cracks in their marble façade. Only much later does Adorno explain what might be affirmative in the illusion of organic unity. When he turns to and salvages "traditional art," he adds an idealist admonition and describes a "conservative moment" that is

> the opposite of the disintegrative one that constitutes the truth of art today. The first lives on in the second to the extent to which it, *qua* forming agent, recognizes the resistance of its underlying material. In terms of this notion *art is similar to peace* [emphasis added]. Without a perspective on peace art would be untrue, just as untrue as it is when it anticipates a state of reconciliation. Even the beautiful in art is the illusion of peace in empirical reality. Even the repressive force of form moves towards that when it unites hostile, centrifugal particulars.[37]

Artistic form as repression redeems itself in two ways: by its recognition of the recalcitrance of its underlying material—in the last analysis, of living human history—to its impositions; by offering the dream, nevertheless, of a peace that has not been achieved. It is the self-confessed false dream of Virgil's Gate of Ivory whose formal completeness or "totality of form"—the punning "*perfecta*" of "*candenti perfecta nitens elephanto*" (6.895)—may itself be illusory but nonetheless speaks for human hope: for what Rome and Augustus might or should be. The Gate of Ivory follows and seems to comment on another version of Roman history viewed in and as a "*longo ordine*" (6.754), the procession of his descendants that pass in front of Anchises in the underworld, and, like the shield of Aeneas, the gate simulates—and in this case explicitly denies—epic totality. Adorno's terms suggest an analogous logic governing Virgil's turn to the self-negating figure of chiasmus: as a means to couple inseparably the utopian aspiration to form with its critique. Chiasmus beautifully patterns hostile elements into both affirmative unity *and* disintegrating contradiction. The *Aeneid* dreams of peace from inside a state of war: like the Roman nation it describes, it is a poem divided against itself.

37. *Ibid.*, 366.

2

Aeacidae Pyrrhi

TROJANS, ROMANS, AND
THEIR GREEK DOUBLES

BOOKS 2 AND 3 are the Greek books of the *Aeneid*. In Book 2, Aeneas narrates at Dido's banquet the destruction of Troy by the Greeks and by the gods. In Book 3, he recounts his subsequent wanderings, for the most part through Greek lands. These books generate structures of doubling, chiasmus, and internal division characteristic of Virgil's art and of the *Aeneid*'s response to Roman history and to Augustan ideology. Some of these are: Aeneas as both narrator and participant in the destruction of Troy, both above and inside the action; divine plan versus human agency in the city's fall; victorious Greeks in Book 2 versus Greek victims and suppliants in Book 3; Greek hostility and hatred versus Carthaginian hospitality and (excessive) love in the surrounding Books 1 and 4; Greeks and Carthaginians as the double historical enemies of Rome.

One link between the two books is the figure of Pyrrhus, the son of Achilles, who leads the final assault on the palace of Priam and who slays the old king in Book 2. In Book 3, we learn that Pyrrhus himself has been killed and that his lands have passed to the Trojan Helenus and Andromache. This turning of the tables on Pyrrhus foretells the future domination of the Greek East by Rome and the descendants of the Trojans, in the same way that the downfall of Dido in the Carthaginian Books 1 and 4 predicts the future fall of Carthage before Roman arms and that rival city's annihilation. History will reverse the fortunes of the Greeks and Carthaginians. The first half of the *Aeneid* appears to deal with the foreign enemies of Rome. The poem's second half, the war in Italy, evokes the recent civil and social wars that followed her foreign conquests: the anguished poet-narrator, we observed in the previous chapter, asks Jupiter why he allows Trojans and Italians destined to live in eternal peace to clash in battle (12.503–504).

But this first half of the poem, and its Greek books in particular, do not, cannot separate Rome's future foreign conflicts from the civil war that is supposed to be its opposite. This is because the *Aeneid* articulates the ideology of the Augustan regime that described the last round of the civil wars, the conflict with Mark Antony, as a foreign war, a war against Cleopatra, of Roman West against Greek East. So the episodes of Books 1–4 not only project a history of Roman conquests over non-Roman peoples, Carthaginians and Greeks, but the victory at Actium that continues and completes that history. In Book 3, Aeneas takes a shield he has won from a Greek warrior and suspends it as a trophy on the shores neighboring the future sea battle at Actium (3.286–288) He anticipates his distant descendant Augustus's achievement over supposedly similar Greek enemies. But the *Aeneid* simultaneously troubles this story and discloses what everyone in any case knew: Romans fought Romans at Actium.

And perhaps they had been doing so from their very Trojan beginnings. This chapter falls into three asymmetrical parts. The first two sections closely read Aeneas's account of the fall of Troy, one of the most elaborately worked passages of the poem. The last night of the city conveys dynastic leadership from the house of Priam to the house of Aeneas and suggests officially unspoken conflicts within the city itself. The headless trunk on the sand that is what is left of Priam evokes the relatively recent, historical death (48 BCE) of Pompey the Great and the internal strife that would divide Rome, the city of Troy's descendants. In the figure of Pyrrhus-Neoptolemus, the destroyer of Priam, the *Aeneid* creates a dark double of its pious hero, who—through the actions carried out by Pyrrhus (and, earlier, by Pyrrhus's father, Achilles)—will inherit Trojan kingship in Priam's and Hector's place. Aeneas even appears to work with Pyrrhus to bring Priam's house down. The chapter's second part (its next two sections) examines the episode of the New Troy built at Buthrotum in Epirus in Book 3, where Aeneas also inherits the heroic mantle of Achilles—and the literal arms of Achilles—that had belonged to the now-dead Pyrrhus. Here the *Aeneid* evokes the later historical King Pyrrhus, Macedonian king of Epirus (318–272 BCE), whose battles against Rome and eventual defeat had occupied a book of Ennius's *Annales*. This Greek Pyrrhus would be coupled in Roman historical memory with Carthaginian Hannibal, both invaders of Italy and the greatest foreign threats to Rome's existence. The greatest, that is, until Cleopatra, the Ptolemaic queen of Egypt, came along, in whom both the poem's Pyrrhus and Dido and history's King Pyrrhus and Hannibal appear to have been reborn as external foe, both Greek and North African. But this enemy queen was—in the real history that ideology could not disguise—an auxiliary to her Roman husband Mark Antony, the main rival, foe, and fellow citizen of Augustus. Part 3 of this chapter looks at how these issues reappear and are built into the structure of the underworld episode in Book 6 that provides a retrospect both on the epic's first half and on Rome's history. The book repeats the pairing of vanquished Carthaginian and Greek enemies, even as it acknowledges internal enemies and civil war that never go away.

Aeneas the Narrator

The narrative of the fall and burning of Troy in Book 2 may be Virgil's greatest achievement. It unflinchingly confronts the consequences of war as well as those forces internal and external, human and inhuman, that annihilate a civilization. It puts the story not in the mouth of the immediate victor, the usual owner and teller of history. *That* version of the city's fall, recounted from the Greek side, was the subject of the lost *Iliou persis*, one of the epics of the Troy cycle. In Book 1 the weeping Aeneas has seen this victors' version of the Trojan War celebrated in the sculpted reliefs on the temple of Juno in Dido's Carthage. Now Aeneas narrates the city's fall from the point of view of the defeated Trojans. Aeneas's descendants, the Romans, the collective heroes of the *Aeneid*, will in their own turn become conquerors, the masters of war. They will subjugate, among other peoples, the Greeks who overturned Troy and the Carthaginians who depict Troy's fall on their central civic shrine. The *Aeneid* itself will portray Rome as history's greatest victor—as the world power of Virgil's own historical moment.

Meanwhile, the fall of Troy also occasions the mythical transfer of Trojan/future-Roman rulership from Priam to Aeneas and to one particular line of his descendants, the Julian family. It thus foreshadows the recent, historical transfer of this rulership to the Julian heir Augustus Caesar, the individual hero whom the *Aeneid* singles out above his fellow Romans. In this scenario, the Troy that falls in Virgil's epic begins to look like the Roman Republic itself, a whole era of history swept away in Rome's civil wars to make way for the new *princeps*—in spite of Augustus's pretenses to preserve the republic and its institutions.

The ideological stakes of depicting the horror of Troy's fall are thus complex. Rome's rise to dominance and the present regime of Augustus may both be mythically justified and legitimated as revenge for the destruction of its ancestral city: the logic of "Never again." On the other hand, the example of Troy, seen through Trojan eyes, shows what it is like to be on the other side of Roman power in the future and in the *now* of Virgil's contemporary readers, the experience of those whom Rome vanquishes, kills, and enslaves, their cities sacked and—in the case of Carthage—obliterated. It may even suggest what it is like to be on the losing side of a civil war. The reliefs on Juno's temple thus not only constitute a sculpted version of the *Iliad* and of the other cyclical epics that celebrate the Greek victory over Troy but, in this case, a model for the ensuing *Aeneid* itself that will depict Rome's ascendancy—and elicit tears, like Aeneas's, for those who perish before her might.[1] Tears for and *of* the vanquished. In the *Odyssey* passage that is Virgil's model, it is rather the victorious Odysseus who weeps at hearing the story of the fierce fighting at Troy retold by a rhapsode in Scheria (*Ody.* 8.521–523). The famous ensuing simile compares his tears to those of a woman captured and enslaved from a city that has been put to sack (*Ody.* 8.523–530). The idea that the sufferings of the returning victor with post-traumatic stress disorder are somehow commensurate with those of his defeated victims might seem Homerically even-handed, as if Odysseus might himself empathize with the woman to whom he is compared. It is a story that the victor likes to tell, popular not only in the *Odyssey* but in the twenty-first-century United States in the wake of its foreign wars. War is hell for everybody: since I, however, am the one left standing, I get the sympathy. But it is bad faith, the Greek poet flattering his own: Odysseus weeps only for himself and his comrades. The *Aeneid* has courted such a reading from its opening lines where it forecasts what Aeneas will have to endure to found the Rome he will never see—"*tantae molis erat Romanam condere gentem*" (1.33)—announcing, it seems, a triumphalist account of Roman history that emphasizes the sorrows of empire, that is, the travails of the victor, whose conquests are the more hard-earned. But the poem also corrects itself and *creates a double* of this reading when Aeneas, the defeated exile, sheds tears at the winners' celebratory depiction of the war at Troy, and

---

1. I owe this line of argument to conversations with Kirk Freudenburg. On the temple reliefs and the various perspectives for reading them, including the perspective of their Carthaginian makers, see Barchiesi, 1999. See also Bellamy, 1992, 60–69; Stanley, 1965; Horsfall, 1973–74; Williams, 1960.

then himself recounts to Dido the last night of the city: *his* city.[2] It corrects Homer.

The narrative of Troy's fall takes us into the mind of the hero who retells it. In the historical long run, the loss of Priam's Troy will be Rome's and Augustus's gain. In the short run it is the political gain of Aeneas himself. The extinction of Priam and his children leaves the collateral line of Anchises, Aeneas, and Iulus as their successors. (From Iulus comes the Julian line of Julius Caesar and Augustus.) Thus Poseidon prophesied in *Iliad* 20, when he removed Aeneas from the battlefield as Achilles was bearing down on him. Poseidon tells us that Zeus cursed Priam and his family (*Il.* 20.306–308) and that it is now the turn of Aeneas and of his sons' sons to rule over the Trojans and to preserve the seed of Dardanus, the mortal beloved above all others to Zeus. The Homeric warrant is crucial to the entire *Aeneid*, which tells how this divinely loved seed returns to its Italian homeland, from which it will eventually rule the world. One book later in the *Iliad*, Poseidon himself and Apollo, too, reveal their own grudge against Laomedon, Priam's father, who had refused to pay them for their labor when they were his servants (*Il.* 21.441–457). Aeneas descends through the line of Assaracus (brother of Tros, uncle of Laomedon) and is thus free from both curses.[3] Homer's Poseidon promises a fresh start when he temporarily covers the eyes of Achilles with

---

2. Aeneas begins his narration in Book 2 with the rhetorical question: what follower of Achilles or of Ulysses would not weep in telling of the fall of Troy? (2.6–8), another recollection of *Odyssey* 8. These Greeks might weep, Virgil suggests, but not for the fate of the Trojans. Murrin, 1994, 205–207, compares the episode in Tasso's *Gerusalemme liberata* (18.92–97), where the archangel Michael grants the *conquering* Crusader Goffredo a vision of his deceased, now sainted comrades fighting alongside the angelic host to assist him in the taking and sacking of Jerusalem during the First Crusade, to its model in the *Aeneid*: Venus showing Aeneas the gods destroying Troy (2.604–622). The victorious crusader sees God and his servants on his side: the opposite of what the dismayed, defeated Aeneas experiences.

3. This does not stop the enemies of Aeneas and of the Trojans in the *Aeneid*—the harpy Celaeno (3.248) and Dido (4.542), the Fama that reaches the Italians in Book 7 (7.105)—from lumping them with Laomedon and his treachery. The narrator of the *Aeneid* himself labels the Trojan Aeneas as the "Laomedontius heros" at the beginning of Book 8 (8.18), a moment of deliberate, glaring carelessness in a book that will shortly go on, through Evander's retrospective narration, to distinguish Anchises, twice in the space of eight verses, *from* "Laomedontiaden Priamum" (8.156–168; 161–163). Something of this ancestral curse may still cling to Aeneas and the Romans; so Virgil had described the recent civil wars—"Laomedonteae luimus periuria Troiae" (1.502)—at the close of the first *Georgic*. It is also the case that Iulus-Ascanius, hence the dynastic Julian line, descends, on the side of his mother, Creusa, daughter of Priam, from the line of Laomedon.

mist and scoops up Aeneas and throws him to the sidelines, where, the *Iliad* has earlier told us, Aeneas has already been something of a resentful malingerer (*Il.* 13.459–461), feeling insufficiently honored by Priam. Achilles himself— who had his own problems about honor and prizes with Agamemnon—has asked Aeneas what he thinks to gain by killing him, since Priam and his sons will still be lords of Troy (*Il.* 20.178–183).[4] A later tradition even suggested that Aeneas owed his survival not so much to divine favor, such as Poseidon's rescue, as to treachery against Priam, from whom Aeneas had already separated himself and some followers on Mt. Ida *before* the fall of Troy.[5] Now, in the *Aeneid*, Priam's death and the end of his ruling house bring Aeneas to center stage: whether the hero, accustomed to playing a secondary role in the wings, is ready for or has aspired to his new prominence or not.

Rescue by a god is epic's dignified way of portraying a hero running away from the fight. So Juno creates a phantom Aeneas to lure Turnus out of battle in Book 10, and Juturna will govern Turnus's chariot to keep him away from the real Aeneas in Book 12, before Turnus will run away from Aeneas in very real panic at the end of the poem. Back in *Iliad* 20, Homer's Aeneas had expressed his diffidence about fighting Achilles to the disguised Apollo (*Il.* 20.86–102), and Poseidon's saving Aeneas to fight another day puts the best light on his encounter with the mighty Greek warrior, although it will not spare him from the taunt of Turnus (of all people) that he was a runaway— "*fugacem*" (12.52)—at Troy. In Book 2, as the city is falling around him, Aeneas is repeatedly told to take flight and to snatch himself from destruction, first by the ghost of Hector in his dream, "*fuge, nate dea, teque his' ait 'eripe flammis*" (2.289), later by Venus, the goddess in question, who admonishes her son with a clear echo of the earlier passage, "*eripe, nate, fugam*" (2.619).

But Aeneas does *not* run away. In between these two moments he leads a band of Trojans into the city in a futile, knowingly suicidal resistance against the invading foes. The result is predictable disaster. Aeneas takes with him the priest Panthus, who has so far escaped from the Greek weapons—"*Ecce autem telis Panthus elapsus Achiuum*" (2.318)—and who is bearing the sacred things and gods of Troy with one hand, his grandson with the other (2.320), much as Aeneas will subsequently consign the sacred things and the Penates to Anchises while he carries his father on his shoulders and leads Iulus-Ascanius by

---

4. Galinksy, 1969, 3–61; Nagy, 1979, 265–275.
5. Heinze, 1993, 18–19; Ahl, 1989, 25, who cites Dionysius of Halicarnassus, 1:42; Horsfall, 1986; Casali, 1999.

the hand, as the three generations of the family finally flee the doomed city later in the book (2.717–724). Panthus had the right idea: get out while you can, hold on to remnants of the cultural past, and save the future. But Aeneas only succeeds in getting Panthus killed (2.429–430) and later can only watch in horror at the death of Polites, who, in an echoing verse that pairs him with Panthus, has thus far escaped from Pyrrhus—"*Ecce autem elapsus Pyrrhi de caede Polites*" (2.526)—just as the son of Achilles catches up with Polites and kills him before the eyes of his father, Priam, and then kills Priam himself. Only now can the appearance of Venus persuade Aeneas to return to his house and flee from Troy. The hero's mad return into the burning city and to the palace of Priam at its center merely postponed his inevitable flight. Had he left at once, he might have saved his wife along with his father and son. Aeneas loses Creusa in the confusion of his escape and must return yet once more into the labyrinthine streets of Troy in a futile attempt to recover her. It is nonetheless with some pride and even defensiveness that Aeneas testifies to his Carthaginian audience and to the poem's readers, swearing by Troy's ashes that he was in on the fighting and that, had the fates allowed it, he would have earned his death in the city—"*et, si fata fuissent / ut caderem meruisse manu*" (2.433–434).

Aeneas may protest too much. He is not the runaway of the *Iliad*. Nor is he a traitor: he loyally fought his way back into the citadel of Priam but was unable to stop Pyrrhus and the slaughter of his king. Frederick Ahl has argued for the carefully self-exculpatory nature of Aeneas's narrative—the ways in which it counters the alternative negative portraits of the hero I have described above. Ahl points, in particular, to the moment when Coroebus comes up with the briefly successful stratagem of donning Greek armor in order to sneak up on the enemy (2.386–401), a ploy that might explain how subsequent accounts thought Aeneas had in fact switched sides, why the temple reliefs at Carthage ambiguously depict him "*principibus permixtum ... Achiuis*" (1.488): *either* fighting against *or* alongside the Greek princes.[6] Aeneas also, I may add, makes part of Sinon's false story the false accusations of treachery—"*falsa proditione*" (2.83)—brought up against Palamedes, an innocent Greek chief unjustly charged and executed for supposedly selling out their side to Priam (2.81–85). Similar stories may be circulating about Aeneas by the time he reaches Carthage, and he refutes them.

The poem invites us to read Aeneas's storytelling in this way and to indulge in the hermeneutics of suspicion. The hero's protestations that he did

---

6. Ahl, 1989, 26–29.

everything he could to find death for himself amid the death of his city may be calculated to wring sympathy from Dido and the reader, and to make us believe in his courage and loyalty to king and country. They also ring true enough to a character whose first words in the poem—a spontaneous response to the storm sent by Juno and Aeolus—is to wish that he had died at Troy.[7] Whether the responses to the tradition of Aeneas-as-traitor really belong to Aeneas or to the poet speaking through him is hard to determine, *but that is the point* continuously raised by Aeneas's first-person telling of the agony of Troy. Virgil's art, I want to argue, probes deep into the psyche of a hero who has survived—mysteriously enough—the destruction of his city and former identity, and who now has greatness, the occasion to be the hero of his own epic and future people, thrust upon him. To modify Ahl's suggestion: Aeneas may not be the master of his own story, and he tells us more than he himself knows.[8] As we shall see, the actions and similes in Aeneas's story couple him with, and make him the (unwitting?) twin of, the vengeful Pyrrhus. *That* is certainly not a message that Aeneas would want to convey to Dido or to the poem's reader. His account also explores, with ever greater complication, the respective responsibility of the gods and of human beings for the historical cataclysm that has taken place. Aeneas may not know his own motives, and these, the drama of Book 2 suggests, are always mixed in historical actors at moments of crisis, as is the apportioning of credit and blame. The *Iliad*'s Poseidon had declared Priam cursed and Aeneas innocent—"ἀναίτιος" (*Il.* 20.297)—but it may not feel that way to the survivor Aeneas, who, simply by living on, may feel himself a traitor and guilty. (How, exactly, did Augustus himself feel when Rome fell into his hands after rounds of civil war? Was he the pious Aeneas or the vengeful, to the point of sacrilegious, Pyrrhus?)[9] The death of Priam was a consummation to be wished for the

---

7. Hanson, 1982, 2:686–688.

8. Aeneas tells us from the outset that he not only saw, but had a large part in the fall in Troy: "*quorum pars magna fui*" (2.6). What does he mean? Gowers, 2011, 93 suggests the usefulness of Freud: "One interpretation of the dreams or dream-like symbolic sequences that mask or reawaken his latent aggression is as a series of murderous memoirs. Acting on Aeneas's behalf, Virgil eliminates each of his relatives in turn. Alibis abound; each rival is seemingly laid to rest through dutiful burial or benediction, but the repressed ghosts return in different, often mutilated forms." See also Bellamy, 1992, 38–81; Johnson, 1999, 54–56.

9. Piety and vengeance can be synonyms. Pandey, 2018, points out the topical resonances of the character Pyrrhus, who seeks to avenge the death of his father, Achilles, at Troy, for Octavian-Augustus, who eliminated his political enemies in the name of *pietas*—filial piety for his adoptive political father, Julius Caesar, that went well beyond the killing of Caesar's assassins and that contrasted with Julius Caesar's own clemency.

ambition of Aeneas's own house—the *Iliad*'s Achilles accuses Aeneas of thinking about it—and it is an unspeakable horror as Aeneas recounts it. Going back into Troy was both heroic and futile; Panthus and the others he led might still be alive. So might Creusa. The hero's storytelling reveals—perhaps below the level of Aeneas's consciousness—the ambivalence, the strata of guilt, of disowned but half-acknowledged desires, that accompanied him on the last night of Troy and that still reside with him.

The Fall of Troy: Aeneas and Pyrrhus

In a classic essay that I have already mentioned in chapter 1, Bernard Knox demonstrated one pattern of action, simile, and language that runs through Book 2. It transfers the destructive imagery of serpents and flames, each with flicking tongues, into the mysterious, harmless fire that plays around the head of little Iulus (2.680–691), an omen of the Julian future of Rome that will rise out of the fall of Troy.[10] The divine sign persuades Anchises to join Aeneas and to escape the doomed city. Knox's famous reading has perhaps caused less attention to be paid to a second, equally impressive chain of action, simile, and language that connects Book 2 from Aeneas's first awareness of the Greek sneak attack to his vision of the city sinking in flames (298–631).[11] Virgil meticulously constructs and unifies the episode, drawing attention to the almost obsessive repetition of its motifs, of the same words, and of the same physical acts that they describe. The following analysis unpacks these passages in close detail and demonstrates how they are linked together. I want to insist on two issues: (1) the ambiguous, no less mysterious, interplay of divine, natural, and human actors, and (2) the disturbing pairing of Aeneas with Pyrrhus/Neoptolemus, the doubly-named son of Achilles.

After the ghost of Hector has appeared to him in his dream, the sounds of warfare in the city reach Aeneas and shake him out of sleep. He climbs to the top of his father's house and listens.

> excutior somno et summi fastigia tecti
> ascensu supero atque arrectis auribus asto:
> in segetem ueluti cum flamma furentibus Austris
> incidit, aut rapidus montano flumine torrens

---

10. Knox, 1950.

11. For some critical discussions of this sequence, see Heinze, 1993, 14–37; Putnam, 1965, 28–48; Kenney, 1979; Di Cesare, 1974, 38–60.

sternit agros, sternit sata laeta boumque labores
praecipitisque trahit siluas; stupet inscius alto
accipiens sonitum saxi de uertice pastor. (2.302–308)

I am shaken from sleep and I climb to the uppermost top of the roof and stand with my ears straining; as when a fire falls on a field of wheat as the south winds [*Austris*] are raging, or when a rapid torrent of a mountain river lays lows the fields, lays low the happy crops and the labors of the oxen, and drags down the forests headlong; an unknowing shepherd is stupefied, hearing the sound from the height of a rocky peak.

Aeneas's position on the roof will be repeated at Priam's palace later in the long episode, during which he will both be on the ground and in the fray as a participant and stand above it as narrator and witness. We have learned to associate such elevation with the godlike vantage point of the omniscient narrator looking down on the action he or she recounts—Helen's review of the Greek troops from the Trojan battlements, the so-called *Teichoscopia*, in Book 3 of the *Iliad* is an epic example (*Il.* 3.122–244). But this initial scene and simile description pointedly call this assumption into question: the shepherd and, by implication, Aeneas are at this moment "*inscius*," uncertain what the noise portends. How much our hero/narrator ever understands is part of the drama. His characterization in the simile as a shepherd detaches him from the farmlands and crops that are being destroyed; in the simile's terms, these are the city of Troy itself. They have associations with human cultivation through the beasts of burden, the oxen, who have worked them, but they are simultaneously coupled with the wild forests the flooding stream drags down—"*trahit*." The absence of human actors is in keeping with the simile that compares the man-made fires consuming Troy first to a wildfire and then to an entirely different scenario, flooding waters that are fire's opposite.[12] The simile thus doubly distances the fall of the city in war from its human agents, comparing it to first one, then another kind of catastrophe (fire, flood) beyond human control. Used in the plural, "*furentibus Austris*" seems to designate the south wind as a weather phenomenon, not as a divine personification, as if

---

12. As we observed in the preceding chapter, Virgil redoubles this pattern at 12.521–525, in the double simile of two fires and two mountain streams that describes Aeneas and Turnus on opposite sides of the battlefield; Di Cesare, 1974, 219–221, notes the connection between the two passages.

the event were a familiar enough but unpredictable natural act. Nonetheless, the phrase returns us to the realm of Aeolus at the very beginning of the poem in Book 1—"*loca feta furentibus Austris*" ("a place teeming with storming south winds"; 1.51)—and the simile recalls the storm sent via Aeolus by Juno that attacks Aeneas's fleet, where the wind, under its alternative name of Notus (1.85; 1.108), *is* so personified.[13] The ensuing complex of action and simile keeps in play these three alternative explanations of what we are seeing in the fall of Troy: man-made calamity, natural disaster, divine act.

Aeneas and his band head into the city.

> lupi ceu
> raptores atra in nebula, quos improba uentris
> exegit caecos rabies catulique relicti
> faucibus exspectant siccis, per tela, per hostis
> uadimus haud dubiam in mortem mediaeque tenemus
> urbis iter; nox atra caua circumuolat umbra. (2.355–360)

> like thieving wolves through a dark cloud, whom the persistent raging of their hunger drives blindly and for whom the cubs they have left behind wait with thirsty jaws, we wade through weapons, through enemies, to no uncertain death and hold our way into the middle of the city; black night hovers about with its hollow shade.

As the Trojan counterattack briefly reverses the battle, so Virgil reverses the preceding simile: its shepherd has become the shepherd's conventional adversary, one in a pack of predatory wolves. The expectant cubs in this simile remind us that these Trojan warriors are fighting on their own domestic ground for family and city, unlike the Greeks who are the real thieves ("*raptores*"). But these cubs who have been left behind or abandoned—"*relicti*"—simultaneously indicate the wrong track that Aeneas and his companions have taken by plunging into the fray instead of taking their young—Iulus, the grandson of Panthus—out of a doomed Troy. Determined to die, they are derelict in their true, harder duty of living on and preserving their offspring in exile. The wolves simile, like so many beast similes in epic, thus reduces warfare, particularly war lust and revenge, to the instinctual and the natural, but it also stealthily imports an idea of human choice. The reversal that turns the

---

13. Wofford, 1992, 120–135, comments on how the opening storm of the *Aeneid*, supposedly calmed by Neptune, keeps returning in the imagery and events of the poem; these examples in Book 2, which *precede* that opening storm in the poem's chronology, bear out her point.

Trojan fighters into their Greek foes appears fulfilled when they follow Coroebus's idea and don Greek arms. Indulging in hyperbole and wishful thinking, the narrator Aeneas describes them driving the invaders back to their ships and back inside the Trojan horse itself. The reversal of the preceding simile is further completed by the faint recollection of a storm in the "*atra ... nebula,*" the black mist or cloud, the darkness of night, in which the wolves move: this simile's language, too, returns us to the opening of the *Aeneid* in Book 1 and its storm scene, where the gathering storm clouds suddenly tear daylight and sky from before the eyes of the Trojans and dark night settles on the sea: "*ponto nox incubat atra*" (1.89). Here the literal, enveloping darkness of the last night of Troy described two verses later—"*nox atra*"—explains the cloud of the simile. Both invading Greeks and defending Trojans become part of the same figurative storm.

This becomes clearer, the reprise of the opening storm scene of the poem more explicit, when the tables are turned again and the Greeks regain the upper hand—a chiastic reversal of the reversal—and in the next, ensuing simile. Coroebus's stratagem backfires when he rushes in to rescue Cassandra; he and his band are assaulted from above by Trojans, who mistake them for Greeks, and cast weapons down on them from a temple rooftop—"*ex alto delubri culmine*" (2.410)—and then on the ground by the rallied Greeks led by Ajax.

> aduersi rupto ceu quondam turbine uenti
> confligunt, Zephyrusque Notusque et laetus Eois
> Eurus equis; stridunt siluae saeuitque tridenti
> spumeus atque imo Nereus ciet aequora fundo. (2.416–419)

> even as when, a storm having broken out, the opposing winds clash:
> Zephyrus, Notus, and Eurus, rejoicing in his eastern steeds; the woods
> scream and foaming Nereus rages with his trident and stirs the sea
> from its lowest bottom.

The simile, as Austin points out, refers to the double attack.[14] It distinguishes, as the episode repeatedly insists upon doing, those on high, the Trojans fighting from their rooftop compared with the winds, from the Greeks' attack below, likened to the upswelling sea. The return to the storm episode that begins the *Aeneid* is clear: Eurus and Notus are paired at 1.85 and strike the

---

14. Austin, 1964, 171.

Trojan fleet in succession in verses 1.106–112; Neptune addresses Eurus and Zephyrus together at 1.130 and threatens them with his *"saeuumque tridentem"* (1.138), if they do not desist and he uses the same trident to open the sandbanks of the Libyan Syrtes and calm the sea (1.146–147). But here in the simile, the winds and seas, whose personified deities were in opposition to each other in Book 1, are no less opposed insofar as they stand respectively for Trojans and Greek fighters—yet they work together to create the storm of war and to assault Aeneas and his men in their disguised arms. Nereus, replacing Neptune as the personification of the sea, uses *his* trident to stir up the sea from its bottom, *"imo ... fundo,"* just as the winds had done in Book 1, *"a sedibus imis"* (1.84). That these winds and sea are personified—Notus has replaced the directional Auster of the earlier simile—suggests a divine presence working through or behind the scene of the battle and prepares for Venus's subsequent revelation to Aeneas of her fellow gods destroying his city. The simile appears to shift comparison (and explanation) from the idea expressed in the relatively recent English figure of speech, *to storm a city,* of war as natural cataclysm, to the figure we use for such disasters, an *act of God,* but here it may not be a mere figure of speech.

The winds of the simile cause the forests to groan and recall the trees that the flood of the earlier simile dragged down headlong—*"praecipitisque trahit siluas"* (2.307). As the action shifts to Priam's palace, the Trojans on high are no longer raining weapons down from the rooftop (*"culmine"*) but wresting away and casting down the rooftops and towers themselves—*"turris ac tota domorum / culmina conuellunt"* (2.445–446)—onto the Greek invaders. The verb *"conuello"* suggests the uprooting of trees or branches, and Troy, particularly its citadel, has imagistically become a forest of falling towers. Other Trojan defenders are massed at the palace gates and doors. Entering the palace through its secret postern gate, Aeneas joins the first group and resumes his position both in but also above the battle. With his sword—*"ferro"*—he helps dislodge another tower, the highest of all,—*"summisque / ... tectis"* (2.460–461).

> adgressi ferro circum, qua summa labantis
> iuncturas tabulata dabant, conuellimus altis
> sedibus impulimusque; ea lapsa repente ruinam
> cum sonitu trahit et Danaum super agmina late
> incidit. (2.463–467)

> attacking this with our swords round about its highest stories which
> offered joints that were giving way, we uprooted and shoved it from its

high foundations; in its sudden fall, it loudly drags down ruin and falls upon the Greek ranks far and wide.

"*Conuello*" reappears here, as does "*traho*" and with them two forms of "*labeo*": to fall. "*Tabulatum*" can in other contexts refer to a level of tree branches and reinforces the arboreal conceit. Troy is falling, but it is ironically its defenders who, in their desperate effort to save their city, are tearing it down. Aeneas, the poem's hero, takes his role among them. He turns his sword upon the top of Priam's citadel.[15]

Aeneas thus describes himself, above and on top of the palace, as the counterpart of Pyrrhus, who leads the Greek assault on the doors below: "*ipse inter primos correpta dura bipenni / limina perrumpit postisque a cardine uellit / aeratos*" (2.479–481; "he among the first, having seized an ax, bursts through the stubborn threshold and wrests the bronze doors from their hinges"). Both heroes are destroying the citadel, one in defending it, one in attacking it. Earlier it was Aeneas and his comrades who were assaulted from on high and on the ground: now it is the turn of Priam's palace, and Aeneas has joined the double assault. The individualized verb "*uellit*" denoting Pyrrhus and his ax echoes the collective "*conuellimus*" that brought down the tower. A corresponding destruction of Priam's palace now takes place on its ground floor that Aeneas's narrative will echo and focalize a few verses later through Priam's own eyes "*conuulsaque uidit / limina tectorum*" (2.507–508; "he saw the doors of his house wrenched away"): "*conuello*" returns again here, and the phrase "*limina tectorum*" brings together both the threshold and palace roof that are being demolished through the two heroes' joint if apparently opposing efforts. Pyrrhus's force wins entry, and the Greeks pour into the domestic, private rooms that are the last bastion of Troy. The flood simile returns.

> non sic, aggeribus ruptis cum spumeus amnis
> exiit oppositasque euicit gurgite moles,
> fertur in arua furens cumulo camposque per omnis
> cum stabulis armenta trahit. (2.496–499)

> not so (furiously) does a foaming river, when dikes have been burst and it has left and overcome with its surge the resisting banks, rush in a mass into the fields and sweep away the herds with their folds all across the plains.

---

15. Marlowe appears to have had this episode in mind when he punningly evokes the "topless towers of Ilium" in *Doctor Faustus* (xviii.100).

There are notably no winds here, no storm, and hence no divinities of wind and sea: foaming Nereus of the earlier simile is a foaming river. Pyrrhus may appear in this simile as a force of nature, but both its pointed "*non sic*" beginning and its content suggest that we should look for another explanation and causality. The mountain stream of the first simile of the sequence indifferently swept away (the same verb "*trahit*") forests and cultivated fields, and indeed appeared to be an uncontrollable natural disaster like the windswept wildfire with which it is coupled. Here, however, human preparations, the man-made dikes, have failed, and the same word, "*agger*," can denote the earthworks of Roman ramparts and camps. These human barriers exclusively protect humanly cultivated fields and flocks: no wild forests here. "*Stabulis*" possesses a particularly pathetic force in the passage, for it corresponds to the fifty bedchambers of Priam's sons in the penetralia of the palace. The Greeks sweep away the human wealth of Priam's house.[16] The simile's emphasis on these human constructions reduce the war at Troy to purely human dimensions: the city falls because its defenses were not strong enough to keep the enemy out. It can draw attention to one of those defenses that is missing, the hero Aeneas himself, who is not downstairs to resist Pyrrhus but looking down with horror on the final playing out of Priam's fate.

Priam goes down before Pyrrhus's sword like his falling city and the falling forests to which it has been compared. The same verbs reappear: as Pyrrhus drags him ("*traxit*") to the family altar where he will dispatch him, Priam is already falling ("*lapsantem*") in the blood of his slain son Polites (2.551). Pyrrhus stabs Priam to death. Nevertheless, in the famous closing lines of the passage, Priam lies as a nameless corpse on the shore, a giant trunk with its head wrenched from its shoulders: "*iacet ingens litore truncus / auulsumque umeris caput et sine nomine corpus*" (2.557–558). The lines refer to the alternate story of how Pyrrhus cut off Priam's head and carried it on a spear down to the tomb of his father, Achilles, built by the Trojan seashore. Servius saw in the same verses an evocation, as well, of the more recent murder (48 BCE) of Pompey the Great, left a headless, unidentifiable corpse on the Egyptian sands. "*Auulsumque*" brings back the verb "*uello*" yet again, and the trunk of Priam's body connects him to the preceding arboreal imagery. As Emily Gowers has pointed out, we are watching the uprooting and destruction of a family tree, the ruling house of Troy.[17] The beheading of Priam by Pyrrhus has had its

---

16. Kenney, 1979, 112–113 also notes the implications of rape in the violation of the palace threshold.
17. Gowers, 2011, 94–95.

counterpart in Aeneas's lopping off the top story of the tower. Aeneas is wearing Greek armor, we remember, when he takes his sword to the tower. He and Pyrrhus are look-alikes.

At this point we may pause and consider why Aeneas and Pyrrhus/Neoptolemus should be so paired and mirrored in the narrative of Troy's destruction. One motive can be termed *literary-historical*. The two warriors are rivals for the heroic mantle of Achilles: who will be the next great epic hero? The issue is already decided in favor of Aeneas: he is telling his story to Dido inside the *Aeneid* that bears his name. Priam enrages Pyrrhus by telling him that he lies in claiming to be the son of Achilles (2.540). Pyrrhus, in turn, mockingly refers to himself as the "*degeneremque Neoptolemum*" (2.549) as he plunges his sword into the king's side.[18] The scene indeed establishes Pyrrhus as the false heroic heir of Achilles in the first half of the *Aeneid*, the same role that Turnus will play in the poem's second half in Italy, where, the sibyl at Cumae predicts to Aeneas in Book 6, another and different Achilles is already born—"*alius Latio iam partus Achilles*" (6.89). For it is Aeneas who will be the unsurpassable warrior and Achilles figure of the second part of the *Aeneid*. So the epic announces in the episode of the Little Troy at Buthrotum in Book 3, when Helenus gives Aeneas as a parting gift the arms of the now-dead Neoptolemus, a breastplate and helmet (3.467–469). More Greek armor for Aeneas, but these have a different symbolic valence. They are presumably the arms not only of Neoptolemus but of his father, Achilles, the same arms over which Ajax and Odysseus contended at Troy as *they* sought to be heir of the greatest warrior, and best of the Achaeans in their own turn: Odysseus won them in debate but gave them to Pyrrhus when he came to Troy. They are in the hands of Aeneas when, a hundred verses later, the Trojans reach the coast of the Cyclopes and learn the fate of "unfortunate" Ulysses—"*infelicis Vlixi*" (3.691). Aeneas has doubly reclaimed the arms and the Achillean heroic status they confer from Pyrrhus and Ulysses, from both the *Iliad* and the *Odyssey*, the latter of which the first half of the *Aeneid* takes as its primary model.[19]

18. On Aeneas's view of Pyrrhus and Achilles both here and on the temple reliefs in Dido's Carthage, a Trojan's reading of *Iliad* 24, see Whittington, 2016, 68–72.

19. The mantle and weavings that Andromache bestows on Ascanius (3.482–491) parallel the arms of Pyrrhus—and Achilles—that Helenus gives to Aeneas and thus also gives to the Aeneas family the legacy of Hector; see Quint, 1993, 60. For the argument that the entire *Aeneid* is based on the *Odyssey*, see Cairns, 1989, 177–214; for the overlapping of the two Homeric poems as models in both halves of the poem, see Knauer, 1964, and Knauer, 1981. It is nonetheless undeniable that Virgil's epic does fall into two respective halves, wanderings based on the *Odyssey* (with its visit to the underworld), a war based on the *Iliad*.

In Book 3 in particular, it rewrites the *Odyssey* in epitome.[20] As has been mentioned above and will be developed further in the next section of this chapter, the question of heroic and literary inheritance—Aeneas and the *Aeneid* taking over the legacy of Achilles and Homer—is inseparable from a future in which Trojan-Roman arms will vie with Greek forces for supremacy in the Mediterranean. In that historical struggle, the Greeks will prove to have degenerated from Achilles and to be as unfortunate as Ulysses.

But, as this last remark suggests, and as I have been arguing above, a second motive lies behind the coupling of Aeneas and Pyrrhus in this sequence, and we can term it *political-topical*. Priam and his sons need *somehow* to be removed from the historical scene so that the descendants of Aeneas, the collateral Trojan lineage, can found Rome. That somehow is Pyrrhus, whom Aeneas watches kill Priam and Polites, while he, Aeneas, is apparently unable to come to their aid from his perch high above the palace floor. Pyrrhus does Aeneas's dirty work for him, and in this way, too, the poem pairs him with its hero. The pious Aeneas is aghast and recounts the story again in its full horror. We cannot tell how much he may consciously or unconsciously second Pyrrhus: *both of them, on literally different levels, destroy the physical house of Priam.* That the scene brutally enacts the transfer of dynastic destiny from Priam to his son-in-law Aeneas explains its evocation of Pompey's headless body on the sands of Egypt.[21] Though the older man, Pompey had been Julius Caesar's son-in-law, as the ghost of Anchises will point out during the parade of Roman heroes in the underworld of Book 6 (830–831). In Virgil's chiastic imaginary, history repeats itself but with reversals. The Julian line, however, always survives and prevails, as it will survive the Roman Republic, of which the Troy of the *Aeneid* might just itself be a figure, to be newly founded as the Rome of Augustus. The future Roman civil wars were—we realize with some shock—already built into the fall of Troy, as Pyrrhus acts as a kind of surrogate for Aeneas and his Julian descendants.

Back to the sequence of action and similes. Only now and for the first time, Aeneas thinks about his own father, wife, and son (2.560–563); but he also looks around and sees that his companions have thrown themselves to the ground or into the flames (2.563–565). The sudden apparition of Venus at

---

20. Putnam, 1980; Quint, 1993, 55–65; Bettini, 1997.

21. Bowie, 1990, 478, suggests the relationship of Pyrrhus's alternate name, Neoptolemus, to Ptolemy XIV Dionysius, whose agents treacherously killed Pompey; one of the latter, Bowie additionally notes, was named "Achillas."

this moment and her subsequent words about Helen and Paris (2.601–602) puzzled early readers of the *Aeneid* and produced the spurious Helen episode (2.567–588).[22] But Aeneas seems virtually to have summoned the goddess by thinking about family and by considering the option of ending it all: facing death, men may cry out for their mothers. Like a sensible mother, Venus tells him not to jump off the roof just because he sees everybody else doing it. With the egotism typical of a god and of her character in particular, Venus denies her own culpability—it's not my fault that the war was fought over Helen she says, contrary to all the evidence—while she casts the responsibility onto the other gods who wanted Troy destroyed (that she goes on to blame Juno and Minerva, her rivals in the beauty contest that she bribed Paris with Helen to judge in her favor, tells against her). She promises to tear away—"*eripiam*" (2.606)—the cloud of mortality surrounding Aeneas's vision and summons him to see the destruction wrought by the gods.

> hic, ubi disiectas moles auulsaque saxis
> saxa uides, mixtoque undantem puluere fumum,
> Neptunus muros magnoque emota tridenti
> fundamenta quatit totamque a sedibus urbem
> eruit. hic Iuno Scaeas saeuissima portas
> prima tenet sociumque furens a nauibus agmen
> ferro accincta uocat.
> iam summas arces Tritonia, respice, Pallas
> insedit nimbo effulgens et Gorgone saeua.
> ipse pater Danais animos uirisque secundas
> sufficit, ipse deos in Dardana suscitat arma. (2.608–618)

Here, where you see broken masses and stones torn away from stones, and waves of smoke mixed with dust, Neptune shakes the walls and their foundations overturned by his great trident, and wrenches up the city from its base. There, fiercest Juno holds foremost the Scaean gates and, garbed with steel, furiously calls fellow troops from the ships. Now look where on the highest citadels Tritonian Pallas sits gleaming with cloud and fierce Gorgon shield. Father Jupiter himself provides

22. Goold, 1970, dismantles, to my mind convincingly, the authenticity of the Helen episode; Heinze, 1993, 26–30 dismisses the possibility that the episode is genuine but feels that there is a narrative lacuna to which the literary forger responded. *Contra*, see Conte, 1986, 196–207. I suggest here the narrative logic for Venus's appearance, not to stop the murder of Helen but to prevent the suicide of Aeneas; Heinze, 1993, 29 reached a similar conclusion.

favoring strength to the courage of the Greeks, he himself spurs the gods against the arms of Troy.

Now the personified winds and seas (Zephyr, Eurus, Notus, Nereus) in the earlier tempest simile that described the fighting in the streets outside the citadel (2.416–419) have been replaced, through Venus lifting of the cloud before Aeneas's eyes, by the Olympian gods themselves. Neptune has taken over the trident that Nereus, his subordinate, had wielded in that simile, and this is Neptune the god not only of the sea but of earthquakes. He shatters the walls that he and Apollo had built without receiving their just compensation from Laomedon. The depths, the *"imo ... fundo"* from which Nereus stirs up the sea in the earlier simile, have been taken over by the *"fundamenta"* of Troy itself, the sea's waves replaced by billowing waves of smoke from the burning city—the idea is reinforced by the glancing wordplay between *"fundamenta"* and *"undantem."* The god's destruction of the city from its base (*"a sedibus"*) also echoes in its language—we note the insistent return of the *"uello"* verbs in *"auulsaque"*—Aeneas's earlier bringing down the tower on top of Priam's citadel: *"conuellimus altis / sedibus impulimusque"* (2.464–465). There is a sly wit in this sequence, too, from the single sword (*"ferro"*) of Aeneas, to the double ax of Pyrrhus (*"bipennis"*), to Neptune's trident. One, two, three: all bring down the city. The shift of perspective from the ground, to the gates, to the highest tower of the citadel, to Jupiter on top of all mirrors the double scene of battle—Pyrrhus and Priam down below, Aeneas up on the roof—that has governed the episode and seems to go it one better, revealing Neptune beneath the action and Jupiter above it.

But how much of a theophany does Aeneas receive? He sees Venus clearly enough, but when she herself disappears into the night and Aeneas turns to look where she has directed him, the language becomes both abstract and gnomic, a mere one and a half verses, the latter incomplete.

> apparent dirae facies inimicaque Troiae
> numina magna deum. (2.622–623)

> dire forms / faces appear and the great powers / godheads of the divinities inimical to Troy.

Does Aeneas see the gods face to face as Venus promises, or does he deduce their hostile shapes and presence from the carnage and ruin around him?[23]

---

23. The question is only complicated further if one hears behind the lines Lucretius, *De rerum natura* 3.18: *"apparet divum numen sedesque quietae,"* the Lucretian speaker's vision of the

Troy falls to human hands as if it were being shattered by an earthquake, the work, in turn, of Neptune: war, natural catastrophe, divine act. Calamity acquires a face, a personification, whether lent to it from the gods or projected upon it by human victims—and by their victors.

The question of agency carries over into the grand conclusion of this whole sequence. Aeneas seems to see one last, great paroxysm of the city that sinks in flames before his eyes and describes it with a long simile.

> Tum uero omne mihi uisum considere in ignis
> Ilium et ex imo uerti Neptunia Troia:
> ac ueluti summis antiquam in montibus ornum
> cum ferro accisam crebrisque bipennibus instant
> eruere agricolae certatim, illa usque minatur
> et tremefacta comam concusso uertice nutat,
> uulneribus donec paulatim euicta supremum
> congemuit traxitque iugis auulsa ruinam. (2.624–631)

Then all Ilium seems to me to sink into the flames and Neptunian Troy to be overturned from its bottom: and as when on mountain peaks farmers rival each other as they strive to tear down an ancient ash tree that they have hacked with iron and frequent blows of the double ax, she threatens to fall and nods, her leaves made to quake, her head shaken, until little by little, overcome by wounds, she has groaned out her last and, torn up from the ridges, drawn ruin after herself in her fall.

The simile, as we shall see, brings back the language of the entire episode: it returns us to the rural world of the first simile describing the Greek assault, where mountain torrents bring down forests headlong (2.307: "*praecipitisque trahit siluas*"). The competition—"*certatim*"—among the farmers to cut down the ash appears to make the simile refer immediately back to the Olympian gods whom Venus has just named, all of them sharing in the destruction of Troy; the verb "*eruere*" echoes Neptune's action in uprooting the city (2.612: "*eruit*") fifteen verses earlier: it is the *Neptunian* Troy he has himself built. Like the opening simile of the epic, where the divinely sent and divinely calmed sea storm—Juno competing with Neptune to contrary ends—was

---

Epicurean gods who have no concern for human events at all. See Delvigo, 2005; Horsfall, 2008, 446–448. I am grateful to Christina Kraus for pointing out to me the deliberate vagueness and abstractness of these lines.

compared to a riot in a city-state, this simile too would bring divine action down to the human (unlike those Homeric similes that do the reverse, comparing men to gods). It is part of a desacralizing strain announced by the *Aeneid* from its beginning.

But the simile does more than this. The competing farmers and the language that describes them refer less clearly to these gods whom Venus points out, but whom Aeneas may or may not see, than to the human protagonists of the poem whom Aeneas has described in his narration: to Pyrrhus with his ax (*"bipennibus"*), to Aeneas himself with his sword (*"ferro"*), each working, at cross purposes but nonetheless together, to bring down the city. As critics have pointed out, the language that anthropomorphizes the nodding, groaning tree—its hairlike leafage (*"comam"*), its trembling (*"tremefacta"*), the choric reappearances of *"traxit"* and *"auulsa"*—restage the killing by Pyrrhus of Priam, last seen as a headless trunk: *"trementem / traxit ... implicuitque comam ... auulsumque umeris caput"* (2.550–552; 558).[24] The straining (*"instant"*) and multiple blows (*"crebris"*) remind us, too, of Pyrrhus beating down the doors of Priam's palace: *"instat ui patria Pyrrhus; nec claustra nec ipsi / custodes sufferre ualent; labat ariete crebro / ianua"* (2.491–493; "Pyrrhus strains with this father's force; neither bars nor the guards themselves avail to hold him off; the gates fall before the frequent blows of the ram"). But the last verse of the simile repeats just as unmistakably the action of Pyrrhus's unwitting partner, Aeneas, as the hero sends the palace tower crashing down on the Greek enemies: *"ea lapsa repente ruinam / cum sonitu trahit"* (2.465–466); that tower had stood on the highest roofs of the palace (*"summisque ... tectis"*), like the ash on the mountaintops (*"summis ... montibus"*). The two warriors have competed to bring down Priam's house: now they—the Greek and the ancestor of Rome—will compete for the future.

This crowning simile raises all over again questions about who or what has brought about the fall and burning of Troy: we do not know if the simile itself refers to the gods whom Venus has made manifest to Aeneas (or has she?) or to the human warriors (Aeneas among them) or to all of them working in emulation and by turns—*"certatim"*—to destroy the city. A divine order may indeed be operating behind the scenes: Venus briefly draws away the curtain and lets Aeneas and the reader watch the stage managers at work, but the revelation of divine malevolence to Troy can bring no comfort to her hero son. The gods themselves are the ironists who turn the faithful Trojan defender

---

24. Putnam, 1965, 39; Gowers, 2011, 95.

Aeneas into the double of the murderous Pyrrhus and into their unknowing, unwilling collaborator.

The immense power that Rome had achieved might require the idea of a divine plan of history or fated necessity: what Virgil's Jupiter promises to Venus in Book 1. Virgil's contemporary, Livy, invokes this idea at the beginning of his great history (1.Preface.7–9) but sets it aside. He drily comments that Rome's claims to have the gods on her side may be a difficult idea to sell to the peoples she has conquered. Livy intends instead to analyze the human behavior, Rome's men and their mores, that caused the city's greatness and that now, in his own times, has brought about her collapse into civil strife: one would not want to hold the gods accountable for *that*. (Livy's metaphor compares the Rome of his day to a falling house, and the language—"*labente*," "*lapsi*," "*praecipites*"—parallels the action and language of the destruction of Priam and his palace in Book 2, nowhere closer than in the episode where Aeneas hews down the tower on the palace roof in verses 460–465, where all three terms appear.)[25] Aeneas's simile may follow a similar logic, by focusing less explicitly on the gods than on the human protagonists, and by offering a picture of human labor.

Unlike the floods and fire of nature that blindly send trees crashing down in the earlier similes, acts of God as inexplicable as the malice of the gods themselves—the farmers cut the tree down for human purposes: to clear the

25. Livy, *Ab urbe condita* 1, preface (7–9): "If any people ought to be allowed to consecrate their origins and refer them to divine makers, so great is the glory in war of the Roman people that when they claim that their father and the father of their founder was most powerful Mars, the nations of men may accept it with the same patience with which they submit to Rome's dominion over them. But to this and things similar to it, however they are considered and judged, I shall not give much importance; let my reader sharply direct his mind to these matters: by what kind of lives and morals, through which men and policies at home and in the army did Rome's empire emerge and expand; let him then note with that same attention, how, as discipline declined little by little, those morals deteriorated, then, as they fell more and more, how they went headlong, until it has come to these times of ours, in which we can neither bear our vices nor the remedy needed to cure them" (*"et si cui populo licere oportet consecrare origines suas et ad deos referre auctores, ea belli gloria est populo Romano ut cum suum conditorisque sui parentem Martem potissimum ferat tam et hoc gentes humanae patiantur aequo animo quam imperium patiuntur. Sed haec et his similia, utcumque animadversa aut existimata erunt, haud in magno equidem ponam discrimine: ad illa mihi pro se quisque acriter intendat animum, quae vita, qui mores fuerint, per quos viros quibusque artibus domi militiaeque et partum et auctum imperium sit; labente deinde paulatim disciplina velut desidentis primo mores sequatur animo, deinde ut magis magisque lapsi sint, tum ire coeperint praecipites, donec ad haec tempora quibus nec vitia nostra nec remedia pati possumus perventum est"*); Livy, 1922–59, 1:4–7.

land for their crops or to turn its wood into tools, weapons, housing. The comparison tells us that war is horrific, even unnatural, but not without its reasons and motives. It also reminds us that human beings can work together constructively as well as fight against each other: this is the force of "*certatim*," which turns rivalry into cooperation. Like Livy, Virgil wants to depict the character that would build the future greatness of Rome, itself a city built by farmers into a world power. It is time for Aeneas to quietly follow Venus home and to get the future started. The simile returns human responsibility to the poem and offers some consolation—a real one, I think—to Aeneas and to the poem's reader, but it is qualified nevertheless. The simile's connection to the preceding episode and to the reminiscence of the fate of Pompey the Great suggests an alternate or supplemental vision of that very future, the one of man-made decline and fall that Livy *also* intends to tell: an updated picture of rivals vying with each other and succeeding in toppling the towers of Ilium, now going under the name of Rome. Thus Lucan intuited when he compares Pompey to a venerable oak ready to come down at the beginning of his epic on the civil wars (*De bello civile* 1.136–143): the tree in Lucan's simile stands for the man and for the Roman Republic itself.[26] Virgil's falling ash already suggests much of the same, and the simile's transformation of weapons—Aeneas's sword and Pyrrhus's ax—into rustic, peacetime tools already foreshadows its reversal in the *Aeneid* itself. When hostilities break out between Latins and Trojans, Virgil's own adumbration of the civil wars in the epic's second half, Tyrrhenus will grab an ax with which he was splitting up an oak tree (7.508–510) and call his Italian troops into battle.

The tree-cutter simile and the relationship that it bears to the preceding complex of similes and symbolically charged actions exemplify Virgil's technique of doubling and the complexity of meaning that it generates. The referents of the simile are themselves doubled—gods and/or men—and in the case of the latter doubled again between Aeneas and Pyrrhus. The episode has from the first placed Aeneas on two planes, above the fray as witness and as present narrator, within it as participant, and it has insisted on this double perspective in the battle itself: Aeneas on the roof of his own house, Aeneas in the streets of Troy attacked by Greeks on foot and by his fellow Trojans from the rooftops; Aeneas now himself on the roof of Priam's house attacking the Greeks beneath, watching from above while Pyrrhus kills Priam. These two planes that the hero occupies may themselves correspond to the question

26. Ahl, 1976, 156–158.

of divine causality and human agency in the fall of Troy: it is while he is on high on the citadel rooftop that Aeneas sees Venus and is bidden by her to behold the gods operating behind the human catastrophe. I have identified this elevated vantage point with the epic narrator—here conflated with the hero—who sees the fuller, divinely authorized story unavailable to the historical actor in the moment. In the *Aeneid* this elevation is also the level of *ideology*, for the story the gods sponsor is the destruction of Troy in order to produce a future Rome—and the much later transfer of power and rulership from the republic to the Julian house of Augustus. Virgil, that is, uses Aeneas to stage his own production of a narrative that will explain the rise of Rome and legitimize Augustus. The hero's story, as we have seen, is self-exculpatory in intent, showing him fighting in support of Priam until the old king's death. But it implicates him, nonetheless, in the violence of the city's fall in ways of which he may be ignorant or which he cannot openly acknowledge and may conceal from himself: the uncanny twinning of his deeds, even when he seems to be above it all on the rooftop, with those of the enemy Pyrrhus. Aeneas (and so, by the poem's long historical foresight, Augustus) disowns the force that brings him kingship and fatherhood of the future Rome; he casts all the blame on the Greek enemy, the impious Pyrrhus below. And yet he cannot shake off the resemblance to Pyrrhus his very narrative creates. Aeneas is the beneficiary of the story he tells, however bloodstained it is, however much it is not his fault. The same may be said for the poet of the *Aeneid*, whose official story from above both reveals and wishes to be blind to the part he plays, his complicity, in a lived history below.

Greeks and Carthaginians

Pyrrhus has more symbolic work to do in the *Aeneid*. In Book 3, Aeneas retells the wanderings of his Trojan remnant after the death of their city through the territory of the victorious Greeks, and it is here that we learn that Orestes has killed Pyrrhus, a version of the story told in Euripides' *Andromache*. The bad end that comes to the son of Achilles is one emblematic part of the general reversal of Greek fortunes between the two books.

The *Aeneid* places these Greek Books 2 and 3 inside the Carthaginian ones, the story of Aeneas and Dido in Books 1 and 4. Aeneas's narrative is enclosed by frame episodes that in Virgilian fashion take the form of a chiasmus or reversal of terms. Two Greek suppliants, each the companion of Ulysses, Sinon at the beginning of Book 2, Achaemenides at the end of Book 3, implore the

Trojans to have mercy on them, and each calls on the stars and the gods to witness his account.

> uos, aeterni ignes, et non uiolabile uestrum
> testor numen (2.154–155)

> I bear witness by you, eternal fires, and by your inviolable divinity.

>   per sidera testor,
> per superos atque hoc caeli spirabile lumen,
> tollite me, Teucri. (3.599–601)

> I bear witness by the stars, by the gods, and by the breathable light of heaven, take me away with you, O Trojans.

Priam himself ("*ipse ... Priamus*"; 2.146–147) frees Sinon, while no one less than Anchises, who has replaced Priam as the authoritative Trojan elder in Book 3, offers his hand ("*ipse pater dextram Anchises*"; 3.610) to the entreating Achaemenides. In fact, the Sinon who begs for his life—"*oro, miserere laborum / tantorum, miserere animi non digna ferentis*" (2.143–144)—is a liar and false suppliant whose treachery leads the Trojans to bring the wooden horse into their city and makes possible the Greek victory engineered by Ulysses in Book 2. But, by the end of Book 3, the situation has been reversed and the real suppliant ("*supplex*"; 3.592) Achaemenides, marooned survivor of the encounter between the cyclops Polyphemus and a now-unfortunate Ulysses, is found to be a true and worthy object of Trojan pity and aid—"*supplice sic merito*" (3.667).

This reversal of the positions of Trojans and Greeks between Books 2 and 3 is mirrored, as Michael Putnam has pointed out, by a second pair of contrasting supplication scenes in Books 1 and 4 and a similar reversal, this time in the situation between Trojans and Carthaginians.[27] In Book 1, the Trojan Ilioneus, playing the same role as ambassador that he will later play to the Latins in Book 7, comes with his companions begging the favor—"*orantes ueniam*" (1.519)—of Dido; he successfully implores her to grant a harbor to their ships: "*Troes te miseri, uentis maria omnia uecti, / oramus*" (1.524). It is a moment that Dido, in her fury at Aeneas's leaving her, recalls to him in Book 4 (373–374). Now she sends her own ambassador, her sister Anna, in the position of a suppliant ("*supplex*"; 414, 424), to seek one last favor from Aeneas—

---

27. Putnam, 1980.

"*extremam hanc oro ueniam (miserere sororis)*" (4.435)—that he put off his sailing until the spring. But Anna can obtain nothing from Aeneas; the fates stand in the way.

The mirroring between these supplication scenes in the poem's narrative present at Carthage and in the inset, retrospective story that Aeneas tells of the Trojans' disaster and ensuing wanderings produces a clear-cut and troubling contrast. The Greek Achaemenides who himself acknowledges that his fighting at Troy may place him beyond the Trojans' mercy (3.602–606), especially, the reader may feel, given his resemblance to the false suppliant Sinon, nonetheless receives their assistance. Anna is refused any comfort for a Dido to whom Aeneas and the Trojans bear a real debt for her own merciful hospitality. Cursing the Trojans and their posterity, the spurned, enraged Dido will have turned at the end of Book 4 into a version of the Homeric Polyphemus from whom Achaemenides is rescued. The *Aeneid* reflects in these two episodes on the future Rome's relationship to the Greek and Carthaginian worlds it will conquer, turning both into its suppliants. With whatever historical injustice and implied Roman culpability—and Virgil may reflect on the cynically calculated destruction of Carthage in the Third Punic War—Punic-Carthaginian culture is cast away and even demonized as something monstrous. With due caveats made against its Sinon-like treachery, Greco-Hellenistic culture is taken onboard for Rome's journey through history. Exhibit A for this absorption of Greek culture is the *Aeneid* itself with its emulation of Homeric epic, which Virgil improves on here by including a character whom both Ulysses and Homer forgot on the coast of the Cyclopes. The poem's myth of Trojan ancestry provides a politically acceptable version of this Hellenization, for Homer's Trojans seem to be culturally Greek—they worship the same gods as the Achaeans—while ethnically and racially distinct from their enemies. When, in the second half of the poem, Virgil uses the convention of giving Greek names to the Trojans fighting against the native Latins in Italy, he does so to suggest not only that they are now assuming the role of victorious Greeks in a replay of the Trojan war, but also that they are the bearers of Greekness to a more backward, rustic Italic world. Aeneas and his Trojan remnant can import Greek civilization into the future Rome on the condition of not being Greeks themselves.[28]

---

28. See Barchiesi, 2017, 156 on the Greek behavior of Virgil's Trojan-Romans in Book 3; see also Lowrie, 2009, 167–168.

Pyrrhus and King Pyrrhus

For the Greeks are enemies, nonetheless. They have been so from Troy to Cleopatra at Actium. The structures of reversals we have described in Books 2 and 3, where Greeks are first victorious over and then suppliants to the Trojans, then in Books 1 and 4, where Trojans first supplicate Carthaginians and then Carthaginians supplicate them in turn, play out in little the larger chiasmus of the *Aeneid*, where defeated Trojans of the first six books set in the Mediterranean go on to be victorious in the last six books set in Italy. They also tell of Rome's historical ascendancy over the Greek-speaking world and of its eventual victory over Carthage in the Punic Wars; the two projects famously coincided in the year 146 BCE when Roman armies sacked both Corinth and Carthage. The unfolding of the poem artfully confuses this historical chronology, presenting the Trojan/Roman contact with Carthage first in the narrative sequence of the poem, but recording, in Aeneas's account to Dido, a still earlier confrontation with the Greeks: Rome thus takes on the Greeks both before and in between its great struggles with Carthage. In fact, Rome had fought a formidable Greek enemy, the Macedonian king Pyrrhus of Epirus, in the wars of 280–275 BCE, *before* the first of the Punic Wars broke out in 264 BCE; it would fight the Second and Third Macedonian wars against kings who claimed, as King Pyrrhus had done, to be descendants of Achilles, before the Third Punic War of 149–146. These events correspond to the sandwiching of the Greek Books 2 and 3 between the Carthaginian ones, 1 and 4; they also suggest the rationale for the continuing prominence of the *character* of Pyrrhus in Book 3.

The contrast of the suppliants Sinon and Achaemenides at either end of the narration of Books 2 and 3 is only one example of how the two books mirror each other.[29] At the center of each book is an episode involving Pyr-

---

29. Aeneas's repeated plunges back into the fallen city of Troy in Book 2 in spite of the repeated supernatural urgings that he leave by the ghost of Hector (289–295), by Venus (589–620), by Anchises after the portent of the flames surrounding Iulus's head (701–704), finally by the ghost of Creusa (771–789), are matched in Book 3 by the repeated sidetracking of his mission to reach Italy by the failed buildings of cities in Thrace (13–68) and Crete (121–171), which are versions of the little replica Troy he will encounter at Buthrotum (293f.) as well as by the stormy seas that carry him off course to the homes of the monstrous harpies (192f.) and cyclopes (554f.). These latter are preludes, we now realize, to the great storm of Book 1 that will take Aeneas and the Trojans to Carthage, one more version of a Troy doomed by history, and to the (eventually) Polyphemus-like Dido. In both books, forward progress toward the future Rome

rhus. Aeneas has gained access to Priam's palace through a secret passageway where Andromache used to bring Astyanax to visit his royal grandfather (453–457), only to watch in horror from the rooftop while Pyrrhus kills Polites before the eyes of Priam and Hecuba. Pyrrhus redoubles this act of impiety by dragging Priam to the sacred household altar before running him through.[30] Aeneas concisely describes again the double killing of Polites and Priam (and alludes to the headless trunk of the latter) when he is trying to persuade Anchises to abandon Troy:

> iamque aderit multo Priami de sanguine Pyrrhus,
> natum ante ora patris, patrem qui *obtruncat* ad aras.
> (2.662–663) (emphasis added)

> Soon Pyrrhus will be here, bathed in the blood of Priam,
> he who strikes down the son before the face of his father, the father at the altars.

In Book 3, retribution has found Pyrrhus out. Aeneas sails into Buthrotum and is astonished to find that Priam's son Helenus is the king there, having taken possession of both the scepter of Achillean Pyrrhus—"*Aeacidae Pyrrhi*" (3.296)—and of Andromache, whom Pyrrhus had taken and then set aside as his wife. Helenus has made over Buthrotum into a small-scale reconstruction of Troy. It now becomes clear that Virgil mentioned Andromache and Astyanax and their passageway just before the great episode of Pyrrhus, Polites, and Priam in Book 2 precisely in order to create a mirroring effect in Book 3, for Andromache soon appears (3.301f.) to tell Aeneas how Pyrrhus met his end: the maddened Orestes surprised him and cut him down on his father Achilles' altars—"*furiis agitatus Orestes / excipit incautum patriasque obtruncat ad aras*" (3.331–332). The echo and the reciprocity are clear.

Pyrrhus's fate, which is felt to be a merited requital for his more-than-Achillean ferocity and impiety at Troy, is a centrally placed figure for the more general downfall of the victorious Greeks in the *Aeneid*'s depiction of the

---

is countered by the regressive pull of the past: by the actual city of Troy in Book 2, by nostalgic versions of it in Book 3.

30. The criminality of Pyrrhus's act was recognized in antiquity; according to Arrian (1.11), when Alexander the Great paid a visit to Troy before embarking on his conquest of Persia, "he offered sacrifice to Priam upon the altar of Zeus the household god"—that is, on the altar where Pyrrhus had killed him—"deprecating the wrath against the progeny of Neoptolemus, from whom Alexander himself was descended." Godolphin, 1942, 2:416.

aftermath of the Trojan War in Book 3. The line of Achilles is cut off. Orestes is himself pursued by the furies of his mother, Clytemnestra, who killed Agamemnon on his triumphant return to Mycenae. Earlier in the book we have learned that Idomeneus has been expelled from his kingdom in Crete, 3.121–122, and Helenus now recounts to Aeneas, 3.400–401, that Idomeneus has settled in the Puglian heel of Italy, while Philoctetes has similarly founded a city, 3.401–402, further south in Calabria. Ulysses is last described as unfortunate. (Later in Books 8.9–17 and 11.225–295, we learn that Diomedes—the other great nemesis of Aeneas in the *Iliad* along with Achilles—has lacked his homecoming and also emigrated to Puglia. To the Latin envoys who unsuccessfully seek to enlist him in another go against the Trojans, Diomedes ticks off, 11.255–277, the various misfortunes that met the Greek victors at Troy.)[31] These retributions reflect the fortunes of historical Greece and Greeks as they were to fall beneath the political domination of Rome.

The Buthrotum episode reflects especially on the beginning of this historical turnaround, for it strongly connects the mythological Pyrrhus of the poem to the historical King Pyrrhus, a nightmarish figure in Roman historical memory where he was routinely paired with Hannibal as one of the two foreign invaders who almost destroyed the republic.[32] King Pyrrhus won two battles over Roman armies at Heraclea (280 BCE) and Asculum (279 BCE), victories so costly that they coined the term "Pyrrhic," before he was defeated at Beneventum (275 BCE) and withdrew from Italy. Virgil's Buthrotum itself lies in King Pyrrhus's old kingdom of Epirus; "*Epirus*" is mentioned at either end of the episode as a kind of verbal frame to it (3.292, 3.505), and it almost rhymes with the hero/king's name. The Pyrrhus of the poem has passed his kingdom on to the Trojan son of Priam, the seer Helenus; King Pyrrhus had *a son named Helenus*, who inherited his father's domain.

Rome's conflict with King Pyrrhus had been the subject of Book 6 of Ennius's *Annales*, of which only fragments have come down to us.[33] Their editor Otto Skutsch suggests Virgil's "*Aeacidae Pyrrhi*" (3.296) may be an echo of Ennius's "*Aeacida Burrus*," and "*Aeacida*" reappears in two other places in the

---

31. Heinze, 1993, 80 points out that Virgil deliberately leaves out of Book 3 one of the traditional stops on Aeneas's wanderings, a meeting with Diomedes, who seeks to return to him the Palladium that he and Ulysses stole from Troy and that has only brought him bad luck.

32. For examples, Cicero, *De officiis* 1.38; Horace 3.6; Livy 22.59, 31.7, 35.14; Propertius 3.11 (cited below); a topos by the time of Juvenal 12.108; 14.161–162.

33. For a consideration of the fragments thought to have come from Book 6 of the *Annales*, the book of Pyrrhus, see Fantham, 2006.

fragments as a patronymic for the Epirote king who asserted his descent from Achilles.[34] More intriguingly, Skutsch connects the inscription that Aeneas, in the episode of Book 3 that immediately precedes the visit to Buthrotum, sets up with a trophy of captured Greek armor at the temple of Apollo near the future site of the battle of Actium,

AENEAS HAEC DE DANAIS VICTORIBUS ARMA

Aeneas won these arms from the victorious Greeks (3.288)

to a scene reported by Orosius where it is King Pyrrhus who dedicates an inscription in the temple of Jupiter in Tarentum in words presumably drawn from the *Annales:*

> qui antehac
> Inuicti fuere uiri, pater optume Olympi,
> Hos ego ui pugna, uici uictusque sum ab isdem.[35]

those men who previously were unconquered, best father of Olympus, those I conquered by force of battle, and am conquered by them.

Ennius's King Pyrrhus already seems to recognize that his victories are Pyrrhic, and that, in spite of appearances, Rome is winning the day. The conjectural link Skutsch suggests between the two passages gains some force, I would suggest, from the proximity of Aeneas's Actium inscription to the Buthrotum episode with its Pyrrhus who recalls the King Pyrrhus in question.

Quite apart from the question of an Ennian model, this proximity, both narrative and geographical, couples these two episodes, as does the narrative detail of Helenus giving the departing Aeneas, as if in substitution for the arms that he suspends as a trophy at Actium, the arms of Neoptolemus/Pyrrhus (3.467–469); these appear to be, I have noted above, the once-disputed arms of Achilles himself. The visit to Buthrotum is framed on either end by arms taken from once-victorious Greeks. The two episodes spell out the same historical destiny: the thwarting of Greek victors and of would-be, but in the end degenerate, descendants of Achilles who find themselves defeated by Roman arms. This destiny will culminate and perhaps be sealed once and for all when Augustus would defeat Antony and Cleopatra and the Greek-speaking East

---

34. Ennius, 1985, 633–634 on fragment 8.28 [?]; see 86 (6.4) and 87 (6.14).
35. *Ibid.,* 87 (6.10) and, for Skutsch's discussion, 345–346.

at Actium.[36] By coordinating Actium and Pyrrhus's Buthrotum in Aeneas's mythic adventures, Virgil can suggest the continuity of Rome's ascendancy from its first repulse of King Pyrrhus to the most recent victory of Aeneas's Julian heir. In between, Rome fought the Second Macedonian War against Philip V, whom, in Livy's account (31.8–14), the Roman consul Publius Sulpicius in his appeal for war depicted as an imminent invader of Italy much more dangerous than King Pyrrhus. Rome fought the Third Macedonian War against his son Perseus; both Philip (see Silius Italicus 15.291) and Perseus (see Propertius 4.11.39) claimed descent from Achilles. After Aemilius Paullus defeated Perseus at Pydna in 168 BCE, Rome subjected Epirus to exemplary punishment: seventy cities were sacked and a hundred and fifty thousand persons were made slaves. In 44 BCE, in spite of lobbying efforts against it by Cicero, a Roman colony was planted in Buthrotum and much of the native Greek population was replaced.[37] In the wake of Actium, Augustus sponsored new building projects and a victory monument at Nicopolis, the site where Aeneas hangs up his trophy and inscription.[38] All these events may be reflected in Virgil's fiction where Epirus is dispossessed from Achillean Pyrrhus and colonized by Trojans who make a city in the image of their lost homeland.

In roughly the same years as the Buthrotum colony, Julius Caesar had sponsored the colonization and rebuilding of Carthage. The *Aeneid* may presage this event, too, when Mercury finds Aeneas himself taking over the construction of Carthage in the following Book 4 (260–261), the hero's misstep in the short term, destined for his descendants in the long run.[39] For Rome will supplant both Greeks and Carthaginians. Books 1 and 4 predict Rome's victory over Carthage, just as Books 2 and 3 are prophetic of Rome's historical conquest of Greece and the Hellenistic East. The epic evokes Hannibal, the Carthaginian scourge, as the mythological Dido's avenger—"*ultor*" (4.625)—

---

36. Costa, 2012, 9–10.

37. The efforts of Cicero and of his friend Atticus on behalf of the Greek inhabitants of Buthrotum whose lands were being confiscated to be given to Julius Caesar's veterans are recorded in the *Letters to Atticus* between 14.10 and 16.16; see especially 15.19, 15.29, 16.2, 16.4, 16.16. See Bergemann, 1999; for the earlier history of the province, see Cabanes, 1976. See also Barchiesi, 2017, on Buthrotum, colonization, and the movement of peoples.

38. Servius, on 3.502, links the little Troy at Buthrotum to Nicopolis. On the link between the two colonies, see Stahl, 1998a. On Nicopolis and the victory monument there, Lange, 2009, 95–123 and Lange, 2016, 141–153.

39. On the colonization of Carthage and the *Aeneid*, see E. L. Harrison, 1984, 95–102; Giusti, 2017.

in her curse that pledges continual war from North African shores, just as it names Hannibal's Greek counterpart, King Pyrrhus of Epirus, beneath the equally mythological Pyrrhus. In the narrative sequence of the poem, it has been pointed out above, these first four books attest to Rome's conquest of the Mediterranean world through foreign war, while its last four books, which depict the conflict between Trojans and Latins in Italy, reflect upon the civil wars that succeeded that conquest.

Actium, however, the latest Roman victory over Greek and eastern arms, complicates this apparent historical sequence. The senate dominated by Octavian had declared war in 32 BCE on Cleopatra, the queen of Egypt, but the real target was Mark Antony, and the war was a civil war.[40] Dido not only stands at the origins of Rome's future conflict with Carthage, but as a North African queen who loves a Trojan-Roman general and eventually commits suicide, she also stands in for Cleopatra. And the Ptolemaic queen Cleopatra was a Greek: the placing of the Greek Books 2 and 3 inside the Carthaginian Books 1 and 4 suggests how these two historical enemies of Rome have been reborn together in Antony's Egyptian consort.

This idea concludes Propertius 3.11, where the poet praises Augustus's victory at Actium over the arch-enemy Cleopatra:

Hannibalis spolia et uicti monumenta Syphacis,	59
et Pyrrhi ad nostros gloria fracta pedes?	60
Leucadius uersas acies memorabit Apollo:	69
tantum operis belli sustulit una dies.[41]	70

(Where are) the spoils and trophies of defeated Hannibal and Syphax and the glory of Pyrrhus broken at our feet? Leucadian Apollo will retell the routed ranks at Actium: one day of battle destroyed so great a work of war.

Cleopatra is the new Hannibal, the new King Pyrrhus; Actium is the continuation, if also the incomparably glorious—one day is all it took!—culmination, of Rome's conquest of dangerous foreign enemies. The testimony of this other Augustan poet spells out the terms of the new regime's propaganda. It also explains how Virgil has coordinated the Carthaginian and Greek books of Aeneas's wanderings and the prominent placement of the mythological Pyrrhus at the respective centers of the latter Books 2 and 3. Following the

---

40. Lange, 2009, 49–71 reconstructs the events of 32 BCE.
41. Propertius 3.11.

terms of this propaganda, the *Aeneid* papers over the last of Rome's recent civil wars as foreign war. Those same terms, however, suggest a converse interpretation of history and its continuities: that Rome's foreign conquests already contain the seeds of, and cannot be separated from, her internecine strife. The chronology that seems to be traced by Virgil's epic, Rome's domination over the Mediterranean in the first half of the poem, her descent into civil strife in the second, is short-circuited when external foes (Dido/Hannibal, Pyrrhus/King Pyrrhus) already seem poised to come back, like a ghostly return of the repressed, as internal ones.

If, in Book 2, the doubling of Pyrrhus with Aeneas casts the violence that brings the house of Aeneas (and of the future Augustus) to power onto the foreign enemy, the association of Pyrrhus with King Pyrrhus in Book 3 does similar ideological work. It turns Augustus's adversary at Actium—Cleopatra—into one more in a historical succession of Greek foes who have been battling Rome ever since the Trojan War. Following A. M. Bowie, we might suggest that the mythological Pyrrhus's other name, Neoptolemus, already punningly places him (and then his later Epirote namesake) into this succession of enemy Greeks leading at last to the Ptolemies of Egypt.[42] If so, Cleopatra, the newest—and last—Ptolemy, hearkens back all the way to Troy. But what, then, of Mark Antony and the Romans who fought against fellow countrymen at Actium? In both cases these Greeks become difficult to distinguish from their supposed Trojan/Roman opposites.

Anchises Explains Roman History in Book 6

The return of the historically repressed is literally reenacted among the ghosts of the underworld in Book 6, and here, too, chronology is short-circuited: in the parade and catalog of Aeneas's Roman descendants that Anchises points out to his son. Virgil constructs the episode through two different ring compositions or chiastic forms. One of these begins with Aeneas's encounters with the shades of Dido (6.450–476) and Deiphobus (6.494–547), who recapitulate the first four books of the poem. The Carthaginian queen turns away in silence from Aeneas who too late expresses his regrets and unwillingness to

---

42. Bowie, 1990, as discussed in note 21, makes a different but, I think, related argument about "Neo-ptolemus." Just to complicate matters further, King Pyrrhus had co-ruled with a kinsman named Neoptolemus, until he had him murdered in 296 BCE.

part from her; she, with her people, remains the enemy—"*inimica*" (6.472)—of the Trojan hero and of the future Rome. Deiphobus, the slain son of Priam, rankling at the treason of Helen whom he wed after the death of Paris, calls for vengeance against all Greeks.

> di, talia Grais
> instaurate, pio si poenas ore reposco. (6.529–530)

> Gods, repay the same to the Greeks, if I ask for their punishment with pious lips.

Dido and Deiphobus respectively play the roles of the angry Ajax and the wronged husband Agamemnon, whose ghosts Odysseus meets in his consultation with the underworld in the *Odyssey* (11.542–567, 387–464). Deiphobus speaks where Dido is silent and takes over, in however reduced and gnomic a form, her cursing in Book 4. His curse is directed not, as hers is, against the Trojans and their Roman descendants but, in an opposite direction, from a Trojan against the Greeks. The retribution he seeks has already been demonstrated in Book 3, particularly in the fate of Pyrrhus, the son of Achilles. In Virgil's Odyssean model (*Ody.* 11.465–540), Odysseus meets the ghost of Achilles between those of Agamemnon and Ajax. The hero of the *Iliad* is momentarily consoled for his underworld existence when he asks about his son and Odysseus gives him a glowing report. The *Aeneid* goes to some length to gainsay the *Odyssey* and to recount Pyrrhus's bad end.[43] The ghosts of Dido

---

43. In *Odyssey* 11, the ghost of Agamemnon similarly asks after *his* son, Orestes (*Ody.* 11.457–461). I have argued elsewhere that Virgil also imitates this underworld scene in Book 3 in the Buthrotum episode, where Andromache seems to answer the questions of both the ghosts of Agamemnon and Achilles by revealing that the maddened Orestes has killed Neoptolemus. Andromache goes on in the same passage to imitate those ghosts by herself asking about the surviving son, Ascanius, who might continue the prowess of his uncle Hector by whose empty tomb Andromache is mourning (3.330–343); she later suggests that Ascanius is also a substitute for her own dead Astyanax (3.482–491). The inference is that Buthrotum, fixed in the Trojan past, is itself a kind of underworld and place of the dead and that Andromache is a living ghost. See Quint, 1993, 58–61. Virgil rewrites the underworld scene of the *Odyssey* twice. Were he to have followed its logic completely in Book 6, Virgil would have included an encounter not only with the Trojan equivalent of Agamemnon, Deiphobus, but also with the Trojan equivalent of Achilles, Hector. But the earlier rewriting of *Odyssey* 11 in Book 3, Andromache at Hector's empty tomb, as well as the still earlier apparition of the ghost of Hector to the sleeping Aeneas in Book 2 (270–297), have already taken the place of such a meeting in the Virgilian underworld. Significantly, the first thing that Aeneas sees on waking from his vision of Hector

and Deiphobus in Book 6 thus repeat, in the same narrative ordering of the *Aeneid* itself, the visit to Carthage and Aeneas's subsequent retelling of the fall of Troy and his wanderings through Greek territories, and they evoke the double historical focus of the first four books on Rome's future victories in the Punic Wars and her conquests over Greeks.

This double focus returns at the end of Anchises' parade of the shades who will be great figures in Roman history. The catalog itself has the form of a chiastic ring composition: Romulus and the kings are succeeded by Brutus and by early republican heroes of the fourth century BCE, then a jump to the civil war between Caesar and Pompey, followed by a return backward into republican history of the second and third centuries BCE that ends with M. Claudius Marcellus, the third winner of the *spolia opima* against the Gauls in 222 BCE during the Second Punic War. In Virgil's apparently deliberate variation of the story, Marcellus dedicates the *spolia* not to Jupiter but to Quirinus, the deified Romulus and first winner of this best of trophies, thus bringing Anchises' pageant back to where it began: Romulus [AUGUSTUS] and kings—republic—civil war—republic—Romulus.[44] This historical overview seems to recoil from the civil strife at its center and to double back on itself to Rome's beginnings. A similar idea initiates the catalog with its jump from beginning to end, from Romulus to Augustus, the second Romulus who turns time back to the golden age (6.792–794). Romulus, born from the line of Aeneas's second son, Silvius (6.760–765), is juxtaposed with Augustus and the Julian line that descends from Iulus, the older Trojan heir—"*Caesar et omnis Iuli / progenies*" (6.789). The at least threefold effect is to cast Augustus as the refounder of the Roman state, to associate him as far as the poet dares with kingship—which no Roman, including the emperors who succeeded Augus-

---

is the burning house of Deiphobus (2.310–311). One might compare Deiphobus's question to Aeneas—

> sed te qui uiuum casus, age fare uicissim,
> attulerint. pelagine uenis erroribus actus
> an monitu diuum? (6.531–533)

to Andromache's earlier question;

> sed tibi qui cursum uenti, quae fata dedere?
> aut quisnam ignarum nostris deus appulit oris? (3.337–338)

both of which depend on *Odyssey* 11.155–162, the question that the ghost of his mother, Antikleia, poses to Odysseus.

44. On the "*spolia opima*," see S. J. Harrison, 1989; Putnam, 1985b.

tus, would claim for himself—and, most radically, to insinuate that all Roman history before Augustus, possibly including Romulus himself, has been a usurpation by the cadet line of Aeneas's descendants and has been waiting all along for the restoration of its rightful Julian dynast.[45] The Augustan regime thus seems to rise from mythic origins rather than from a more recent history of civil war: it seems to lie both in and outside of Roman history.

In fact, the subsequent unfolding of Anchises' catalog quickly jumps forward through the history of the Republic to reach an impasse with the civil conflict between Julius Caesar and Pompey. It is both a historical and logical leap: Caesar's war against his son-in-law Pompey is aligned with the slayings of their sons by Brutus and Torquatus (6.819–825) and suggests a killing off of the future that has been built into the Republic since its beginning.[46]

> aggeribus socer Alpinis atque arce Monoeci
> descendens, gener aduersis instructus Eois! (6.830–831)

> The father-in-law (Caesar) descending from Alpine camps and the fortress at Monoecus (Monaco), the son-in-law (Pompey) provided against him with armies of the East.

45. Casali, 2009, 323–325, shows Virgil finally choosing in Book 12 to trace Romulus back to Silvius: the Julians can only claim so much of Roman history. Bettini, 2005, 90 argues, *contra*, that the name of Romulus's mother, Ilia, denotes descent from Iulus: "*Assaraci quem sanguinis Ilia mater / educet*" (6.778–779). The genealogy of Romulus through Silvius in Book 6 contradicts the genealogy of Book 1 (267–277), where Romulus seems to descend from Iulus. On the double, contradictory genealogy, see O'Hara, 1990, 144–147 and O'Hara, 2007, 88–90. Book 8 tells us that the shield which Vulcan makes for Aeneas shows the Roman stock that will descend from *Ascanius* (8.628–629), but here Virgil may equivocate. Livy (1.3) suggests that there were *two* different sons of Aeneas named Ascanius, the elder one the son of Creusa, from whom the Julian House claims descent, the younger the son of Lavinia and the father of Silvius. See R. M. Ogilvie, 1965, 42–43. Dionysius of Halicarnassus (*Roman Antiquities* 1.70.3–4) tells us that Silvius, the ancestor of Romulus, ascended the throne of Alba Longa, after the death of his older brother Ascanius-Iulus, and in opposition to Ascanius-Iulus's son Iulus, from whom the Julian lineage descended, thus dispossessing it from its rightful place in Roman history that Augustus, the new Romulus, was to reclaim. The root question is just how continuous is Augustus with Romulus after the long interruption: is he continuous with Romulus as Julian, with Romulus as king, or does he refound Rome on different terms? I think that all these possibilities are in play: I am inclined toward the last. See Barchiesi, 2012, who stresses the apartness in the *Aeneid* of the imperial house of Augustus that enables a cosmopolitan idea of Roman-ness for everyone else.

46. For an opposite reading of Brutus, see Lefèvre, 1998, especially 103–107. That account leaves out Virgil's qualification of the first Brutus's motives: "*laudumque immensa cupido*" (6.823).

It appears that history cannot go forward from this point of national cataclysm. (A related, if different, question arises with the natural death of the possible heir Marcellus [6.860–865] in the mournful supplement to the pageant, discussed below in chapter 4.) Instead, Anchises starts going *backward* to celebrate the heroes of Rome's foreign wars.

> ille triumphata Capitolia ad alta Corintho
> uictor aget currum caesis insignis Achiuis.
> eruet ille Argos Agamemnoniasque Mycenas
> ipsumque Aeaciden, genus armipotentis Achilli,
> ultus auos Troiae templa et temerata Mineruae.
> quis te, magne Cato, tacitum aut te, Cosse, relinquat?
> quis Gracchi genus aut geminos, duo fulmina belli,
> Scipiadas, cladem Libyae, paruoque potentem
> Fabricium uel te sulco, Serrane, serentem?
> quo fessum rapitis, Fabii? tu Maximus ille es,
> uno qui nobis cunctando restituis rem. (6.836–846)

> There is he (Mummius) who, having triumphed over Corinth, will drive his chariot as victor to the high Capitol, famous for the Achaeans he has killed; that one (L. Aemilius Paullus) will overturn Argos and Agamemnon's Mycenae and that descendant of Achilles (Perseus), from the lineage of Achilles strong in arms, he (Paullus) the revenger of his ancestors of Troy and of the violated temple of Minerva. Who would leave you in silence, great Cato, or you, Cossus? Who the family of the Gracchi, or the twin Scipios, two thunderbolts of war, calamitous to Libya? Or you Fabricius, rich in poverty? Or you, Serranus (C. Attilius Regulus), sowing the furrow? Where do you carry away my tired voice, O Fabii? You are that (Q. Fabius) Maximus who alone restored our state by delaying.

The list moves generally backward in time and from victories over Greeks to victories over Carthage, although it contains its own minichiasmus between its opening mention of the destruction of Corinth in 146 and the mention of the two Scipios in verses 6.842–843, the second of whom, L. Aemilius Scipio, conquered and razed Carthage in the same year. In between, in the longest vignette, the poem celebrates the victory of Aemilius Paullus—L. Aemilius Scipio's father—at Pydna in 168 over Achillean Perseus—"*Aeaciden*" (6.839)—as revenge against the Greeks for the Trojan War. Deiphobus's earlier call for retribution has been fulfilled. "*Aeacides*" was also the poem's earlier epithet for Pyrrhus and had been used by Ennius for his King Pyrrhus; the latter is recalled by the naming of his Roman foe Fabricius at verses 6.843–844. The catalog alternates between Greek and Carthaginian enemies:

Greece:
> Mummius 146 BCE
> L. Aemilius Paulus against Perseus 168

Carthage:
> Scipio Africanus 202
> Scipio Aemilianus 146

Greece:
> Fabricius against Pyrrhus 278

Carthage:
> C. Attilius Regulus 257
> Q. Fabius Maximus 217
> M. Claudius Marcellus (co-consul with Fabius Maximus) *spolia opima* 222

By placing the Roman victors over Carthage last in this sequence, the passage thus closes the ring-composition that opened earlier in the book with Dido and Deiphobus: just as Dido precedes Deiphobus and the narrative of the larger poem begins in Carthage before turning, in Aeneas's inset narration, to tell of Greece, so here, in a reverse sequence the catalog moves from Rome's more recent conquests over Greeks to its earlier confrontation with Carthage. In doing so, however, it chronologically "misplaces" the still earlier defeat of King Pyrrhus, much as Aeneas's recounting of the earlier crimes and death of Pyrrhus is contained within the larger Carthage episode.[47]

In this switch in Book 6 from the showdown between Julius Caesar and Pompey to a backward rehearsing of Roman republican heroism against Carthaginian and Greek foes, the *Aeneid* repeats in miniature and makes explicit the ideological stakes that govern the fiction of its first half. The civil wars that

---

[47]. In this scheme, M. Claudius Marcellus is described as fighting the Gauls—from whom he won the *spolia opima* in 222—and the Carthaginians: "*sternet Poenos Gallumque rebellem*." But during the Second Punic War, he also conquered the Greek city of Syracuse that had allied itself with Carthage, sacking it in 212 BCE. So, although the poem does not spell it out, Marcellus also brings together Rome's victories over Carthaginians *and* Greeks at the end of Anchises' parade of heroes. See Freudenburg, 2017.

brought Augustus to power cannot be told and, in fact, led to a dead-end. The way out of this impasse is to disguise them as foreign wars, as latter-day versions of Rome's earlier conquests in the Mediterranean. These conquests have been the historical corollary and references of the mythological wanderings of Aeneas and his defeated Trojans through Greece and Carthage in the preceding books of the poem. The fiction has invoked the future specters of King Pyrrhus and Hannibal, but the reader knows that history has turned prior defeat into Roman victory, already suggested by the fates of Pyrrhus and Dido. Moreover, the *Aeneid* constructs a typology of Rome's twofold history of conquest over its foreign enemies so that Augustus, Aeneas's descendant, may be seen to have fulfilled it in his crushing the Greek/African Cleopatra at Actium. Virgil may suggest here in Book 6 that Julius Caesar's battles against Pompey's eastern armies of the Greek-named dawn—"*Eois*" (6.831)—are already transformed into foreign conflict: at the battle of Actium depicted on the shield of Aeneas in Book 8, Antony will be characterized as "*uictor ab Aurorae populis*" (8.686).[48] But the struggle between the in-laws Caesar and Pompey is unmistakably civil, and its juxtaposition with the history of Rome's encounters with Greece and Carthage makes the strategy of the poem glaringly visible. Civil war remains at the center of Anchises' pageant, however much its ring composition and retreat to the past may seek to contain it, and the same may be true for the *Aeneid* as a whole.

48. Bowie, 1990, 479–480; Reed, 2007, 159–161; Oliensis, 2004, 42–43.

3

The Doubleness of Dido

THOUGH HE IS Rome's mythical progenitor through his marriage with Lavinia, Virgil's Aeneas never does found Rome itself. He walks through its future precincts in Evander's Pallanteum in Book 8, unaware that he is doing so. The actual foundation of the city by Romulus only appears in the prophecies of Anchises and on the shield that Vulcan makes for Aeneas; he does not recognize or understand the images on the latter. Aeneas does wander into the foundation story of another city, Dido's Carthage, carried there, almost by accident, by the storm of Book 1. In doing so, Aeneas and the *Aeneid* transform the tale of Dido, the Punic city's own national myth. At the same time, I shall argue in the second half of this analysis, Virgil's rewriting criticizes that myth on its own terms.

That Aeneas and Dido were never lovers, that they lived in different epochs, was well known to ancient readers.[1] Perhaps Naevius had also invented their meeting: the evidence is fragmentary and inconclusive. But Virgil's episode, the most famous section of the *Aeneid*, was a supplement to the tradition and a fabrication, and it declares as much. Even as Virgil tells it, there is no narrative need for Dido to fall in love with Aeneas. Jupiter has sent Mercury ahead to make the Carthaginians well disposed to and ready to host the Trojans, Dido foremost among them (1.297–304). Perhaps Venus is unaware of this, but her sending Cupid to take the form and place of Ascanius and to kindle Dido's passion becomes literal overkill. It is an add-on within the Dido episode that marks the add-on quality of the episode itself. Critics have pointed out that Virgil acknowledges that he is making up a new story of Dido

---

1. Hardie, 2014, 52–55.

through the figure of Fama.² Fama is earthborn, but she has the power to reach the skies and to found or to conceal—the poem's overdetermined verb, *"condere"*³—her head or her origin (*"caput"*) in the clouds: *"caput inter nubila condit"* (4.177). Earlier we have been told that Dido was founding—*"condebat"* (1.447)—her temple to Juno on the spot where the head of a fierce horse—*"caput acris equi"* (1.444) was dug up. Fama, that is, the *Aeneid* itself, replaces the traditional foundation story of Carthage with one of its own. That new story claims, in a kind of regress, its own foundation in the clouds. It is an official story with apparent divine sanction. Or it comes murkily out of thin air.⁴

Servius neatly sums up the other, superseded story of Dido:

DIDO she was first called by her real name Elissa, then after her death she was named Dido by the Phoenicians, that is, virago, in the Punic language, because when she was urged by her allies to wed one of the African kings and she held on to her love for her first husband, she with a strong soul killed herself and threw herself on the pyre which she had feigned to have built to placate the spirit of her first husband. (on 1.340)⁵

---

2. Feeney, 1991, 186–187; Hardie, 2012, 98. For an analogy of Virgil's doubled Dido to the Helen of Homer and Stesichorus, see Hexter, 1992, 332–384, 341–342.

3. James, 1995.

4. Fama can make us suspicious about Jupiter's ensuing pronouncement, carried down to earth by Mercury—whom Hardie has shown to be an inverse double of Fama—ordering Aeneas to leave Carthage and set sail for Italy. The divine command issues from similarly cloudy origins in the heavens. See Hardie, 2012, 92–98 as well as Hardie, 1986, 276–285. This is all a poetic fiction, the poem allows the skeptical reader to conclude. In between these moments, Iarbas has complained, with a Lucretian emphasis on thunderbolts sent from the clouds (*"caecique in nubibus ignes"*; 4.209), that the Jupiter he worships is just an empty fame: *"famamque fouemus inanem"* (4.218). Iarbas believes himself to be the son of Jupiter in the role of Hammon (4.198); it's better than thinking of oneself as a fatherless bastard. The most famous claimant to such Hammonian sonship in antiquity was Alexander the Great. Romans had looked down on such Hellenistic god-kings, though Augustus was now becoming one himself. Virgil's replacement of Dido's prior fame with a new one threatens to reveal the whole religio-political establishment that the *Aeneid* depends on and serves as a house of cards or, rather, as a hard fact of power. I return to the issue of divine sonship below in the next chapter. On *fama* as part of the imperial ideology of the *Aeneid*, see Boyle, 1986, 87–89; Hejduk, 2009.

5. Servius, 1881, 1:120. "DIDO vero nomine Elissa ante dicta est, sed post interitum a Poenis Dido appellata, id est virago Punica lingua, quod cum a suis sociis cogeretur cuicumque de Afris regibus nubere et prioris mariti caritate teneretur, forti se animo et interfecerit et in pyram iecerit, quam se ad expiandos prioris mariti manes extruxisse fingebat."

This is a Greco-Roman story about Carthage, just as Virgil's is.[6] We do not know if this was the story that the Carthaginians liked to tell about themselves since we do not have Punic sources. I shall treat it, as the *Aeneid* does, *as if* it were the national myth. In this account, not only does Dido establish her new Phoenician colony in Libya. She also maintains, at the cost of her own life, the self-rule of the city by refusing to wed a king from among the neighboring North African peoples. In the course of time, Carthage would make these peoples subject to its empire.

Virgil's version keeps the story of African suitor kings, aligning Dido with the Penelope of the *Odyssey* besieged by her suitors and faithful to a husband she presumes to be dead. It aligns Dido, too, with the *Odyssey*'s Nausicaa, courted by local Phaeacians, a Homeric double of Penelope. The episode of the entertainment of the shipwrecked Odysseus by King Alcinous, Nausicaa's father (*Odyssey* 6–13), during which the hero recounts his wanderings, is the largest of the many Odyssean models (Calypso, Circe, the cave of Polyphemus, the Laistrygonians, the Lotus Eaters) that Virgil recombines in the depiction of Aeneas's stay with Dido in Carthage. Iarbas, the rejected suitor, triggers the queen's tragedy as he or other neighboring kings do in the traditional story. Virgil keeps, too, Dido's building of a funeral pyre under false pretenses. But he writes over the story of Dido's exemplary marital fidelity to her murdered husband Sychaeus and, even more important, of how her self-immolation preserved Carthage's independence from the African peoples it would come to dominate. "I have not kept the faith I promised to the ashes of Sychaeus"—"*non seruata fides cineri promissa Sychaeo*" (4.552)—Dido guiltily confesses, after she has prepared the pyre that is supposed to destroy the remnants of her affair with Aeneas and break its love spell. Virgil offers an alternative, "true" version of Dido's death on her pyre. Its motive was irrational, desperate eros, after Dido, like Iarbas, found herself spurned, in her own turn, by the Trojan hero. Carthage in this version was not founded by an extraordinary act of female self-sacrifice—on a par with Lucretia's suicide that founded the Roman Republic—but instead on self-destructive passion whose consequences would haunt the city through three Punic wars and its annihilation in 146 BCE.[7]

6. A longer account of Dido's story is found in Justin's *Epitome of the "Philippic History" of Pompeius Trogus*, 18.4–6. For possible Punic components in Virgil's portrait of Dido, see Hexter, 1992.

7. Boccaccio, following Tertullian, compared Dido to Lucretia in *De claris mulieribus*; see Hardie, 2014; Hardie, 1986, 283.

One might say that this history of how Carthage turned out *required* a rewriting of the Carthaginians' own account of their origin story. With revisionist irony, Virgil explains that once Rome, already in the person of Aeneas, came into the picture, Carthage could no longer cling to its myth of sovereign autonomy, personified in the chaste widow. Virgil, that is, *expects* us to know that, from historical hindsight, he is writing over the traditional story—the story we already know—and telling a new version that corresponds to the city's ultimately tragic end. The mourning that rises from the palace when Dido kills herself evokes the fall of Carthage itself, foes rushing into the city, its houses and temples burnt to the ground (4.669–671). Virgil's model, the Trojans' lament at the killing of Hector described in *Iliad* 22.408–411, evoked Troy in flames, the destruction, burning, and sacking of the city that Aeneas has narrated in Book 2. Carthage is itself one of the series of false, doomed Troys that Aeneas went on to describe himself trying to found or visiting in Book 3. Dido might have listened more carefully, were Cupid not nestled in her lap.

As Richard Heinze noted, Virgil's rewriting of Dido's story creates a palimpsest.

> Even in Virgil, the original picture of Dido shines through beneath his new over-painting; not only in the importance that Virgil still assigns to the motif of her loyalty to her dead husband: when Dido laments that she has allowed her sense of shame to die and has ruined her reputation, the one thing by which she has been hoping to gain immortality (4.322), there is a memory—no doubt unconscious—of that Dido who went to her death for the sake of loyalty, and so won for herself immortal fame.[8]

I want to contest Heinze's qualification, "no doubt unconscious." Virgil writes over the traditional story but, as I have just noted, leaves enough traces of it visible so that we can compare and contrast. The two competing versions color the way that we judge the Carthaginian queen. Dido says that she has lost her *"fama prior"* (4.323), that is, the earlier version of her story that this character almost seems to know about as she (more literally in this context) laments the loss of her good name. Both she and Aeneas have, Jupiter observes, been oblivious to their better fame—*"oblitos famae melioris amantis"* (4.221)—and Virgil's invented episode will not do credit to his uxorious (but blundering lover) hero either.

---

8. Heinze, 1993, 95.

Virgil *must* include details from the familiar story of Dido in order to explain how it came into being in place of the one he is now telling to supersede it. Dido enters the poem as a wise lawgiver to her own people (1.507–508), generously willing to aid the Trojans driven to her coast, either by sending them on to Italy or Sicily or by inviting them to settle in her new city (1.569–574). Up to this point, she is Dido the city-founder of the traditional story, before Aeneas breaks forth from the misty cloud—"nebula" (1.412; 439), "nubis" (1.580; 587)—in which Venus has sheltered him from view. Virgil's use of the Homeric motif (*Ody.* 7.40–145) might just lead the reader to conclude that Aeneas was never present in the first place: like one of Fama's fictions, he has come from the clouds. But once he has entered Dido's story, how could he have been forgotten and subsequently written out of it? Dido claims to erect her pyre, following the order of the Massylian priestess she has invented, in order to remove all memories that Aeneas has left behind: "*abolere nefandi / cuncta uiri monimenta iuuat monstratque sacerdos*" (4.497–498). She is lying but tells an unintended truth: the pyre will take with her the indications that Aeneas had ever been in Carthage. The effect is something like the opposite of the palimpsest, of the original, traditional story of Dido peering through the story that is being written over it. Here it is Virgil's own story that is going up in flames. It explains to us why the affair of Dido and Aeneas was lost to history until the *Aeneid* could come along and set things straight. Dido's death destroyed the evidence.

The conflict between Virgil's version and the traditional story reaches its apex in Dido's last two scenes in Book 4. When she sees the Trojan fleet sailing away, Dido briefly imagines a different fiery end in the pluperfect subjunctive: "*faces in castra tulissem / implessemque foros flammis*" (4.604–605). While they were still in Carthage, she should, she says, have played the role of Hector, burning the camp and ships of Aeneas, as the Trojan hero had tried to do to the Greek fleet in the *Iliad*—and as Turnus will try to do, mistakenly thinking that he is playing the role of Achilles, in Book 9 (the Trojan matrons have their go at it in Book 5).[9] Dido already announces here the reversal of the Trojan War that will take place in the second half of the *Aeneid* and aligns herself with the doomed Italian hero. She would, she says, have wiped out

---

9. Iris, disguised as Beroë, invokes Hector (5.634) just before she urges the matrons to burn the ships; Ascanius tells them that they are not attacking the Greek enemy camp, as if they were still in the *Iliad* following Hector in his quest to burn the Argive ships, but are instead burning up but their own hopes for a future: "*non hostem inimicaque castra / Argiuum, uestra spes uritis*" (5.671–672).

Aeneas and Ascanius and thrown herself on the conflagration—"*memet super ipsa dedissem*" (4.606)—extinguishing both Roman and Carthaginian futures.

Would have, could have, should have. The poem still leaves open, as it has done thus far through the episode, whether Dido is indeed the threat to Aeneas that Mercury says she is—you'll soon see torches and flames, the god says, if you don't clear out of Carthage (4.566–568).[10] It may be Aeneas's leaving her and the *way* he leaves her that push Dido to these fantasies of revenge which may be nothing more than fantasies.[11] She has been burning with love from the start of Book 4, but *that* is a metaphor. Dido's immediately ensuing curse (4.607f.), however, makes fantasy real, just as the pyre she has built will literally burn her dead body. The fantasy of Virgil's myth itself shifts into history, as Dido projects recurring warfare between Carthage and Rome, the avenger rising from her bones and ashes who will be Hannibal, the shores battling shores with fire and sword—"*face ... ferroque*" (4.626)—down to the latest North African queen, Cleopatra. Dido at the last turns—however she may be driven to turn—into a monster: her terrible curse is modeled on the curse of the cyclops Polyphemus in the *Odyssey*. Aeneas had cut the cable of his ship in order to make a quick escape from the shores of the cyclopes in Sicily toward the end of Book 3 (667), and he repeats the action in his haste to depart from Carthage (4.575; 579–580): just in time, it now seems.

But the Dido who now mounts her pyre sounds a different note. Sandwiched between her address to the relics of Aeneas and her wish that her Trojan lover see her burning funeral pyre from the deep, Dido speaks her epitaph.

---

10. Schiesaro, 2008, demonstrates, at length and in detail, that Virgil does some careful stacking of the deck against Dido. Allusions to both the Medea of Euripides, asking for time (in which to carry out her revenge), and to Apollonius's Medea, who betrays her brother Apsyrtus to murder, should give us pause about the Dido with whom the larger poem makes its readers sympathize. Mercury, Schiesaro argues, may know what he is talking about. His intervention and the ensuing events of the poem will never let us know for sure; Virgil has it both ways.

11. The initial delay of Aeneas in confronting Dido, his barely credible story of a divine messenger ordering him to leave, his tactless assertion that, were he freed by the fates to pursue his wishes, he *still* would not stay with Dido but return to vanquished Troy, his failure to weep, his refusal to wait out the winter (on which occasion he may weep before her sister Anna, if the tears of verse 449 are his, and not Anna's, and *that* might be as bad or worse than not weeping at all), his sailing in the secrecy of night: this series of actions by Aeneas keeps ratcheting up Dido's fury and her literature-soaked imagination: she could have been a Medea or a Procne (4.600–602) as well as a ship-burning Hector.

uixi et, quem dederat cursum Fortuna peregi,
et nunc magna mei sub terras ibit imago.
urbem praeclaram statui, mea moenia uidi,
ulta uirum poenas inimico a fratre recepi,
felix, heu nimium felix, si litora tantum
numquam Dardaniae tetigissent nostra carinae. (4.653–658)

I have lived and completed the course that Fortune gave, and now my image will descend in grandeur beneath the earth; I founded a splendid city, I have seen walls of my own, as an avenger of my husband I have punished my enemy brother; happy, alas, too happy, if only the Dardanian ships had never touched our shores.

Seneca later admired these verses for their acceptance of death, and even more for the gratitude they express for the life that is now coming to its end.[12] This Dido has much to be grateful for. In the third and fourth lines she sums up her achievements: she has founded her city, seen its walls rise, and obtained some revenge for her murdered husband. This is the Dido, in other words, of the traditional story that stares out at us beneath Virgil's retelling, the Dido who commits suicide on her pyre to save the city she has founded. Hence the peculiar effects of the last two verses—again in the pluperfect subjunctive—she would have been too happy had the Trojans never touched her shores. Dido echoes Catullus's abandoned Ariadne wishing Theseus had never reached Crete—"*ne tempore primo / Gnosia Cecropiae tetigissent litora puppes*" (64.171–172)—but in her case, her contrafactual wish may be no more than the truth: Aeneas's ships never did make a landing on Dido's shores (just as she never attempted to burn them).[13] She and Carthage would have been only too happy with this foundation story: with Dido's heroic self-sacrifice, with Rome nowhere in sight. But first history and now Virgil have rewritten it.

Monster or wife devoted to husband and city? As it has long been recognized, the question is kept alive in Book 6 by the company Dido keeps in the underworld, the group of women among whom Aeneas encounters her shade.[14] They are victims of cruel love ("*durus amor*"; 6.442), but of what kind? Phaedra (445) and Pasiphae (447), daughter and mother, succumb to monstrous, unnatural passion for stepson and bull. Pasiphae has been

---

12. *De Ben.* 5.17.5.
13. Catullus, 1966, 108.
14. Perret, 1964; Tatum, 1984; West, 1980.

mentioned earlier in the book, the mother not only of Phaedra but of the Minotaur pictured earlier on the gates sculpted by Daedalus at Cumae (6.25–26), where the Cretan labyrinth anticipates in miniature the underworld itself, presided over by *its* Cretan judges, Minos (6.432) and Rhadamanthus (6.566), a labyrinth from which Theseus does not return but sits and will sit forever (6.617–618; cf. 6.393–394). Perhaps Carthage posed another hellish, deadly trap for Aeneas, Dido not so much the helpful, then abandoned Ariadne (6.28) as the monster at its center. Love of another sort, love of riches, drove Procris and Eriphyle (445) to betray their spouses. But alongside these bad wives are Evadne and Laodamia (447), who, out of marital love and devotion, both threw themselves on pyres in order to perish with their dead husbands, a kind of Indian suttee, as Propertius comments on Evadne (3.13.15–24; cf. 1.15.21–22). The Carthaginians recounted that Dido similarly perished in a patriotic blaze, remaining true to the ashes of Sychaeus, and it is to Sychaeus that her shade returns at the end of episode, to her *fama prior*.[15]

This return seems to be signaled by the last of these companions mentioned before the appearance of Dido herself: Caeneus. This is the masculine shape into which Caenis was transformed; in Virgil's version of the myth, she returned to her earlier female form and gender. We may read this figure, as other critics have done, as a commentary on Virgil's episode, where Dido the beloved wife takes on, after the murder of Sychaeus, the masculine role of leader of her new city—"*dux femina facti*" (1.364)—only to fall back, as the victim of Venus and of Aeneas's charms, into womanly passion: "*uarium et mutabile semper / femina*" (4.569–570).[16] Alternatively, we can read it as a metaliterary pointer: the Dido of the Carthaginian foundation story has been transformed into the Dido of Virgil's corrective rewriting only now, in the underworld to return to her original shape, the queen who committed patriotic suicide and stayed true to her husband's ashes.

Thus the (over)loaded nature of the question that Aeneas addresses to Dido's shade:

infelix Dido, uerus mihi nuntius ergo
uenerat exstinctam ferroque extrema secutam?
funeris heu tibi causa fui? (6.456–458)

---

15. Perret, 1964, 352–353 remarks that Evadne and Laodamia, faithful to their husbands on their respective pyres, recall the traditional story of Dido.

16. Tatum, 1984, 436–437; West, 1980, on Dido's androgyny.

> Unhappy Dido, was the message that came to me truthful that you were dead and had sought your end with the sword? Was I, alas, the cause of your death?

The message was "true" that Dido had killed herself by the sword—so both the preexisting and Virgil's competing version of her story agree. Was Aeneas the cause? *That* may be the question which the *Aeneid* opens here about its own fiction. Dido does not answer one way or the other. She angrily—"*torua*" (6.467)—looks the other way with her eyes fixed on the ground. The model is the shade of Homer's Ajax who, in the underworld episode of the *Odyssey* 11 (543–564), refuses to acknowledge Odysseus's not fully sincere apology for having won the arms of Achilles in Ajax's stead. The Homeric model, Dido's anger, the recent wound in her breast (6.450): these all seem to indicate that this is Virgil's Dido who has killed herself for love of Aeneas in Book 4. Yet her silence, her acting as if Aeneas is not there equally suggest that he is not part of her story at all. Dido's shade is likened in simile here to the moon one sees or thinks one sees behind the clouds ("*aut uidet aut uidisse putat per nubila lunam*"; 6.454). Like Fama herself, the publicizer of the love of Aeneas and Dido, the queen's shade is lost in the clouds. Fama is herself both the messenger of truth—"*nuntia ueri*"—as well as the upholder of wicked fictions—"*ficti prauique tenax*" (4.188). So, too, in Book 1, Aeneas behind his cloud both was and was not on the scene in Carthage. Now, too late, Aeneas weeps and expresses his love for a Dido who, the poem simultaneously suggests, is both there and not there, a Dido whom he may never have encountered and whom we as readers only think we are seeing in Virgil's story. For the "true" Dido—still a shade and a fiction—lives on in the underworld with Sychaeus in another story entirely.

Dido the Phoenix

Virgil preserves that other story of Dido's suicide in a separate, if related way. He revises but nonetheless takes it seriously as the founding myth of a city-state that maintains its autonomy and refuses marital alliances with its neighbors. For once Aeneas is indeed out of the picture, Dido's ghastly death at the end of Book 4 associates her, "Phoenissa," as the poem has heretofore named her, and Carthage itself with a different myth: the self-generating *Phoenix*. The larger *Aeneid* contrasts this foundation of Carthage with the foundation of Rome through Aeneas's marriage to Lavinia and the late child he will have with her.

Virgil's Dido would indeed like to have a child by Aeneas: the prospect of maternity is one of the enticements that Anna places before her sister's mind at the beginning of Book 4 when she encourages Dido to embrace the Trojan who comes bearing gifts (4.31f.). Anna adds that settling the Trojans beside her Phoenicians, an offer that Dido had herself already made to Ilioneus (1.572–574) before Aeneas broke through his cloud, would also help populate and defend Carthage. The new city, Anna points out, is threatened by their brother Pygmalion (4.43–44) and surrounded by African tribes: Gaetulians (4.40), Numidians (4.41), and the Barcaei (4.43). The last of these names is overdetermined, for it both denotes a preexisting people and the future Carthaginian Barcid dynasty of statesmen to which Hannibal would belong: Virgil also suggests a purely Punic origin for the dynasty in Sychaeus's old nurse Barce (4.632), a family retainer who must also be a living reproach to Dido in her new love affair. The passage indicates the future conquest by Carthage over these North African neighbors as far as Cyrene (Barca did not exactly border on Carthage, but was, as Austin's commentary points out, seven hundred miles to the east).[17] Dido herself, in her first speech of complaint to Aeneas upon learning of his planned departure, wishes that he had at least given her a child, a little Aeneas playing in her palace—"*si quis mihi paruulus aula / luderet Aeneas*" (4.328–329). Here, too, strategic as well as personal emotional ends are involved, for in the preceding verses (4.320–326) Dido, in a clear echo and reprise of Anna's speech (4.36–44), considers her vulnerability to attacks from Tyre and from Iarbas and the Africans.

Let us briefly switch to Virgil's contemporary times, in order to acknowledge the double historical scheme that the Dido episode serves. The child that Dido wants, but does *not*, in fact, obtain also points to, in order to deny, Julius's Caesar's fathering of a son, Caesarion, on the recent North African queen Cleopatra. Antony and Cleopatra designated Caesarion as the true dynastic Julian heir—a rival to Augustus, the adoptive son of Julius Caesar. This love child, the *Aeneid* suggests, here and at the earlier moment when Cupid, in the guise of Ascanius, pours his poison into Dido during her banquet (1.657–722), was a phantom stand-in for a true Julian child. Caesarion, that is, was illegitimate, fathered by who knows whom: just to be safe, Augustus had

17. Austin, 1955, 36.

Caesarion killed after Actium. Meanwhile, the epic criticizes Aeneas for acting like an Antony banqueting, consorting with, and even marrying Cleopatra in name as well as in deed, until Mercury brings the Trojan hero to his senses and sends him on his true Roman and Julian way, triggering Dido's mad suicide. Cleopatra would also take her own life, and Virgil, on the shield of Aeneas sculpted by Vulcan in Book 8, pairs her through textual echo with Dido, both pale in prospect of their coming suicides (4.644; 8.709).

Back to Carthage and to Dido's suicide itself. In an elegant article, Jane E. Phillips demonstrates how Dido's taking of her own life with the sword of Aeneas not only mimes the sexual act but also the childbirth in which sex can result. Servius had noted that when Dido approaches the altars by her pyre with one sandal off and unloosed garment: *"unum exuta pedem uinclis, in ueste recincta"* (4.518), she behaves as a worshipper of Juno Lucina, the goddess of childbirth. All clothing must be loosened, all knots untied, in order, through symbolic sympathy, to ensure an easy delivery. But that is what is denied to Dido in her death pangs. Her struggling soul cannot leave her body until Juno, taking pity on her protracted pain and difficult departure, sends down Iris *"quae luctantem animam nexosque resolueret artus"* (6.695): the verb governs both objects, freeing the soul and unloosing the binding limbs. Phillips points out that death in childbirth was far more common in the classical world than in our own. Dido dies giving birth not to the child she hoped for from Aeneas but to the Carthage that would be Rome's most terrible enemy. She had called upon an avenger to rise from her ashes—*"exoriare aliquis nostris ex ossibus ultor"* (4.625).

This is Hannibal and other Carthaginian foes of Rome, but the symbolic birth has shifted into a different mythological key. Phoenician Dido, "Phoenissa," so Virgil calls her four times (1.670, 714; 4.348, 529), has become a phoenix, the bird that regenerates itself through self-immolation on the pyre it builds for itself, its successor born from its ashes.[18] So Carthage itself rose from defeat after the first and second (Hannibalic) Punic wars to be burnt to the ground in the third. Dido's thwarted sexuality and maternity turn into a monstrous parthenogenesis. To repeat, Dido has played a man's role as ruler (*"dux femina facti"*), and her giving birth in death, Phoenissa become Phoenix, implies a switch in gender similar to Caenis–Caeneus: the phoenix is a male bird that reproduces asexually.

18. I have advanced an earlier version of this reading in Quint, 1993, 108 on Dido's curse.

By bringing Aeneas onto the scene of Carthage's foundation myth, Virgil supplies the eros that the story of the chaste widow Dido had repressed, and that eros, awakened and then thwarted by the hero's departure, transforms the myth which tells how the Phoenician city could retain its autonomy without intermarrying or mingling with its neighbors into a dark version of the phoenix that regenerates through its own, repeated self-destruction. For Virgil appears to detect the real historical weakness that would destroy the Carthaginian empire, at least as the Greco-Roman sources present it: its refusal, so proudly declared in the other Dido story, to admit its subject African peoples into its citizenry. Carthage might well, like the phoenix, reproduce by itself rather than through and with its neighbors, but this exclusivity limited the size of the citizenry that manned her armies and fleets, and made the city depend on mercenary soldiers.[19] So, in a famous passage comparing the constitutions of the two cities, Polybius commented on the Carthaginian neglect of infantry and suggested why the city lost out to Rome.

> The reason of this is that the troops they employ are foreign and mercenary, whereas those of the Romans are natives of the soil and citizens. So that in this respect also we must pronounce the political system of Rome to be superior to that of Carthage, the Carthaginians continuing to depend for the maintenance of their freedom on the courage of a mercenary force but the Romans on their own valor and on the aid of their allies. (6.52.4–5)[20]

Rome had citizens and allies enough to fill its armies. By contrast to Carthage, it conquered its Italian neighbors and at the same time began to intermarry with and admit them into its citizenry. These peoples had a stake, Polybius affirms, in Rome's future—they shared in the booty of Rome's victories—in

---

19. On this question see Ameling, 2013; see also Ameling, 1993, 262–263. Ameling, 1993, 189–190 sets out the conventional historical view that Carthage's mobilization of citizen armies gave way in or after the First Punic War to the use of mercenaries and that citizens' participation in warfare took place predominantly in her fleets, where their abilities were particularly valued. He then, 203–210, offers a more complicated picture: citizens were conscripted into both army and navy, but, like any other ancient state, Carthage found it difficult to man both land and sea forces at the same time. For brief remarks on the question of Carthage's closed citizenship, see Lancel, 1993, 119–120. Fantar, 1993, 1:170 citing epigraphic evidence, argues that against the Greco-Roman tradition, Dido *did* marry Iarbas: that is, there was a degree of intermarriage between Phoenicians and Libyans.

20. Polybius, 2011, 3:426–429.

a way that few of Carthage's dominated subjects did for hers.[21] The extension of Roman citizenship was a long-term process and proceeded by fits and starts.[22] It eventually required the Social Wars of 90–88 BCE to complete the integration of Rome's Italian allies into fully shared citizenship: in 49 BCE the inhabitants of Virgil's Cisalpine Gaul, and these may have included Virgil's own family, were similarly enfranchised. In his depiction of Actium on the shield of Aeneas, the poet depicts Augustus leading the unified *Italians* into battle, his name surrounding them in the verse: "*hinc Augustus agens Italos in proelia Caesar*" (8.678). Before the third century BCE, Rome had offered her colonies and neighbors in Italy the intermediate status of *Latini*, between ally and citizen. The loyalty of these Latini to Rome, even after her disastrous defeat at Cannae, frustrated the victor Hannibal, doomed him to defeat in the second Punic War, and led to the end of Carthage itself.

Livy depicts this practice of Rome's expansion of her citizen base beginning with Aeneas's marriage to Lavinia, the Italian princess. The historian tells us that Turnus, formerly betrothed to Lavinia, allied himself with the Etruscans. Facing this enemy coalition, Aeneas began state-building.

> Aeneas, that he might win the good will of the Aborigines to confront so formidable an array and that they all might possess not only the same rights, but also the same name, called both nations Latins; and from that time on the Aborigines were no less ready and faithful than the Trojans in the service of Aeneas. (1.2.4–5)[23]

21. See Ameling, 2013, 379: "Enriching the citizens at the subjects' expense provided stability for Carthage—the rationale behind the sharp division between citizens and subjects: any integration of the subjects into the state, for instance by means of large-scale citizenship grants, would have reduced the possibility for the exploitation of subjects and would thus have endangered the enrichment of the people—and the rule of the aristocracy. This had its consequences: Carthage always retained the status of a city with its limited possibilities. Its subjects never identified themselves with Carthage." The readiness of Carthage's subject North Africans to join with the mercenaries against the city in the great revolt of the Mercenaries' War (241–238 BCE) is telling; see Lancel, 1993, 372–376 and the narrative in Polybius 1.66–88, who describes, 1.71–72, the provincials' resentment at extortionate taxes paid to their Carthaginian masters. As a counterexample but perhaps exception to the rule, Livy reports, 21.45.6, that Hannibal, on the eve of the battle of Ticinus (218 BCE), promised citizenship to his allies in the event of victory.

22. Nicolet, 1976, 37–68. On the diaspora of Roman citizens in the conquered provinces and client states of the empire, see Purcell, 2005.

23. Livy, 1922–59, 1:12–13. "Aeneas, adversus tanti belli terrorem ut animos Aboriginum sibi conciliaret, nec sub eodem iure solum sed etiam nomine omnes essent, Latinos utramque gentem appellavit. Nec deinde Aborigines Troianis studio ac fide erga regem Aeneam cessere."

Livy retrojects what would be future Roman policy to the first settlement of the Trojans in Italy, and he adds the idea that Aeneas gave to the Trojans themselves the name of Latini in order to join the two peoples as one. These are much the same terms that Virgil's Juno imposes on Jupiter at the end of the *Aeneid*, when she consents to the marriage of Aeneas and Lavinia. But here the Italian natives are already called Latins, and the goddess's goal is the obliteration of the Trojan name.

> ne uetus indigenas nomen mutare Latinos
> neu Troas fieri iubeas Teucrosque uocari
> aut uocem mutare uiros aut uertere uestem.
> sit Latium, sint Albani per saecula reges,
> sit Romana potens Itala uirtute propago;
> occidit, occideritque sinas cum nomine Troia. (12.823–828)

> Do not command the native Latins to change their ancient name nor to become Trojans or be called Teucrians, nor to change their language or dress. Let Latium be, and the Alban kings, through the ages; let there be a Roman stock potent in Italian virtue; Troy has fallen; command that it stay fallen, together with its name.

This is the poetic, mythic version—the result of the divine colloquy—of what the historian Livy depicts as Aeneas's own political decision, the beginning of a practice of intermarriage and absorption of bordering peoples that would continue among his Roman descendants. By insisting on the Trojans themselves becoming Latins and Italians, Juno, still at this point the enemy of Rome, actually ensures the city's future greatness—a Roman seed powerful with Italian *virtus*—as a peninsular, then world power.[24]

---

24. Bettini, 2005, argues that Juno does not quite get her way and that an *echt* Trojan stock, principally the *gens Iulia*, survives within the larger absorption of Trojans into the new Roman people. Bettini writes in response to Giardina. Giardina, 1997, 62–77 explores the various valences of the Trojan myth for the Romans and for their neighbors and enemies; he notes, 67–68, that it could both indicate something of the mixed, expansive nature of Roman citizenship *and* preserve the idea of an exclusively Roman-Trojan pedigree as opposed to a greater Italian identity: the two ideas worked together to make Roman-ness. Casali, 2009, 323–325 convincingly demonstrates, however, that in Juno's *and Jupiter's* decree of an admixture of Trojans and Romans the *Aeneid* implicitly chooses to trace the lineage of the Alban kings and Romulus back to Aeneas's marriage with Lavinia and to their son, Silvius Postumus, rather than to the elder, Trojan son, Ascanius, and to the Julian line. For a further overview, see Barchiesi, 2012. Dupont, 2011, reads the *Aeneid*'s story of the foundation of Rome by the exile, nonnative

Juno does so at the expense of her favorite, Carthage.[25] The *Aeneid* contrasts this foundation of Rome's future with the foundation of Carthage it has treated in its first half. At issue is how these empires were to reproduce themselves through subsequent history. Virgil's Dido had offered to settle the Trojans in Carthage and to make no discrimination between them and her Tyrians (1.574). She claimed that Aeneas was her husband. But the epic's hero leaves her, taking his followers with him, in order to reach Italy and instead to marry his Latin princess. Beneath its mythmaking, the *Aeneid* reflects upon two real and different demographic destinies, the consequences of political choices and institutions, that would turn out to be decisive for Rome and Carthage. The son, Silvius of Alban name (6.763), that Lavinia will produce for Aeneas sets the pattern for the building of Rome's population through its mingling with, and extending citizenship to, its conquered Italian neighbors. By contrast the barren Dido in *either* of her versions, whether as the chaste widow of the story the *Aeneid* writes over or as the love-maddened woman whom the *Aeneid* depicts, establishes Carthage's closed model of citizenship, which in the long run made the Punic city unable to compete with Roman manpower. Virgil's rewriting, that is, still allows us to see beneath it—indeed, the phoenix myth brings it further out—the catch-22 in the other story of a noble Dido sacrificing herself on her pyre in order to foil her African suitors and preserve her city's independence. Even if Aeneas never arrived on her shores (and he never did), this Dido had already doomed Carthage to its inbred, unsustainable future.

Aeneas as a model for the city's future openness and inclusive citizenship: outsiders become insiders.

25. Juno may not, then, obtain what she wants or thinks that she has obtained; I would qualify the critical views of Feeney, 1984, and Johnson, 1976, 124–127, who grant the goddess a more than partial victory at the poem's end. There is some irony in her insistence that the name of Troy be lost, since it allows for the category of the *Latini* and Rome's demographic expansion. The whole *Aeneid* bears witness, in any case, to the fact that the name of Troy has *not* been lost, although it may have had to be reinvented.

4

Sons of Gods in Book 6

AT THE CENTER of the *Aeneid*, Virgil confronts the central question asked by the genre of epic. In the face of the universal condition of death, what deeds do men, can men do to assure their memories live on—and live on in good renown? Following Homeric precedent, Virgil shapes the underworld of Book 6 as a Hall of Fame or a memory theater.[1] The shades of the dead are distinguished there, broadly speaking, between those who make others remember them (6.664) and who become permanent residents, and those who forget their earthly lives (6.750)—lives that are unmemorable—and who are recycled out of the underworld to start over again in new lives and identities, a transmigration of souls. (Some evildoers imprisoned in Tartarus achieve notoriety, even if they deserve to be forgotten in its darkness with the innumerable rest of the wicked: no second chances for them.) The famous few versus the nameless many. The upper limit of such fame and place in human memory is divinization, an escape from the realm of death and oblivion that the sibyl of Cumae attributes to a very few, "offspring of gods"—"*dis geniti*" (6.131)—and one of these is Augustus, son of the deified Julius Caesar.

This chapter explores the possible meanings of the sibyl's words. Deification of ruler-heroes was both an old phenomenon of Roman myth (Romulus) and normal practice among orientalizing Hellenistic monarchs.[2] The cults around succeeding Roman emperors have made the idea too familiar to us.

---

1. On the larger issue of poetic fame and its various paradoxes, see Hardie, 2012.

2. Romulus, but Aeneas perhaps not so much. The deification in store for Aeneas announced by the *Aeneid* may be a recent construction of Augustan propagandists, such as Varro in his *De gente populi Romani*, intended to bolster the claims to divine honor that Octavian (Augustus) obtained for Julius Caesar and might expect for himself; see Cole, 2013, 194–195, who notes that Cicero does not mention Aeneas or Rome's Trojan (Julian) origins in the *De re*

When first employed by Julian dynasts, it was a recent and revolutionary development on the Roman political scene, a scarcely credible Big Lie. Virgil contributes mightily to this propaganda but, as usual, tells another story inside it. The *Aeneid* takes a hard, distanced look at its own making of the divine image of Augustus.[3] Book 6 understands deification, in Euhemerist terms, as a hyperbolic metaphor for deathless fame and earthly power, and Virgil's views about such god-men impinge on the "real" gods themselves. But, as if in exchange for this hollowing out of the godhood it officially promotes, the book offers Augustus a rationalized alternative: enshrinement in its own verses, a lasting name in an enduring poem.[4]

My argument is organized around the inversion—a chiasmus, a double cross—that Book 6 makes of the sibyl's pronouncement that the way into the kingdom of death is easy, that the way back out is the real trick: "*hoc opus, hic*

---

publica, where he discusses the deification of Romulus (2.10). Livy (1.2.6) reserves judgment on the matter of Aeneas the god.

3. Virgil's earlier poetry does the same. How should one read the apprehension of Virgil's narrator at the opening of the *Georgics*? He worries that Augustus as a god, that is, after his death, might—out of dire desire for rulership (*"regnandi ... dira cupido"*) and because the Greeks have so many good things to say about the Elysian Fields—wish to conquer and dwell in Tartarus (*Georgics* 1.36–39). The tone is teasing, but it provides a model for Lucan's more clearly ironic address to Nero at the beginning of the *De bello civili*, auguring that emperor's apotheosis and removal from earth, ASAP. Virgil suggests to Augustus that he might want to go down to the dead—like everybody else. Or go to hell. If the deified Daphnis of the *Fifth Eclogue* is a figure of the apotheosized Julius Caesar, he is transparently raised to heaven by poetry: "let us carry Daphnis to the stars"—"*Daphnin ad astra feremus*" (52)—says Menalcas, and, presto chango, four lines later Menalcas describes Daphnis staring down at the floor of heaven (56).

4. Feeney, 1986, 5–8 discusses the issue of names, both family names and place names in Book 6, one aspect of the book's meditation on fame. (The two are related in the giving by both Misenus [6.235] and Palinurus of names [6.383] to the places where they have died.) Feeney points out that the Alban city tellingly named *Nomen*tum (6.773), as yet unbuilt and prophesied by Anchises, had by Virgil's time fallen into obscurity. Both families and cities, even possibly Rome, may become *mere* names. On Virgil, Augustus, and divinization, see Thomas, 2001, 45–51. The reading I propose about poetic fame as a substitute for divinization is informed by my earlier study, Quint, 1983, 81–92, of Ariosto's lunar allegory in Cantos 34–35 of the *Orlando furioso*, where John the Evangelist, after telling us that Augustus was not so "sainted and benign" as Virgil's trumpet makes him out to be (35.26), turns his euhemerist logic upon the divine son, Jesus Christ, the product of the literary fame John has made for him (35.29). Virgil, I argue here, already anticipates Ariosto's desacralizing episode, which targets Dante's *Divine Comedy*.

labor est" (6.129). Transmigration, to the contrary, makes leaving the underworld the rule, staying there in Elysium the exception. Writing over Odysseus's consultation with the dead in *Odyssey* 11, Virgil marginalizes most of the Greek figures in that Homeric museum of poetic and heroic renown, pushing them into its offstage corners or consigning them as criminals, like Theseus, to its Tartarean basement. He makes room for the characters of his poem (Dido, Deiphobus, Aeneas himself) and for a Roman pantheon: Anchises' roll call of patriots, of heroes and Caesars raised to godhood.[5] In doing so, Virgil raises questions about justice in a book where the dead are judged and sorted out, and about *poetic justice* in particular—whom should the *Aeneid* praise and blame? what about Theseus? He acknowledges the complicity of poetry with power in shaping historical myth and memory. The long-standing Roman state and the new ruling Julian house (with its claims to divine honors) sanction Virgil's project to write a Latin epic that vies for fame with the Homeric poems. The *Aeneid*, in turn, buttresses these political arrangements by promising them eternity in its poetry, a guaranteed afterlife. The chapter concludes by turning its attention to the episode of young Marcellus at the end of Book 6, a last-minute supplement that upsets the best-laid plans of the poem and its projected endpoint in 29 BCE. It troubles the future of a dynasty of immortals.

Anchises and His Body Double

The opening of Book 6 tells us that Daedalus first landed at Cumae after he took wing to escape from Crete, the realm of Minos—*"Minoia regna"* (6.14)— and home of the labyrinth that Daedalus had himself designed and that he later depicted on the gates of the Cumaean temple of Apollo. With its *"inextricabilis error"* (6.27), the labyrinth is an evident figure for the underworld that follows, presided over by Cretan judges, old Minos himself (6.432) and his brother, Rhadamanthus (6.566). It is easy to descend—*"facilis descensus"* (6.126)—into this underworld, says the Cumaean sibyl to Aeneas, the hard part is to recall one's steps—*"reuocare gradum"* (6.128)—and get out, something like the return path that the compassionate Daedalus granted to Ariadne, as she guided Theseus out of the maze. Sergio Casali points out that the reference to Ariadne as a queen—*"magnum reginae sed enim miseratus amorem"*

---

5. Feldherr, 1997, on the Roman colonization of Homer's underworld.

(6.28)—hauntingly recalls Queen Dido, the *Aeneid*'s own version of Ariadne. When Dido cannot die after she has committed suicide, Juno takes pity on her—"*longum miserata dolorem / difficilisque obitus*" (4.693–694).[6] Going down to the underworld—dying—can, in fact, not be easy and, as we saw in chapter 3, Juno sends Iris to free—"*resolueret*" (4.695); "*soluo*" (4.703)—the soul of Dido, so that she can be found later on in Book 6 among the shades of the "*campi lugentes*." Daedalus freed up—"*resoluit*" (6.29)—the twists and turns of his labyrinth for Ariadne.[7] The Virgilian underworld will turn out for Theseus to be a second labyrinth from which he is not going to escape—"*sedet aeternumque sedebit / infelix Theseus*" (6.617–618). He is just plain dead. Aeneas, who cites Theseus, along with Hercules and Orpheus, as a precedent for his own underworld journey (6.122), is one of those rarities, offspring of the gods, described by the sibyl, who negotiate their way back up to the air of heaven, sometimes to the heavens themselves. In this poem, the abandoned Ariadne figure Dido does *not*—as Hesiod, Apollonius of Rhodes, and Catullus tell of Ariadne before her—earn herself Bacchus, immortality, and a place for her crown among the stars.[8] Dido says that she had been making her way to the stars before Aeneas came along—"*sidera adibam*" (4.322)—but she self-destructs and goes down to the dead. Aeneas, the Theseus who abandons her, will be carried by Venus to the starry heaven; so the prophetic Jupiter tells Venus in Book 1: "*sublimemque feres ad sidera caeli / magnanimum Aenean*" (1.259–260). The real Theseus meanwhile fares badly in the underworld, even

---

6. Casali, 1995, connects the Theseus depicted on the doors of the temple to the Aeneas who has abandoned Dido. See also Zarker, 1962. Zetzel, 1989, 270 discusses the alternate stories of Theseus and the underworld. One might further note that Homer includes Phaedra, Procris, and Ariadne in one verse of the underworld in *Odyssey* 11.321, where he tells an alternate story of Ariadne's death; Virgil echoes the line at 6.445, where he couples the first two women but substitutes Eriphyle for Ariadne. He pointedly leaves Ariadne out of his underworld so that he can go on to feature his own Ariadne figure, Dido. In *Odyssey* 11, Odysseus is waiting to learn about Theseus and Pirithous, glorious sons of gods (*Ody.* 11.631), when he is overtaken by fear and the episode comes to an end; the two had attempted to carry Persephone out of the underworld. Virgil provides the information about these heroes that Homer leaves out.

7. One can also compare the difficulty that the unburied dead, condemned to a hundred-year wait, have in going down to the underworld; Aeneas pities their lot: "*sortemque animo miseratus iniquam*" (6.332).

8. Hesiod, *Theogony*, 947–949; Apollonius, *Argonautica*, 4.430–433, 3.992–1004; Catullus 64.251–264.

though, Charon later tells Aeneas, he, too, was one of those divine offspring: "*dis quamquam geniti*" (6.394). Virgil turns the earlier Ariadne-Theseus myth chiastically inside out and, in doing so, invites a mixed response: who belongs where after death, and how does one get there? This may restate the question I have initially posed and be *the* question of Book 6.

The sibyl's words to Aeneas, extraordinarily double-edged, set out terms that resonate throughout the book. Aeneas has just claimed descent from highest Jupiter—"*et mi genus ab Ioue summo*" (6.123)—the privilege that should allow him, like Theseus, like Hercules, to visit the underworld. The sibyl answers:

> sate sanguine diuum,
> Tros Anchisiade, facilis descensus Auerno:
> noctes atque dies patet atri ianua Ditis;
> sed reuocare gradum superasque euadere ad auras,
> hoc opus, hic labor est. pauci, quos aequus amauit
> Iuppiter aut ardens euexit ad aethera uirtus,
> dis geniti potuere. (6.125–131)

> Offspring of the blood of the gods, son of Trojan Anchises, it is easy to descend into Avernus: day and night, the gates of black Dis stand open; but to recall your step and escape to the higher air, that is the task, that is the work. A few, whom just Jupiter loved or whom fiery virtue carried up to the heavens, have succeeded, born of gods.

Her pronouncement begins and ends with what appears to be a repetition and a kind of tautology. "You, divine offspring, should know that a few human beings manage to go down to the realm of death *and* come back up, and they are divine offspring." Does being the offspring of a god allow you to live beyond death, or does such afterlife confer divine sonship: birth and heredity confirming themselves or action and merit creating their own genealogy? There are other problems. What is the relation between the "*superas ... auras*" of v. 128 and the "*aethera*" two lines later in v. 130? The first might be taken as the air above the underworld itself, that is, the world we inhabit as living, if mortal beings, the second as the heavens in which immortal gods dwell. But they could be synonyms and mean either the first or the second. Virgil uses *both* words to mean both things. He employs "*aether*" to convey the first of these meanings, the air that we breathe, later in Book 6 itself (6.436); he uses "*auras*" to suggest the second, notably in Book 4 when Fama lifts her head to the heavens—"*in auras*" (4.176)—as a kind of earthborn rival to the gods.⁹ (We shall return to this below.) Does one rise to the heavens through divine favor or through one's own virtue, and are these related? Does Jupiter love virtue, and in that case does the "*aequus*" that describes Jupiter mean "just," as it might and which matters in a book that includes judgment of the dead? Or does it mean, as it can and as the verb "*amauit*" could suggest, "favorably disposed to"—not a question of an even playing field in human events, nor of divinely guaranteed justice, but rather of special consideration and particularly of nepotism, if Jupiter loves these sons of gods because they are his sons? The question of what it means to be the son of a god looms large in a book that leads up, as does the entire *Aeneid*, to "Augustus Caesar, *diui genus*" (6.792), predicted by Anchises as he points out a parade of souls ready to exit from the underworld into the Roman future. It, alternatively, could be *the* question of Book 6.

The immediate father-god in question is Julius Caesar, assassinated at the Ides of March in 44 BCE. He had designated his grand-nephew, the then Gaius Octavius, later Augustus, his adopted son and heir. In 42 BCE Gaius, in return, began to construct a temple, dedicated in 29, to the deified Julius Caesar and to the comet, the Julian star, that had appeared after Caesar's murder, and he added *Diui Filius* to his own name.[10] In the loose-fitting historical allegory of the *Aeneid* that makes Aeneas into Augustus's mythic avatar, the role of Julius Caesar is played by Anchises, the hero's biological father. When the

---

9. For "*auras aetherias*" see *Georgics* 2.291–292 and *Aeneid* 4.445–446: the tree whose branches reach up to heaven as far as its roots extend down to Tartarus. The same noun and adjective describe the vital air we breathe in Lucretius, *De rerum*, 4.305. Virgil uses "*superas … auras*" to describe the land of the living as opposed to the underworld in his retelling of the Orpheus story in *Georgics* 4.486.

10. For a fundamental discussion of the consolidation of the doctrine of divinized savior-heroes in the writings of Cicero and the Augustan poets, see La Penna, 1988. Weinstock, 1971, argues that Julius Caesar was gradually establishing his own ruler-cult in Rome at the time of his assassination, in part to solidify his position in the city before departing on a campaign against the Parthians. In the second *Philippic* (2.110–111), composed in the fall of 44 BCE, Cicero inveighs against Antony for not having taking up his appointment as a priestly *flamen* to Julius Caesar; but he notes his own disapproval of this and other such honors, tantamount to treating Caesar as a god. Cole, 2013, 17–184, argues that Cicero in *Philippics* 3–14 is more willing to grant divine honors and status to Julius Caesar, in order to drive a wedge between Octavian and Antony. Syme, 1939, 52–53, had contended *contra* that, autocrat that Julius Caesar undoubtedly was, there is little conclusive evidence that he, unlike Pompey before him, aspired to divine honors or, like Augustus after him, sought to establish hereditary monarchy.

sibyl refers to Aeneas as a divine offspring, she does not seem so much to refer to his divine mother Venus—the hero is called "*nate dea*" eleven times through the poem, but notably not in Book 6—as to Anchises, the human parent whom she goes on to name and whom Aeneas has come to seek out in the underworld.[11] A literal burden to Aeneas while he is alive in Books 2 and 3, Anchises, once dead, shows up in dreams as a sponsor of Aeneas's national mission in Books 4–5,[12] appears to be divinized during his funeral and games in Book 5,[13] and in Book 6 becomes the mission's prophet. Residing now among the blessed in Elysium, Anchises shows Aeneas a parade of future famous Romans and instructs Aeneas on the more immediate future, how to wage successfully the wars coming up in Books 7–12 in Italy. The two versions of Anchises, living and dead, adumbrate the analogy to Julius Caesar. The career of the living, historical Caesar, fomenter of civil war and aspiring autocrat, was an embarrassment to his "son," who officially claimed to uphold the senate and the institutions of the Roman Republic.[14] But the dead, deified Caesar just as officially granted Augustus both dynastic and heavenly legitimacy; his star appears in the heavens over the head of the victorious Augustus in Vulcan's depiction of Actium on Aeneas's shield (8.681). He also provided a model for Augustus's own deification, also prophesied by Jupiter to

---

11. The sibyl's address to Aeneas at 6.322 further rubs in the point: "*Anchisa generate, deum certissima proles*" ("Sired by Anchises, most certain offspring of the gods").

12. Anchises at first refuses to budge from the burning Troy in Book 2; he misinterprets the oracle of Delos and steers the Trojans off course to Crete in Book 3 (102–191). In Book 4, Aeneas tells an unbelieving Dido that his father has appeared to him in dreams as a disturbing ghost—or introjected superego—that bids him give up his erotic life with her. Book 5 depicts such a dream (5.722–745), in which Anchises invites Aeneas to visit him in the underworld at Avernus, an instigation for Book 6 itself. In the tree of dreams at its beginning (6.282–284) and the gates of horn and ivory at its end (6.893–899), the book suggests that the visit to the dead is one large dream.

13. The funeral games for Anchises in Book 5, especially the arrow of Acestes that bursts into flame like a comet (5.521–528), suggest the Julian games, the *ludi Victoriae Caesaris* of 44 BCE, during which the Julian comet appeared. See Camps, 1969, 100–102; Weinstock, 1971, 370–375. Virgil's description contains typical ambivalence: the seers/poets of later years will be terrified as they sing of the omen—"*seraque terrifici cecinerunt omina uates*" (5.524). I shall argue below that these games and the dedication of the grave and grove of Anchises at 5.760–761 also suggest the more recent dedication of the temple of Divus Julius by Augustus in 29 BCE.

14. Syme, 1939, 317. Quint, 1993, 56–65 on Anchises and Julius Caesar. For an interpretation of Anchises' actions that argues he is a figure for the father-poet Ennius, see Casali, 2007.

Venus in Book 1: she personally will welcome Augustus to heaven as she will raise Aeneas to the stars. The family is turning into a constellation.

> nascetur pulchra Troianus origine Caesar,
> imperium Oceano, famam qui terminet astris,
> Iulius, a magno demissum nomen Iulo.
> hunc tu olim caelo spoliis Orientis onustum
> accipies secura; uocabitur hic quoque uotis. (1.286–290)

> Trojan Caesar will be born, of beautiful lineage, who will confine his power with Ocean, his fame with the stars, a Julius, his name descended from great Iulus. Him, laden with the spoils of the East, you will one day receive in heaven, your mind set at rest; he will be invoked in prayers.

The language refers to Augustus *as* a Julius and confuses Augustus with his divine father to the point that the commentator Servius thought the passage was, in fact, about the earlier deified Caesar, and controversy over the identification has continued since then.[15] The *Aeneid* can both depict Augustus's career as a replica of that of Julius, power leading to divine honors—Virgil had celebrated Augustus as a living god by the sixth verse of his *First Eclogue* and by the twenty-fourth verse of the *First Georgic*—even as it tries to distinguish the questionable deeds of the warmongering father from the peacekeeping, furor-binding son (1.291–295). Like father, like/unlike son. Augustus's own waging of civil war is passed over or refigured as foreign conquest—those Eastern spoils, presumably of Actium, in the passage above—or silently pondered in the acts of his divine predecessor.

There is a suggestion of Julius Caesar's comet in the sibyl's declaration that fiery virtue—"*ardens ... uirtus*"—may carry you up to the heavens. But who, to return to the question the sibyl poses, legitimated or divinized whom? Ovid gives one answer, laying the process bare in the last book of the *Metamorphoses*: it was not so much his triumphs, domestic deeds, or glory that turned Julius Caesar into a star, the poem declares, but rather his offspring. So that Augustus would not be born of mortal seed, Julius Caesar was to be made a god: "*ne foret hic igitur mortali semine cretus, / ille deus faciendus erat*" (*Met.* 15.760–761). As Ovid and everyone else knew, Julius did not in fact sire

---

15. O'Hara, 1990, 155–163 argues that the confusion of the Caesars is deliberate.

Augustus but adopted him (although from within his lineage): the fiction of sonship, let alone divine sonship, was already transparent.

Virgil does not share Ovid's cheekiness. The effects he seeks are more double and uncanny. As the parade of heroes unfolds, the Anchises of Book 6 speaks to the shades who will be Julius Caesar and Pompey and begs them to desist from the future civil wars he knows they will nonetheless fight. He speaks to Caesar in particular,

> ne, pueri, ne tanta animis adsuescite bella
> neu patriae ualidas in uiscera uertite uiris;
> tuque prior, tu parce, genus qui ducis Olympo,
> proice tela manu, sanguis meus!— (6.832–835)
>
> Do not, young men, do not accustom your souls to such warfare, nor turn your valiant strengths against the bowels of your country; and you be first to forbear, you who derive your descent from Olympus, throw down the weapon from your hand, my own blood!

The *Aeneid*'s own Julius Caesar figure, Anchises, addresses the shade—who has not yet been embodied and who has a long time to wait to be born—of Julius Caesar. But these represent two different Julius Caesars, the dead and the living (or about to be living) one. Anchises, who is a permanent denizen of Elysium, corresponds to the divinized postmortem Julius Caesar—the god Caesar whose star shines over Augustus at Actium (8.681). He speaks to the Caesar who, in the lived history that Anchises foretells and that Virgil and his contemporary Romans remember, will cast the city into civil war. The alliteration of verse 833 and the repetition of "*ne*" and "*tu*" in verses that surround it intensify this plea from the deep past that will be to no avail—and Anchises knows it. Nor will avail the divine bloodline drawn from Olympus that makes Caesar himself a "*sate sanguine diuum*" or one of the "*dis geniti*." As is the case of Theseus, being a divine offspring in Book 6 does not guarantee that you will do the right thing.

There is, furthermore, a quibble about how far Anchises' bloodline extends. The Trojan ancestor addresses both Pompey and Caesar as "*pueri*," young men, perhaps, in their larval stage in the underworld, but also—so Fairclough translates the word—"sons." Here, too, the *Aeneid* wavers about who are included among the *Aeneadae*. For it is here, in Anchises' parade of future Romans in Book 6, that the *Aeneid* offers a *second* genealogy, differing from the Julian one that Jupiter offers Venus in Book 1 and to which we have referred above. This bloodline traces Romulus back not to Iulus but to Silvius, the child that Aeneas will bear to the Latin Lavinia (6.760–779). The epic may be telling the story of the whole family of the Roman people, figurative as well as literal descendants of Aeneas and hence of Anchises, as in the case of 8.648, where the "*Aeneadae*" in question are the people fighting the tyranny of Tarquin and founding the republic. Books 1 and 6 contain parallel passages, both juxtaposing Romulus and Augustus (1.274–296; 6.777–807). In Book 1, Romulus founds the original walls of Mars—"*et Mauortia condet / moenia*" (1.276–277). In Book 6, under the auspices of "*Mauortius ... Romulus*" (6.777–778), this Roman family will have enclosed all seven of the city's hills within its vastly expanded wall (6.783). Collectively, it is a godlike family: the ensuing simile compares them to the offspring of the divine mother Cybele, *all of them gods and dwellers in heaven*—"*omnis caelicolas, omnis supera alta tenentis*" (6.787).

Or it may be the story of just one Julian clan—"*sanguis meus*"—culminating in Augustus, whom Book 6, in its next breath, proclaims to be a second and better founder, not just godlike, as are the Roman people, but the son of a god, who refounds a golden age for Rome—"*Augustus Caesar, diui genus, aurea condet / saecula qui rursus*" (6.792–793). The clan descends from Iulus, "*Aenide*" (9.653). The epithet is used only once in the *Aeneid*, when Apollo addresses Iulus-Ascanius in Book 9 after Iulus shoots an arrow into the boasting Italian Numanus Remulus and seems himself to kill off the beginning of that early chapter of Roman kingship (Numa and a combination of Romulus and Remus) of which Tarquin was the end.[16] In this passage, Apollo encourages and reins in Iulus: "so one goes to the stars, son of the gods and begetter of future gods"—"*sic itur ad astra, / dis genite et geniture deos*" (9.641–642).[17] The echo of the sibyl in Book 6 is clear. Now it is the tyro Iulus, rather than his grandfather Anchises, who is associated with his notable Julian descendants.

---

16. Barchiesi, 1997, commenting on Norden, 1916, 326–327, notes how Virgil strategically places Augustus in *Aeneid* 6 as a kind of golden mean between the martial Romulus and the peaceful Numa (6.776–811), only in the ensuing lines on Tullus Hostilius to appear to criticize Numa's inactivity. On Numanus Remulus's name, see Hardie, 1994, 186–187.

17. See the rich discussion in Casali, 2009, who notes that the anti-Eastern diatribe of Numanus is the ideology of Augustus's victory at Actium: Iulus/Ascanius appears to shoot this ideology down along with Numanus, and, Casali suggests, Apollo's praise of Ascanius may be ironic. Casali notes that the episode replaces a Julian version of the Trojans' war against the Italians in which it is Iulus who kills Mezentius. Apollo and Virgil remove Ascanius from the fighting in the rest of the poem. See also Miller, 2011, 149–160 on the episode.

Both are distinguished from the hero Aeneas himself, who through his marriage to Lavinia and through the younger son Silvius (6.760–765), will engender the early kings of Alba and Rome *and* the liberty-loving republicans who succeed them, that is, *all* of Roman history up until the new regime of Augustus. Like Julius Caesar, Iulus will sire gods, and that may be his main role and accomplishment. Apollo sidelines him for the rest of the poem, and his more exclusively Trojan Julian progeny are effectively bypassed, too, in Rome's story. They have been waiting for their big moment that at last will come to pass. But when Iulus has earlier unleashed his arrows, he kills the stag of the Latin Silvia (7.475–539), whose name suggests Silvius and that other, larger side of the Aeneas family. However innocently and through Allecto's machinations, Iulus starts the war between Trojans and Italians in the *Aeneid*'s second half, setting two sides of the future family at odds in fraternal conflict. It is a foretaste of what can happen when the Julii are *not* placed on the sidelines of history.[18]

Iulus is nonetheless, Apollo tells him, on his way to the stars, as is Julius Caesar who will *not* throw down his weapons of civil war as Anchises implores him to do. Augustus needed a divine father, one visible in the heavens. Had Julius Caesar not pursued his ambition, taken power, and been deified, Anchises would not be the character that he is in the *Aeneid*, Virgil's figure of that future divinized Caesar and authorizing father in the afterlife, and Anchises would not now be addressing Caesar, his historical alter ego to-be on earth. Such foresight/hindsight can appear to be a tired trick in the *Aeneid*, but here the startling confrontation of the two versions of Julius Caesar, one divinely enshrined in propaganda, the other about to embark on his all-too-human career, exposes the fault lines in the poem's ideology as sharply as possible. Augustus, demigod refounder of a golden age here in Anchises' parade, wager of civil war on earth, may come in two such versions himself.

Getting Out or Staying Put

The deified Julius Caesar becomes a star in the heavens; someday the sky, Jupiter tells Venus, will welcome Augustus, too. But Anchises is found in the underworld in an Elysium that pointedly possesses it own heaven and stars:

---

18. The two lineages, Trojan-Julian and Italian, seem to have come together and been reconciled in Marcellus at the end of the book: "*nec puer Iliaca quisqam de gente Latinos / in tantum spe tollet auos*" (6.875–876). But Marcellus will die young and leave the promise unfulfilled. On Silvia and Silvius, Jenkyns, 1998, 504–505, 512–513.

largior hic campos aether et lumine uestit
purpureo, solemque suum, sua sidera norunt. (6.640–641)

here a wider aether invests the fields with purple light, and they know their own sun and their own stars.

Anchises' account of Hades *reverses the sibyl's declaration and its terms*. It is normal, he tells Aeneas, for the souls of the dead to go back to earth, reincarnated, as the Roman shades whom Anchises points out are lining up to do. The real task for the few (*"pauci"*), as opposed to the *"pauci"* the sibyl earlier describes carried by virtue into the *"aethera"* (6.130), is to remain in the fields of the blessed forever—*"pauci laeta arua tenemus"* (6.744)—and to be purified in soul into the simple elements of aether and of fiery air: *"purumque relinquit / aetherium sensum atque aurai simplicis ignem"* (6.746–747): *"aether"* and *"aura"* return as virtual synonyms here. These *few* residents in Elysium—*"pauci ... tenemus"*—are pointedly contrasted both to *all* those other souls—*"has omnis"* (6.748)—returning to new existences and identities beneath the *"supera ... conuexa"* (6.750) of heaven and, another forty verses later, to the *all* of Cybele's brood who reside in the heavens themselves—*"omnis supera alta tenentis"* (6.787)—the "real" gods. Burning virtue does not so much raise you to the higher air or aethereal heavens, as the sibyl says, but turns you into them, for this Platonic-Stoic starstuff has been inside you all along.[19] If you are one of the lucky few who know it: perhaps *this* is what it means to be truly an offspring of the gods, the secret revealed in Aeneas's trip to the underworld that has overtones of a mystery rite.[20] It might make you little different from the bees of Virgil's *Georgics*, gifted, some say, with a part of the divine mind and a quaff of aether (*"haustus / aetherios"*), and, like all living souls, destined at the death of their bodies to fly up and return to the stars and high heaven from whence they come—*"uiua uolare / sideris in numerum atque alto succedere caelo"* (*Georgics* 4.220–221; 226–227)—a reabsorption into a World Soul. But human beings, unlike bees and beasts, can recognize the god within.[21]

---

19. Cicero, *De re publica*, 6.15: "to humans is given a soul out of those eternal fires which you call stars and planets"—"*hisque animus datus est ex illis sempiternis ignibus, quae sidera et stellas vocatis.*" Cicero, 1970, 266–267.

20. Bremmer, 2009.

21. In good Stoic terms, Scipio is instructed (*De re publica* 6.24): "Know then, that you are a god, if a god is that which lives, feels, remembers, and foresees, which rules, governs, and moves the body over which it is set, just as the Supreme God above us rules this universe"—

This internalizing or spiritualizing revision of the sibyl's words and the narrative scenario of Book 6 sets in relief the conflict of models that Denis Feeney has shown to underlie Virgil's episode, the Platonic myth of Er in the *Republic* and the *Somnium Scipionis* in Book 6 of Cicero's *De Republica*, which looks back on and modifies Plato's myth for Roman use.[22] The Scipio of the *Somnium* learns, on one hand, to disdain the smallness of earthly achievement, even and especially Rome's *imperium*, and to know the limits of mortal fame. On the other, he is instructed that those who have conserved, supported, and extended their fatherland can earn themselves a place in the heavens, in the Milky Way. The second of these doctrines—in which empire counts for something after all—underlies the parade of future patriots that Anchises will point out to his son. But it is in the Platonically flavored context of the first, Feeney points out, that we should understand Aeneas's question to Anchises about why anyone would want to return to earth and to life in the body: what dread desire—"*dira cupido*" (6.721)—drives them on?[23] One answer is that the souls who are being reincarnated are not doing so as themselves: they are compared, in fact, to anonymous bees (6.707–709). They have drunk from the river of Lethe (6.713–715; 748–751) and forgotten their earlier existence and identities.[24] Virgil's fiction may be a prettier way of pic-

---

"*deum te igitur scito esse, siquidem est deus, qui viget, qui sentit, qui meminit, qui providet, qui tam regit et moderatur et movet id corpus, cui praepositus est, quam hunc mundum ille princeps deus.*" Cicero, 1970, 278–281.

22. Feeney, 1986. Otis, 1964, 299–304 emphasizes the lack of fit between the philosophical and patriotic models of the underworld and concluded that the first was a kind of alibi for the second. The various models and analogues for Virgil's underworld, Pindaric, Platonic, Ennian, and Ciceronian, are conveniently assembled in Fletcher, 1968, ix–xxviii. See also Norden, 1916, 16–48; Bremmer, 2009.

23. Feeney, 1986, 3. On the apotheosis of the patriotically virtuous in *De re publica*, see Cole, 85–103.

24. Anchises' account of such Pythagorean reincarnation appears to owe much to the preface of Ennius's *Annales*. See Casali, 2007. But Ennius (1.2–10) recounts that Homer not only remembers his being Homer before transmigrating into Ennius's body but also remembers his reincarnation as a peacock. The forgetting of the souls at Lethe, I have argued elsewhere, is connected to the need of Aeneas and his companions to let go of their Trojan past and to embrace a Roman future in Italy (where the past, ironically enough, comes back in a repetition of the Trojan War in which, this time, they will play the roles of the victorious Greeks)—and it is also an injunction for Virgil's contemporaries to let the bygones of the civil wars be bygones and to move forward under the new Augustan regime, a kind of political amnesia if not quite an amnesty (Quint, 1993, 62, 65, 75–76).

turing death as personal annihilation, but it comes down to much the same thing as Lucretius's mortalism.

So the declaration of the sibyl might be amended again. The vast mass of humanity, as many as the falling leaves at the first frost of autumn (6.309) *and* as many as the flocks of birds flying south to sunny lands (6.310–312)—already suggesting their transmigration—find it easy to die *and* to recall their steps out of the labyrinthine underworld. They, too, undergo purgation, for a thousand years according to 6.748–751, so the steps are not *that* easy—but they do so only to prepare themselves for Lethe and reincarnation. They go back to earth *"immemores"* (750), but also leaving no more trace of themselves than the nameless, aether-drinking bees of the *Georgics*. The task and labor for the few, the sons of gods, is to escape death with their own identities intact, to survive oblivion. But that may mean staying put, as Anchises does, inside an Elysium that begins to assume the contours of a gallery of fame: built within the confines of the poetic underworld that Virgil—the new Daedalus—has designed and built.

The *Somnium Scipionis* tells us that, in addition to good citizens, a second class of human beings rise up to the stars, "Learned men, by imitating this harmony [of the heavenly spheres] on stringed instruments and in song, have gained for themselves a return to this region, as others have obtained the same reward by devoting their brilliant intellects to divine pursuits during their earthly lives" (*De re publica* 6.18).[25] That is to say, poets and philosophers. Virgil has this passage in mind when the sibyl describes the denizens, the *"pauci"* of Elysium.

> hic manus ob patriam pugnando uulnera passi,
> quique sacerdotes casti, dum uita manebat,
> quique pii uates et Phoebo digna locuti,
> inuentas aut qui uitam excoluere per artis
> quique sui memores aliquos fecere merendo:
> omnibus his niuea cinguntur tempora uitta. (6.660–665)

Here are the many who suffered wounds fighting for their fatherland, and here the priests who passed their lives in chastity, and the pious poets who spoke things worthy of Phoebus, and those who improved

---

25. Cicero, 1970, 272–273: "*quod docti homines nervis imitati atque cantibus aperuerunt sibi reditum in hunc locum, sicut alii, qui praestantibus ingeniis in vita humana divina studia coluerunt.*"

life with their discoveries, and those who made others remember them because of their merit; snowy white fillets bind the brows of all.

Patriotism first, religion second, then poetry and philosophy and other arts; finally anyone who did anything deserving that makes others remember them (*"memores"*). Those who have been forgotten, forget their own selves (*"immemores"*) at Lethe and make the return trip to earth. Those who are remembered hold the happy fields: the qualification, spelled out at the end of the list and of verse 664, is that they be meritorious.

Poetry and poets are conspicuous, in alternation with *disarmed* heroes, in vv. 642–659.[26] Athletes wrestle in sport, then sing—*"carmina dicunt"* (6.644)—while the Thracian priest Orpheus accompanies them; then appear the progenitors of the Trojan house back to Dardanus, with their lances fixed in the earth and their horses, loosed from their chariots, grazing the plains; meanwhile others in a chorus sing a paean within a fragrant grove of laurel—*"choro paeana canentis / inter odoratum lauris nemus"* (6.657–658). The sibyl turns to Musaeus, *"optime uates"* (6.669), who towers head and shoulders at the center of a throng of the blessed, to ask where to find Anchises. Musaeus is Orpheus's son in some mythic accounts, and the passage appears to offer a double genealogy, suggested by its depiction of the underworld source of the Po amid the grove (6.658–659): a return to the mythical origins of the Trojans in Italian Dardanus, whose Roman posterity Anchises will now unfold and which will rise, like the river, to the world above—and a return to the origins of poetry itself. For poetry is the vessel of memory, and it is telling that the singers of Apollonian paeans do so in a laurel grove sacred to the god, the laurel that binds the foreheads of triumphant generals *and* of poets. The grove, as an epitome of Elysium, itself an epitome of the underworld, itself an epitome of the larger *Aeneid*, is a stand of poetry. Evergreen—as opposed to the autumn leaves—it makes and preserves the fame of the dead. Virgil stakes his own claims to remembrance, to poetic immortality, in this passage.

Dardanus is son of a god, in his case the ur-Roman son of Jupiter-Zeus, as Aeneas himself declares in the *Iliad* (*Il.* 20. 215) and, as Homer's Poseidon subsequently confirms (*Il.* 20.304), the best loved among all such sons. He

---

26. Horsfall, 2013, and, in response, Spence, 2013. See Horace, *Odes,* 2:13.21–40 for another underworld of poets and poetry. The ur-Trojans and patriotic Roman war dead in Elysium proper are distinguished from the heroic combatants at Thebes or Troy, Deiphobus among them, in the fields of those famous for war (6.477–547).

lives on here in his own fame in this underworld Elysium that substitutes for the aethereal heavens and higher air to which the sons of gods aspire in the sibyl's declaration. It is possible, according to Virgil's model in Book 11 of the *Odyssey*, for a son of a god to occupy both places at once. Odysseus does not go down to the underworld but raises its shades through necromancy: the last he sees is Hercules, the human hero who became a god.

> I was aware of powerful Herakles;
> his image, that is, but he himself among the immortal
> gods enjoys their festivals, married to sweet-stepping
> Hebe, child of great Zeus and Hera of the golden sandals.
> (*Ody*. 11. 601–604)

It is Hercules' "*eidolon*" that Odysseus sees; earlier he has lamented that Persephone has sent him an "*eidolon*" of his mother, Antikleia (*Ody*. 11.213), to make him grieve. In the *Aeneid*, Hercules has indeed reached the heavens, worshiped as a new god by Evander, Pallas, and the Arcadians in Book 8 (301–302), shedding tears, in turn, on account of Pallas's upcoming death in Book 10 (464–471). The *Odyssey* both places Hercules/Herakles on Olympus and reproduces his image among the shades of its underworld. Glenn Most has described the *Odyssey*'s underworld as an encyclopedic storehouse of the previous tradition, Homeric and Hesiodic, of Greek epic poetry.[27]

The episode's insistence on the image is equally metapoetic. The Homeric/Virgilian underworld shades may disclose the nature of all literary representation, including that of the "living" characters Odysseus and Aeneas who consult them: they are all dead words on the page that create the illusion, thin and ungraspable, of living beings. As man *and* god, the divine son Hercules lives on in the poets, and possibly only there. So, with the *Odyssey* passage in mind, Horace declares in *Odes* 4.8 that it is the poets who grant Hercules a share in the wished for banquet of Jupiter: "*sic Iovis interest / optatis epulis impiger Hercules*" (4.8.29–30).[28] The *Aeneid* does something similar for the

---

27. Most, 1992. Most relates the spatial layout of Virgil's underworld to literacy; it is, he suggests, a kind of library.

28. Lyne, 1995, sees Horace in *Odes* 4.8 correcting and "sapping" his earlier promise of divinization to Augustus in *Odes* 3.3; I see Virgil doing something similar here. See also La Penna, 1988, 281; Barchiesi, 1996b, 42. The poem follows *Odes* 4.7, which declares that Aeneas himself is dust and shadow. (The fourth book of the *Odes* dates to 13 BCE, six years after Virgil's death, and these poems presumably were written after the composition of the *Aeneid*.) *Epodes* 17.39–41,

still living *"Augustus Caesar, diui genus,"* whom Book 6 presents as a greater divine son and savior hero than Hercules himself (6.801–803). It both promises him apotheosis in the prophecy of Jupiter to Venus in Book 1 and places his shade—before its time on earth but also, for projected future readers of the poem, during and after it—among the famous in the underworld. As commentators have pointed out, this shade and others in the procession Anchises shows to his son have something of the quality of the *"imagines,"* the masks of ancestors, that, as Polybius describes them (6.54), a distinguished Roman family would wear and carry in a funeral procession or on other ritual occasions.[29] Anchises is himself an *"imago"* (6.701) whom Aeneas vainly tries to embrace. The shade of Augustus, too, is an *"eidolon,"* in which the poet's making of images and of fame finds a reflection. Jupiter's words to Venus couple fame and deification: *"famam qui terminet astris ... hunc tu olim caelo ... accipies."* Augustus's fame already borders the stars—*"terminet"* nicely quibbles whether it reaches or stops short of them—and Augustus cannot be far behind. Or deification may be a hyperbolic figure for his fame, as the sibyl herself quibbles on *"aethera"* and *"auras"*—heavenly or mortal air: the *"auras"* into which Fama herself pokes her head in Book 4. In that case Augustus may have to settle for having his image perpetuated in the alternative heaven inside Virgil's underworld, both escaping and not escaping the labyrinth of death.[30]

Before Augustus, subject peoples in the East granted divine honors and built temples to Roman warlords and grandees of the late republic; these people's Hellenistic rulers, following the examples of Alexander the Great and of their Persian and Egyptian predecessors, had been worshipped as god-kings. Cicero turned down divine honors offered to him in Asia; his brother did receive a cult on Samos.[31] But such veneration had been largely kept outside of Rome itself. The extravagant honors granted to Julius Caesar may have

---

where Horace, seeking to get the witch Canidia off his back, promises to raise Canidia to the stars with his untruthful (*"mendaci"*) lyre, seems to be a *reductio ad absurdum* of the trope of poetic immortalization.

29. Feeney, 1986, 5; Skard, 1965; Burke, 1979. When the panicked Aeneas draws his sword on the gorgons and harpies near the entrance to the underworld, the sibyl reminds him that these are only images—*"caua sub imagine formae"* (6.293)—located near a tree of false dreams. The underworld episode of the *Odyssey* ends when Odysseus is afraid that Persephone might send up the head of a gorgon—real or image—from Hades (*Ody.* 11.633–635).

30. Horsfall, 2013, 27 argues that Augustus logically should return to Elysium: but then, what about the heavens?

31. Weinstock, 1971, 55n5.

already introduced his cult into the city before his assassination. In its aftermath, Augustus implemented and exploited the cult of his divine father, blending foreign divine rulership with local precedents in Roman ancestor worship. The dead were appropriate subjects for deification. Antonio La Penna has shown that by the time of Augustus, Romans distinguished a second order of divinities, heroic mortals who had become gods and, already in Cicero (*De Legibus* 2.9), had established a small canon of such gods: Hercules (Alcides), Dionysius (Liber), Castor and Pollux, and Romulus, the city-founder who would become the god Quirinus.[32] Book 6 names *Augustus Caesar, diui genus* directly after Romulus, depicted with the twin-plumed helmet that is the attribute of *his* divine father Mars (6.776–780)—Augustus is the re-founder of Rome, who at the Actium portrayed on the shield of Aeneas will shoot twin flames from his brows as he goes into battle (8.680–681). The conquests of Augustus, west and east, Anchises goes on to say in Book 6, make him a greater hero than Alcides (6.801) and Liber (6.805). It is propaganda, normative in the Greek world, more unusual until recently in Rome, and also speaks to a belief system that cannot quite be reduced to poetic metaphor—although I have been arguing that Virgil is doing just that.

Mary Beard notes, "So far as we can tell, Roman thinkers and writers took the idea of deification (that is, of a human being literally becoming a god) with no greater equanimity than we do ourselves."[33] Divinized rulers might make one wonder about the gods themselves.[34] In Cicero's *De natura deorum*, the academic skeptic Cotta lumps with Epicureanism the doctrine, equally destructive to religion, of Euhemerism.

> [What religion is left] by those who teach that brave or famous or powerful men [*aut fortis aut claros aut potentis viros*] have been deified after death, and that it is these who are the real objects of the worship, prayers, and adoration which we are accustomed to offer—are not they entirely devoid of all sense of religion? This theory was chiefly developed by Euhemerus, who was translated and imitated by our poet Ennius. Yet Euhemerus describes the death and burial of certain gods; are we then to think of him

---

32. La Penna, 1988.
33. Beard, 2007, 233–234.
34. La Penna, 1988, argues that Euhemerus attacked the gods and did not go after divinized mortals, although he admits that the two categories are inevitably confused. Euhemerus's connection with Cassander might suggest, to the contrary, that Euhemerist doctrine arose from the scrutiny of a specific divinized mortal, Alexander.

as upholding religion, or rather as utterly and entirely destroying it? (I.42.119)[35]

The Macedonian Euhemerus lived in the wake of the death of Alexander the Great, who had claimed Libyan Ammon-Zeus as his divine father and who had sought *proskynesis*—the ritual prostration offered to a Persian god-king— from his Greek as well as Persian subjects. The Greeks refused.[36] The teaching of Euhemerus can be read as a similar rationalizing refusal to make famous and powerful men into gods. Euhemerus lived under and was an agent of Cassander, the king of Macedon who had an interest in debunking Alexander's claims to divinity. His doctrine leads to a recursive logic that turned the gods themselves into former human beings and the byproducts of their fame.

This logic is voiced in the *Aeneid* in Book 4 by another divine son, Libyan Iarbas, disappointed in his courtship of Dido and—Alexander-like—the reputed offspring of Ammon-Jupiter (4.198). "We cherish an empty fame in you," he complains to Jupiter: *"famamque fouemus inanem"* (4.218). Not only is his parentage by Jupiter doubtful; Jupiter himself may have been a human being famous enough to have become a god.[37] Such skepticism would only be reinforced by the antics of King Salmoneus, whom the sibyl describes in Book 6 as suffering punishment in Tartarus.

> quattuor hic inuectus equis et lampada quassans
> per Graium populos mediaeque per Elidis urbem
> ibat ouans, diuumque sibi poscebat honorem,
> demens, qui nimbos et non imitabile fulmen
> aere et cornipedum pulsu simularet equorum. (6.587–591)
>
> He, borne by four horses and brandishing torches, went triumphing through the Greek peoples and his city in the middle of Elis, and sought divine honors for himself. Madman, who simulated storms

---

35. Cicero, 2000, 114–115: "*Quid qui aut fortis aut claros aut potentis viros tradunt post mortem ad deos pervenisse, eosque esse ipsos quos nos colere precari venerarique soleamus, nonne expertes sunt religionum omnium? quae ratio maxime tractata ab Euhemero est, quem noster et interpretatus et secutus est praeter ceteros Ennius; ab Euhemero autem et mortes et sepulturae demonstrantur deorum; utrum igitur hic confirmasse videtur religionem an penitus totam sustulisse?*"

36. Arrian 4.9–12; La Penna, 1988, 282–283.

37. Iarbas also frames his complaint to Jupiter in Epicurean terms; do we create gods out of our superstitious fear of lightning, he asks (4.208–210)? See Hardie, 2012, 88–93; Feeney, 1991, 186–187.

and the not imitable thunderbolt with bronze and the beat of horn-footed horses.

In the version of Virgil's contemporary, Diodorus Siculus (6.6–7), Salmoneus is a skeptic. He imitated Zeus not so much to promote himself but *in order to ridicule belief in the gods*: he refused to sacrifice to them or to celebrate their festivals and told his people that they might as well worship him. Diodorus makes him a mythical precursor to Euhemerus.[38] In the *Aeneid*, Jupiter, the real god, intervenes to save his own reputation. He answers Iarbas by ordering Mercury to send Aeneas packing from Dido and Carthage.[39] In the myth the sibyl tells, he fulminated Salmoneus with real thunder and sent him down to Tartarus. So yes, Iarbas, there *is* a Jupiter, the *Aeneid* piously declares—or archly denies. In either case, Salmoneus, like Theseus, the son of a god sitting forever in Tartarus nearby him, is a clear counterexample in Book 6 to its climactic view of Augustus on parade, the son of the deified Caesar, already on his way to becoming a god himself. However ridiculous—and Greek—he may be, Salmoneus's chariot ride does not look that different from that of a triumphing Roman general, who might seem to be playing god-for-a-day, Jupiter the god in question.[40] Both risk reducing godhead itself to fame, a human fiction.

Tartarus, the realm of eternal punishment, appears as the counterpart to the fields of the blessed in Virgil's Platonic sources (*Phaedo*, *Gorgias*, the Myth of Er in the *Republic*), and Homer's Odysseus, too, raises the shades of the punished Tityos, Tantalus, and Sisyphus toward the end of his visit to the underworld (*Ody*. 11.576–600), before the quasi-theophany of the *"eidolon"* of Hercules. From *Odyssey* 11, too, Virgil draws the first two of the four main locales of his underworld and their sequence. The Campi Lugentes offer a shortened version of Homer's catalog of women, in which Dido substitutes for Ariadne.[41] The fields of famous warriors—"*bello clari*"—name Trojan heroes and allies in place of the Greeks whom Odysseus summoned (Agamemnon, Achilles, Ajax) and who now keep their distance from Aeneas; the episode features Deiphobus and his diatribe against Helen instead of Homer's

---

38. Diodorus Siculus, 2000, 3:340–341; the stories about Salmoneus follow shortly after Diodorus's exposition of the ideas of Euhemerus in the fragmentary Book 6.

39. Hardie, 2012, 88–95.

40. Beard, 2007, 219–256. For the coupling in Book 6 of Salmoneus with Misenus, figure of the epic poet, see the preface above.

41. See note 6 above.

Agamemnon complaining darkly against Helen's sister, Clytemnestra. These first two episodes read like Virgil's filling out of Homer's poem. They give space to his character Dido and to his Trojan side of things and remove Homer's heroes to the shadows. But all three of these underworld sites—the Campi Lugentes, the fields of the heroes of Thebes and Troy, and especially Tartarus—are as much receptacles of fame as Elysium. Deiphobus may leave Aeneas to continue on his journey by saying that he will go and fill out the numbers of the dead and return to the dark—"*explebo numerum reddarque tenebris*" (6.545)—as if he is falling back into anonymity, but he has had his day in the sun, if not in Elysium with its own sun, at least on the pages of the *Aeneid*.

In the Tartarus episode that follows, the sibyl and the poet list the Aloides, Salmoneus, Tityos, Ixion, and Perithous, and then seem to back away from naming names—don't ask, the sibyl says (6.614). "Some roll a huge stone, others are suspended, stretched out on the spokes of wheels"—"*saxum ingens uoluunt alii, radiisque rotarum / districti pendent*" (6.616–617). These are so many stone-rolling Sisyphuses, so many who suffer the traditional punishment of Ixion on his wheel—while Ixion and Perithous receive the punishment usually reserved for Tantalus (neither Tantalus nor Sisyphus is mentioned by name here as they are in the *Odyssey*). And Perithous should be seated next to Theseus, not Ixion.[42] The confusion, surely deliberate, suggests the multiplicity and interchangeability of the prisoners of Tartarus, as if loss of identity is part of their punishment. But the sibyl nonetheless returns to naming Theseus and Phlegyas—the latter explains why when he proclaims with a loud voice ("*magna ... voce*") that his exemplary punishment is a warning: "*discite iustitiam moniti et non temnere diuos*" ("admonished by these, learn justice and not to scorn the gods"; 6.619–620)—only again to fall into the anonymity of the "this one here, this one there" ("*hic ... hic*") construction in verses 621–623, and finally into the topos of inexpressibility. A big voice, like that of Phlegyas, is not enough. The sibyl cannot enumerate all the evildoers of Tartarus, "not even," she says, "if I had a hundred tongues and a hundred mouths and a voice of iron" ("*non, mihi si linguae centum sint oraque centum, / ferrea uox*"; 6.625–627). The phrase adapts and imitates Homer's introduction to his catalog of ships in Book 2 of the *Iliad* (*Il.* 2.488–493), where the narrator calls on the Muses to remember the numbers of the Greek ships and the names of their leaders that he goes on to list at exhaustive length and preci-

42. Zetzel, 1989, 264–272.

sion. In pointed contrast, the sibyl stops here; she will not name the wicked, too many to be counted, but also, because of their crimes, deserving of *damnatio memoriae*, of being erased from human memory.[43]

In Virgil's Hades, some are remembered for their loves and sins of love, some for their martial heroism, some for their crimes, some for their blessed memory, in a kind of alternation of negative and positive renown that leads up to the immortality of the last of these in Elysium. The underworld holds fame, both good and bad, in the case of the Elysian residents very good indeed—they have become godlike. The distinction between these kinds of fame, praise and blame, is made in the name of justice—"*discite iustitiam*"— the poetic justice of the *Aeneid* that reaches an ethical sublime in these verses, their naming, from the apparent perspective of eternity, what will always be human crimes and what will always be human deeds of merit. Virgil makes Dante's project possible but also criticizes it in advance.[44] What is the basis of such justice? Is it unchanging? Book 6 equivocates when it shows its Cretan judge Minos at work: "*nec uero hae sine sorte datae, sine iudice, sedes*" ("but these places in the underworld are not assigned to shades without lot, without a judge"; 6.431). The ensuing verses, in which Minos shakes his urn, show that this line apparently refers to Roman court procedure, where the order of cases was assigned by lot: the dead are getting due process but have to wait their turn. But the line can equally suggest that justice, in the life after death as well as in this one, can be a question of luck.[45] It returns us to the sibyl's earlier speech to Aeneas about those whom "*aequus*"—equitable or biased— Jupiter loved or who through their own fiery virtue have been raised to the stars, the sons of gods. Is there a godly thumb on the scales of divine justice, favoring those lucky sons?

The situation of Theseus, with which we started, is a case in point. Virgil insists that Theseus sits forever in the underworld and couples him for his sacrilege with the worst of all criminals, Phlegyas. But Virgil knew that in most alternate versions of the myth, Hercules had freed Theseus from the underworld. He knew, more importantly, that Theseus was a culture hero of Athens, a human hero transformed into a god with his own cult and rites— like Hercules, like Dionysius, like Romulus.[46] Aristotle in the *Poetics* (8.20)

---

43. Dante picks up on this ambivalence in the *Inferno*, where some sinners want to be remembered, others to bury their ill fame: compare *Inferno* 13.75–78; 15.119–120; 27.61–66.
44. Hardie, 2012, 371–376.
45. See the great rewriting of these verses in Thomas Kyd's *The Spanish Tragedy*, I.1.32–85.
46. Den Boer, 1969.

testifies to more than one *Theseids*, epic poems devoted to the hero. Plutarch cites one of these a century after Virgil.[47] Theseus was credited with setting up the Athenian constitution, and Plutarch parallels Theseus and Romulus as founder-kings. Plutarch also tells how Theseus had appeared in gigantic form at the battle of Marathon helping the Athenians against the Persians, much as Virgil shows the star of Julius Caesar shining over the head of Augustus in what he depicts as a similar battle of West against East at Actium. The holy days of the cult of Theseus in Athens commemorated the event depicted by Daedalus on the gates of the temple of Cumae at the opening of Book 6, his having slain the minotaur and freed the city from the yearly tribute of seven unlucky sons—"*sortibus urna*" (6.22)—and demanded by Minos, as retribution for the Athenians' killing of his son Androgeus. Seven for one; the condemned chosen by lot. This Minos is the son of the Minos who shakes his urn in the underworld, but his labyrinth seems to be a perverted model—or is it a mirror ("*nec ... sine sorte*")?—of the justice his father dispenses in the afterlife. The sentencing judge may be both partial and arbitrary. And so, in this light, may be Virgil himself, who punishes Theseus while letting his own Theseus, Aeneas, not only go scot-free but become a god.

But this arbitrariness is itself a judgment of history and a sign of Jupiter's favor. Roman power—for which Jupiter might be another name—now rules the world. The *Aeneid* condemns Athens's hero-god as part of its larger hostile takeover of Greek literature and culture, a project it shares with much of Augustan poetry. In well-known lines, Anchises acknowledges that other peoples—Greeks—may be better sculptors, orators, and astronomers (he does *not* mention poets or concede Greek superiority on that score). It is Rome's talent to rule such peoples, "*tu regere imperio populos, Romane, memento*" (6.851): Anchises addresses the Roman reader as much as Aeneas. Rome has conquered Greece, and as the new political capital it also claims to replace Athens, Greece's most prestigious capital of culture.[48] Thus, the *Aeneid* not only demotes Theseus, Athens's Romulus, from divine kingship but places him at the bottom of its underworld, a Homeric underworld entered at

---

47. Cingano, 2017, considers the evidence for epics based on the career of Theseus.

48. Feeney, 2016, 120–121 points out that the first Roman authors of the mid-third century BCE who translated Greek tragedy already chose as target texts the canonical works of fifth-century Athens. They probably followed the cultural projects of Macedonian kings and other non-Athenians who (121) "wanted access to the charisma and authority of the cultural center of Greece." For telling remarks on the Augustan urban projects carried out by Marcus Agrippa on Athens itself, see Zanker, 1988, 261–263.

Greek Cumae but already rearranged for Trojan-Roman uses. The Athenians paid Theseus divine honors, but Roman Virgil has stripped those honors away and made Theseus no more of a deity than Salmoneus, who dressed up as a god in order to debunk godship itself.

Theseus falls victim to cultural politics. Yet by placing Theseus in the same underworld occupied, if in a different sector, by the shades of the future Romulus, Julius Caesar, and Augustus Caesar (those Roman mortals who will become gods), Virgil spells out not only the mechanisms, the "justice," by which his poem confers fame tantamount to divinity but also the power relations that underlie them. Justice, at least some justice, is not eternal, even if depicted in the afterlife. Should Rome's own power fail, or the power of their dynasty, these Roman god-men will no longer retain their cult status. Perhaps, like Theseus, they will even be seen as criminals. The *Aeneid* will continue to enshrine them, for it will outlive—like the poetry of the Greeks (if not the *Theseids*)—the politics of its moment.[49] The verdict on their godhood, however, is still out.

In and Out of the Labyrinth

The doors at the temple of Cumae are missing one of their sculpted panels at the beginning of Book 6.

> tu quoque magnam
> partem opere in tanto, sineret dolor, Icare, haberes.
> bis conatus erat casus effingere in auro,
> bis patriae cecidere manus. (6.30–33)
>
> You, too, Icarus, had sorrow allowed, were to have a large part in this work: twice he tried to depict your fall in gold, twice the father's hands fell away.

The grief-stricken Daedalus is unable to depict the fate of his son, Icarus, who briefly escaped from Crete and its labyrinth and flew into the higher air with his father, only to fall along the way, his life cut short. His fate is coupled with the climax/anticlimax at the book's end, the mourning that Anchises makes for the younger Marcellus, whose shade still waits to leave the labyrinth of

---

49. Or will it? See the address of Virgil's narrator, promising memory to Nisus and Euryalus, at 9.446–449, so long—only so long?—as the house of Aeneas dwells by the immovable rock of the Capitol.

death to which it is fated to make a premature return (6.860–886). In Marcellus's case, the task that the sibyl declares, *"hoc opus, hic labor est,"* comes down to staying alive.

Anchises appears to have finished his roll call of Roman heroes with M. Claudius Marcellus, the hero of the Gallic and Punic wars.[50] Aeneas notices a youth of exceptional beauty and shining arms—*"egregium forma iuuenem et fulgentibus armis"* 6.861)—arms and the young man, a figure haunted, however, by the black shades of night that encircle his head: *"nox atra caput tristi circumuolat umbra"* (6.866). He asks Anchises, and learns that this is the M. Claudius Marcellus of the same name, the nephew of Augustus through his sister Octavia. When he married Augustus's daughter Julia in 25 BCE, Marcellus appeared to be a presumptive heir to the princeps.[51] But Marcellus died at the age of nineteen or twenty in 23 BCE (four years before Virgil's own death). He was buried in the family mausoleum that Augustus had just built— the *"tumulum ... recentem"* of 6.874. Augustus himself delivered the funeral eulogy, which may be echoed in Anchises' ensuing lament over Marcellus and his unrealized virtues (6.868–886), a poetic set piece invested with the same number of verses, nineteen, that Anchises / Virgil has earlier allotted to Augustus himself (6.789–807). Anchises concludes by calling for lilies and violets to be scattered upon young Marcellus's shade. The parade of Roman heroes in Book 6 that evokes the *"imagines"* of the funeral of a prominent *gens* suddenly resembles such a funeral procession for real. Marcellus takes up the head—as the image of the deceased would have preceded those of his ancestors carried by the mourners—rather than the rear of the parade. This about-face, A to Z become Z to A, may be the most unexpected among the many reversals of the *Aeneid*.[52]

Like *"aequus"* Jupiter, Virgil appears to play favorites. Nowhere does the *Aeneid*'s special treatment of the Julii appear more blatantly than in this commemoration of an otherwise insignificant young man whose early death makes him a footnote to the grand Roman history that Anchises unfolds in his parade of dignitaries. It is unclear whether Anchises intends to mention

---

50. See Freudenburg, 2017, on the older as well as younger Marcellus. See Feeney, 1986, on the motif of the continuity of the *gens*, but also on sons who degenerate from their ancestors or, in the case of Marcellus, simply do not survive. See also Goold, 1992.

51. Velleius Paterculus, 2.93, who notes that Marcus Agrippa would have had his say in the matter.

52. Burke, 1979, has excellent remarks on this reversal. He reads the episode as constituting Aeneas's own funeral.

Marcellus at all until Aeneas points him out. Anchises almost gratuitously rescues Marcellus from the darkness surrounding him by addressing and naming him—"*tu Marcellus eris*" (6.883)—as Virgil's narrator has earlier addressed and named Icarus—"*tu ... / ... Icare haberes*"—when Icarus's own artist father failed to memorialize him.[53] Corresponding to the Daedalus-Icarus vignette at the book's opening, the mourning over Marcellus is made to feel at once part of the book's design and an add-on, a *supplement*, in Jacques Derrida's term, that adds to what is now revealed to have been incomplete without it.[54] That is what Marcellus himself should have been, an heir to Augustus, but was not: you will be *that* Marcellus, Anchises says to him, only if you can break the bitter bonds of fate (6.882). In Marcellus's place, Book 6 gives a final say to death, the precondition of its projects to build fame for a nation and its new ruling house. The episode of Marcellus casts last-minute irony on these projects: it both universalizes poetic commemoration and mourning in this book of the dead *and* addresses a dynastic crisis in the single clan that counts above the collective Roman family and the rest of humanity together.

Universality first. The lament over Marcellus briefly switches the register of Book 6 from epic to elegy. We are no longer asked to contrast the nameless all to the famous few—those who, a few verses later, are said to inspire Aeneas upon his mission: "*incenditque animum famae uenientis amore*" (6.889). The focus is now on a single individual who died before he could achieve renown, and in this sense Marcellus is a stand-in for all the nameless dead, dear to their immediate family, to be forgotten with the passage of time, a figure of ordinary human loss. Virgil has told this story once before in his *Fourth Georgic*, in the myth of Orpheus and Eurydice. After his wife Eurydice dies, Orpheus tries to rescue her from the underworld through the power of song.

The Orpheus story and its version in the *Georgics* haunt Book 6 and its images of the famous dead. Aeneas mentions four precedents for his descent into the underworld, Orpheus, Pollux, Theseus, Hercules (6.119–123), an alternation of failure (to restore Eurydice to life), success (to restore Castor to the heavens even if that means that Pollux stays in the underworld himself in alternation with his brother), failure (for Theseus to get out of the underworld), success (Hercules makes his way back to earth and even to the heavens). Orpheus has, in fact, a mixed success, for he does manage to recall his steps and return to earth, *and*, as we have seen, he also turns up in Elysium,

---

53. Bartsch, 1998, 336.
54. Derrida, 1967, 208.

the Thracian priest playing his lyre to the blessed (6.645–647). But he does not get what he came for: he looked back on Eurydice and thereby lost her. The shades clamoring to enter the underworld of Book 6 are described in successive verses that Virgil repeats verbatim from the Orpheus episode of the *Fourth Georgic* (6.306–308 = *Georgics* 4.475–476): included among them are youths placed on their funeral pyres before the eyes of their parents— "*impositique rogis iuuenes ante ora parentum*" (6.308)—so many Marcelluses. The comparison to bees of the countless ("*innumerae*"; 6.706) shades, Marcellus among them, assembled to leave the underworld and to return to earthly lives, also recalls the *Fourth Georgic*'s tragic vision of poetry. The earlier poem contrasts the restoration of his bee colony by the shepherd Aristaeus to Orpheus's failure to bring Eurydice back to life: the anonymous species survives en masse, but the individual, particularly the loved, named human individual, dies.

Virgil's Orpheus looks back on Eurydice while nature and time move forward on their one-way path: "*immemor*" of the gods' command, he nonetheless *remembers* her (*Georgics* 4.491), first in his journey down to Hades, now as he looks back on her, and even after his own death, when, in Virgil's account, Orpheus's disembodied head continues to repeat the name of Eurydice in three successive verses (*Georgics* 4.525–527) as it is carried away down the Hebrus, the river of time. Plato, the enemy of poets, had maintained that the underworld gods had only granted Orpheus an "*eidolon*" of his wife in the first place (*Symposium* 179d). Perhaps that is all that poetry can do, its words and images only ghostly representations of life. But the capacity to know individual loss and not to accept substitutes defines human beings. Virgil's myth of the archetypal poet defines poetry as giving a name or image to this loss and as preserving it in song that outlives the poet himself.

Virgil now does something of the same for Marcellus. In this vignette the poetic fame that Book 6 confers upon the great and good is both distinguished from, but also ironically reduced to, something more basic: to a compulsion of poetry, evidenced in the story of Orpheus, to bring the dead back, to represent them, to keep alive their memory as well as the poet's own.[55] Virgil's poetry does so against its better knowledge. The dreamlike "imago" of Anchises

---

55. Anchises' description of Greek sculptors insists on their ability to make "life" out of their sculptures and their portraits, "*spirantia ... aera*"; "*uiuos ... uultus*" (6.847–848). Photography has changed our modern understanding of artistic commemoration, and our lives now will indeed rise to the heavens in the digital "Cloud."

escapes three times—"*ter conatus... ter frustra*" (6.700–702)—from Aeneas's embraces, echoing the double failure of the artist Daedalus—"*bis conatus... bis*" (6.32–33). The lines also echo verbatim Aeneas's attempt in Book 2 to embrace the "*imago*" of his wife Creusa, the Eurydice of the *Aeneid* (according to Ennius, the name of Aeneas's wife *was* "Eurydice"), whom Aeneas searches to recover through the streets of a burning Troy, now become a labyrinthine underworld of death (2.792–793).[56] In the first book of his *Odes*, Horace addresses Virgil himself, mourning for their friend Quintilius, and admonishes his fellow poet that, even if he outdid the song of (Virgil's own) Orpheus, blood would not return to the empty image of Quintilius—"*num uanae redeat sanguis imagini*" (*Odes* 1.24.15)—both underworld shade and image made of words. Anchises would strew flowers, by Roman funerary convention, as gifts for Marcellus. These are also the flowers of Virgil's poetic eloquence itself, which recognizes an emptiness in the fame it would bestow in place of a lived life—"*fungar inani / munere*" (6.885–886).

Now for the politics. According to the story preserved in Servius, Octavia broke down and fainted at the eulogy for her son when the poet gave a private reading to her and Augustus. But private grief in a ruling family is tragedy for the nation. In a political-historical key, the death of Marcellus reads as disaster for the imperial house and its plan of succession. As we have observed in chapter 2, Anchises' parade of heroes appears to double back from the civil war impasse of Caesar and Pompey to figures of the earlier republic and, perhaps as a final gesture of closure, to the *spolia opima* that M. Claudius Marcellus won in 222 BCE and, in Virgil's account, dedicated to Quirinus, the now divinized Romulus (6.859). Earlier in its sequence, the parade made a chronological jump from Rome's founder to Augustus, its refounder, as Jupiter's prophecy also does in Book 1. The mention of Quirinus-Romulus triggers another such leap to the Augustan present, but this time it is a failed one. The mourning over Marcellus seems to have brought Rome's present history, and the *Aeneid* with it, to another impasse, a dynastic dead end. It is the latest chronological event mentioned in the poem.

This is not where Virgil appears to have planned to cut off the chronology of the *Aeneid*. The middle books of the *Aeneid*, 5–8, begin with the funeral

---

56. Putnam, 1965, 41–48; Grillo, 2010. The verses are based on Odysseus's attempt to embrace the *eidolon* of his mother, Antikleia, in *Ody.* 11.205–207. Ennius calls the wife of Aeneas "Eurydica" in the dream of Ilia in the fragment left to us from Book 1 of the *Annales*; Ennius, 1985, 73 (1.19).

games for Anchises in Book 5 in Sicily, including a performance of the "*Lusus Troiae*," a series of equestrian exercises performed by Iulus and other Trojan boys, and the dedication of a priest and sacred grove to Anchises (5.759–761). They end with the ekphrasis of the shield of Aeneas in Book 8, scenes of Rome's future that culminate in the victory of Actium and the triumph of Augustus. This frame alludes to two events three days apart in 29 BCE, whose order the poem reverses. Augustus celebrated his triple triumph on August 13–15; he dedicated the temple of Divus Julius in the Forum on August 18, during which he staged the *Lusus Troiae*. Together these events proclaimed the end of the civil wars, the victory over Antony and Cleopatra, and the final putting to rest—by his exaltation to divinity—of the ghost of the assassinated Caesar. They offer an ending to the larger *Aeneid* in the middle of the epic.

These coupled events of 29 BCE that afford pillars to the structure of Virgil's poem not only placed Augustus in a dynastic succession but also featured a display of the dynastic future. Suetonius (*Tiberius* 6.4) reports that during the triple triumph Marcellus rode the right trace horse next to the chariot of Augustus, while Tiberius, the son of Augustus's wife Livia, rode the left one. Marcellus and Tiberius were both born in 42 BCE and would have been about thirteen years old. Suetonius also reports that in the festivities surrounding the temple dedication three days later, Tiberius led the band of older boys through their equestrian paces of the *Lusus Troiae*. Did Marcellus take part? We might be led to think that Marcellus had received the top (righthand) honors during the triumph; Tiberius may have been compensated by top (and exclusive) billing during the Troy game. Or perhaps both boys and possible heirs were again displayed together, either in the same miniature cohort, or as friendly rivals, each leading one of his own in the cooperative, choreographed maneuvers and mock combat of the horse ballet. The message would have been clear in both triumph and temple games: here was a vigorous younger generation ready to continue the lineage of the ruling family and to renew the ranks of the city's aristocracy.

Sulla had earlier revived the *Lusus Troiae* in association with his personal devotion to Venus-Fortuna. But it was Julius Caesar, flaunting his Trojan descent from Venus, who made this pageant of Roman youth a particularly Julian event; he staged the Troy game during his own dedication of the temple of his ancestress, Venus genetrix, in the Forum in 46 BCE.[57] Virgil tells us that

---

57. Virgil may recall this event, too, in verses 5.759–761, where Aeneas founds in Sicily a shrine for Venus as well as a grove and cult for Anchises. He may conflate the two temples fac-

Iulus himself, the founder of the clan, reinstituted the *Lusus Troiae* in Alba Longa, and in Book 5 Iulus leads one of three bands of boys in the equestrian exercise. It is the culmination of the funerary games in commemoration of Anchises, by now the poem's figure, as we have seen, of the divinized Julius Caesar. When Augustus dedicated the temple to his deified father in 29 BCE, he had the horse games performed as part of a family tradition and as a demonstration of family continuity.[58]

The *Lusus Troiae* of Book 5 appears to be the one unequivocally happy moment in the *Aeneid*. The interweavings of the boys' ranks in a kind of mock battle (*"pugnaeque ... simulacra sub armis"*; 5.585), are compared in simile to the windings of the labyrinth on Crete.

> ut quondam Creta fertur Labyrinthus in alta
> parietibus textum caecis iter ancipitemque
> mille uiis habuisse dolum, qua signa sequendi
> frangeret indeprensus et inremeabilis error; (5.588–591)

> As once they say the Labyrinth in lofty Crete held a path woven
> with blind walls and a maze that forked uncertainly in a thousand
> directions, where undiscovered and irretraceable error broke the signs
> of which way to follow.

As many commentators have noted, the simile anticipates the labyrinth-like underworld of death in the following book and provides a solution to it.[59] The general idea is that these boys who replenish the family stock guarantee the Trojan-Roman future as it passes through the deathly perils of history and in spite of Troy's own extinction. Aeneas's and the Trojans' own wanderings come to an end at the conclusion of Book 5; having left the old and the women behind in Sicily, he and his band of young and fit-for-duty warriors

---

ing each other in the Forum, the one to Divus Julius, the other to Venus genetrix, and their dedications.

58. On the *Lusus Troiae*, see Sumi, 2007, 61, 218–219; Doob, 1990, 27–33; Deremetz, 1993. On Suetonius's interest in the Troy game, see Wallace-Hadrill, 1983, 47. For a reading connecting the Troy Game episode in Book 5 to the death of Marcellus, see Miller, 2003, 64–75.

59. In addition to *"inextricabilis error"* describing the Cretan labyrinth (6.27) depicted on the gates of the temple at Cumae, see the use of *"inremeabilis"* to modify the waves of Styx at 6.425. On the figure of the labyrinth in the *Aeneid* and its relationship to this passage, see Doob, 1990, 27–33, 227–253, on Books 5 and 6, 234–241; Fitzgerald, 1984; Deremetz, 1993; Barchiesi, 1994, 443n22, Bartsch, 1998.

coast by their destination of Italy.⁶⁰ The boys perform before the delighted eyes of their parents—"*ante ora parentum*" (5.553). In a repetition of the same "*ora parentum*" at the end of the verse, they reproduce the features of their parents and ancestors (5.576). It is a reassuring sign of generational continuity that contrasts with all those young men subsequently described in Book 6 placed on funeral pyres "*ante ora parentum*" (6.308). It partially compensates, too, for the horror of the exterminating Pyrrhus of Book 2, who kills Polites before the eyes of his parents, Priam and Hecuba, "*ante ... ora parentum*" (2.531; cf. 2.63).⁶¹ We are further reminded of the latter by the presence of Polites' son, little Priam, leading one of the bands (5.563–565). Spitting images of their forefathers, these boys are living, flesh-and-blood replicas, *unlike* the illustrious shades conserved in Virgil's Hades in the half-life images of poetry. The fertility of Rome, particularly of its Julian dynasty and aristocratic elite, overcomes death; Book 6 compares it to Cybele and her divine offspring and depicts it in the innumerable shades ready to get out of the labyrinthine underworld and assume new Roman bodies. This is the city's true eternity.

But what about young Marcellus, then, the last of those shades lined up for earthly existence? Anchises addresses Marcellus as an afterthought and as Virgil's update. The bookends of Books 5 and 8 that recall the events of August in 29 BCE which still give the month its name in the West may be supposed to have constituted the end and limit of the *Aeneid*'s historical plot. But time has somehow leaked through, and here in Book 6, at the center and hinge of the *Aeneid* itself, the plot has led up to the funeral of a Julian heir, a new unlooked-for ending. When Augustus himself dies and becomes a god, who is next in line to be the son of a divine father? Who will succeed Augustus, and into what kind of civil strife may Rome descend to answer that question? In this light, the presence of little Priam in the *Lusus Troiae* of Book 5 may not be entirely hopeful and reassuring. As Emily Gowers has noted, here is a potential rival dynast for Ascanius/Iulus, one, moreover, from the old ruling house.⁶² The mock warfare of the horse games may suggest real internecine struggle starting all over again between competing imperial heirs—the much later *Lusus Troiae* of 47 CE, where little Nero made a better impression than Britannicus, seems to have staged just such a rivalry before the Roman

---

60. Doob, 1990, 234.
61. Smith, 2005, 176–182 on the instances of "*ora parentum*" throughout the *Aeneid*.
62. Gowers, 2011, 112–113.

public.⁶³ If Marcellus did participate with Tiberius in the Troy games of 29 BCE, three days after they had been paired in Augustus's triumph, the emulation of these boys of the same age may not have been so friendly after all. It may be for this reason that Virgil describes *three* cohorts of boy horsemen, while Suetonius describes two cohorts, one of older boys, one of younger ones, as the normal participants of the *Lusus Troiae* (an aspect of the game's presentation of ever succeeding generations). Virgil avoids a direct confrontation between Iulus and young Priam, although, in doing so, he just might make us think of a triumvirate.⁶⁴ Even at its happiest moment of collective Trojan-Roman unity in Book 5, the *Aeneid* brushes with the ghost of civil war. Now, in Book 6, the poem asks if the death of Marcellus will constitute a full-blown crisis in the consolidation of the regime of Augustus instead of the bump in the road that Virgil could not have known it would turn out to be.

Augustus lived longer than anyone expected and survived Agrippa on whom Virgil appears to have been betting. (See 8.682, where the favoring winds at Actium—"*uentis...secundis*"—also seem to name Agrippa as second in line behind the *princeps*.) Several bumps named Gaius and Lucius later: *Tiberius Caesar Diui Augusti Filius Augustus*.

---

63. Suetonius, *Nero*, 7.1; Tacitus Ann. 11.11.5. I thank Kirk Freudenburg for pointing out this event to me.

64. Fratantuono and Smith, 2015, 533–534.

5

Culture and Nature in Book 8

BOOK 8 IS VIRGIL'S BOOK of green and gold—golden objects shining against the green backdrop of nature, green thickets now where golden Rome will later be, memories of a past golden age and anticipations of a future one. It is equally a book of green and bronze ("*aes*"), the metal of Homeric, heroic weaponry *and* a metal of ancient Roman coinage: the *aerarium*, the national treasury, contained gold and the booty of empire within it. Bronze is in Aeneas's name, and the book's opening simile (8.22–25) that compares his thoughts to light reflecting off of waters in bronze vessels ("*labris ... aënis*") is a kind of pun that suggests, as will the book's ensuing action and motifs, the coupling of arms and the man in the *Aeneid*'s opening verse. Gold and bronze flow together, along with steely iron, the metal of modern Roman weapons—"*fluit aes riuis aurique metallum / uulnificusque chalybs*" (8.445–446)—to make the shield of Aeneas in Vulcan's forge and to make the Roman history the shield represents. Together they light up the sea at Actium in the long ekphrastic description of the shield that concludes the book: "*classis aeratas ... auroque effulgere fluctus*" (8.675–677). The Rome of Augustus will indeed be golden, enriched beyond precedent by the "gifts"—"*dona*" (8.721)—of the subject peoples led in his triumph in the shield's final scene. They have been conquered by Roman arms, of which the shield is the prototype, along with the new helmet, sword, corselet, greaves, and spear that Vulcan fashions for Aeneas.[1]

Various woods and groves—"*lucus*," "*nemus*"—of the Italian natural world provide the book's greenery, whether the woods along the Tiber (8.92) or out-

---

1. For some discussions of the shield and readings of its episodes, see Putnam,1998, 118–188; Hardie, 1986, 336–376; Binder, 1971, 150–282; Casali, 2006; Zetzel, 1997, 198–203; Quint, 1993, 21–49; West, 1975–76, 1–7; Feldherr, 2014; Rossi, 2010; Gurval, 1995; McKay,1998.

side Pallanteum where Evander conducts the rites of Hercules (8.103–110), whether inside the walls of the future Rome, in the Asylum, the Argiletum, the very Capitoline Hill (8.342–352), or in the wild sanctuary of Silvanus (8.597–599). Venus places the radiant shield against an oak tree in this latter shrine. Gold glittering on green is Book 8's figure for the imposition of human power and culture on nature: the overarching issue that organizes its various episodes into a repeated argument and that invites reflection on the epic's own poetic art, on the making of meanings that are precisely not natural. The shield depicts the rise of the city of Rome from its origins in the green, pastoral cave (*"uiridi ... Mauortis in antro"*) of Mars and the she-wolf (8.630). The larger book continuously adjusts the reader's perspective on the now of Rome's present-day world power and wealth under Augustus, he who, according to the prophecy of Anchises back in the underworld of Book 6, will found a golden age in the fields of Latium where Saturn once reigned—*"aurea condet / saecula qui rursus Latio regnata per arua / Saturno quondam"* (6.792–794)—and on the rural Italian world encountered by Aeneas, already a post–golden age world but still poor and simple. Virgil mythologized this world of fields and flocks in the *Georgics* and *Eclogues*, and associations with those earlier, generically "lower" works cling, respectively, to its Latin and Arcadian inhabitants in the *Aeneid*. Now the Trojans enter Italy, bringing with them from Troy the high style and riches of epic.[2] In a series of overlapping oppositions, Book 8 sets the art of the shield (and of the *Aeneid*) against the green trees and flowing rivers of the Italian landscape, technology versus nature, civilization versus rusticity, history versus myth. This is a Roman poem: the first terms in these oppositions cannot be uncoupled from warfare, the bronze that is inseparable from the gold.

Italians and Arcadians, *Georgics* versus *Eclogues*

Aeneas founds the Roman future in Italy through arms, the first word of the *Aeneid*. So, depicted on his shield, his Julian descendant Augustus will restore a Saturnian golden age of peace by waging war at Actium. The whole of Book 8 is an arming scene of the hero.

---

2. Putnam, 1998, 183–187 notes the echo of *Eclogues* 1.75–76 in the green cave of the she-wolf and notes how the shield might recapitulate Virgil's career. The Arcadian scenes earlier in Book 8, I shall argue below, also evoke the world of the *Eclogues* as part of its meditation on the distance that Rome has traveled from humble, pastoral beginnings to military world power—something like the shape of the Virgilian career from *Eclogues* to the *Aeneid*. On the landscape of Books 7 and 8, see Jenkyns, 1998, 463–563, especially 470–484, 535–542.

Evander, the poor Arcadian king and strategist-Nestor-figure, comes up with the ploy of allying Aeneas with the Etruscan enemies of Mezentius who are in need of a foreign general, giving Aeneas the troops he needs to fight the Latins; Evander also contributes horses (8.551–553) and his own Arcadian troops, including his son Pallas. Venus meanwhile obtains armor for Aeneas, especially the shield with its sculpted scenes of future Roman history, from her artificer husband Vulcan. Aeneas arrives at Evander's settlement in Pallanteum, on the future site of Rome, on August 12. The day, Evander tells him, commemorates the victory of Hercules over the fire monster Cacus, the half-bestial son of Vulcan; it was on the following day of Aeneas's visit, August 13, that Augustus in 29 BCE began his triple, three-day triumph, celebrating his victory at Actium (31 BCE) over Mark Antony and Cleopatra, the last events the book describes on Vulcan's shield.[3] Aeneas seems to be inducted into a heroic space and identity, in a kind of ideological arming, between mythology and history. Sergio Casali observes that the shield is Virgil's own version of the *Aeneid* itself as a propaganda weapon for the new principate.[4] Aeneas ends the book by shouldering the shield and the Augustan Rome that is to come, *urbs* and *orbis*, much as Hercules or Atlas, the common ancestor that Evander claims for both Aeneas and himself, once held up the heavens and earth (8.137; 141).[5]

The book responds to, and copies with a difference, the previous Book 7 where Turnus, urged on by the fury Allecto, has called for arms, even in his own bedchamber—"*arma toro tectisque requirit*" (7.460). The ensuing simile (7.462–466) that compared his seething emotions and warlust to water boiling over in a *bronze* ("*aëni*") vessel, the dark smoke flying into the air above ("*uolat … ad auras*"), anticipates and contrasts with the description in simile of Aeneas's darting thoughts—"*peruolitat … sub auras*" (8.24)—at the beginning of the following book: the instinctive versus the reflective hero. Turnus's call for arms becomes universal among the Italians after the incident of Silvia's stag—"*omnes arma requirunt*" (7.625)—where five Italian cities have set up forges to make arms out of bronze, silver, and gold (7.629–640). Book 7 ended with a catalog of the Italian forces, including a son of Hercules named Aventinus (7.655–669) for the very hill where his father, we will now learn, killed Cacus. Turnus himself bears a shield with golden artwork; it depicts Io, transformed into a cow, beside her father, the River Inachus.

---

3. Drew, 1927, 6–41; Galinsky, 1966; Gransden, 1976, 14–17; Binder, 1971, 42–45.
4. Casali, 2006.
5. Binder, 1971, 60–65; Hardie, 1986, 336–376.

They, the Italians, have started it. Aeneas must now be armed in return, but an escalation has taken place: those five cities are no match for one divine smithy. Book 8 depicts a whole different level of arms invading the Italian rural landscape and finally into all parts of the universe itself. Virgil uses the conceit of the four elements to organize his fiction.[6] Both on the Tiber at the book's beginning and at Actium at its end, where the sea gleams with gold and bronze, arms have entered water. They are forged in Vulcan's subterranean realm of fire (8.416–453). They sound and flash in the air and aether of heaven (8.524–529) as a sign to Aeneas.[7] They come down to earth in the grove of Silvanus. The shield of Aeneas is an image of the cosmos itself, where, in the future that is the present of Virgil and Augustus, Roman power and arms will be everywhere. The reciprocity of the two initial books of the second half of the *Aeneid*, in fact, appears one-sided, but, as we shall see, it affords more than one opportunity for the chiastic reversal—contrast become comparison—that characterizes Virgil's art.

The shield of Turnus is a giveaway, so incommensurate as it is to the shield of Aeneas. The story of Io attests to Turnus's Argolic ancestry (7.371–372) and to the power of Turnus's patron Juno. The bull, the *uitulus*, was the symbol of Italy, quite possibly the Oscan etymon of "Italy" itself, and appeared on the coinage of the Italians allied against Rome in the Social Wars recalled in the warfare of the second half of the *Aeneid*.[8] But it is still a cow that Turnus bears on his shield as he marches into battle. Virgil does not go in much for jokes, but he appears to indulge in a silent one here at the expense of his Italian hero and his rustic compatriots, no match for the Trojan survivors of a once rich and great city and bearers of the future of the greatest city the world will know.

The farmer-soldiers of rural, central Italy would, nonetheless, be decisive instruments of Roman power—Mark Antony lost out when Octavian blocked him from recruiting troops in Italy. The *Aeneid* will wed them, through Lavinia, to Aeneas's Roman destiny. The virtues of their hardscrabble poverty were part of the national ideology enshrined in Virgil's own *Georgics*. But the *Georgics* separate these virtues *from* warfare, in what can alternatively be seen as a criticism of this ideology or as a furthering of its mystification, and in either case a denial of the actual state of affairs. The fertile Saturnian Italian

6. For the motif of the four elements elsewhere in the *Aeneid*, see Hardie,1986, 325–329.
7. See the rich discussion of the episode in Barchiesi, 1984, 74–90 [Barchiesi, 2015, 53–67].
8. Morgan, 2004, 200–201 discusses the *vitulus*-Italy connection in a discussion of the myth of Hercules and the cattle of Geryon that includes *Aeneid* 8; on the particular memory of the Social Wars in the civil war scenario of the second half of the *Aeneid*, see Marincola, 2010; Barchiesi, 2008. On the shield of Turnus, see Putnam, 1998, 18–22.

earth of *Georgics* 2 bears not only crops and livestock but also the "*genus acre uirum*," the tough race of men who include the toughest of all, Augustus, conqueror of Asia and protector of the hills of Rome from Eastern threats (*Georgics* 2.167–172). But the happy farmer celebrated at the book's end, happy if he knows his happiness, is happiest when he and the rural youth who bear toil and are used to want—"*et patiens operum exiguoque adsueta iuuentus*" (*Georgics* 2.472)—stay untouched by the affairs of Rome itself (*Georgics* 2.498) and by all of urban civilization's discontents: war, commerce, law courts, luxury. This farmer of the *Georgics* recaptures both the age of just Astraea at the beginning of this passage and the age of golden Saturn at its end (*Georgics* 2.474; 2.538–540), an age without the swords and trumpets of war.[9] It is from this early, rustic stage of her existence—when Remus lived peacefully alongside his brother in old Etruria, a world without *civil* war in particular—that Rome drew in the first place the virtues and strengths that made her the most beautiful of things (or states)—"*et rerum facta est pulcherrima Roma*"—and enclosed her seven hills inside one wall (*Georgics* 2.533–535). But now, in Virgil's time, those country values appear to be lost beneath the corruption of city life even as the *Georgics*, repeating the patriotic myth, call for their renewal.

When Virgil returns in Book 7 of the *Aeneid* to this poor and primitive Italy, he sees it through the language of the *Georgics*. But he also rewrites the earlier poem and restores their bellicosity to the Italian farmers. They are indeed poor, particularly in comparison with the Phoenician Carthage of the first half of the poem, and with Troy itself. Galaesus, the Italian richest in fields—"*Ausoniisque olim ditissimus aruis*" (7.537)—with his five herds of cattle and five of sheep, is pointedly compared with Dido's husband Sychaeus, the wealthiest of the Phoenicians in Tyre—"*ditissimus agri / Phoenicum*" (1.343), whose buried treasure is carried away by Dido to found Carthage: the point is that there is no comparison between the Latin peasantry and Phoenician commercial urbanites.[10] The Italians commemorate their ancestors *ab origine*

---

9. Galinsky, 1996, 90–121 describes the use of the motif of the Golden Age in the national and moral program of Augustus and presents, 121–125, a thoughtful assessment of Virgil's idea of renewal-as-struggle. See also Perkell, 2002; Ryberg, 1958.

10. Mynors, 1969, accepts Huet's emendation "*ditissimus auri*" for 1.343, but it is not necessary to emphasize further the mercantile nature of the wealth of Tyrian Sychaeus, and the change only weakens the intended contrast to 7.537; the formula "*ditissimus agri*" is also used at 10.563. I follow Conington and Nettleship, 1883–98. On Galaesus's identification with the river of his name, which would enrich the fields around it, see Jones, 2005, 33–34. Against this view of the poverty of the Italians, see La Penna, 2004, 243–247.

in wooden carvings (7.177–182); the Carthaginians celebrate the deeds of theirs engraved on their golden dinnerware (1.640–642). Galaesus dies caught in the middle of the skirmish over Silvia's stag while Sychaeus is murdered *because* of his riches and because of Pygmalion's blind love of gold—"*auri caecus amore*" (1.349)—while it was the wealth of Troy, the "*Troia gaza*" seen strewn on the waves in the opening storm scene of the poem (1.119; cf. 2.763), that made the city a target for conquest and depredation. Tyre and Carthage would themselves follow Troy's example at the hands of Alexander and Rome (cf. 4.669–671). So there is a danger in wealth as well as a virtue in poverty: Galaesus had sought to be a peacemaker.

But these farmers are no strangers to war. Latinus, we are first told, has been ruling over his fields in a long peace, and he seems only three generations removed from Saturn himself: he is the son of Faunus, the son of Picus, the son of Saturn. Latinus's own efforts to avoid war, like those of Galaesus, add to this first impression of a peaceable kingdom undone by Juno and the fury Allecto. But we realize that Faunus is a god and outside of historical succession, and that, as the carved images of Latinus's palace and senate hall recount, there have been other kings between Saturn and the present day. Moreover, these kings have fought and suffered wounds in wars—"*aliique ab origine reges, / Martiaque ob patriam pugnando uulnera passi*" (7.181–182): their arms and trophies decorate the walls. Allecto's reminding Turnus of the perils he has undertaken against the Etruscans to defend the Italians (7.425–426) casts a different picture of the peace of Latinus's own reign, as does the testimony of the Tiber in the following book that the Arcadians and the Latins are perpetually at war (8.55). Evander shortly confirms the river's account (8.146–150). The golden age of Saturn seems to have been just yesterday and long gone.[11] When the Italian peasants turn from the makeshift weapons of their farm tools to real arms in the uproar that breaks out after the wounding of Silvia's stag (7.505–527), we understand the hostilities either/both as the violation of their naturally peaceful rustic world or/and as the disclosure of the violent nature just beneath its surface and of these farmers' ready aptitude for war: a similar ambiguity lies in the final verse of Book 7, Camilla's dart, a herdsman's myrtle staff tipped with a spear point—"*pastoralem praefixa cuspide myrtum*" (7.817).

The language of the *Georgics* in praise of the Italians' rustic poverty—"*et patiens operum exiguoque adsueta iuuentus*" (*Georgics* 2.472)—returns almost

---

11. Lowrie, 2005, 950–952; O'Hara, 2007, 96–98.

word for word in the Book 9 speech of Numanus Remulus, the brother-in-law of Turnus, which presents, in almost caricature form, the national myth of the farmer-soldier:[12]

> at patiens operum paruoque adsueta iuuentus
> aut rastris terram domat aut quatit oppida bello;
> omne aeuum ferro teritur, uersaque iuuencum
> terga fatigamus hasta; (9.607–610)

> but our youth, bearing toil and used to making do with little, tames
> the earth with the hoe or shakes cities with war; our whole life is worn
> out with the use of iron, and we goad the backs of our cattle with an
> inverted spear.

The Italian farmer's tool and weapon are one and the same thing. The verses also suggest a kind of rhyme and connection between "*iuuentus*," and "*iuuencum*."[13] Virgil's evocations of his *Georgics* tie Turnus and, through Turnus, the Italians to the cattle they are prodding at the plow. The depiction of Io and Inachus on the shield of Turnus alludes not only to Moschus's own ekphrasis of Io in his poem on Europa but also to the teachings on the care of livestock that is the subject of the third book of the *Georgics*, and to their description of the gadfly that maddens cattle, *asilus* in Latin, *oestrus* in Greek (*Georgics* 3.147–148): this was the monster that Juno used as a pest to vent her wrath on the Inachian heifer Io: "*hoc quondam monstro horribilis exercuit iras / Inachiae Iuno pestem meditata iuuencae*" (*Georgics* 3.152–153). The Greek term lends a technical quality that connects the external goad of the insect pest to the internal sexual drives of the rut that Book 3 of the *Georgics* goes on to describe (3.209–283). The stirrings of blind love—"*caeci stimulos ... amoris*" (3.210)—universally disturb beasts and men alike. By the time we learn of the contents of the shield of Turnus at the end of Book 7, we have seen the hero himself prodded into battle by the monstrous Allecto. In Book 12, it is his own love, set afire by the sight of the blushing Lavinia, that sends him into his duel against Aeneas, and he becomes in simile what his shield depicts, compared to a bull stirring himself to battle (12.104–106) in three verses that directly repeat three verses from the farming lore of the *Georgics* (3.232–234) and bring its barnyard perspective squarely into the epic. Turnus and now Aeneas himself square off for their final duel, in a second simile, as two bulls fighting over who will be

---

12. Horsfall, 1971; Casali, 2009.
13. See Horace's transfer of "*iuuencus*" to sexually enthralled young Roman men in *Odes* 2.8.21.

the stud of the herd (12.715–722). The latter simile is recalled at Turnus's fall, when the hillside surroundings echo or bellow, "*gemitu ... remugit*" (12.928; cf. 12.722), perhaps an indecorous lapse at this moment of high tragedy. The Italian rustic primitivism of the *Aeneid* not only arms the idealized farmer of the *Georgics*; war frenzy makes him difficult to distinguish from the animals he raises.

But in Book 8 cattle also graze and low in the Roman Forum and in the lavish Carinae residential district of Augustan Rome: "*Romanoque foro et lautis mugire Carinis*" (8.361); it is one of the *Aeneid*'s most famous and startling verses. They graze, that is, in Arcadian Evander's Pallanteum where a rich and powerful Rome will later stand.[14] The story that Evander tells of Hercules' victory over Cacus is the tale of the punishment of a cattle thief. Sharing *pecunia* (from "*pecus*"/cattle) as their first form of currency, Latinus's and Evander's realms are poor and rural, but Evander's is poorer still—"*pauperis Euandri*" (8.360). And whereas the Italians of Book 7 are associated with the farming Italy of the *Georgics*, Evander and his Arcadians in Book 8 are bathed in the pastoral nostalgia of the *Eclogues*, Virgil's other predecessor work. The action of Book 8 ends in the grove of Silvanus, god of shepherds, who in *Eclogue 10* comes with Arcadian Pan to visit the lovestruck Gallus (*Ecl.*10.24–26; for Pan, see *Aen.* 8.343–344).[15] The *Eclogues*, too, connect their pastoral world of Arcady with the golden age, through the prophecy of an imminent new order of things in the "messianic" *Eclogue 4*.[16] Evander describes the now-distant golden age in Italy, when Saturn first gathered into settlements and gave laws to a race of men sprung from trees, who did not know the rudiments of agriculture and how to accumulate wealth ("*opes*"), and who fed themselves from those trees and their hunting (8.315–318).

> aurea quae perhibent illo sub rege fuere
> saecula: sic placida populos in pace regebat,
> deterior donec paulatim ac decolor aetas
> et belli rabies et amor successit habendi. (8.324–327)

> Under Saturn's reign were those ages that are called golden: so he ruled over those peoples in tranquil peace, until little by little there succeeded a worse generation of discolored hue, and the madness of war and the love of gain.

---

14. G. Williams, 1983, 151–152; W. Fowler, 1917, 71–78.
15. On Silvanus, see Dorcey, 1992.
16. Ryberg, 1958. Arcadian shepherds of Evander's former homeland appear in *Eclogues* 7 and 10.

If the golden age is long gone, Evander's poor realm—"*res inopes*" (8.100)—and its woody, animal skin accoutrements—a lion hide on a maple throne (8.177–178), a bed made of a bearskin over leaves (8.367–368), the panther hide that Evander himself wears (8.460), even the poplar branch and leaves with which he wreathes his hair for the rites of Hercules (8.276–277)—link his Arcadian town to the moment when Saturn first drew men from hunting and gathering in the forests into communities. So do the groves that stand inside Pallanteum (8.342–354), particularly the Capitol, golden now but at that time bristling with woodland thickets—"*aurea nunc, olim siluestribus horrida dumis*" (8.348)—and that also reveal the foundations of Saturn's old citadel (8.355–358). Both Arcadians and Italians have cattle-raising in common, but the cows in the future Forum particularly identify the Arcadians as herdsmen, like the speakers of the *Eclogues,* and associate them with the pre-agricultural golden age—as opposed to the Italian farmers.[17] When Evander, inviting Aeneas to share the same hospitality he has offered Hercules, urges him to *dare* to scorn riches in order to make himself worthy of heroic godhood—"*aude, hospes, contemnere opes et te quoque dignum / finge deo*" (8.364–365)—he gives voice to an ethos that is both Arcadian and of the golden age.[18] The Rome of Virgil and Augustus may well be golden now and the peace that Augustus imposed after civil war a new golden age, as Anchises predicts in the underworld in Book 6, but what remains of her Arcadian origins, the honest poverty that makes Evander the good man of his name? "*Amor … habendi*" destroyed the original golden age. Romans, too, once claimed to be austere in the days of the elder Cato. But who spurns riches nowadays?

Chiasmus

In Books 7 and 8, Virgil offers two different perspectives on the imposition—through the culturally more advanced Trojans—of Rome's civilized future upon the rural, green world of Italy, viewed in Book 7 in the harsher light of his *Georgics,* seen in Book 8 through the soft shade of the *Eclogues.* The effect is the chiasmus roughly mapped in the table below.

17. See the comments of Hardie, 1994, 193 on *Aeneid* 9.609: "these Italians live in the Age of Iron." La Penna, 2004, 236–237 measures the pastoral economy of the Arcadians against the diverse agriculture of Ithaca in the *Odyssey*; the hospitality of the swineherd Eumaios to the disguised Odysseus is one of the models behind Evander's hosting of Aeneas.

18. On the Golden Age in Book 8, see Binder, 1971, 84–105; Zetzel, 1997; Ryberg, 1958; Perkell, 2002.

Book 7	Book 8
Civilization (+)	Civilization, war, gold (−)
Rusticity, war, animality (−)	Rusticity, simplicity (+)
Italians, *Georgics*	Arcadians, *Eclogues*

These perspectives overlap and are not stable: as I have noted, the Italians are initially depicted at peace, and the pious Arcadians have been incessantly at war. The potential collapse of differences, I have been arguing, lies at the heart of Virgil's art, and through the distinction of Italians and Arcadians he is presenting two sides of the same issues of historical process, of culture versus nature. Nevertheless, the dominant feelings the mirroring books produce is of a gain achieved by the future Rome over the hard primitivism of the Italians *and* of a loss sustained by this same Rome of the Arcadians' harmony with the natural world, the virtues of their poverty—and their Greekness.

This chiastic pattern is worked out *narratively* in the second half of the *Aeneid*. Aeneas will gain Lavinia's hand in marriage, and he and the Trojans, per Juno's demands, will be incorporated with the Italians. Meanwhile, the death in battle of Pallas, the son and heir of Evander, will mean the extinction of his royal line and the disappearance of the Arcadians. A similar scheme, we have observed in chapter 2, prevailed in the epic's first half. The sympathetic Dido and her Carthaginians hosted the Trojans in Book 1; Aeneas recounted the destruction and sacking of his city by the Greeks in Book 2. But, in an apparently unjust reversal of the poem's events and according to the verdict of history, it is the Greek Achaemenides whom Aeneas and the Trojans pity and take on board on their travels in Book 3, Dido and her city whom they abandon in Book 4. Roman culture will take on Hellenistic features, rather than Punic ones. The pattern repeats itself, *but with a reversal*, in Books 7–12. The Italians declare war on the Trojans in Book 7; the Arcadians host and come to the aid of Aeneas in Book 8, help, the Cumaean sibyl had predicted in Book 6, that will surprisingly come from a *Greek* city (6.96–97). But, in a no less unjust turn of events, it will be the Italians with whom Aeneas and his compatriots will finally intermarry at the end of the *Aeneid*, while Pallas dies and Evander mourns for him in Books 10 and 11. Rome will be a rougher, energetic Italian culture, aligned with the real farmers of the *Georgics*, rather than, certainly more than, with the fictional Arcadian shepherds of the *Eclogues*. The expansionist, superwealthy world power will outgrow the model of the small-scale and self-contained Greek *polis*; the *Aeneid* asks how much will survive, in the grand city that will stand on its site, of the gracious simplicity of Evander's Pallanteum, itself a half-utopian pastoral fantasy. These chiastic patterns in the two halves of the poem thus themselves form a chiasmus—Greek civilization supersedes Carthaginian wealth only to be superseded in turn by Italian-Roman *virtus*. In both halves, the poem makes us *feel* the loss involved in these historically dictated choices in the loss of possible love-objects of Aeneas: the suicide of Dido and the slaying of Pallas, whose beautiful corpse Aeneas covers with even more beautiful robes of Tyrian purple woven by Dido herself (11.72–75).

By virtue of her sex, the Italian heiress Lavinia affords Aeneas a marriage choice and the opportunity for the Trojans to join with the Latins and form a new Roman people: she is the "*regia coniunx*" whom the ghost of Creusa had predicted for Aeneas (2.783) and whose place Dido had attempted to take. But the peculiarity of Roman practices of adoption make an analogous integration of the male Pallas and of the Arcadians into the family and people of Aeneas less unlikely than it might appear.[19] The crush that the young, stripling Evander had experienced back in Arcadia itself for the tall Anchises, whom he took by the hand (8.160–165), appears to be repeated in the next generation when Pallas takes the hand of Aeneas (8.124).[20] The loss that Aeneas feels at the death of Pallas is steeped in both homoerotic and paternal sentiment. "How great," he says, "is this loss to you, Iulus"—"*et quantum tu perdis, Iule!*" (11.58). Conington commented in the nineteenth century, "Had Pallas lived, he would have supplied the place of an elder brother to Ascanius, and would have been a protection to the new kingdom, in the event of Aeneas' dying prematurely."[21] Aeneas refers to Pallas at the end of the poem as one of my own—"*meorum*" (12.947)—as he plunges his sword into the breast of Turnus.

It might be nice to think so. But the prospect that Pallas might become a member of the Aeneas family is more probably the reason that he had to die beneath the spear of Turnus. The *Aeneid* depicts history jealously guarding the Roman *gens* from misalliances with foreign peoples who would change the

---

19. According to Suetonius (*Augustus* 68), Mark Antony accused Augustus himself of having submitted to homosexual relations with Julius Caesar as the price for his adoption—"*M. Antonius adoptionem auunculi stupro meritum.*" Suetonius professes to be skeptical about this political calumny (71) but characteristically repeats it.

20. On the erotic dimension of Aeneas's relationship to Pallas, see Putnam, 1985a. See also chapter 7.

21. Conington and Nettleship, 1883–98, 3:333.

national character, even when, in the case of Pallas and the Arcadians, they just might improve it. Dido will have no little Aeneas to cherish (4.327–330), as she had thought she was cherishing a little Ascanius when Cupid took the place of the son and heir in her lap back in Book 1 (657–722), a nightmare scenario both of Roman-Carthaginian union and, of much more recent topicality, of Cleopatra mothering her Julian heir Caesarion, a little "brother" to Augustus.[22] Similarly, Ascanius will have no big brother in Pallas. It may be bad enough that he finally *will* have a little brother in Silvius, the child that Lavinia will bear to Aeneas (6.760–766). For through that Italian younger son, Ascanius-Iulus and his elder, legitimate *gens Iulia*—*echt* Trojan—would be sidestepped by Roman history until they are restored to their pride of place by Augustus, who, by his separate lineage, may also escape from the fratricidal curse that Silvian Romulus placed on that history by killing his twin Remus.[23] In this case, the homosexual charge surrounding the family of Evander and the body of Pallas, still beautiful like a newly cropped flower even in death, may indicate their alien Greekness as well as the sterility and historical dead end, from a Roman point of view, of Greek culture itself: the inappropriateness of their Arcadian version of Rome, in spite of its beauty and of the, perhaps, ethical superiority of its poverty, for the great city that is to come. But this charge, within the drama of the epic, nevertheless intensifies the grief that Aeneas feels at the death of Pallas and that fuels his rage against the suppliant Turnus at its ending. Focalized through the hero's emotion, the *Aeneid* mourns for a Rome that might have been.

All That Glitters

Aeneas's own volatile thoughts, compared to sunlight or radiant moonlight striking water in vessels of bronze and reflecting off of gold-fretted ceilings (8.22–25), sets a chain of imagery in motion in Book 8. Objects glisten with unnatural light and suggest a superimposition, human or divine, on the green world that is their silent backdrop. Nature, in fact, talks back at the beginning of the book, when the river god Tiberinus appears to the sleeping Aeneas and predicts the portent—already predicted by Heleneus in Book 3 (388–393)—that will shortly appear to him in the form of a gleaming white ("*candida*")

---

22. Quint, 1993, 28; Eidinow, 2003; for other possible Ptolemaic heirs and rivals, see Hardie, 2006.

23. See chapter 2, note 45.

sow and thirty piglets recumbent on the Tiber's green shore ("*uiridique in litore*"), the "*mirabile monstrum*" that is something between natural and supernatural (8.81–83).[24] Thereafter the gleaming objects will be metallic and fit into the book's thinking about culture and nature, civilization and arms. A few verses later, the sow is replaced by the glittering shields of Aeneas's warriors that cause the groves and waves of the river to wonder as his twin ships makes their way upstream to Pallanteum / future Rome.

> mirantur et undae,
> miratur nemus insuetum fulgentia longe
> scuta uirum fluuio pictasque innare carinas.
> olli remigio noctemque diemque fatigant
> et longos superant flexus, uariisque teguntur
> arboribus, uiridisque secant placido aequore siluas. (8.91–96)

> The waves wonder, the woods, unused to such things, wonder at the shields of men gleaming far and wide and the painted keels that swim up the river. The Trojans wear out day and night with rowing and put the long bends behind them; they are shaded by different kinds of trees and they cleave the green woods in the placid water.

The natural world of Italy appears unaccustomed to warships and flashing shields in a book that leads up to the single radiant shield of Aeneas and its culminating depiction of effulgent naval battle. For the wondering—"*mirantur*"— groves and woods, these shields are as much of a "*mirabile monstrum*" as the fecund sow. The passage furthers the notion of a long peace now shattered by the outbreak of hostilities between the Trojans and native Latins, although we have seen how the poem also corrects this impression. Only a few verses earlier, the god of the Tiber himself has reported a constant state of war between Arcadians and Latins, and the present placidity of the river itself is a special dispensation granted by the god to the Trojan ships (8.55–58).

The appearance of these painted "*carinis*" seems to be the first step in the human transformation of this apparently virgin landscape that will lead to the expensive *Carinae* in the future metropolis. Trees will have to fall, land cleared, for the city that is to come. There may be something prophetic in Virgil's daring description of the oars and keels of the ships cutting through the reflections the shoreline trees make in the river. For the moment, the

---

24. See Jenkyns, 1998, 531 on the sow gleaming on a woodsy backdrop.

woods seem safe enough, their chopping down merely metaphorical in the watery images that can be a self-conscious figure of figuration itself. No real trees were damaged in the making of this scene, no harm done, and at the book's end Venus presents the shield forged by Vulcan to Aeneas in a grove—"*lucus*" (8.597), "*nemus*" (8.599)—sacred to Silvanus, the pastoral exurban god who has "woods" in his name.

> arma sub aduersa posuit radiantia quercu. (8.616)

> She placed the shining arms before him beneath an oak.

Arms and nature seem able to inhabit the same space side by side. By the end of the *Aeneid*, however, war has changed matters. In Book 12 the Trojans have cut down the oleaster outside of Laurentium consecrated to Faunus, the woodland associate of Silvanus, to level the field for battle.[25] The stump of the fallen tree, now associated with oak—"*morsus / roboris*" (12.782–783)—holds fast the spear of Aeneas stuck in its root until Venus frees it. Nature and human invader are now in conflict, and nature, however holy, takes the worst of it.

Book 8 insists on this imagery of arms and gold gleaming against green nature and on drawing out the implications of its description of the Roman Capitol, golden now, but once crowded with woodland thickets ("*dumis*"). The thickets were still there when, in the scene depicted on Vulcan's shield, the Gauls attacked Rome and its Capitol in 390 BCE.

> Galli per dumos aderant arcemque tenebant
> defensi tenebris et dono noctis opacae.
> aurea caesaries ollis atque aurea uestis,
> uirgatis lucent sagulis, tum lactea colla
> auro innectuntur, duo quisque Alpina coruscant
> gaesa manu, scutis protecti corpora longis. (8.657–661)

> The Gauls lurked in thickets and made for the citadel, protected by darkness and the gift of a shadowy night; their hair is golden as are their garments, and they shine in their striped cloaks, their milk-white necks are encircled with gold, and each flashes two heavy Alpine spears, their bodies protected by long shields.

---

25. Dorcey, 1992, 33–40 sharply distinguishes the cults of Faunus and Silvanus. On the cutting down of trees, see Thomas, 1988.

The inset vignette neatly incorporates the terms of Book 8 but now reverses their historico-political logic: we are made to feel what it might be like to be on the other side of things. Where Aeneas and the Trojans bring the gold, shields, and weaponry of the future Rome into the green world of Italy, here Rome and its sacred center are menaced by foreign invaders bearing the gold and shields, and creating the telltale glint of metal—*"lucent," "corruscant"*— on a leafy backdrop. Vulcan has used literal gold, we assume, on the highly wrought shield to burnish the blond hair of the Gauls as well as to depict the literal gold that they wear around their necks. Philip Hardie has noted the associations of these Gauls with the giants of the gigantomachy, a myth, he further notes, that is evoked a few verses later in the shield's depiction of Actium, where the huge battleships make one think of the islands and mountains the giants uprooted and tossed about (8.691–692).[26] What had been a close call for Rome in 390 has now been reversed. Augustus defeats Antony and his foreign troops, the new giants threatening Rome's universal rule, who join the vanquished peoples led in Augustus's subsequent triumph depicted on the shield. These include the farthest of men, the Gallo-Belgic Morini (8.727). Augustus's lieutenant Gaius Carrinas had put down their rebellion in 29 BCE (he co-triumphed with Augustus on the first of the triumph's three days); they were subdued by 23 BCE, the completion of Julius Caesar's conquest of Gaul under the auspices of his adoptive son.

The trees and waves of the Tiber may appear unused to ships and shields. The Arcadian Pallas genuinely experiences them for the first time, for he is a novice to battle (11.155). There is a special pathos, reinforced by Evander's tearful farewell to his son (8.558–584), in the little set piece that describes Pallas leaving Pallanteum amid his Arcadian horsemen. He will not return alive.

> ipse agmine Pallas
> it medio chlamyde et pictis conspectus in armis,
> qualis ubi Oceani perfusus Lucifer unda,
> quem Venus ante alios astrorum diligit ignis,
> extulit os sacrum caelo tenebrasque resoluit.
> stant pauidae in muris matres oculisque sequuntur
> pulueream nubem et fulgentis aere cateruas.
> olli per dumos, qua proxima meta uiarum,
> armati tendunt. (8.587–595)

26. Hardie, 1986, 120–125; 100–110.

and in the middle of the troops Pallas himself, conspicuous in his
cloak and painted arms, as when Lucifer the morning star, bathed in
the Ocean's wave, whom Venus loves above all the other fiery stars, has
raised his sacred face into the heavens and dissolved the shadows of
night. The frightened mothers stood on the walls and followed with
their eyes the dusty cloud and the ranks gleaming with bronze. They
took their way in their armor through the thickets, the shortest way to
their destination.

The scene is a worthy of a John Ford cavalry film: one thinks of his horse soldiers' yellow scarves.[27] Pallas's cloak bears an exotic name—"*chlamys*"—and the garment, usually enwoven with gold, is associated with Trojans and Trojan gift-givers. Andromache gives one to Ascanius in Book 3 (483–484), Aeneas gives one to Cloanthes, victor in the boat race, in Book 5 (250), Chloreus sports one in Book 11 (775–776) that evokes in Camilla a fatal, womanly love for booty. This one, too, has an exotic Trojan history. Evander tells us earlier in Book 8 that when Anchises had visited Arcadia, he gave to Evander, then a stripling youth, a gold-embroidered cloak, together with some golden horse bits, "*chlamydemque auro dedit intertextam*" (8.167): guest gifts, perhaps, the poem lightly suggests, love tokens. Evander has passed these gifts on to Pallas, and this is presumably the cloak he now sports. It is another instance of gold, particularly Trojan gold, entering the Italian world. For a moment this gold turns Pallas in simile into a thing of beauty, the morning star, and the associations with Venus are also Trojan, if misleading.[28] Venus, who appears less than twenty verses later with Vulcan's golden shield for her son, loves only the Aeneas family, and it is the Julian star that will shine over the sea at Actium on the shield (8.681). The shining morning star here disperses the shadows of night, but it is also short-lived and evanescent. In the shift of focalization to the eyes of the fearful mothers, the distant Pallas is quickly swallowed up into the dust and into the general effulgence of his companions' armor. Gold again becomes indistinguishable from bronze. Then they and their arms disappear into the "*dumis*" (thickets) of a still-wild natural world.

The departure from Pallanteum begins with another golden gift of Evander, this time *to* Aeneas, which epitomizes the motifs of Book 8. Evander

---

27. "I can't see him. All I can see is the flags," says the wife of Captain Collingwood in *Fort Apache*, as the doomed cavalry regiment disappears in the dust it raises.

28. Holzberg, 2006, 176 notes that the beautiful morning star denotes transitoriness and presages the death of Pallas. See also Feldherr, 2014, 315–316; Jenkyns, 1998, 548.

gives horses to a cohort of Trojans, and to the poem's hero a specially selected steed

> quem fulua leonis
> pellis obit totum praefulgens unguibus aureis. (8.552–553)

> whom the yellow hide of a lion entirely covers, shining with golden claws.

The lion's skin lends Aeneas the attributes of Hercules, the savior demigod celebrated in the first part of the book.[29] Aeneas had already placed a lion's skin over his shoulders and played a Herculean part when he carried Anchises out of the Trojan past in Book 2 (721–723); he will raise the shield of the Roman future onto his shoulders in Herculean style at the end of Book 8.[30] But this caparison for Aeneas's horse is also a miniature emblem of the imposition of culture upon nature that is the book's subject. Evander's poor, primitive realm is furnished with the skins of lion, bear, and panther. The hide here is already naturally golden in color—as the wordplay between "*fulua*" and "*praefulgens*" suggests. The gilded claws are another shiny object that attests to a human addition to nature. On one hand, they are a decoration, an enrichment of art—like Vulcan's golden shield and the poem itself. On the other, the fact that they are claws and, again like the shield, weapons, tells a lot about Book 8's repeated story about gold and golden ages.

The Taming of Fire

The lion skin recalls the tale of Hercules and Cacus, the little epyllion that Evander retells to Aeneas earlier in Book 8 (185–275) and that balances the narrative digression describing the shield of Aeneas at the book's end. It is a much commented upon episode, and I build on the work of earlier scholars and readers in situating it inside what I describe as the book's larger scheme and its argument about human culture and the natural order.[31] Cacus the

---

29. Aeneas gives a lion skin with gilded claws as a prize to Salius, after the latter is fouled by Nisus in the footrace during the games of Book 5 (351–352); the passage hints at an alternative origin for the Salii priesthood, who are already present in Book 8, celebrating the rites of Hercules (8.285f.). See Hardie, 1986, 373n117. The Salii reappear on the shield at 8.663–664. For further discussion of the hymn the Salii sing in honor of Hercules, see Miller, 2014.

30. Hardie, 1986, 369–376; Galinsky, 1966.

31. See, among others, Gransden, 1976, 14–20, 36–41; Binder, 1971, 2–4, 141–149; Buchheit, 1963, 116–133; Lyne, 1987, 27–35; Galinsky, 1966; Putnam, 1965, 130–141; Hardie, 1986, 110–119; Morgan, 1998; Labate, 2009; Holzberg, 2006, 180–187.

fire-monster is a cattle thief, and the lowing heifer that gives him away links him—and his conqueror Hercules too—to the rusticity of both the georgic Latins and pastoral Arcadians. Cacus, however, represents a wilder, precivilized Italian primitivism, something still closer to elemental nature: Evander describes him as half-man and half-beast—"*semihominis*" (8.194); "*semiferi*" (8.267).[32] Yet he is also, like Hercules, half-god: he is child of Vulcan, the fire-god and artificer, whose making of the shield and whose shield itself takes up much of the space of the book and provides its unifying narrative thread. Evander's narrative provides Book 8 with two distinct, if interrelated, strands of thinking about myth and history, brute nature and civilization. One strand links Hercules in a heroic genealogy to Aeneas and to Augustus at Actium. The other opposes Cacus, who embodies in his fire a primordial violence in nature, to his father, the smithy Vulcan who channels that violence into technology and art. But both genealogy and opposition have a way of breaking down through Virgilian chiasmus.

One of the structuring devices of *Aeneid* 8, K. W. Gransden has pointed out,[33] is the threefold analogy it sets in place among

(1) Hercules, the story of whose victory over the cattle thief Cacus, the fire-vomiting son of Vulcan, is told to Aeneas by Evander as he and his fellow Arcadians commemorate it in festival;
(2) Aeneas himself, who is about to go to war against the Italian Turnus, in whose breast the fury Allecto has fixed her torch (7.456–457), and whose fiery Achillean nature is displayed in his helmet shaped into a Chimaera breathing Aetnean flames associated with Vulcan—"*Aetnaeos efflantem fauciibus ignis*" (7.786)—near the end of the preceding Book 7. Aeneas will also war against the Etruscan tyrant,

---

32. The analysis of Labate, 2009, shows how both Cacus and Hercules belong to a fantastic, precivilized world with which Virgil carefully makes sure that his more "modern" hero Aeneas—both more physically limited and also piously self-restrained—does not interact.

33. Gransden, 1976, 14–20; I have deliberately left out, for purposes of simplification, a fourth term that Gransden includes: Romulus, with whom Hercules and Aeneas are identified as predecessor heroes who achieved deification. Aeneas is the ancestor of Romulus. Both he and Romulus foreshadow Augustus, the contemporary refounder of Rome. The hut of Romulus was supposed to have been preserved on the Palatine both near the hut of Evander in Book 8 and near the temple of Apollo and residence of Augustus near or on the same spot. Morgan, 1998, 185–187 explores geographical resonances that might identify Aventine Cacus with Remus. I have tried to suggest above that the *Aeneid* wishes to free Julian Augustus of descent from the younger Silvian Romulus—and thus capable of a refounding of Rome that is also an escape from its history of civil war. But the poem is inconsistent in its genealogies.

Mezentius, who, we learn from Evander in Book 8, would join his living victims face to face with dead bodies oozing with gore and rot, "*oribus ora, / tormenti genus, et sanie taboque fluentis*" (8.486–487). This practice also makes Mezentius a second Cacus, before whose den were affixed as trophies faces of men pale with gruesome rot, "*ora uirum tristi pendebant pallida tabo*" (8.197); his fellow citizens drove Mezentius into exile by setting fire to his palace (8.490–491), much as Hercules destroyed the house of Cacus, which the monster himself fills with fire and smoke; and

(3) Augustus Caesar, who overcomes Mark Antony and Cleopatra at the battle of Actium in 31 BCE, the scene pictured on the shield that Vulcan, the fire-god, has forged for Aeneas in his Aetnean caverns— "*antra Aetnaea*" (8.419)—beneath the island Volcania.

The analogy extends to both the geographical and temporal references of Book 8. The shield's ensuing depiction of the triumph of 29 BCE that Augustus led to celebrate his victory ends at the temple of Apollo on the Palatine. It takes Augustus to the same place where Evander currently holds residence in Pallanteum. Here Evander hosts Aeneas in his humble dwelling where, Evander tells Aeneas, Hercules himself once was a guest; the next day Aeneas receives his shield from Venus. As we have observed above, the two days during which the book takes place correspond to the poem's glimpse at the mythological past and the historical future that the shield is turning into myth: August 12, the date of the annual sacrifice to Hercules at the Ara Maxima, the great altar that the poem tells us Hercules himself set up after killing Cacus (8.271–272); and August 13, the date on which Augustus celebrated his triumph. The final books of the *Aeneid*, the war in Italy, take place in the month of Augustus, a month that got its name from the victorious entry of his troops into Alexandria and the end of the war against Antony and Cleopatra on August 1, 30 BCE.

The book thus presents a simple A versus B opposition: Hercules, Aeneas, Augustus on one side, Cacus, Turnus and Mezentius, Antony and Cleopatra on the other. The moral contrasts seem clear and build up a typology and apology for the political establishment of Augustus. Savior heroes, sons of gods, put down monsters: Cacus is a monster—"*monstro*" (8.198)—while Cleopatra is associated with Egyptian monster-gods of all kinds, "*omnigenumque deum monstra*" (8.698); the raging Mezentius commits unspeakable killings, "*infandas caedes*" (8.483), "*infanda furentem*" (8.489); Cleopatra is herself unspeakable, "*nefas*" (8.688).

But, as usual in the *Aeneid*, things are not so simple. The opposition breaks down into potential identity and chiasmus, A = B. Fire is a term that moves from one side to the other. Commentators, particularly R. O. A. M. Lyne and, revisiting Lyne, Llewellyn Morgan, have noted how the rage of Hercules metaphorically kindles him in his battle with Cacus—"*his uero Alcidae furiis exarserat atro / felle dolor*" ("the wrath of Hercules furiously broke into flame with black gall"; 8.219–220)—and makes the hero hard to distinguish from the foe he overcomes: Cacus spouts real black flames ("*atros / ... ignis*"; 8.198–199) and later a black cloud ("*nebulaque ... atra*"; 8.258) of smoke. The same might additionally be said about Aeneas who is likened to *his* foe Turnus by the helmet that Vulcan crafts for him: the resemblance is no longer metaphorical.[34]

> miraturque interque manus et bracchia uersat
> terribilem cristis galeam flammasque uomentem (8.619–620)

> He admires and turns about in his arms and hands the helmet,
> terrifying with plumes and vomiting flames.

The fire-spouting helmet is a close counterpart to the Chimaera-helmet of Turnus, but this one is made by Cacus's father, Vulcan, and forged in real Aetnean fire. The two heroes enter combat wearing nearly identical helmets, and we might conclude that once armed and in battle, the identity of individual soldiers is difficult to distinguish, all the more so when that battle has overtones of civil war: the similarity of the armor in fact produces those overtones. Moreover, because it spouts or vomits fire rather than exhales it, as does the helmet of Turnus, this helmet of Aeneas seems even closer to Cacus, who vomits his father's fire—"*huic monstro Volcanus erat pater; illius atros / ore uomens ignis magna se mole ferebat*" ("this monster's father was Vulcan, and it was Vulcan's black fires that he vomited as he moved his great body about"; 8.198–199)—and who vomits them in vain in his effort to elude Hercules: "*incendia uana uomentem*" (8.259). The verb further links Aeneas to the Augustus at Actium depicted on the shield, whose happy brows vomit twin flames associated both with the two-crested helmet of Mars and Romulus and with the comet star of his deified father, Julius Caesar: "*geminas cui tempora flammas / laeta uomunt*" (8.680–81). It is a reprise of the prodigy of Book 2, where flames play harmlessly around the temples of the child Iulus (2.684) while a flaming star falls from heaven (2.693–698), marking him and his line

---

34. Lyne, 1987, 27–35; Morgan, 1998, 177–180, 190–192.

for this future moment that the shield puts on display. In the battle of Book 10, moreover, it will be the golden shield of Aeneas itself that appears to spout fire with same verb: "*et uastos umbo uomit aureus ignis*" (10.271). Already at the end of Book 8, then, the attribute of vomiting fire has moved from the monster Cacus to the hero Aeneas and to the conqueror Augustus, from the literal bad guy ("Cacus" means "evil one") to the figures glorified by the *Aeneid*. (Even in the relatively minor vignette of Mezentius, as I have noted above, it is the righteous Etruscan enemies of Mezentius who use fire against *him*.) Moreover, while fiery Hercules and Aeneas counteract fiery Cacus and Turnus, Augustus seems to have a monopoly on this firepower at Actium: no such associations of fire cling to Antony and Cleopatra on the shield. At the level of realistic description of the sea battle, *both* sides shower the other with flames of tow—"*stuppea flamma*" (8.694). One may have no choice but to fight fire with fire—and Virgil will describe Turnus and Aeneas in Book 12 as fires started on two sides of a dry woods (12.521–522). But such mutual, equivalent violence threatens to collapse the oppositions, moral and political, that Book 8 has carefully set in place.

Moreover, the parallel between Hercules and Augustus at Actium already represents a hostile takeover or reversal of the official mythological identifications of Roman political ideology. In the precincts of the Temple of Apollo on the Palatine, the goal to which the reliefs on the shield of Aeneas and hence of the entire Book 8 are leading, the walls were decorated with beautiful terra-cotta plaques in a faux early classical style that depict the archer Apollo and Hercules, with lion skin and club, contending with each other for the tripod of Delphi that the god prevented Hercules from carrying away. The tripod is adorned with winged victories, and the plaques, repeated across the walls, symbolically depicted Augustus's defeat of Antony at Actium.[35] For it was *Antony* who ostentatiously claimed descent from and affinity with Hercules, while Augustus chose Apollo as his patron. Plutarch reports that Antony had

> a noble dignity of form; and a shapely beard, a broad forehead, and an aquiline nose were thought to show the virile qualities peculiar to the portraits and statues of Heracles. Moreover, there was an ancient tradition that the Antonii were Heracleidae, being descendants of Anton, a son of Heracles. And this tradition Antony thought that he confirmed, both by

---

35. Zanker, 1988, 247, figure 193; Strazzulla, 1990, 17–22. Lange, 2009, 172–177 strongly rebuts Gurval, 1995, 125–126, who cautions against reading too much into the plaque.

the shape of his body, as has been said, and by his attire. For whenever he was going to be seen by many people, he always wore his tunic girt up to his thigh, a large sword hung at his side, and a heavy cloak enveloped him. (4.1–2)[36]

After Octavian-Augustus had the senate declare war against Cleopatra, Plutarch further recounts, a bolt of lightning struck the temple of Hercules in Patrae on a day when Antony was himself in the city: his enemies took it as a bad omen, and so Actium would prove it to be (60.2). The mythological outcome of the struggle of Hercules with Apollo at Delphi was, in fact, erotic servitude for Hercules to the Lydian queen, Omphale. The Palatine plaques may have reminded viewers, indeed may have been intended to remind them, of Antony's subjection to Cleopatra and her eunuch and hairdressers, all too like the fate of his claimed ancestor.[37] G. Karl Galinsky briefly observes that Virgil's fiction in Book 8 wrests the mythic identification with Hercules away from Antony in order to vest both Aeneas and Augustus with the traits of the hero demigod.[38] The real modern Hercules prevails at Actium over the dress-up one. But the Roman reader who had experienced the propaganda of both triumvirs would have been the more struck by the chiastic pattern by which Book 8 depicts near its beginning a Hercules defeating the fire-spouting Cacus and toward its end a fire-spouting Augustus collaborating with Apollo to defeat the Herculean Antony and his Egyptian *coniunx*.

Cacus, I further wish to point out, is not the only, nor the first, victim whom Hercules has killed over the cattle of Geryon in the *Aeneid*. In Sicily during the funeral games in honor of Anchises held beneath Eryx in Book 5, the boxer Entellus produces the fearsome gloves of his own former pugilistic teacher, Eryx himself, after whom the town has been named. Everyone is dazed at the sight of them. Entellus tells Aeneas:

> quid, si quis caestus ipsius et Herculis arma
> uidisset tristemque hoc ipso in litore pugnam?
> haec germanus Eryx quondam tuus arma gerebat
> (sanguine cernis adhuc sparsoque infecta cerebro),
> his magnum Alciden contra stetit. (5.412–414)

---

36. Plutarch, 2014, 9:145–147.
37. Strazzulla, 1990, 18, who cites Propertius 3.11.17–20, which spells out the parallel between Omphale and Cleopatra.
38. Galinsky, 1972, 141; see also Galinsky, 1981, 1004–1005.

> What if one were to have seen the gloves and arms of Hercules himself, and the fatal match on this very shore. Your brother Eryx once bore these arms (you can see them stained here with blood and spattered brains); with these he stood against mighty Hercules.

In the myth that lies behind this passage, Eryx, the son of Venus and hence half-brother to Aeneas, either steals a runaway bull from the herd of Hercules or covets the cattle. He challenges or is challenged to a fight with Hercules and loses his life: perhaps his are among the brains and blood splattered on the gloves. In some versions, this contest is more of a wrestling than a boxing match, and hence a mythical repetition of Hercules' defeat of Antaeus.[39] Virgil appears to recall this latter combat when Evander tells how the hero squeezes the life out of Cacus (8.259–261).

Evander's celebration of the deliverer Hercules at the Ara Maxima might thus be tempered for Aeneas by the sobering memory that the same Hercules had killed one of his brothers. Cacus, however monstrous, is also Aeneas's stepbrother. Evander is himself largely modeled on Homer's Nestor. They are not only roughly the same age but are actual contemporaries, members of the same heroic generation that preceded that of Aeneas and the Greek combatants at Troy. Both thus knew Hercules. But whereas Evander knew Hercules as a monster-killer, Nestor knew Hercules as the killer of his whole family of *eleven* brothers (*Il.* 11.689–692). In one version of the story, Hercules killed them because they, too, stole the same cattle of Geryon.[40] In the *Metamorphoses* (12.536–576), Ovid's Nestor, mourning his family, declines to praise Hercules in his account of the battle of the Lapiths and Centaurs. Roman readers of the *Aeneid* may have similarly looked upon Augustus, the Herculean savior of their country, as they remembered their own relatives who had perished on the other side during the civil wars.

The question of relations between and among divine offspring structures Book 8. The monster Cacus is the son of Vulcan. The hero Aeneas is the son of Venus. As Anthony J. Boyle has emphasized, the shield of Aeneas that represents Roman-history-as-it-culminates-in-Augustus is the product of the

---

39. Seneca pairs the two myths at *Her. Fur.* 480.

40. Isocrates 6.19. The story is repeated in Philostratus, *On Heroes* 26.1. The same text, an admittedly late (second- and third-century CE) source with respect to the *Aeneid*, describes, 26.4, the attraction of Hercules to the young ephebe Nestor, a version that, *if* it reflects older traditions, might lie behind the story of Virgil's Nestor-like Evander about his meeting with Anchises during his own youth back in Arcadia (8.160–165). Philostratus, 2014, 195.

lovemaking of Vulcan and Venus. It is, figuratively at least, their joint child: "Is this intercourse with Venus, herself underscored as 'mother' (8.370), to generate another firemonster?"[41] Through her union with Vulcan, the love-goddess Venus might be thought, on the contrary, to instill creativity into the fire-god who is also divine craftsman, channeling fire that is destructive in its raw, natural state into works of art and culture. That is the role she plays in a model that stands behind the episode: the opening invocation to Venus, mother of the Romans, the race of Aeneas—"*Aeneadum genetrix*"—and mother of generation itself, in Lucretius's *De rerum natura*. Lucretius implores the goddess to couple with Mars and to put to sleep the works of (civil) war, bringing peace to Rome (*DRN* 1.29–40).[42] Following on the lovemaking of Venus and Vulcan in *Aeneid* 8, the homey simile at the book's center (8.408–413) parallels Vulcan as he rises while it is still night to go to work at his forge with a modern matron who keeps the household fire and lamps burning so that she and her handmaids can keep weaving into the wee hours. It indicates, by its transfer of gender, the passive role that Vulcan plays in the lovemaking, just as Mars in Lucretius's passage lies recumbent in Venus's lap, conquered by the eternal wound of love.[43] It also testifies to a domestication of fire at the very center of Roman civilization. In his description of the rise of human progress in Book 5 of *De rerum natura*, Lucretius places animal hides and fire at its primitive beginnings (5.1011), textile-making toward the end (5.1350–1360). Virgil's Book 8 is distinguished for its animal pelts, indicating the still relatively backward state of Evander's Italy.

But the simile is also discordant with the ensuing action—the clothing that Vulcan is going to make is armor: greaves, helmet, breastplate. Similarly, the relationship of Virgil's fiction to its Lucretian model is, at least on the face of it, inverted and ironic. Virgil's Venus is no peacemaker: she lies with Vulcan in order to induce him to make weapons of war for her son Aeneas, weapons that are beautiful and highly wrought, like the poem that describes them, but weapons nonetheless. She and Vulcan give birth to the Roman history the

---

41. Boyle, 1993, 157.

42. See the brilliant discussion of Virgil's reuse of Lucretius in Casali, 2006, 189–196. Hardie, 1986, 358–362 notes the recall of the opening tableau of *De rerum natura* inside the shield in the she-wolf who repeats the recumbent posture of Lucretius's Mars, as she suckles Romulus and Remus (8.630–634): the shield promises peace as well as war, peace achieved through war. See also Hardie, 2012, 356–357.

43. Casali, 2006, 194–197; for some of the ironies of the scene and simile, see Putnam, 1965, 138–140; Putnam, 1998, 167–180; Lyne, 1987, 42–44.

shield depicts. Both Cacus and Aeneas are half-brothers to this shield, and they are stepbrothers to each other. All three spout flames. How we untie the tangle of this relatedness determines readings of the poem, but the point is the chiastic tangle itself. Book 8 depicts Aeneas as a new Hercules, and it ends with Aeneas striking a Herculean and Atlas-like pose, holding up the shield, a cosmos dominated by Rome. But whereas the book has described the real Hercules squeezing the life out of one son of Vulcan, the Aeneas who plays Hercules sustains another child of Vulcan on his shoulders. As the shield testifies, moreover, the primitive fire of Cacus may be transferred by the master artist Vulcan into the products of civilization, but a result is to organize, and hence magnify, violence: the shield depicts future Roman wars laid out in order—"*pugnataque in ordine bella*" (8.629). Indeed, Augustus commands at Actium technological means of killing on an unprecedented scale. The images of cosmic dissolution that describe the fighting—of islands uprooted and mountains clashing with mountains as in the gigantomachy—not only compliment the *princeps* as the earthly master of the cosmos but also reflect on the literally earth-shattering powers of human civilization. Augustus is not just Jupiter, a queller of giants, but a giant himself.

The fires of Cacus that Hercules extinguished, "*extinctos ... ignis*" (8.267), in the mythical past come back as a constitutive part both of Aeneas's fire-spouting helmet and shield in the poem's narrative present and of the Roman history the shield depicts, culminating in Virgil's own Augustan present. Gransden argues that the movement of fire in Book 8 is an allegory of human progress.

> Cacus represents primitive man at his most bestial, man in the era before Vulcan, before the domestication of fire; he eats his flesh raw, he fights with stones—the fire he belches forth is forest fire, dangerous fire, useless and destructive.... In contrast the fire in the Cyclopes' cave where the arms are forged under Vulcan's tutelage is controlled and constructive.[44]

Virgil's fiction undeniably represents a scenario of this kind. Yet it also, equally, suggests the return of the not so deeply repressed of Rome, the state built on war. The pattern suggests the "Dialectic of Enlightenment" that Max Horkheimer and Theodor Adorno describe: barbarity that has been supposedly conquered by a more advanced stage of civilization returns under the

---

44. Gransden, 1976, 39.

guise of that civilization itself, in its instrumental reason and improved technology of violence. The analogy may be all the closer because Horkheimer and Adorno chose as their classical test case the victory of Odysseus over the cyclops Polyphemus in the *Odyssey*.[45] Virgil's Cacus is the Polyphemus figure of Book 8, closely related to the Polyphemus the *Aeneid* depicts in Book 3: both live in vast, dark, gore-stained caves (3.618–619; 8.193f.), both are monsters (3.658; 8.198) whose bodies are of huge bulk, "*uasta se mole mouentem*" (3.656); "*magna se mole ferebat*" (8.199) and yet shapeless, "*informe*" (3.658; 8.264).[46] Polyphemus, moreover, lives next to Mount Aetna and the fires of Vulcan along with his brother cyclopes, "*Aetnaeos fratres*" (3.678). Three of those Aetnean cyclopes, "*Aetnaei Cyclopes*" (8.440), Brontes, Steropes, and Pyracmon, work in Book 8 at the forge of Vulcan beneath his volcanic island in its Aetnean caverns—"*antra Aetnaea*" (4.419). They drop their work on divine weapons and collaborate with the artificer god in making the armor of Aeneas. Horkheimer and Adorno comment: "The vengeance wreaked by civilization on the prehistoric world is a fearful one, and makes civilization approximate that very world"[47]—so much so that we may even begin to feel sympathy for the primitive monster, for the terrified cow thief Cacus or for Virgil's blinded shepherd-cannibal Polyphemus groaning as he washes out his empty eye-socket in the sea (3.655–665), perhaps for the Gauls and other "barbarian" peoples led in triumph on the shield.[48] Questions arise about what kind of progress has been made when the book substitutes for Cacus's den the military-industrial complex of Vulcan's underground armory, each described as a vast cave: "*uasto ... antro*" (8.217; 8.424). The now-tamed Cyclopes "construct" Rome, a weapon of mass destruction.

45. Horkheimer and Adorno, 1969, 43–80.
46. Labate, 2009, 131–133; Hardie, 1986, 115–117; Putnam, 1965, 131.
47. Horkheimer and Adorno, 1969, 78.
48. Virgil's blinded Polyphemus is said to find his sole consolation and pleasure in his flock of sheep: "*ea sola voluptas / solamenque mali*" (3.660–661). The passage make us recall the moving address of Polyphemus to his ram in *Odyssey* 9.446–460, where Homer humanizes his monster and makes him the subject of the reader's compassion. Virgil transfers this Homeric model to the speech that Mezentius, wounded and bereft by Aeneas of his son Lausus, addresses to his beloved horse Rhoebus (10.858–866); the steed had been the tyrant's consolation—"*hoc solamen erat*" (10.859). Mezentius is aligned with both Cacus and Polyphemus: they all get what is coming to them, but Virgil makes us feel for and with them, nonetheless. See Glenn, 1971.

Time and the River

From fire to water: Book 8 rephrases the questions we have seen it ask about the interactions of culture and nature in the river personifications that frame it at either end.[49] The book begins with Virgil's depiction of the personified Tiber. Tiberinus, the very god of the pleasant river—"*deus ipse loci fluuio Tiberinus amoeno*" (8.31)—appears to the sleeping Aeneas in what may or may not be a dream. The god welcomes the Trojan hero as a native son: Virgil may have invented the idea that Dardanus, whom Homer describes as the founder of the royal Trojan lineage (*Il.* 20.215f.), originally came from Italy and that Aeneas and his companions are returning home to a land that already belongs to them.[50] Tiberinus prophesies Aeneas's success, directs him to an alliance with Evander's Arcadians, and at the end identifies himself as the blue Tiber, the stream most loved by heaven—"*caeruleus Thybris, caelo gratissimus amnis*" (8.64). The awakened Aeneas then piously scoops up the nearby river's waters and prays to its resident numens, to the nymphs and to their river father by his newly disclosed name (8.72). Book 8 ends with Vulcan's depiction on the shield of images of personified rivers carried in Augustus's triumph that indicate the borders of Roman power and the peoples on either of their banks, subject to Rome within, a potential threat without. The last three lines of the shield's description name in succession the Euphrates, the Rhine, and the Araxes (8.726–728), the first and last facing the Parthians, the second the Germans. This frame is extraordinarily self-conscious. In a series of Chinese boxes, the Roman poet describes the work of the artificer god who, in turn, describes the work of the Roman artists who have made the river-god images of these foreign rivers: we are three times removed from the physical rivers themselves. Earlier the shield has shown the personified, mournful Nile welcoming the defeated Antony and Cleopatra into its own blue lap—"*caeruleum in gremium*" (8.713)—at two such poetic removes. Both reflect on Virgil's own personification of the Tiber, who already names himself as a kind of fiction by his dreamlike apparition to Aeneas. The poem invites its reader to remember that rivers do not naturally have names, do not naturally serve as borders between peoples. These are the creation of human beings and their history, as they seek to "naturalize" their own relationships to the world they live in. The

---

49. For discussion of how Book 8 is framed by the motif of rivers, see Feldherr, 2014. On the dream of the Tiber, Pontani, 2011.

50. Casali, 2007, 119; Buchheit, 1963, 151–172; Dupont, 2011, 152–156.

Aeneid does its best to denaturalize these relationships, to make us see them as habits of thought and see the force of such habits: that is, the power and ideology that inform them.

Book 8 takes a particularly Roman point of view. The Italian Books 7 and 9 that flank it on either side offer parallel treatments of the Tiber and of other rivers that both belong to nature and have become part of human settlement and culture. Book 7 similarly begins with the appearance of the Tiber, in this case the physical river as the Trojans first sight its mouth from the sea and enter its stream (25–36): to mark the parallel, Virgil uses the phrase, "*fluuio Tiberinus amoeno*" (7.30; 8.31) in almost the same position in each book. Book 7 similarly ends with a description of a shield with the depiction of a river-god on it, the shield of Turnus with the river Inachus next to his daughter, the heifer Io (7.789–792) The deity is at least two removes—on the shield inside the poem—from the river he represents, and perhaps one remove further if the urn he holds marks him as a statue, like the images of rivers carried in Augustus's procession, or if the reader recognizes the citation of Moschus's Europa poem, where the story of Io is already an engraved scene by Vulcan on Europa's basket—although the figure of urn-bearing Inachus is Virgil's pointed *addition* to Moschus's scene, put there to establish the parallels I am describing.[51] Turnus's shield and Turnus too, moreover, are figures here in the catalog of Italian warriors and troops that is a set piece standing in Book 7 where the shield of Aeneas and its historical overview of Rome stand in Book 8. The catalog of Book 7 is also a catalog of rivers: in addition to the Tiber, the Anio, Amasenus, Himella, Fabaris, Alia, Vulturnus, Sarnus, and Ufens. Most of these rivers are tributaries of the Tiber, and the peoples by them will share, as eventual future Romans, in the great national history that will put the Tiber on the shield of Aeneas in the company with—and the master over—the great world rivers of the Nile, Euphrates, and Rhine. But they also suggest here local stories and traditions that stand apart from Rome. Pointedly named last (7.802), the Ufens bears the same name as one of the lead Italian warriors of the catalog (7.745) who is later killed in battle in Book 12 (460; 641–642). It is unclear whether he got his name from the river or the river from him. Earlier in Book 7, the first named casualties of the new war that breaks out between the natives and the new foreign arrivals are the Latins Almo and Galaesus (7.531–537), who also, not coincidentally, share the names of local

---

51. Putnam, 1998, 18–22. "Again, we are reminded that we are seeing an artifact" (18).

streams.⁵² These Italians have their own claim to the land—some may have died for it—even to the Tiber itself.

Book 9 begins with Turnus sitting in his own sacred vale and grove (9.3–4), dedicated to his ancestor Pilumnus, similar to the one where we left Aeneas at the end of Book 8 (597–98; 609). Turnus scoops up the waters of the river—the Tiber—in prayer, "*aethera uotis*" (9.22–24), just as Aeneas had done back at the beginning of Book 8, "*aethera uoces*" (8.70). The troops of Turnus scouring the plain toward the Trojan camp are then compared in simile to the overflowing Ganges and *ebbing* Nile (9.30–32), and Virgil allows a cruel deflation of the Italians and their hero: this may *not* be part of the world battlefield of Rome's future, but a little squabble in primitive, rustic Italy. The aggrandizing simile no sooner gets going than it reverses and cancels itself out, as the Nile retreats from the fields it fertilizes and hides itself in back its banks: "*cum refluit campis et iam se condidit alueo*" (9.32).⁵³ Nonetheless, Book 9 ends by bringing Turnus back to the river where he started—just as Book 8 begins and ends with rivers. Wearied by his single combat against the combined Trojan troops, Turnus leaps in full armor into the Tiber.

> ille suo cum gurgite flauo
> accepit uenientem ac mollibus extulit undis
> et laetum sociis abluta caede remisit. (9.816–818)

the river with its yellow flood received him as he came and bore him
up with its calmed waves and sent him back, joyful, to his companions
cleansed of slaughter.

There is Virgilian irony in this ring composition bordering on chiasmus: Turnus ritually washes his hands in order to pray at the beginning of the book, only to go out into combat and to be in need of the Tiber's ablutions at its end. The wiping away of the bloodshed as if it had never happened applies to the whole inconclusive action of Book 9, which, in the absence of the poem's true hero, Aeneas, has been an exercise in futility on both sides (think of Nisus and Euyalus). Things might have been different had Turnus, too intent on his own bloodlust and glory, opened the gates of the Trojan camp to his troops. But this ending of the book also shows the Tiber softening its waves to bear up the armed Turnus, as the Euphrates under Roman pressure had

---

52. Jones, 2005, 33–34.
53. Hardie, 1994, 76, points out the coupling of Ganges and Nile in *Georgics* 3.26–28, as a reference to Augustus's victory at Actium.

flowed more softly on Vulcan's shield—"*iam mollior undis*" (8.726)—and as the Tiber itself had calmed his swelling waters at the beginning of Book 8 to ensure smooth rowing for the ships of Aeneas (8.86–89). The river favors the native Italian as well as (as much as) the Trojan / future Roman settler.[54] Or, indifferent to both, it may do nothing of the kind: these are poetic fictions.

At the basis of such fictions is power. In the last book of the *Aeneid*, we are formally introduced to Juturna, the goddess who presides over standing pools and sonorous rivers—"*stagnis quae fluminibusque sonoris / praesidet*" (12.139–140). We learn that she is the sister of Turnus who made a fleeting, unnamed appearance at 10.439. Native land and native hero could not be closer, their relationship could not be more loving. Yet Juturna is brought onstage in Book 12 in order to share in the defeat of Turnus and the Italians. She descends moaning, "*gemens*" (12.886), into the river's depths shortly before the dying soul of Turnus itself descends, "*cum gemitu*," to the shades in the poem's final verse. Perhaps a wound is left in nature and in cultural memory, but these receive new masters, who tell their own narratives—the *Aeneid* itself—about place and its history. A *lacus Juturnae* had been relocated and consecrated within the Roman forum itself.[55]

The framing of Book 8 by rivers, the Tiber at its opening, the foreign rivers at the end, takes on the familiar Virgilian structure of chiasmus and symbolic reversal. Where the Tiber spontaneously welcomes its new Trojan inhabitants and calms its waters, the Euphrates has been compelled by Roman arms to flow more gently, while the last river of the shield's description, the Araxes, is indignant at the bridge—"*pontem indignatus Araxes*" (8.728)—that Augustus builds across it. Seneca (*Natural Questions* 6.17.1) understood Virgil's verse to mean that the Araxes will eventually wash the bridge away. Nature appears to cooperate with or struggle against human attempts to control it.

Within the sequence of episodes pictured on the shield, as opposed to the larger book that contains it, the Araxes completes a separate chiastic construction. Michael Putnam has pointed out that it answers to Horatius Cocles' famous defense and tearing down of the wooden bridge over the Tiber against the troops of expelled King Tarquin and his *indignant* Etruscan ally Porsenna—"*indignanti ... / ... pontem auderet quia uellere Cocles*" (8.649–650).[56] This event founded the Roman Republic that Augustus, the new Romulus,

---

54. Hardie, 1994, 248–250 points out the parallel framings of Books 8 and 9.
55. See Valerius Maximus, 1.8.1. On Juturna's lament, see Barchiesi, 1978 [2015, 95–113].
56. Putnam, 1998, 157–158.

was in the process of returning to a new form of monarchy. Resented by its river, the Araxes bridge correlates foreign conquest with domestic civil war and the quelling of those who fought to keep a king out of Rome. Inversely, the shield depicts the civil strife at Actium as war against the foreigner and queen, Cleopatra. Moreover, as Philip Hardie comments, it is Horatius Cocles' throwing himself in his armor into the Tiber and swimming safely to his friends—after he held off multitudes almost single-handedly—that Turnus will appear to prefigure at the end of Book 9.[57] It aligns the Italian resistance to Aeneas and his royal house inside the action of the *Aeneid* with a later Roman opposition to kingship. Both with and without irony. Heir presumptive to Latinus's throne and suitor to Lavinia, Turnus is no republican, as his treatment of the rather unsympathetic orator-figure Drances attests; he seems like the warlord Antony, who had little patience for the niceties of the senate and the likes of Cicero and who married the Ptolemaic dynast Cleopatra. Or he is like the warlord Octavian-Augustus, who ruled through the façade of the senate (he agreed with Antony to the proscription and murder of Cicero). Vulcan may portray the "*patres*" of the senate on the side of Augustus at Actium (8.679), but it was a battle between two autocrats who lacked only the title of king. In the contrast of the vignettes of the bridge-destroying Cocles and the newly spanned Araxes, Virgil suggests how Rome's far-flung conquests have caused it to outgrow its political institutions, too rich, too big, too complex abroad to evade one-man rule at home. At Actium, both foreign peoples and the Roman Republic have received a new master. The moral is Sallustian, as is the shield's placement of Catiline and Cato in the underworld, which houses the now-dead republic (8.666–670), in the verses that directly precede its depiction of the sea battle. Loss of freedom is a price of the enormous enrichment of the expanded city, the riches flowing into Augustus's triumph, of its new Golden Age.[58]

The placement of the Araxes, named at the end of the final verse of the ekphrasis of the shield, has an additional, unsettling effect of asking who has the last word on history. Rivers not only are permanent features of the land but, in their steady flow, also figure the continuing passage of time. So Ovid's famous image of time-as-river, wave upon wave, in the final book of the *Meta-*

---

57. Hardie, 1994, 249.

58. Sallust, *Bellum Catilinae*, 10–13. It is to Julius Caesar, however, more than to Catiline, that Sallust contrasts Cato, 51–54.

morphoses (15.179–184), his perpetual poem of change. The imperial conquest depicted in the bridge over the indignant Araxes suggests control, not just over defeated Parthians or Dahae, but over time itself, the time that power shapes into history.[59] The multiple removes, one inside the other, that place the Araxes and the other rivers of the triumph in images-within-the-images-of-the-shield-within-the larger-*Aeneid* seem an effort to box time into the permanence of the artwork. The poem transfers its own fame-producing timelessness to (or makes that timelessness depend on) Rome's and Augustus's political achievement: *"imperium sine fine dedi"* (1.279), says Jupiter, supreme god and Virgil's poetic character. Power and poetry mutually support their having the final say on events, as if history not only were leading up to the triumph of Augustus but stopped in 29 BCE.

In the long run, such "Hindsight as foresight makes no sense," W. H. Auden complains about Vulcan's shield in "Secondary Epic," and asks

> Why a curtain of darkness should finally drop
> On Carians, Morini, Gelonians with quivers,
> Converging Romeward in abject file,
> Euphrates, Araxes, and similar rivers
> Learning to flow in a latinate style,
> And Caesar be left where prophecy ends,
> Inspecting troops and gifts for ever?
> Wouldn't Aeneas have asked—'What next?' (15–22)[60]

Citing Auden's poem has become an almost obligatory gesture for an anglophone critic of Virgil. But the great poet sells the greater poet short. Virgil does ask what will happen next, though he cannot provide an answer. As we remarked in chapter 4, the mourning over the potential heir Marcellus lets history continue past Anchises' grand overview to a dead end at the conclusion of Book 6, and the effect is similar here at the conclusion of Book 8. The Araxes is different from the Euphrates. It may take its place in Latin poetry in Virgil's verses, but it has its own history. Servius comments:

> this is a river in Armenia which Xerxes was unable to mount with bridges, and upon which Alexander the Great built a bridge, but the flooding of the

---

59. Quint, 1993, 29–31.
60. Auden, 1976, 455; Zetzel, 1997, 200 cites the Auden passage to make much the same point; see also Gurval, 1995, 209, 244.

river broke it; later Augustus bound it with a stronger bridge, whence it is called, to the glory of Augustus, "the Araxes indignant at its bridge."[61]

Modern scholars suspect that Servius is making this up.[62] There is no other record of this bridge in ancient literature, and the commentator may project its existence out of Virgil's verse, which itself might be expressing an aspiration for Augustus rather than a fact. It is unclear to which eastern river Virgil refers: *three* go by the name of Araxes in classical sources. The prime and likely candidate is the one named by Servius, the Armenian river Aras, which was a sometimes border with the Parthian empire. Augustus would be seen here bringing the Parthians to heel after they had inflicted defeats on Antony in 36 BCE and, more disastrously, on Crassus, killed earlier with his legions by the Parthians at Carrhae in 53 BCE. (Augustus wisely chose a diplomatic settlement with Parthia in 20 BCE.) The coupling with the Dahae, however, can suggest the even more distant Volga, which Herodotus calls the Araxes (1.202), and herald a still greater expansion of Rome's dominion.[63] Virgil's geographical sources may have confused these rivers as one and the same. Or Virgil may intentionally confuse them—as well as a third river in southwestern Iran, the modern-day Kor. Alexander *did* build a bridge over this last Araxes on his way to Persepolis in 330 BCE; he vanquished Persia and the East, but his empire fractured at his death.[64] Servius possibly associates this bridge with the pontoon bridges built over the Hellespont by Xerxes a century and a half earlier in 480 BCE, an event recalled in Latin poetry by Ennius before Virgil and by Lucan after him.[65] These were twice washed away by storms, and Xerxes lost the war.[66] Servius's identification of a river that has twice foiled its would-be conquerors, a Persian invading Greece, a Greek invading Persia, may be too neat, but it catches the last-minute twist at the end of the description of the shield. Earlier empires have risen and fallen. So the de-

---

61. Servius, 1881, 2:305. "ARAXES hic fluvius Armeniae, quem pontibus nisus est Xerxes conscendere. cui Alexander Magnus pontem fecit, quem fluminis incrementa ruperunt. postea Augustus firmiore ponte eum ligavit, unde ad Augusti gloriam dixit 'pontem indignatus Araxes.'"

62. Gurval, 1995, 243; Fordyce, 1985, 287–288.

63. Propertius, 4.3.35–38, places the Araxes in proximity with both Parthians and Dahae, as Arethusa pores over maps to follow the campaign of her husband, Lycotas.

64. Diodorus Siculus 17.69.2; Quintus Curtius 5.5.3–5.

65. Ennius, 1985, 102 (13.1); Lucan, *De bello civile*, 2.672–676.

66. Herodotus, 7.33–35, 8.117. On the relationship among Xerxes, Alexander, the Troy myth, and Roman conquests of the East in the second century BCE, see Feeney, 2016, 244–247.

feated Araxes—indignant like the dying Turnus and Camilla but still alive and rolling—may eventually throw off the power of Augustus, whether by the river's flood or by a flood of invading Parthians. Or by a squabble among Augustus's successors. Like the river, history does not stand still. *Araxes* is the last word on the shield.

It is Evander's remarks earlier in Book 8 on the Italian past, however, that most clearly place the achievement of Augustus's Rome and of the poet who celebrates it into the long-term perspective of nature and time. Between a now long-ago golden age under Saturn and the present of Evander and Aeneas, waves of human invasions and settlement swept in succession over the peninsula.

> tum manus Ausonia et gentes uenere Sicanae,
> saepius et nomen posuit Saturnia tellus;
> tum reges asperque immani corpore Thybris,
> a quo post Itali fluuium cognomine Thybrim
> diximus; amisit uerum uetus Albula nomen. (8.327–332)
>
> Then came the Ausonian horde and the Sicanian tribes, and often the land of Saturn set aside her name; then came kings and harsh, huge-in-body Thybris, from whom we Italians have since called the river Tiber (Thybrim); ancient Albula has lost its true name.

The reader of Book 8 adjusts bearings with a measure of surprise. The river-god who rose to announce himself to Aeneas as Tiberinus/Thybris was operating, it turns out, under an assumed name. Or, rather, the name that a fierce and physically powerful king has imposed on it and left behind. The river may not so much have welcomed Aeneas as a long-lost Dardanian native son as yielded to another, new conqueror of the land. The personification now seems all the more dreamlike, an expression of the hero's wishes.

In Livy (1.3.8), there is a King Tiberinus who is a descendant of Aeneas and an Alban king: he drowned in the Albula and gave it its new name. (Similarly: Ufens, Almo.) Virgil deliberately moves Thybris back into a time that is lost and primordial, an age of giants.[67] Human intervention continually reshapes and renames the land of Italy. Evander's own Pallanteum, the reader knows as Aeneas does not, will be renamed as Rome. The river remains. But against that geological constant, human history fades into the successive rise

---

67. Binder, 1971, 105–108.

and fall of conqueror-kings, some of their names now forgotten entirely or only recalled in the features of the land. Neither Aeneas, Romulus, nor Augustus is the first nor the last.

This Virgilian passage would have a particularly rich fortune in the Renaissance, a period whose signal achievement was the recovery of the classical past and a recognition of its pastness. In his epigram "*De Roma*," the neolatin poet Janus Vitalis (1485–1560) described the experience of the newcomer looking in vain for Rome and its greatness in what were now the ruins of the ancient city. "Rome," he says, cannot be found in Rome. The poem concludes:

> Albula Romani restat nunc nominis index:
> Quin etiam rapidis fertur in aequor aquis.
> Disce hinc quid possit Fortuna. Immota labascunt,
> Et quae perpetuo sunt agitata manent.[68]

> The Albula remains the sign of the Roman name: even as its surface is constantly borne away by its headlong waters. Learn hence what Fortune can do. The permanent falls away, and what is in perpetual flux endures.

Even the name "Rome" no longer corresponds to the city that Vitalis sees; it is as lost as "Albula," replaced by "Tiber." But the flowing river the former once named persists, part of an unchanging nature, indifferent to the human settlements that appear and vanish beside it, and an image of time's inexorable forward movement. Vitalis's poem was adapted by, among others, Quevedo, Szarzynski, and Du Bellay; Spenser translated the final couplet of the latter's version in *The Ruines of Rome*: "That which is firme doth flit and fall away / And that is flitting, doth abide and stay."[69] This moral gloss from the future about the mutability of the world under Fortune's sway declines to register—and hence naturalizes, mystifies—Virgil's insistence on power and conquest: on man-made change. Book 2 of the *Aeneid* had already shown at length what other epics often avoid or condense: the capture and death of a city. In Evander's words hindsight *does* become foresight in the *Aeneid*. Gazing with the Arcadian king into an immemorial past, Virgil envisioned a time to come when Rome and its empire might be barely remembered; the cattle

---

68. García-Castañón, 2001, 20. It is noteworthy that in the Renaissance translations and adaptations of Vitalis's poem, the learned, Virgilian "Albula" disappears and is replaced by the Tiber, thus blunting some of the force of the original.

69. Oram, Bjorvand, et al., 1989, 387.

who graze in the Forum that is to come may return to graze there when the Forum is no more.[70] Or, as is the fate of once powerful cities which great poets celebrate, its ruins might be the later object of literary pilgrimage: as Troy's ruins were a tourist attraction in Virgil's own day.[71] Rome is not yet founded in the *Aeneid*; the poem can imagine a Rome-less future.

70. Hardie, 1992, discusses Augustan poets contemplating the transience of Rome. The celebrated verses 8.360–361, describing cattle lowing in the Roman forum, might point to a devastated Rome of the future: see Isocrates 14.31. I am indebted to Bakker, 2013. See also the remarks in Barchiesi, 1999, 338–341 on the prophetic dimension of the *Aeneid*; Kraus, 1994.

71. On the tourism at Troy, see Rose, 2014; Sage, 2000.

6

The Brothers of Sarpedon

THE DESIGN OF BOOK 10

IN THE FIRST WORDS he speaks in the *Aeneid*, Aeneas imagines himself vanquished on the plains of Troy along with two other remembered Trojan heroes, Hector and Sarpedon (1.94–101). The *Aeneid* continually remembers Hector, whose death at the hands of Achilles in *Iliad* 22, evoked here and subsequently in Book 1 by the reliefs of the temple of Juno in Dido's Carthage (1.483–487), will be reenacted in the duel between Aeneas and Turnus that closes the poem in Book 12.[1] To a lesser but nonetheless important extent, the *Aeneid* also remembers Sarpedon, particularly in the battle scenes of Book 10, though also in the surrounding Books 9 and 11. As the war in Italy produces a second *Iliad*, it produces many versions of the Sarpedon whom the gods of Homer's poem refused to save from death. Virgil, in fact, meditates on the relationship that the *Iliad* already draws between its Aeneas and the other two Trojan heroes, between a hero twice rescued by the gods and destined to survive and those they leave to perish on the battlefield.

The textual memory of Sarpedon dictates the logic of Virgil's imitations of Homer in Book 10. These reveal a repeated pattern whose systematic nature and artistic intricacy have not been fully explored by previous commentary on the poem. Virgil constructs each of the heroic duels of the book by superimposing at least two scenes from the *Iliad*. He practices a *contaminatio* of

---

1. See *Aeneid* 1.273, 1.750, 2.270f., 2.540f., 3.300f., 5.190, 5.371, 5.634, 6.166f., 9.155, 11.288f., 12.440. The last of these passages, Aeneas's words to his son before he goes off to the final battle with Turnus, enjoins Ascanius to be roused by the examples of both Aeneas and of his uncle Hector: "*et pater Aeneas et auunculus excitet Hector.*"

Homer with Homer. Commenting on the technique of combinatory imitation that is named by this nonclassical term, Stephen Hinds insists, as I also want to do, on its dynamic, unstable nature: the multiple models compete with one another, and the reader cannot be sure which of them determines meaning.[2] Virgil's warriors shift back and forth between possible Homeric models and identities, at times from one verse to the next. The larger emblem of this confusion is the modeling of *every* major protagonist of Book 10—at some point in the book's fiction—*both* upon Homer's Sarpedon *and* upon Sarpedon's own slayer, Patroclus. It is another case of Virgilian doubling, and here, too, behind the similarities among apparently interchangeable combatants lies the poet's experience of civil war. Brothers fight side by side in Book 10, but the book also produces an image of warriors as identical as brothers fighting on opposite sides. The ingenuity and virtuosity of Virgil's imitation is displayed in his reworking the same Iliadic prototypes over and over again, in his ability to produce so many different replicas of Sarpedon and Patroclus. At the same time, his insistent reprises of the same heroic models lend the book an underlying tonal and thematic unity.

Book 9: Nymphs, Ships, and Pines

The *Aeneid* has already remembered the dying Sarpedon at a significant moment in Book 9, when Turnus kills Antiphates, Sarpedon's bastard son (9.696–698). This mention of Sarpedon is part of a larger symbolic complex that takes the form of yet another Virgilian chiasmus. It prepares the ground for Book 10, where two of Sarpedon's brothers are in the fighting and where one combatant after another becomes a version—or brother—of Sarpedon.

At the book's opening, Turnus attacks the Trojan encampment and is on the verge of setting fire to their ships, much as Hector had sought to burn the Greek ships in the *Iliad*. A miracle transpires to thwart the Italian hero. The ships are built from pines of Mount Ida sacred and dear to Cybele—"*pinea silua mihi multos dilecta per annos*" (85)—and the goddess has obtained from Jupiter the promise to transform the ships that survive the trip to Italy (thirteen of the original twenty are at hand) into immortal sea nymphs. The apotheosis duly occurs, in an episode that readers have had difficulty in connecting to the rest of the *Aeneid* and that is often criticized as an Alexandrian excess unworthy of the poem: Ovid, naturally, seizes on it as one of the few

---

2. Hinds, 1998, 141–142.

episodes of the *Aeneid* really worth retelling in his miniaturized version of Virgil's epic in the *Metamorphoses* (14.530f.).[3]

But Virgil *does* link the transformation of the ships to a part of the subsequent action of Book 9. The final sequence of the book, the *aristeia* of Turnus inside the Trojan camp, begins at 672 when the young Trojan warriors Pandarus and Bitias unwisely fling open its gates and come out to fight hand-to-hand. The poem initially describes them and their parentage.

> Pandarus et Bitias, Idaeo Alcanore creti,
> quo Iouis eduxit luco siluestris Iaera
> abietibus iuuenes patriis et montibus aequos ... (672–674)

> Pandarus and Bitias, born of Alcanor of Ida, whom sylvan Iaera bore in the grove of Jupiter, youths tall and massive as their native pines and mountains ...

Pandarus and Bitias are natives of Mount Ida, and they are equal in height to or equated with the pines of their homeland, the same pines that are transformed into nymphs earlier in the book. They are, moreover, the offspring themselves of a sea-nymph, for Iaera appears in the list of Nereids in *Iliad* 18.42. She is now a wood-nymph and, as Philip Hardie notes, "in literary historical terms she has undergone a passage opposite to that of the ship nymphs."[4] This passage is completed, however, in her sons, turned by metaphor into pines, producing an elegant chiasmus: pine trees of Ida cut down to be turned into ships, then into nymphs, a nymph who produces Idaean tree-like sons. This arboreal conceit is reinforced and neatly sutured to Virgil's principal Iliadic model by the ensuing simile five lines later that compares the two youths to twin oaks—"*geminae quercus*" (681)—a simile that closely imitates Homer's simile in *Iliad* 12.132f., which describes the oaklike Polypoites and Leonteus, the heroic pair who defend the gates of the Greek camp against the Trojans seeking to destroy their ships.[5] The Homeric model is ironic, however, subject to characteristic Virgilian inversion: for while Polypoites and

---

3. See the commentary of Hardie, 1994, 88. The corresponding Homeric episode is the transformation of the Phaeacian ship, blocking the harbor of Phaecia, in *Odyssey* 13.125–164. See also Ovid, *Amores*, 3.12.28.

4. Hardie, 1994, 215.

5. Here, as throughout this chapter, I am indebted to the table of Homeric passages imitated in the *Aeneid* compiled in Knauer, 1964; see 298–301 on Pallas, Patroclus, and Sarpedon. I have also found helpful the commentary on Book 10 of S. J. Harrison, 1991.

Leonteus hold back the Trojan onslaught, Pandarus and Bitias are slain by Turnus. The action of Book 9 is thus framed by two rewritings of the fighting over the ships in the *Iliad*, though in the second instance the Trojan ships are no longer there but have swum away in the form of nymphs. So, in this second episode closing the chiasmus, Turnus does not destroy the pines of Ida but instead the pine-tree-like warriors from Ida. The book's frame contrasts pines that are cut down to be turned first into ships, then into immortal goddesses, and the fate of men "equal" to trees who are simply cut down in battle, reduced to inanimate matter.

The contrast is commented on by another, more obliquely signaled reminiscence of the *Iliad*. The first victim of Turnus's *aristeia*, the first to face him before he goes after Pandarus and Bitias, is one Antiphates. There is an Antiphates among the victims of Leonteus in the fighting before the Greek camp in *Iliad* 12.191, and his namesake here turns us back to the Homeric episode that Virgil is imitating. But the parentage of this Antiphates contains a further indication to the reader.

> et primum Antiphaten (is enim se primus agebat),
> Thebana de matre nothum Sarpedonis alti,
> coniecto sternit iaculo. (8.696–698)

> and first of all Antiphates (for he first came against him), the bastard
> son of lofty Sarpedon by a Theban mother, Turnus lays low with a cast
> of his spear.

Antiphates is the son of Sarpedon, a hero of the first order in the *Iliad*—"*Sarpedonis alti*"—killed by Patroclus in *Iliad* 16 (419–525).

Such references to a relation or offspring of a figure in earlier epics are a repeated device in the *Aeneid*, textual markers by which Virgil indicates the literary affiliation of his episode and asks his reader to look for a new version of the figure from the earlier poem. In Book 10, Messapus kills Erichaetes, the son of Lycaon—"*Lycaoniumque Erichaeten*" (10.749)—in the same book in which Aeneas's merciless encounters with Magus, Tarquitus, and Liger (10.521–601) imitate the episode of Achilles and Lycaon in *Iliad* 21.34–135. The suppliant Italian warriors whom Aeneas refuses to spare are all "sons of Lycaon," new versions of the Iliadic Lycaon who pleads for his life only to be killed by Achilles. In Book 12 (346–352), Turnus kills Eumedes, the son of Dolon whom, we are reminded, Diomedes killed in *Iliad* 10. The reader is tipped off to see Turnus, in killing this new Dolon, as a new Diomedes—or at least as trying to stand in place of the Diomedes who in Book 11 is reported to have declined to come from Arpi to fight once more against Aeneas and the Trojans. And in Book 5, during the funeral games for Anchises, we are told that the boxer Dares had defeated Butes, sprung from the race or people of Amycus—"*Amyci de gente*" (5.372–374). It is a signal that Dares and, it will turn out, his present opponent Entellus are new types of Amycus, the boastful pugilist of *Argonautica* (2.1–97); their boxing match rewrites Apollonius's telling of the fistfight between Amycus and Polydeuces. The appearance here late in Book 9 of an illegitimate son of Sarpedon is complemented by the announcement early in Book 10 that two brothers of Sarpedon are fighting in the Trojan forces (10.125–126); the implication is that the reader should be looking there for new versions of the Trojan hero. So, by the same token, the death of Antiphates, a new if bastard version of his heroic father, Sarpedon, suggests the presence in Book 9 of other Sarpedon-like figures, and his appearance in the sequence that leads to the deaths of Bitias and Pandarus at Turnus's hands makes them the likely candidates.

The dying son of Sarpedon is the poem's cue to remember the moment of Sarpedon's own death, narrated by Homer in *Iliad* 16.482–484, a death that links him, in fact, both to the young warriors from Ida and to the ships that have earlier been turned into nymphs.

Aeneas describes Sarpedon in Book 1 as huge: "*ingens*" (1.99); here he is lofty ("*alti*") in size as well as in heroic rank—like the tall-as-trees Pandarus and Bitias. When Patroclus kills Sarpedon with his spear in the *Iliad*, Homer compares the warrior's collapse into the dust of the battlefield to the felling of a tree.

> He fell, as when an oak goes down or a white poplar,
> or like a towering pine tree which in the mountains the carpenters
> have hewn down with their whetted axes to make a ship-timber.[6] (*Iliad* 16.482–484)

In Homer's simile, the dying Sarpedon falls as a tree and, as the simile becomes more specific, as a mountain pine that is cut down to build a ship.[7] The

---

6. English citations of the *Iliad* are taken from Homer, 1951. Citations of the Greek text are taken from Homer, 1931.

7. The same simile appears earlier at 13.389–391 to describe the death of the minor character Asios, a Trojan ally. For other tree similes in the *Iliad*, see the commentary of Janko, 1994. Perhaps of special relevance to my argument here is the simile at the end of Book 17 that compares the carrying of the body of the dead Patroclus to the conveying of a ship timber (17.742–745);

simile contains both of the opposed figures of Book 9: the pine as warrior, the pine as ship. Already in this Iliadic passage, the comparison suggests the difference between the human death of the warrior and the afterlife as a ship into which human art has transformed the pine. The immobile tree will now be freed of its roots to roam the sea; the living warrior falls into the stillness of death. Virgil's framing episodes of Book 9 enact the Homeric simile and do it one better; the pine trees of Mount Ida live on not only as the ships of Aeneas but finally as immortal nymphs. Meanwhile the nymph-born, pinelike and oaklike natives of Mount Ida, Pandarus and Bitias, are felled by Turnus in battle, as is Antiphates, Sarpedon's own son. Virgil supplements the pathos of Homer's simile with a further inescapable thought: the gods, at least Grandmother Cybele, care more about trees than they do about men and women. As Virgil's Jupiter recalls to Hercules in Book 10 (469–471), Sarpedon was Jupiter's own son, but he, too, fell at Troy.

The Brothers of Sarpedon

Pandarus and Bitias are brothers, unlike their Iliadic counterparts, Polypoites and Leonteus; the comparison to the *"geminae quercus,"* another Virgilian variation on his Homeric model, suggests that they may be twins. We may think back on the doomed brothers from Ida when we learn toward the beginning of Book 10 (125–126) that two brothers of Sarpedon, Clarus and Thaemon, are fighting among Aeneas's Trojans in this, their first appearance in the *Aeneid* or, for that matter, in any classical texts that have come down to us. They briefly reappear in one verse in Book 12 as the Lycian brothers— *"fratres Lycia missos"* (12.516)—who fall to the sword of Turnus.[8] But the

---

the parallel similes suggest the likeness in death between Sarpedon and his slayer, Patroclus. Barchiesi, 1996, notes that the falling tree simile at the death of Sarpedon is the evident model for Simonides, fragment 11, describing the death of Achilles, a passage that, Barchiesi argues, stands, in turn, behind Horace, *Odes*, 4.6.9–12.

8. These brothers introduce the Sarpedon motif that is the subject of this chapter. They also introduce into Book 10 the lesser but clearly plotted out motif of warrior brothers, a motif familiar from the *Iliad* that Virgil has just employed with the brothers Pandarus and Bitias in the final episode of Book 9. See Harrison, 1991, 94. See 10.128–129; 10.317–322, 10.336–341; 10.226–341; 10.351; 10.390–396; 10.575–600. These brothers fighting and dying together contribute to the book's larger picture of interchangeable victims of war, particularly in the case—a Virgilian invention with respect to Homer—of the identical twins Larides and Thymber slain by Pallas, no longer identical in the modes of death inflicted upon them (10.390–396).

obvious Sarpedon-figure of Book 10 itself is Pallas. It is in relationship to the imminent death of Pallas at the hands of Turnus that Jupiter explicitly reminds the weeping Hercules of the death of his own son Sarpedon at Troy. The rather indirect, even subliminal evocation of Sarpedon's death in the contrast between the ship-nymphs and Pandarus and Bitias in Book 9 can be viewed as an anticipation of the action of Book 10, just as, we shall see below, the still further echoes of Sarpedon's death in the death of Camilla in Book 11 look back on the book that precedes it. The background presence of the dying Sarpedon connects all three of these books of the *Aeneid*, framing Book 10 and the death of Pallas that lies at the book's center.

But Pallas is not the only warrior in Book 10 to fight and die like the *Iliad*'s Sarpedon. The book's early reference to the presence of two brothers of Sarpedon in the battle announces that it will feature multiple versions of Sarpedon— and thus multiple versions, too, of Patroclus, the warrior who killed him in *Iliad* 16. For Pallas's function in the *Aeneid* is also to play the role of the *Iliad*'s Patroclus, the beloved comrade whose death Achilles avenged by killing his slayer Hector; just so Aeneas avenges Pallas—"*Pallas te hoc uulnere, Pallas / immolat*" (12.948–949)—by killing Turnus at the end of the poem. In the death of Pallas, Virgil imitates and combines the two episodes of *Iliad* 16: both the slaying of Sarpedon by Patroclus *and* the slaying of Patroclus himself by Hector.

This combination of Homeric models sets the pattern for *all* of the subsequent duels and confrontations of Book 10. Virgil's repeated strategy in each episode of the warfare he stages in the book is to juxtapose the models of two or more different duels from the *Iliad*. These are chosen from the chain of heroic duels and death that begin in *Iliad* 16 with Sarpedon, who is killed as the major trophy of the *aristeia* of Patroclus, who is then himself killed, with the help of Apollo, by Hector; in *Iliad* 22, Hector is killed, in his turn, by Achilles. Something like this succession of ever mightier warriors occurs in Book 10, which also depends on age gradation, beginning with the death of the immature Pallas at the hands of Turnus, who is himself a younger warrior than Aeneas and whose fate is postponed, like Hector's in the *Iliad*, until later in the poem at the end of Book 12; Aeneas instead dispatches Mezentius who, it is suggested, is an even more formidable opponent than Turnus, though in this case *older* than Aeneas and a bit over the hill (his son Lausus is older than Ascanius and the same age as Pallas, the son of the decrepit, Nestor-like Evander). Aeneas never gets to pick on someone his own age. At different moments of the fighting of Book 10, each of Virgil's warriors will imitate more than one of the figures of the Iliadic chain: Sarpedon–Patroclus–Hector–Achilles.

Virgil can place these Homeric models in successive *abab* alternation; sometimes he creates a kind of *ababa* ring composition or chiasmus. He exploits the resemblances among these killings, particularly the gesture that Patroclus makes of stepping on Sarpedon's body to remove his spear and that Hector repeats when he removes his spear from Patroclus. The effect, surely carefully meditated and deliberate, is to blur at each successive moment the identity of Virgil's own characters. Depending on which Homeric role they play, they are cast as victor or victim, or as victor soon to become victim in turn. In fact *all* the major characters—Pallas, Turnus, Aeneas, Lausus, Mezentius—will at one point be cast as Sarpedon. All will play Patroclus as well, the central protagonist and exemplary victor-*and*-victim of *Iliad* 16. This blurring of identity suggests the equalizing effect of war, especially of fraternal, civil war: the future Roman civil wars that are built into Virgil's replaying of the Trojan war in Italy. That future, more than the decree of Jupiter early on in Book 10, erases distinction between Trojan and Italian adversaries: "*nullo discrimine habebo*" (10.108), says the father of the gods, apparently refusing to take sides and allowing the fates to have their way. Like brothers, these warriors will resemble both their Homeric models and one another.[9]

The following map of the battle of in Book 10 will help the reader orient my analysis.

THE SEQUENCE OF BATTLE IN AENEID 10

Aeneid X	*Iliad*
125–126 SARPEDON's brothers Clarus and Thaemon are fighting against Rutuli	
(a)	
362–379 PALLAS rallies Arcadians	16.419–426 SARPEDON rallies Lycians vs. PATROCLUS

---

9. One calculated resemblance—and implied equivalence—between the Trojan and Italian forces is that each, in a book that features Hercules weeping tears for Pallas at its center (10.464–465), can claim family members of a former companion of Hercules fighting—and dying—in its ranks. Aeneas kills Cisseus and Gyan, club-wielding sons of Melampus, "*comes*" of Hercules during the hero's labors (10.317–322). Mezentius, aiming for Aeneas, instead kills Antores, who was himself a "*comitem*" of Hercules; he stayed on with Evander and now dies thinking of his native Argos (10.777–782). In addition to Pallas, there are victims for Hercules to mourn for on both sides of the battle and of the book itself.

380–425 PALLAS *aristeia*

426–432 LAUSUS rallies Latins against PALLAS

434–438 PALLAS not fated to fight LAUSUS

439–441 Juturna to TURNUS

454 TURNUS lion

464–465 Hercules grieves for PALLAS; dialogue with Jupiter

486 PALLAS pulls spear out and dies

495 TURNUS steps on dead body of PALLAS

501–505 narrator on TURNUS with belt of PALLAS

510 news of death of PALLAS reaches AENEAS

16.692–697, 399–418 PATROCLUS

16.419f. SARPEDON rallies Lykians vs. PATROCLUS

16.707–709 PATROCLUS not fated to win Troy

16.712–730 Apollo to HECTOR

16.756–758 both HECTOR and PATROCLUS lions

16.431–434 Zeus grieves for SARPEDON; scene with Hera

16.503–505 PATROCLUS takes spear out of SARPEDON

16.862 HECTOR steps on dead body of PATROCLUS

17.200–208 Zeus on HECTOR with arms of PATROCLUS/ Achilles

16.508 news of death of SARPEDON reaches GLAUCUS

(b)
532 AENEAS and Magus

541 armor of Haemonides, killed by AENEAS

557–560 AENEAS and Tarquitus

592–594 AENEAS taunts Lucagus

600 AENEAS and Liger

21.98 ACHILLES and Lycaon

16.663 armor of Sarpedon, killed by PATROCLUS

21.122–127 ACHILLES and Lycaon

16.745–750 PATROCLUS taunts Kebriones (cf. 16.616–618: AENEAS taunts Meriones)

21.106 ACHILLES and Lycaon

(c)
606–632 Jupiter and Juno discuss fate of TURNUS

16.431–461 Hera and Zeus discuss fate of SARPEDON; 20.291 Poseidon and Hera discuss fate of AENEAS

THE DESIGN OF BOOK 10 (BOOKS 9–11)   159

615 Juno will remove TURNUS as Juno recalls (10.81)

636 Juno makes false Aeneas for TURNUS

687–688 TURNUS returns to homeland

(d)

736 MEZENTIUS steps on ORODES

737 MEZENTIUS exults over ORODES

739–41 ORODES to MEZENTIUS

743–744 MEZENTIUS to ORODES

744–746 MEZENTIUS takes spear out of ORODES

749 MESSAPUS kills son of Lycaon

(e)

794 wounded MEZENTIUS retreats, protected by companions, trailing spear

819–820 death of LAUSUS, killed by AENEAS

829–830 AENEAS to LAUSUS

831 AENEAS lifts up LAUSUS

833–835 MEZENTIUS under tree

843–844 MEZENTIUS mourns over LAUSUS

Venus removed AENEAS in *Iliad* 5 and Neptune did in *Iliad* 20

21.600 Apollo imitates Agenor for ACHILLES; 5.449 Apollo makes a false Aeneas

16.676–683 dead SARPEDON's body returned to homeland

16.503 PATROCLUS steps on SARPEDON (16.862 HECTOR steps on PATROCLUS)

22.393 ACHILLES exults over HECTOR

16.851–855 PATROCLUS to HECTOR (22.358–360 HECTOR to ACHILLES)

22.365–366 ACHILLES to HECTOR

16.503–505 PATROCLUS takes spear out of SARPEDON

21.34f. ACHILLES kills Lycaon

5.663–667 wounded SARPEDON removed by companions, trailing spear

16.856–857 death of PATROCLUS killed by HECTOR = 22.362–363 death of HECTOR killed by ACHILLES

21.106–109 ACHILLES to Lycaon

24.589 ACHILLES lifts up HECTOR

5.692–695 SARPEDON under oak

18.23–25 ACHILLES mourns over PATROCLUS

861–866 MEZENTIUS talks to horse	19.400f. ACHILLES talks to horses; 8.185f. HECTOR to horses; 17.442f. Zeus to horses; *Ody.* 9.447–460 POLYPHEMUS to ram
873 MEZENTIUS calls three times	16.783–785 PATROCLUS calls and charges three times
885 MEZENTIUS circles three times	
891f. AENEAS wounds RHOEBUS, horse of MEZENTIUS	16.467 SARPEDON wounds PEDASOS, horse of PATROCLUS (8.81 arrow of Paris wounds Nestor's unnamed horse)
897–898 AENEAS taunts MEZENTIUS	5.472 SARPEDON spurs HECTOR (22.331–336 ACHILLES taunts HECTOR)
904 MEZENTIUS asks AENEAS for burial	22.338 HECTOR asks ACHILLES for burial

Pallas

The death of Pallas occupies the center of Book 10. He enters the scene of battle trying to rally his Arcadian troops, who are yielding to the shock of the Latin attack. His actions and his subsequent speech to his followers (10.362–379) are modeled on those of Sarpedon in *Iliad* 16.419f., rallying his Lycians in flight before the onslaught of Patroclus, who has now entered the war in the armor of Achilles. Thus, the scene prepares us to read the ensuing duel between Pallas and Turnus as a rewriting of the Iliadic duel between Sarpedon and Patroclus. No sooner has it done so, however, than Pallas is allowed an *aristeia* of forty-five verses that culminates in his killing of Halaesus (10.380–425): there is no such equivalent moment for Homer's Sarpedon, and instead these verses, which list Pallas's victims in order of their deaths, recall Homer's descriptions of the warriors who fall to *Patroclus* in *Iliad* 16 (692–697; 399–418). In fact, at verse 10.426, when Lausus must rally the Latins, in turn, against this onslaught of Pallas, he, Lausus, now plays the role of a Sarpedon holding the line against a Patroclus. Pallas and Lausus, the warriors of equal age and prowess, are not, however, fated to meet (10.434–438)—the language recalls

Apollo's warning to Patroclus that he is not fated to win Troy at *Iliad* 16.707–709, and when Juturna a few verses later (10.439–441) moves Turnus to fight against Pallas, the action appears to have jumped ahead to this later moment in *Iliad* 16 (712–730) when Apollo subsequently spurs Hector to battle against Patroclus.

By this point the Homeric model for the upcoming fight between Pallas and Turnus has shifted to the duel between Patroclus, the slayer of Sarpedon, and Hector. It begins, however, to shift back again to the model of Sarpedon and Patroclus, a shift that is effected in the simile that compares Turnus to a lion eyeing a bull at verses 10.454–456; it recalls Homer's simile comparing *both* Hector and Patroclus to lions, fighting over a deer, at *Iliad* 16.756–758. Even as Virgil's simile refers us to the later Homeric duel, the likeness of the leonine Turnus to Patroclus as well as to Hector suggests that his slaying of Pallas may be reenacting the earlier duel as well. In fact, the model of Sarpedon and Patroclus now takes over: in response to the prayer of Pallas, Hercules weeps at verse 10.465 and recalls the grief that Homer's Zeus suffered over his son Sarpedon's imminent death (*Il.* 16.459), an Iliadic moment that Virgil's Jupiter now expressly evokes: "*quin occidit una / Sarpedon, mea progenies*" (10.470–471). When at verses 10.486–487 Pallas pulls the spear of Turnus out of his own chest and tears out his life with it, he echoes the action of Patroclus, who steps on the chest of Sarpedon in order to pull his spearhead and the life out of the vanquished Sarpedon (*Il.* 16.503–505).

Now the *Aeneid*'s perspective on the *Iliad* changes again, once more with a moment of ambiguity and uncertainty about which scene from Homer's epic is being reenacted. When Turnus steps on the now-dead body of Pallas at verse 10.495 in order to strip him of his baldric, the action seems to recall *both* Patroclus taking his spear out of Sarpedon and Hector's stepping on the body of Patroclus similarly to remove his spear (*Il.* 16.862), a Patroclus, we should point out, whose soul has already left his body. The moment also evokes Hector's stripping Patroclus of the armor of Achilles in the *Iliad*, and the ensuing warning of the narrator that Turnus will get his comeuppance for spoiling Pallas of his baldric at verses 10.501–505 echoes Zeus's spelling out the doom of Hector, destined to be killed by Achilles, at *Iliad* 17.200–208.

Alessandro Barchiesi has written revealingly about the moral valences of this moment, and he points out what he calls the "optical illusion" that is taking place.[10] In the *Iliad*, both Patroclus and Hector step on the bodies, respectively,

10. Barchiesi, 1984, 34 [2015, 18].

of the living Sarpedon and the dead Patroclus to retrieve their spears; in this instance in *Aeneid* 10, the act of stepping on the body of Pallas, Barchiesi shows us, turns out to have nothing to do with spears—Pallas removes the spearhead himself from his body—and everything to do with treading on the already defeated, with stripping him of his armor, and with a lack of restraint ("*seruare modum*"; 10.502) and piety.[11] For my purposes the initial ambiguity that Turnus's gesture creates is equivalent to the effect of the earlier lion simile: as he moved from the role of Hector to that of Patroclus and now moves back here to the role of Hector, his Iliadic identity blurs.

Virgil shifts his Homeric model one final time. The moment when the news of the death of Pallas reaches Aeneas at verse 510 imitates *Iliad* 16.508 when Glaucus, the cousin of Sarpedon and the addressee of his famous speech in *Iliad* 12 (309–328), learns that his kinsman has been killed. So Pallas ends up the episode where he started, as a new Sarpedon, and we can recognize a kind of chiastic ring composition in Virgil's imitation and switching back and forth between his alternative Iliadic models: Sarpedon–Patroclus–Sarpedon–Patroclus–Sarpedon.

Aeneas

We can detect a similar ringlike *ababa* pattern in the next episode of the battle of Book 10, the savage *aristeia* upon which Aeneas embarks at the news of the death of Pallas. The principal Homeric model of his actions is Achilles, the pitiless avenger of Patroclus in *Iliad* 21, and, as we have noted above, the three Italian warriors whom he vanquishes and who ask, in vain, for his mercy—Magus (521–536), Tarquitus (550–560), and Liger (595–601)—all play the Iliadic role of Lycaon, the son of Priam whom Achilles meets at *Iliad* 21.34. Achilles had once before captured but spared Lycaon by selling him into the social death of captivity and slavery; ransomed and brought back to Troy, he reappears to Achilles as a kind of revenant from Hades, and this time—because of the death of Patroclus—Achilles makes certain to kill him (21.54–107). When later in *Aeneid* 10 the Italian warrior Messapus kills a son of Lycaon, Erichaetes (10.749), we may feel that here, too, is a return of the dead man in his progeny who is just as surely dispatched. Meanwhile, Virgil's imitation has produced not just one but three "sons" or versions of Lycaon. Aeneas's speeches to Magus (531–533), Tarquitus (557–560), and Liger (600)

---

11. Barchiesi, 1984, 30–43 [2015, 15–25].

respectively echo sections of Achilles' terrible words to Lycaon (*Il.* 21.98; 123–127; 106) before and after he kills the suppliant Trojan.

We expect Aeneas to imitate the actions—even the more barbaric ones—of Achilles; he is the hero and greatest warrior of his epic as Achilles was of the *Iliad*. But in this episode, too, Virgil shifts back and forth between models and, somewhat surprisingly, Aeneas is also cast as the Patroclus of *Iliad* 16. Between his confrontations with Mago and Tarquitus, Aeneas kills the splendidly armored priest Haemonides at verses 10.537–542; at verse 541 Serestus gathers up the armor of the slain warrior. The moment is of considerable interest because it shows that Aeneas, no less than Turnus, the spoiler of the baldric of Pallas, and no less than Camilla who pursues the richly armored priest Chloreus in Book 11 (768f.), is not above carrying away the armor of those he kills, a trophy, the narrator declares, to Mars—"*tibi, rex Gradiue, tropaeum*" (10.542)—even if he has it done by the surrogate, Serestus. At the opening of Book 11, Aeneas personally constructs a similar "*tropaeum*" (7) to the god of war out of the arms of Mezentius (11.5–8).

The carrying of the arms of Haemonides out of the fray returns us, however, to the death of Sarpedon in *Iliad* 16; it is Sarpedon's armor that Patroclus gives to his companions to carry back to the Greek ships at *Iliad* 16.664–665. For a moment, then, Aeneas reminds us not so much of the *Iliad*'s vindictive Achilles as of the Patroclus Achilles is out to avenge; and this moment is repeated between his merciless killings of Tarquitus and Liger. Liger is acting as charioteer for his brother Lucagus, but as Lucagus himself urges on the steeds with his sword, he is struck by Aeneas's spear and tumbles from the vehicle (10.586–591). Aeneas taunts him for jumping from the wheeled chariot and deserting his yoked team: "*ipse rotis saliens iuga deseris*" (10.594). The grim battlefield humor recalls one of the most famous moments of the *Iliad*, when Patroclus launches a stone that kills Kebriones, the charioteer of Hector, then compares him to an acrobat and diver (*Il.* 16.745–750). Virgil has included the elegant variation of making the victim of this death and mockery not the charioteer Liger but his brother Lucagus, though by showing Lucagus himself urging on his horses—another optical illusion of the kind to which Barchiesi refers—Lucagus seems to be a charioteer like Kebriones; and the real charioteer Liger will soon meet his own death together with his brother.

Virgil also remembers that Homer's Aeneas was himself a mocker in *Iliad* 16. He called Meriones a dancer when the latter avoided his spear (*Il.* 16.616–618), and Meriones' response earned the rebuke of Patroclus, who urges fighting rather than talking (*Il.* 16.629–631). Patroclus's own subsequent jests about

Kebriones now liken him to the Aeneas he earlier criticized and show how much his success in battle has gone to his head, how much warlust has maddened him: Homer is preparing the reader for his upcoming downfall. The taunting Aeneas of *Aeneid* 10 is imitating an Iliadic Patroclus who was, in turn, imitating an earlier, perhaps discreditable, Homeric Aeneas. There is thus a resemblance, Virgil implies, between the merciless Achilles and the armor-stripping and mocking Patroclus his Aeneas alternately imitates in this episode, creating the configuration of models: Achilles–Patroclus–Achilles–Patroclus–Achilles. Both Iliadic figures are out of control and—like the Turnus we have just seen—do not restrain themselves in their moments of victory. And we may feel that Aeneas is acting like his old Homeric self, or the self he would have liked to have been, one whose spear hits rather than misses adversaries, one who does not have to meet a greater adversary in Achilles himself.

Turnus

It is this last-mentioned Iliadic Aeneas who is recalled in the next episode when Juno removes Turnus from the battlefield. Wounded by Diomedes in *Iliad* 5 and about to meet and be killed by Achilles in *Iliad* 20, Homer's Aeneas is twice taken out of the fighting by protecting gods, first by Venus-Aphrodite and Apollo, who cloaks him in mist (*Il.* 5.311–346; 444–453), then by Poseidon, who throws mist before the eyes of Achilles (*Il.* 20.291–329). Poseidon announces to an adamant Hera that Aeneas is reserved by destiny to preserve the descendants of Dardanus and to replace the House of Priam (302–308)—the Homeric basis, as have earlier seen, for the legends of Aeneas that Virgil turned into the *Aeneid*. The hero cannot die because he is reserved for a sequel. Earlier in Book 10, during the council of the gods, Juno has reminded Venus of her rescuing her son in *Iliad* 5: "*tu potes Aenean manibus subducere Graium / proque uiro nebulam et uentos obtendere inanis*" ("You were able to remove Aeneas from the hands of the Greeks, and to substitute for the hero cloud and empty air"; 10.81–82). Now Juno turns around and does the same for Turnus.

If Juno seems a bit hypocritical, given her earlier words to Venus, she seems especially so when we recall her conversation—as Homer's Hera—with the Zeus of *Iliad* 16, when he toyed with the idea of saving his son Sarpedon. In effect, Virgil rewrites that Homeric scene *twice* in *Aeneid* 10, first in Jupiter's consolation of Hercules for the upcoming death of Pallas (10.464–

473), then in the dialogue between Jupiter and Juno over the fate of Turnus (10.606–632); he thus casts Turnus, too, as another Sarpedon.[12] Like Hercules in the earlier passage, Juno weeps (10.628) at the prospect of Turnus being killed by Aeneas; unlike Hercules, she is allowed by Jupiter to do something about it. But when Zeus considered lifting Sarpedon out of the battle of *Iliad* 16 and putting him down in his homeland of Lycia, it was Hera-Juno who stood firm. She argued that other gods would want to follow his example and save their children from falling at Troy; they would resent the rescue of Sarpedon (*Il.* 16.440–449). The same Hera was later unyielding when Poseidon proposed the rescue of the "guiltless"—"ἀναίτιος"—Aeneas (*Il.* 20.297) in *Iliad* 20; she and Athena would have nothing to do with saving any Trojans (*Il.* 20.310–317): they were especially reluctant, we may suspect, to save the son of the Venus-Aphrodite who had bested them in the judgment of Paris that brought about the Trojan War in the first place. (The question of rescuing a doomed warrior comes up one more time in the *Iliad* when Zeus asks his fellow Olympians whether to spare Hector at *Iliad* 22.168f.; here it is Athena who brusquely argues in the negative and descends to earth in person to help Achilles kill Hector.)

Virgil understands the relationship between the two Iliadic scenes, each concerned with the removal of a hero fighting on the Trojan side from imminent death in battle, each preceded by a divine conversation with Hera. Zeus decided to let Sarpedon die, Poseidon decided to save Aeneas; the Aeneas of the *Iliad* was thus a Sarpedon who was allowed to live. But in both cases, Hera spoke against divine intervention. Now, in a similar conversation with Jupiter, the Juno-Hera of the *Aeneid* has reversed herself, wishing to save the "guiltless"—"*insontem*" (10.630)—Turnus.[13] The war in Italy has itself reversed the *Iliad*, so that now Aeneas and the Trojans find themselves playing the roles of Achilles and the Greeks, while Turnus and the Italians have to play the roles of the doomed Trojans.[14] Turnus is put in the position of *both* the Homeric Aeneas and Sarpedon: he is saved and not saved by Juno, who only succeeds in buying him a short reprieve. The question of whether this now

---

12. On this doubling of the model of the dialogue of Zeus and Hera over the fate of Sarpedon, see Feeney, 1999, 186–189.

13. The adjective "*insontem*" applied to Turnus not only links him to the "ἀναίτιος" Aeneas of *Iliad* 20 but also contrasts him to Mezentius later in Book 10, who declares himself "*sontem*" (10.854), guilty of crimes against his people and indirectly responsible for the death of his son Lausus.

14. For these reversals of roles, see Anderson, 1957; Lyne, 1987, 104–113.

Aeneas-like Turnus will be saved from death is not answered until the final moment of the poem, when Aeneas indeed seems to kill an alter ego or former self.[15] In the *Iliad*, Hera offers a kind of compromise to Zeus; let Sarpedon die, but let his dead body be removed from the fighting and sent back to his homeland in Lycia by the divine transport of Death and Sleep (*Il.* 16.450–457); her proposal is duly carried out by Apollo (*Il.* 16.666–683).[16] (In still another Virgilian reprise of this scene in Book 11.593–594, Diana, Apollo's twin sister, promises to carry the corpse and armor of Camilla, enclosed in a hollow cloud—"*nube cava*"—back to her homeland.) The boat that carries Turnus out of battle takes him back to his homeland and the city of his father, Daunus—"*Dauni defertur ad urbem*" (10.688). This, too, is a compromise— "*hactenus indulsisse uacat*" (10.625)—now offered *by* Jupiter *to* Juno, even as he warns her not to get her hopes up: Turnus gets home alive for now, but he is living on borrowed time.

The tactic by which Juno lures Turnus into the boat recalls still another Iliadic passage and affords him another heroic role. At the end of *Iliad* 21, as Achilles is bearing down upon the city gates of Troy, open to receive the Trojan warriors whom the Greek hero is driving before him, Apollo first sends out Agenor to face Achilles, then encloses Agenor in a cloud of mist and takes his place. In the likeness of Agenor, the god runs away from Achilles, who chases him up and down the battlefield, while the routed Trojans reenter the city (*Il.* 21.600–611). Virgil's imitation combines these two moments: Juno makes a phantom likeness of Aeneas out of mist, who runs fleeing from the pursuing Turnus. He also asks his reader to remember *Iliad* 5.449–453, where the same Apollo creates an image of Aeneas, left on the battlefield for the Greeks and Trojans to fight over, while he has meanwhile covered the real Aeneas with a cloud of mist and carried him out of battle. Again Virgil puts together scenes that Homer himself had linked in the *Iliad*. The effect of these blurred Homeric identities is brilliantly ironic. Turnus, who earlier laid claim in Book 9 (742) to the role of Achilles, the top warrior, only gets to play Achilles in Book 10 at the moment that he runs away from the battlefield. Chasing the phantom Aeneas, Turnus briefly resembles the Achilles from whom the Aeneas of the *Iliad* needed to be rescued. In Book 12, with tables turned, it will be Turnus who flees before the Achilles-like Aeneas (12.742–765) in a reprise of Hector's flight before Achilles in *Iliad* 22. In effect, Turnus is already

---

15. Quint, 1993, 68–80; Lyne, 1987, 132–135; Lipking, 1981, 86–88.
16. Barchiesi, 1984, 18 [2015, 6–7].

running away here in Book 10 without realizing it.[17] By following the false Aeneas into the waiting boat that floats away and carries him out of combat, Turnus proves to be the warrior who needs to be rescued, and he is overcome by shame (10.666–688). He ends up playing the Homeric self of his enemy Aeneas, the hero's *doppelgänger*.[18] The scene, moreover, may exorcise that Homeric Aeneas, along with Turnus, from *Aeneid* 10. The Aeneas who appears in the rest of Book 10 is less like his old mocking Iliadic self, less like the mocking Patroclus or merciless Achilles. He now begins to show some glimmerings of humanity and piety, a Virgilian hero rather than a Homeric one.

Mezentius and Orodes

Turnus's departure clears the field for Mezentius. If Turnus fails in his self-proclaimed role as the Achilles of Italy, the irony against him is complicated by Mezentius's assumption of the model of Achilles for much of the rest of the book. Mezentius, not Turnus, is a worthy opponent for the Achillean Aeneas. Virgil aligns the Homeric models according to the age distinctions I have mentioned above: the youthful Pallas and Lausus do not imitate Achilles; the mature but still young and unmarried Turnus imitates Achilles for one brief moment, illusory and ignominious; the older Mezentius and Aeneas, both of them fathers, repeatedly imitate Achilles. The narrative of Book 10 leads us to the confrontations of increasingly older and mightier fighters.

But Mezentius—like Aeneas—plays other Iliadic roles as well, as Virgil continues his practice of alternating and juxtaposing Homeric models. Mezentius's brief exchange with another warrior, the minor character Orodes, during his *aristeia* that precedes his meeting with Aeneas produces another chiastic ring composition—*abcba*—of Homeric imitation. After felling Orodes, Mezentius at 10.736 strives to recover his spear and places his foot

---

17. In Book 12, Aeneas is not the fleet-footed Achilles, because of the residual effects of the arrow wound to his knee (746–747). Homer suggests something similar about the Achilles who pursues Apollo-in-the-likeness-of-Agenor, for Agenor has struck Achilles on the greave beneath his knee (*Iliad* 21.594); it may have slowed Achilles down. By the time he meets Hector in *Iliad* 22, however, Achilles appears fully recovered.

18. Or a double of the Aeneas of the *Aeneid* itself, who escapes in flight from the fighting at Troy, builds ships and sails to his distant paternal homeland of Italy. Turnus also looks here like Cleopatra (and Antony), fleeing by ship from Actium on the shield of Aeneas (8.707–713); Turnus briefly considers suicide (10.680–686), like the vanquished rivals of Augustus and, in the poem, like Dido at the end of Book 4. Juno restrains him.

on the prone but still breathing Orodes, a gesture that recalls Patroclus placing his foot on the living Sarpedon (*Il.* 16.503). When in the next two verses, 10.737–738, Mezentius boasts to his followers that he has killed the tall Orodes, a hardly contemptible part of the battle, he is exaggerating, since Orodes has just been brought onstage for his only appearance in the *Aeneid*, scarcely more important than the other warriors whom Virgil lists as the victims of Mezentius's *aristeia*; the extent of the boast becomes evident when measured against its Homeric model: Achilles boasting to *his* followers after killing Hector in *Iliad* 22.391–394. The expiring Orodes now responds at verses 10.739–741 and prophesies that Mezentius does not have long to live and will die on the same battlefield; the model has shifted again, this time to the words of the dying Patroclus to the victorious Hector at *Iliad* 16.851–854, announcing that Hector will soon fall to Achilles. Mezentius's smiling response, verses 10.743–744, commanding Orodes to die and placing himself in the hands of the king and father of the gods, brings us back to that very moment later in the *Iliad* prophesied by Patroclus and to the Achilles who tells the now-dead Hector to die and who leaves Zeus to determine his own death (*Il.* 22.365–366). In verses 10.744–746, Mezentius now wrests his spear out of the body of Orodes and Orodes dies, just as Sarpedon died when Patroclus retrieved his spear from Sarpedon's chest. The vignette has thus come full circle, creating an *abcba* pattern: Orodes has played in succession the victims Sarpedon–Hector–Patroclus–Hector–Sarpedon, Mezentius the victors Patroclus–Achilles–Hector–Achilles–Patroclus.

One effect of this almost too precious Alexandrianism is to suggest the formulaic interchangeability of the Homeric models that Virgil is following: one heroic death is much like the next, and we may remember that Hector too stepped on the body of Patroclus to remove his spear as Patroclus had stepped on the body of Sarpedon (*Il.* 16.862; *Il.* 16.503–505), that the last words of the dying Hector too had predicted the eventual death of his conqueror Achilles at the Skaian gates (*Il.* 22.358–360). The same Homeric models, moreover, underlie the death of Pallas at the center of the book and the death of the nonentity Orodes; in the *Aeneid* as well as the *Iliad*, these deaths seem interchangeable.

Mezentius, Lausus, and Aeneas

Mezentius has so far played the roles of Iliadic victors (although these will become victims, in turn, inside and beyond Homer's poem): Achilles, Hector, Patroclus. Now, when he meets Aeneas and his own eventual defeat and death, Mezentius for a moment plays the role that Virgil's fiction has designated as the emblematic Homeric victim: Sarpedon. The spear of Aeneas passes through Mezentius's shield and wounds him in his groin; with the aid of Lausus and his followers, Mezentius is conveyed out of the fighting. His progress is impeded by the spear that is still embedded in the shield, which he drags along behind him—"*ligatus / cedebat clipeoque inimicum hastile trahebat*" (10.794–795). The somewhat unexpected Homeric model for this scene is the wounding of Sarpedon, not in Book 16, but earlier in the *Iliad* in Book 5 (660–667). There a spear strikes Sarpedon in the thigh and remains stuck there, rather than in the hero's shield, weighing him down and dragging behind him as his companions carry him out of battle (*Il.* 5.664–665). Subsequently Mezentius recovers beneath a tree, surrounded by his companions (10.833–835); Sarpedon similarly lies beneath an oak tree to have the spear removed from his thigh and to recover at *Iliad* 5.692–698. The Iliadic reminiscences are clear, and they include the mighty but now vulnerable Mezentius among the other "brothers" of Sarpedon of Book 10; his time, too, is numbered.

Mezentius's two imitations of the Sarpedon of *Iliad* 5 frame the death of Lausus, who now takes his father's place in combat against Aeneas. An immature warrior "equal," we have been told earlier (10.431), to Pallas, Lausus is no more of a match for Aeneas than Pallas was for Turnus. So Aeneas tells Lausus in words that are both a battlefield taunt and a warning not to get carried away by filial piety: "*quo moriture ruis maioraque uiribus audes / fallit te incautum pietas tua*" (10.811–812); then, his wrath kindled (10.813–814), Aeneas kills the young man. The moment of Lausus's death, as his life leaves his body and descends to the shades (10.819–820), contains a double Iliadic echo, since it imitates the formula Homer used to describe both the deaths of Patroclus (*Il.* 16.856–857) and Hector (*Il.* 22.362–363). Here, too, Virgil exploits links already made by the *Iliad* to suggest how heroic deaths have become identical and to blur together the models he evokes: Lausus plays both Patroclus and Hector, Aeneas both Hector and Achilles.

This doubling of models superbly focuses the different perspectives of Mezentius and Aeneas on Lausus's death. For Mezentius, Lausus is his Patroclus whose death has rendered life meaningless and that he now seeks, like Achilles, to revenge—just as Pallas is the Patroclus of Aeneas, who avenges Pallas by killing Turnus in Book 12. For Aeneas, however, Lausus is a dead Hector to whom he can show the pity and civilized restraint of the Achilles of *Iliad* 24, the Achilles moved and appeased by the appeal of Priam, Hector's father. He acknowledged the "*pietas*" of the living Lausus. Now, as the young man's corpse evokes the image of his own filial piety (*"pietatis imago"*; 10.824), the pious Aeneas (*"pius Aeneas"*; 10.826) speaks to the dead Lausus. He promises to give his body back for burial and also lets Lausus keep his armor (10.825–828): this last, of course, in pointed contrast to Turnus, who spoiled Pallas of his baldric (but who *did* return the body of Pallas for burial). At verses 10.831–832, he himself lifts up the body of Lausus, recalling the gesture of Achilles in *Iliad* 24.589–590, who lifts the body of Hector onto a litter and then into Priam's wagon. Here is the better side both of Aeneas and of his Achillean model: it is contrasted to Mezentius, who will now himself play Achilles opposite Aeneas, but an Achilles in this case in furious pursuit of vengeance and of his own death.

It is of course not so simple: Turnus might otherwise be spared when he makes a similar appeal to Aeneas's filial piety at the end of the poem (12.932–936).[19] The kind words that Aeneas speaks are addressed to a Lausus who is already dead, and whom Aeneas earlier taunted and killed in savage Achillean anger. When, in verses 10.829–830, he offers the dead Lausus the consolation of having fallen before the hand of the great Aeneas—*"Aeneae magni dextra cadis"*—there is a suggestion of boasting, not unlike Mezentius vaunting his killing of Orodes. The moment, furthermore, recalls the words of the Achilles who refuses to spare the live suppliant Lycaon at *Iliad* 21.106–109. The tone is very different: Achilles tells Lycaon not to complain since even he, the mighty Achilles, will also die in battle. The reminiscence brings us back to the Aeneas who earlier in the fighting of Book 10 imitated this Iliadic episode and, in his anger at the death of Pallas, killed the suppliants Magus, Tarquitus, and Liger. The first sought mercy with a double appeal to the piety of Aeneas, filial and paternal, invoking both the spirit of his father Anchises and his hopes in his son Iulus (10.524–525); the last appealed to the parents who bore Aeneas (10.597). In that context, the epithet *"pius"* attached to Aeneas as he taunted Lucagus (10.591), Liger's dying brother, had seemed particularly loaded. Virgil now appears to ask the reader to measure the distance that Aeneas has come from his earlier merciless behavior, from the behavior of the Homeric model of Achilles. The fact remains, however, that Aeneas—like the Achilles of the *Iliad*—only shows piety to dead rather than living victims.

---

19. The relationship between the scene of Aeneas and Lausus and the end of the *Aeneid* has been explored by Barchiesi, 1984, 66–70 [2015, 45–49]; Putnam, 1981, 139–156. On the tension between the subjectivity of Aeneas and the imperatives of his mission in this episode, see Conte, 1986, 176–179.

Aeneas does demonstrate a new restraint and defensive passivity in the way he fights. He hesitates before he attacks Lausus, and he twice shelters himself behind his shield, first before the shower of weapons that Lausus and his companions cast at him (10.801–810), then before the missiles of Mezentius (10.886–887).

I return to this scene in the following chapter.

It is Mezentius, grief-stricken over the death of Lausus, who takes the offensive, cast initially in the role of an Achilles out to revenge Patroclus. Mezentius throws dust over his head (10.844), just as Achilles had befouled himself at the news of the death of Patroclus in *Iliad* 18.23–25. He speaks to his faithful horse Rhoebus (10.861–866); Achilles had spoken to his horses (*Il.* 19.400–403), rebuking them for not bringing Patroclus safely out of battle.[20] But, once again, Virgil shifts Homeric models, and Mezentius's actions in battle recall not those of Achilles but rather of Patroclus. He calls three times and circles Aeneas three times on horseback, recalling the Patroclus who calls three times and charges three times against the Trojans at *Iliad* 16.783–785, just before Apollo strikes him down. It is appropriate that Mezentius, the *"contemptor diuum,"* as he is called at *Aeneid* 7.648, and who has just declared that he does not give any regard to the gods—*"nec diuum parcimus ulli"* (10.880)—should imitate Homer's Patroclus at the latter's moment of fatal hubris: Achilles had admonished Patroclus not to pursue his success in battle too far lest some god, Apollo in particular, lay him low (*Il.* 16.91–95), and Apollo himself had warned Patroclus off as he tried—three times here as well—to storm the wall of Troy (*Il.* 16.702–711). Mezentius's impiety—even as he attacks Aeneas in the name of paternal piety—contrasts him to the Trojan hero, and one of its measures is that Mezentius does not fight fair. It is true that the wounded Mezentius has no choice but to reenter battle on horseback, but his attack on an Aeneas who is on foot presents both an unequal combat—*"pugna ... iniqua"* (10.889)—and an anachronistic one: a modern Roman cavalryman against a Homeric warrior. (His being on horse *does* even the odds between the older, almost elderly Mezentius and the younger, in-his-prime Aeneas.)

Mezentius is still in the role of Patroclus when Aeneas vanquishes him, yet Aeneas is not playing the role of Hector, the slayer of Patroclus, but, in an odd twist, of *Sarpedon* in the earlier duel with Patroclus in *Iliad* 16. Aeneas wounds

---

20. See Thome, 1979, 139–151. The scene also imitates the words of the blinded Polyphemus to his head ram in *Odyssey* 9.447f.; see Glenn, 1971, 129–155.

and kills Rhoebus (10.891–894), whose fall brings down and traps Mezentius beneath him; Sarpedon had cast his spear, missed Patroclus, and inadvertently killed Pedasos (*Il.* 16.467), the mortal horse attached to the team of steeds drawing the chariot of Patroclus, the horses whom Achilles later speaks to and rebukes.[21] It is, in fact, surprising that Aeneas—who, as the mightiest warrior of the *Aeneid*, ought to correspond to Achilles at the top of the Homeric ladder of victors and victims on which Virgil constructs the fiction of Book 10 (Achilles–Hector–Patroclus–Sarpedon)—should, in the final heroic act of the book, assume the role of Sarpedon at the ladder's bottom rung. Like all the other main characters of the book, Aeneas too plays Sarpedon, but a Sarpedon who, in this case, wins. Unlike Sarpedon, he deliberately wounds the steed of his adversary to overcome the disadvantage in which he finds himself when fighting the mounted Mezentius—the disadvantage that may make Aeneas *seem* like the weaker Sarpedon in the duel. By the end of Book 10, Aeneas does indeed assume the role of Achilles, as Mezentius's plea that Aeneas guarantee his burial (10.904–906) corresponds to Hector's plea to the still unappeased Achilles to return his body for burial in *Iliad* 22.338–343.[22] The book thus closes where one would expect, with the normative epic model of Achilles and Hector—and it looks forward to Book 12, where the final duel of Aeneas and Turnus will elaborately replay the duel of Achilles and Hector in *Iliad* 22. The narrative transition of Aeneas from the role of Sarpedon to that of Achilles is managed, however, with one more virtuoso instance of Virgil's combinatory imitation of Homer. In verses 10.897–898, Aeneas taunts the fallen Mezentius: "*ubi nunc Mezentius acer et illa / effera uis animi?*" ("Where now is fierce Mezentius and that untamed might of soul?"). Structurally this moment recalls the taunt of Achilles over Hector in *Iliad* 22.331–336, but the

---

21. This is a parallel omitted by Knauer, 1964, who, 420, notes the model of the killing of the unnamed horse of Nestor at *Iliad* 8.81–86 by an arrow from the bow of Paris. Nestor's horse is wounded in the head like Rhoebus and similarly rears up. But Virgil is also imitating the killing of Pedasos, who (a), like Rhoebus, has a name, (b) is wounded with a spear like Rhoebus, (c) is wounded in the shoulder (16.467), while Rhoebus, in falling, dislocates his shoulder "*eiecto ... armo*" (10.894). See Janko, 1994, 378–379, on the relationship of the two Iliadic scenes through the cyclic epic *Aithiopis* in which, in the battle against Memnon, Nestor's horse is wounded by an arrow of Paris, leading to the death of Antilochus; see Pindar, *Pythian*, 6.28–39. The resonance of this allusion for the Nestor-Antilochus-Memnon story will be discussed in the next chapter. In a way that is typical of his art, Virgil probably recognized the kinship already existing between the two slayings of horses in the *Iliad* and combined them together in the slaying of Rhoebus.

22. On the question of what happens to Mezentius's body, see Fratantuono, 2007, 322–324.

words of Aeneas, with their *"ubi nunc"* formula, recall a different Iliadic passage, the friendly taunt of *Sarpedon* who urges Hector back into the fighting at *Iliad* 5.472: "Where now, Hector, has gone that spirit that was yours?" Even as Aeneas goes from being a Sarpedon to become an Achilles, his identity blurs between the overlapping Homeric models: between the *Iliad*'s designated victim and glorious victor. He is both Sarpedon *and* Achilles at once.

A Question of Survival

Sarpedon finds a sister in the *Aeneid* along with so many brothers. The death of Camilla in Book 11 (532–867) follows a familiar model. Here is the analysis of K. W. Gransden.

> Camilla's death is a re-enactment of some aspects of the deaths of Sarpedon and Patroclus in *Iliad* XVI and thus to some extent "doubles" the death of Pallas in *Aeneid* X. Arruns' prayer to Apollo to allow him to kill Camilla and return safely corresponds to Achilles' prayer on behalf of Patroclus in *Iliad* XVI, while the divine removal of Camilla's body to her homeland for burial is modelled on the divine removal of Sarpedon's body in the *Iliad*. Arruns' prayer, like Achilles', is only half granted: Patroclus kills Sarpedon but is himself killed by Hector, while Arruns kills Camilla but is himself killed by Opis. Apollo blinds Patroclus in a mist, and it is Apollo who allows Camilla to die: she too goes blindly (*caeca*, 781) to her doom. When Arruns kills her he assumes the Homeric role of Euphorbus, the otherwise unknown soldier who gave Patroclus his first wound and was subsequently killed; Arruns like Euphorbus is overcome with fear at his own deed and seeks refuge in flight (*fugit ... exterritus*, 806).[23]

Camilla, too, plays the roles of both Sarpedon and Patroclus, her identity shifting between the two Homeric figures. As Gransden points out, the heroine's death repeats the pattern of the death of Pallas, and, we can now add, it repeats the pattern of Book 10 as a whole in which all the major fighters are cast, at one moment or another, as Sarpedon and Patroclus. Yet it is the identification of Camilla with Sarpedon upon which the *Aeneid* insists at the moment of her introduction into the poem. She is the *last* Italian warrior listed in the catalog of Book 7 (803.f), closing the book, just as Sarpedon is placed last

---

23. Gransden, 1991, 19.

in the muster of the Trojans and their allies in the corresponding final lines of *Iliad* 2 (876–877).

The larger *Aeneid* also insists upon our remembering Sarpedon more than Patroclus. It takes a Trojan point of view and names Sarpedon four times, in Aeneas's opening words in Book 1, in his bastard son Antiphates in Book 9, twice, as we have seen in Book 10, in the brothers of Sarpedon and when Jupiter himself remembers Sarpedon. By contrast, the poem never mentions Patroclus by name. Its versions of Patroclus might be seen as the necessary corollaries or attributes of its versions of Sarpedon: so many Sarpedon-like victims imply as many Patroclus-like slayers.

But Virgil's evocations of Patroclus have their own independent logic. In the wake of the *Iliad, all* epic warriors may be versions of Patroclus, dressed in the armor of Achilles but merely an imitation of him. That is, they all testify to their belatedness with regard to the great epic model of the *Iliad* and its central hero. Turnus, at the height of the glory of his *aristeia* in Book 9, boasts that an Achilles has been found in him in Italy (9.742), although one who does not need the armor of Vulcan (9.148), and he appears to confirm the dire prophecy of the sibyl at Cumae that another Achilles has been born in Latium (6.89). Turnus later has to admit in Book 11 that it is Aeneas who indeed wears armor made by Vulcan similar—"*paria*"—to that of Achilles (11.439–440), and that the Trojan hero might even excel Achilles himself: "*uel magnum praestet Achillem*" (11.438). The subjunctive mood here is telling: Virgil, if not Turnus, might like to claim that Aeneas and the *Aeneid* overgo Achilles and his poem, but it is more likely that Aeneas is only the next best thing, a later, facsimile Achilles: a Patroclus whose armor is itself an imitation of the armor of Achilles.

Virgil nonetheless couples Sarpedon and Patroclus, not only as victim and slayer but also as parallel victims. When the *gods* of the *Aeneid* mourn for a hero about to die—Hercules for Pallas, Juno for Turnus, Diana for Camilla—they do so as the Zeus of the *Iliad* mourned for Sarpedon. When Virgil's *human* characters mourn and seek revenge for a hero's death—Aeneas for Pallas, Mezentius for Lausus—they do so as the *Iliad*'s Achilles mourned for Patroclus. Patroclus's death looks back on the death of Sarpedon—we remember those spears being pulled out of bodies—and anticipates the death of Patroclus's own slayer, Hector, in Book 22, while both Patroclus and Hector prophesy the future deaths of their killers, Hector and Achilles.

Virgil exploits these likenesses and the interchangeability of victor and victim in the close alternation of models that has the warriors of the *Aeneid* switching between Iliadic roles from one verse to the next. He does so in part to suggest the problem of distinguishing *morally* among his characters once they are engaged in battle, particularly the problem of judging his hero who at times seems only minimally different from the other combatants—an Aeneas who can at one moment go after the spoils of enemy armor just as much as Turnus, forswear them at another; who can first imitate a merciless Achilles, then a compassionate one; a Mezentius who shares the familial love and piety of Aeneas but also impiously disdains the gods. War is the leveler of differences, especially in Book 10, where Jupiter himself sits back in neutrality and leaves matters to the fates. The problem is only compounded when the war in question looks like a civil one, a war—as Book 12 comments—between peoples destined to live together in eternal peace. How does one judge the victor and loser of such a conflict? The *Aeneid* comes to a mixed verdict.

At the same time, by allowing all his warriors to play Sarpedon—and by allowing Turnus, Mezentius, and Aeneas all three to play Sarpedon in alternation with Achilles—Virgil offers a reading of the chain of heroic deaths in the *Iliad* on which the warfare of Book 10 is modeled. Sarpedon and Achilles at either end of this chain may be equivalent because Achilles, no less than Sarpedon, is fated to die, even if his death, prophesied to him by Hector but already known to Achilles, *will* take place outside the action of the epic. Each Homeric warrior's glorious moment of victory implies that he will become the victim of the glory of another—and the supreme irony of Achilles' fate is that he will be brought down by the most inglorious warrior of all, Paris. The *Iliad* is a poem from which it is hard to get out alive.[24]

Some heroes manage to escape, however. The Trojan exception, as we have seen, was Aeneas himself, and the *Aeneid*, like the *Odyssey*, is an epic of survivors. The logic of the multiple Sarpedons in the second, Iliadic half of the *Aeneid* is spelled out in the epic's first mention of his name, in those first words Aeneas speaks in Book 1. We return to this passage already discussed in chapter 1. As he faces the storm sent by Juno to wreck his fleet, Aeneas regrets that he has survived at all; when he thinks of those who died at Troy, we find that Sarpedon occupies an important place in the hero's imagination.

> o terque quaterque beati,
> quis ante ora patrum Troiae sub moenibus altis

---

24. Perhaps no one was supposed to survive. See Slatkin, 1991, 118–122, for the argument that behind the *Iliad* lies a myth in which the Trojan War was designed to wipe out the race of heroes.

contigit oppetere! O Danaum fortissime gentis
Tydide! mene Iliacis occumbere campis
non potuisse tuaque animam hanc effundere dextra,
saeuus ubi Aeacidae telo iacet Hector, ubi ingens
Sarpedon, ubi tot Simois correpta sub undis
scuta uirum galeasque et fortia corpora uoluit! (1.94–101)

O three and four times blessed whose lot was to perish before the eyes of his fathers beneath the lofty walls of Troy! O Son of Tydeus, bravest of the Greek folk! why was it not possible for me to fall before your hand on the Ilian fields and pour out my life-spirit, where fierce Hector lies beneath the spear of the grandson of Aeacus, where huge Sarpedon ..., where the Simois has seized so many shields and helmets and brave bodies of men and rolls them beneath its waves!

Aeneas first recalls his own rescue by the gods, carried out of battle by Venus and Apollo when he was about to be killed by Diomedes in *Iliad* 5; then he contrasts it with the death of Hector, whom the gods refused to save but instead allowed to perish beneath the spear of Achilles in *Iliad* 22, the same Achilles from whom Aeneas had to be rescued for a second time in the *Iliad* in Book 20, when Poseidon and Hera debated his fate. (We may note that this opening scene of the *Aeneid* seems to restage that Iliadic moment, as Juno-Hera sends the storm that would wreck the fleet of Aeneas, while Neptune-Poseidon quiets the waves and once again saves the Trojan hero.) Aeneas cannot bear to call the Greek foes who almost killed him by their real names, but only by patronymic displacement, which only increases as his thoughts move from the lesser to the greater Greek hero. And he then evokes Sarpedon, whom, like Hector, the gods refused to rescue, but whose dead body they removed from the dusty battlefield. Patroclus, the killer of Sarpedon, is conspicuously not named.

Commentators, arguing that "*ubi ingens / Sarpedon*" has to be understood to be the subject of the same verb "*iacet*" in verse 99 of which Hector is also the subject, have chided Virgil of nodding and of having forgotten that Sarpedon's body does *not* lie in the fields of Troy but was instead carried back to his Lycian homeland.[25] But Virgil knows what he is doing. The grammatical ambiguity suggests that Aeneas himself has been brought up short when thinking about Sarpedon, over whose lifeless body he himself thought he was

---

25. See, for example, Conington, 1884, 2:16.

battling in *Iliad* 16 (536f.): the mortal Aeneas would presumably not have seen Apollo lift the dead hero out of the fighting. The body of Hector lying on the battlefield is surrounded in these verses by two missing bodies: that of the living Aeneas rescued by the gods, that of the dead Sarpedon removed by the gods. The verse seems to turn into the question: "where, indeed is/was huge Sarpedon?"; one grim explanation of what became of the hero's body is offered in the final memorable lines that describe the river Simois sweeping away armor and bodies under its waves into anonymous burial. Sarpedon is assimilated here with all the victims—here, it appears, Greek as well as Trojan—of the killing fields of Troy. Why, Aeneas asks, was he rescued in their place? Why, especially if he is only to drown now, in a similar watery grave, off the shores of Carthage?[26]

Aeneas's words suggest that he is aware, at least in some part of his mind, conscious or unconscious, of what Virgil himself has gleaned from careful study of the relations of Homer's Aeneas to the other Trojan heroes of the *Iliad*. This Aeneas is already in the *Iliad* a kind of mirror-figure or double of Hector and Sarpedon. He is the more minor character whose rescue by divine intervention suggests a way out of the epic slaughter that is denied to these preeminent Trojan victims. These opening words of Virgil's Aeneas also predict the patterns of reversal in the imitations of the *Iliad* that characterize the warfare in Italy in the second half of the *Aeneid*. The Italian foes of Aeneas will themselves be cast as the Trojans of the *Iliad*, and they will have to play the roles of these victims, including the former Iliadic self of Aeneas. Thus the Aeneas of the *Aeneid* plays Diomedes and Achilles to the Homeric *Aeneas* of Turnus, Achilles to the Hectors of Mezentius and Turnus—and *all* the victims of battle, on both the Italian (Turnus, Lausus, Mezentius, Camilla) and the Trojan side (Pallas, Orodes), play Sarpedon. The second *Iliad* of the *Aeneid* is hardly less of a death trap than Homer's original.

And once again, Aeneas survives. The *Aeneid* conserves the Roman future at the expense of all those peoples and their possible futures that history leaves behind: young Italy dies—the Arcadian Pallas, the Etruscan Lausus, the Italians Turnus and Camilla—so that Aeneas and his ever diminishing Trojan remnant can survive. The hero will marry Lavinia and create the Roman *gens* that will replace and absorb those other peoples as well as submerge, so

---

26. O'Hara, 1990, 104–111, tellingly associates these verses with the story of the later disappearance of Aeneas after a battle beside the river Numicius. The hero's body was not recovered, either deified in heaven or simply lost beneath the waters.

Jupiter decrees to the appeased Juno, the identity of the Trojans themselves: "*subsident Teucri*" (12.836). Aeneas himself may play Sarpedon at the end of Book 10, bringing this entire book of Sarpedon to an appropriate ring-composition close or chiasmus. But just as the Iliadic Aeneas was a Sarpedon whom the gods, in his case, decided to save, so Virgil's Aeneas is a Sarpedon who defeats his Patroclus-like foe Mezentius and fights on to see another day. The haunting presence of Sarpedon, not only in Book 10 but in the surrounding Books 9 and 11 as well, thus names all those who do not make it out of the *Aeneid*, those who fall in epic battle and who are submerged beneath the violent tides of history. They do so in contrast to the survivor Aeneas, the exception who proves a grim historical rule.[27]

This history, Book 10 suggests, possesses a further, not-so-secret irony. The Roman nation that Aeneas begins to found will be handed over so many centuries later *not* to his and Lavinia's posterity but to that of Iulus—the Julian line of Augustus that refounds a state to which, as the heir of the older son of Aeneas, it may have all along been entitled. At the beginning of Book 10, verses 44–50, Venus professes her willingness to sacrifice her son Aeneas provided that her grandson Iulus be preserved: she may be disingenuous, but she nonetheless reveals her priorities, which may be the priorities of the poem's dynastic ideology as well.[28] In the chiastic structure of Book 10, Aeneas loses his young comrade Pallas as Mezentius loses his son Lausus, and readers may well feel that Mezentius has a greater cause of grief.[29] But this structure also suggests that the death of Pallas—the central Sarpedon-Patroclus figure of the book—substitutes for the death of Aeneas's own son: Iulus. It is in the group of warriors symmetrically arranged in verses 10.123–134 as a kind of cornice and defensive ring around Iulus in the middle, himself described as a jewel mounted in gold—"*qualis gemma micat, fuluum quae diuidit aurum*" (10.134)— that we meet Clarus and Thaemon, the brothers of Sarpedon (10.125–126), themselves doomed to fall before Turnus with a scarce, barely recognizable

---

[27]. It is tempting to see these deaths as somehow sacrificial substitutions for the hero who survives, and the logic of sacrifice does appear in the *Aeneid*, particularly in the opening scene where only *one* of Aeneas's companions, the steersman Orontes, dies, a one-for-many substitution that will be repeated in the death of Palinurus at the end of Book 5. See O'Hara, 1990, especially 19–24, 82–84, 106–110; Nicoll, 1988; Hardie, 1993, 32–35; Quint, 1993, 83–96; Miller, 2003, 52–91. But the collective victims of war and history do not seem to qualify as sacrifices except to a very cruel deity.

[28]. See chapter 2, note 45.

[29]. But see the argument in chapter 7 below, a further complication.

mention in Book 12, two supernumeraries.[30] Like Pallas, perhaps all the Sarpedon-like victims of the *Aeneid* are dying—all the casualties on both sides of Rome's civil wars have died—for the sake of Iulus and a specifically Augustan future. In this case, the survival of Aeneas is of secondary importance: the poem's hero may himself be one more expendable brother of Sarpedon.

30. The passage is a good example of Virgil's use of chiasmus described in this study. Here it is employed to describe what is itself a circular situation. The Rutulians have encircled the walls of the Trojan camp (*"circum"* … *"cingere"*; 118–119), and the thinly ranked Trojans themselves now form a defensive ring on the walls that is compared to a crown (*"cinxere corona"*; 122). The Trojans form the first line of defense (123–125) and are accompanied, whether in this first line or not, by the Lycian Clarus and Thaemon (125–126), followed by Mysian allies (127–131). In their midst and in the middle of the passage is the uncovered (without the protection of a helmet, but also as yet uncrowned) head of Iulus (132–138), who is not only compared to a gem mounted in surrounding gold but who, in the last words of the lines devoted to him, wears a gold circlet (*"circulus auro"*; 138) that binds his hair in back. (Is a crown far away?) He is enclosed on the other side of the passage by Ismarus, the ally and specialist in poisoned arrows who hails from the golden Pactolus in Lydia (139–142), and then by the Trojans Mnestheus and Capys (143–145). So the order and sense of the passage shows Trojan warriors on the outside, allies and then Iulus on the inside: Trojan/Lycian–Mysian–Iulus–Lydian–Trojan. The concentric structure suggests a hierarchy in battle prowess: the Trojans fight man to man at the front of the fighting, the allies behind them use projectiles, whether Mysian Acmon's huge rock (127–128) or the corresponding envenomed arrows of Ismarus (139–140)—blunt force balanced on one side of Iulus against fraud on the other—and we have seen Iulus himself back in Book 9 make his first battle kill, shooting Numanus from afar with his bow and arrow (9.590–671) after Numanus has called the Trojans to come out from behind their camp and fight like men. The play between the names of Mysian Menestheus (129) and Trojan Mnestheus (143) adds to the patterning as does the implicit play between Lycia and Lydia; the latter is not named, but in the ensuing passage we are reminded that Aeneas's new Etruscan allies are the *"gens Lydia"* (10.155). The mention in the last line (145) of Capys, from whom Capua will take its name, seems to bring us to Italy from Asia Minor where the passage began in line 123 with its naming of Asius, and foretells the happy end of what is now the Trojan camp's desperate situation. Iulus will be saved.

In this light, Hardie, 1994, 14–18 suggests a similar pattern in Book 9: Pandarus and Bitias, those pinelike warriors from Mount Ida, die, like Euryalus and Nisus, as immature adolescents who fail to cross the initiatory threshold to warrior adulthood that Iulus himself does cross by shooting Numanus with an arrow in verses 9.590f. Young warriors fall around the chosen Iulus.

7

The Second Second Patroclus and the End of the *Aeneid*

VIRGIL ADDS ANOTHER LAYER of allusion to Book 10, on top of the patterns observed in the preceding chapter. Those, we saw, unified the battlefield action of the book through the models of the deaths of Sarpedon and Patroclus. Virgil also structures the book by basing *both* of its key heroic duels—the slaying of Pallas by Turnus and the killings of Lausus, then Mezentius, by Aeneas—on another epic model, a non-Homeric one, that describes the post-Iliadic fighting at Troy. This is the death of Antilochus, the son of Nestor and the beloved of Achilles, at the hands of Memnon the Ethiopian; Achilles subsequently slew Memnon in turn.[1] The model not only shapes Book 10 but returns to govern the final moment of the *Aeneid*, Aeneas's vindictive killing of the suppliant Turnus.

The story of Antilochus, Memnon, and Achilles was recounted in the cyclical epic known as the *Aithiopis*, a text that is now lost to us. We know about it from other ancient sources. This model stands behind the apparent erotic, homosexual dimension of the relationship between Aeneas and the ephebe Pallas. The intensity of Aeneas's grief over Pallas is otherwise surprising: he has only known the young man for a couple of days. The more familiar epic

---

1. In an important, neglected article, Manton, 1962, notes many of the same parallels between the *Aeneid* and the Nestor-Antilochus-Memnon story that I am presenting here. We draw different conclusions. Fraenkel, 1932, pointed out the modeling of Lausus's death on the death of Antilochus. Kopff, 1981, 941 suggested that Evander's lament over Pallas in Book 11.151–181 was based on Nestor's mourning over Antilochus and, 944, hypothesized that a possible model for the final duel between Aeneas and Turnus in Book 12 might lie in Achilles' killing of Memnon in the lost *Aithiopis*. See also Gärtner, 2015, 557–558.

model of the *Iliad* makes Aeneas a second Achilles and Pallas a second Patroclus. But the relationship of the Homeric warriors is not an erotic one; even when Plato's character Phaedrus does make it erotic in the *Symposium* (179e–180b), he notes that Patroclus, not Achilles, was the older of the pair. But the Homer of the *Odyssey* and the heroic tradition had already produced a substitute Patroclus in Antilochus. After the death of Patroclus, Antilochus replaced Patroclus as a companion to Achilles, in this case a younger companion and, so ancient readers assumed, a sexual beloved. By identifying Pallas, the son of the Nestor-like, aged advisor Evander, with Antilochus, Virgil plays self-consciously with the secondary relationship of the *Aeneid* to the *Iliad*: his second Patroclus figure is modeled not only on Patroclus but on a second Patroclus figure. Moreover, as we shall see, Virgil distributes the model of Antilochus between Pallas and Pallas's counterpart in youth, Lausus, on the Italian side of the war in the second half of the *Aeneid*. By rewriting the death of Antilochus *twice* in Book 10, he makes not just Pallas and Lausus doubles of each other, he also makes doubles of their slayers, Turnus and Aeneas. In so doing, he further splits into characteristically chiastic doubles the Aeneas who, *as a Memnon*, kills Lausus in Book 10 and the Aeneas who kills Turnus at the end of the poem in Book 12 as an Achilles taking revenge *on a Memnon*.

Let us review the story of Antilochus and Achilles. The final book of the *Odyssey* describes Achilles' tomb and thus puts to rest not only its own story but the story of the *Iliad* as well. It recounts that while the bones of Achilles and Patroclus were buried together and mixed in a single golden jar, the tomb also contained in a separate urn the remains of "Antilochus, whom you prized above all / the rest of your companions after the death of Patroclus" (*Ody.* 24.78–79). Antilochus appears, paired with Patroclus in the same identical verse, as shades in company with the shade of Achilles, both in this underworld scene (*Ody.* 24.16) and in the earlier one of Book 11 (*Ody.* 11.468). Back in Book 3, Nestor had mourned for the death of his son Antilochus, whom he names directly after Achilles and Patroclus among the casualties at Troy (*Ody.* 3.109–112); in Book 4, Peisistratos sheds tears for his brother, "stately Antilochus / one whom the glorious son of the shining dawn had cut down" (*Ody.* 4.187–188). Pindar (*Pythia* 6.28–43) records that Ethiopian Memnon, the son of Aurora, killed Antilochus as the latter was coming to the rescue of Nestor on the battlefield, an exemplary case of filial piety. The *Aithiopis* recounted this incident and Achilles' subsequent killing of Memnon in revenge for Antilochus's death; it is an evident replaying of Hector's killing Patroclus and being killed, in turn, by the vengeful Achilles.

Where did the story that the *Odyssey* takes for granted come from? Antilochus appears in the *Iliad*, where we are told, through Menelaos, that he is youngest of the Greeks and fastest on foot (*Il.* 15.569–570). It is presumably because of his foot speed that Menelaos sends him to deliver the catastrophic news of Patroclus's death to Achilles (*Il.* 17.685–699; 18.1–34). Later at the funeral games in Book 23, Achilles specially favors Antilochus in the distribution of prizes, and the narrator explains that Nestor's son was Achilles' "beloved companion"—"*philos ... hetairos*" (*Il.* 23.556)—the same term used by Achilles himself to describe his relationship with Patroclus (*Il.* 18.80; cf. 17.411; 17.655).[2] Homer could be alluding to a preexistent tradition about Achilles and Antilochus. It is equally possible that this single verse of the *Iliad* provided the hint for the story of Antilochus as a second Patroclus that is known and registered in the *Odyssey* and that the *Aithiopis* poet would develop.[3] I do not wish to enter into this Homeric Question, nor do I have the competence to do so.

The youth of Antilochus made him an appropriate object of sexual love for Achilles in a way that the older Patroclus could not be. So the second-century CE Philostratus describes the heroic pair in his *Imagines*, rereading the *Iliad* in the process.

> That Achilles loved (*èran*) Antilochus you must have discovered in Homer, seeing Antilochus to be the youngest man in the Greek host and considering the half talent of gold that was given him after the contest [i.e., the footrace during the funeral games, *Il.* 23.796]. And it is he who brings word to Achilles that Patroclus has fallen, for Menalaüs cleverly devised this as a consolation to accompany the announcement, since Achilles' eyes were thus diverted to his loved one; and Antilochus laments in grief for his friend and restrains his hands lest he take his own life, while Achilles no doubt rejoices at the touch of the youth's hand and at the tears he sheds. (*Imagines* 2.7)[4]

In this account, Antilochus has already assumed the role of a replacement for Patroclus, even, it appears, before the death of Patroclus, in Achilles' affective life. Patroclus was his friend, the younger Antilochus was his lover.

---

2. Nagy, 1979, 105.
3. Burgess, 2004.
4. Philostratus, 1960, 155.

So Virgil's Pallas, a second Patroclus in literary history like Antilochus himself, plays the part of an ephebic younger companion to Aeneas. (Aeneas has a loyal friend in the rather shadowy Achates.) Pallas is the son of the Nestor figure Evander. Virgil models Aeneas's visit to Pallanteum in Book 8 on Telemachus's visit to Nestor in Pylos in Book 3 of the *Odyssey* (where Nestor mourns for Antilochus). As chapter 6 noted, Evander and Nestor are about the same age and are contemporaries in the time schemes of the *Aeneid*, the *Iliad*, and the *Odyssey*—and so are their sons, Pallas and Antilochus. (The *Odyssey* episode would, in fact, have taken place *a little after* Aeneas's meeting with Evander: who is imitating or being modeled on whom?) Evander plays the Nestor-like role of strategist too old for combat who recalls his own glory days: he provides an Etruscan alliance for Aeneas, then cites the prowess of his own youth at Praeneste (8. 560–567) as he sends young Pallas to fight in his place. It is apparently Pallas's initiation as a warrior (11.154–156). Evander's subsequent lament over the dead body of Pallas in Book 11 (151–181), G. R. Manton and E. Christian Kopff argued, inevitably recalled the mourning of Nestor over Antilochus that had become the *locus classicus* in Roman poetry for paternal grief over the untimely death of a son, and it likely imitated the Nestor of the *Aithiopis*.[5] And if Pallas plays the role of an Antilochus, Turnus, his slayer, takes on the part of the Ethiopian Memnon.[6]

Evander also provides, as we observed above in chapter 5, a model for same-sex attraction from an earlier heroic generation. He recalls that, back when he was an ephebe, he had burned with love to join hands with the older Anchises, then a visitor to Arcadia (8.160–165). His son Pallas has already taken the hand of Aeneas in embrace, repeating the gesture from one generation to the next. "*Amplexus*" (8.124), as Michael C. J. Putnam has shown, suggests something more than a handshake, and it is next seen in Book 8 to describe the lovemaking of Vulcan and Venus, Aeneas's other parent (8.388; 405).[7] Pallas sits beside Aeneas onboard the Etruscan ship toward the beginning of Book 10 (160–162), eagerly asking the hero about the stars and about what he has endured on land and sea. The scene recalls, Putnam points out, the lovestruck Dido at the banquet in Carthage listening to Aeneas's narrative

---

5. Manton, 1962, 5–11, citing Juvenal 10.246–255; Kopff, 1981, 941.

6. Knauer, 1964, 305–307 connects Turnus's killing of Pallas to Achilles' killing of Troilus in another cyclic epic, the *Cypria*, evoked on the reliefs of Dido's temple at 1.474–478.

7. Two different primal scenes. See Putnam 1985a, 6–8. On the homoeroticism of Roman military culture depicted in the *Aeneid*, see Miller, 2001, 88–91.

of his wanderings in Books 2 and 3, the storytelling that follows her own bard Iopas's song about the constellations (1.744).[8] Aeneas may indicate, or Virgil may indicate for him, the erotic charge of his relationship to Pallas, when he takes a cloak woven by Dido, a personal love token, and uses it to cover the corpse of the slain youth in Book 11 (11.72–77). Pallas, not Lavinia, replaces Dido as love-object in the second half of the *Aeneid*. The simile that compares the still beautiful corpse to a plucked flower (11.68–71) links Pallas to the slain Euryalus in Book 9 (434–437), another homosexual beloved, though, it appears, a slightly younger one than Pallas.

The distraught Nisus kills Volcens, the killer of Euryalus, as an anticipation and reflection of Aeneas's killing of Turnus at the end of the *Aeneid*, when the hero sees the baldric that Turnus has stripped from the body of Pallas—it is Pallas, Pallas, Aeneas proclaims, who delivers the death blow and sends Turnus to the shades.[9] The climax of the epic thus replays two scenarios of Achillean vengeance: the Achilles of the *Iliad* killing Hector to avenge Hector's killing of Patroclus, and the Achilles of the Cyclic epics who kills Memnon to avenge the killing of the second Patroclus, Antilochus, who was Achilles' young lover. The presence of this second model, well known and present to mind in antiquity, confirms Putnam's argument that the furies which overtake Aeneas in the poem's final scene include an irrational, sexual dimension.[10]

It is a model that Virgil announces from near the *beginning* of the *Aeneid*, when the poem looks through the eyes of Aeneas at the sculpted reliefs on Dido's temple of Juno at Carthage—these conclude, as the epic cycle itself had, with the coming first of Penthesilea, then of Memnon, to the aid of Troy: "*Eoasque acies et nigri Memnonis arma. / ducit Amazonidum lunatis agmina peltis / Penthesilea*" ("The Eastern forces and arms of black Memnon. Penthesilea leads her ranks of Amazons with their crescent-moon shields"; 1.489–491). Virgil's description reverses (one feels that such reversal is almost a reflex of his imagination) the traditional sequence of the arrivals of Amazon and Ethiopian warrior at Troy, but this ordering also corresponds to the order of appearance of their avatars in the *Aeneid* itself, and it is a preview of the epic's coming attractions. The playing out again of the Trojan War in Italy will feature versions of both of these figures: Turnus as Memnon, killer of Antilo-

---

8. Putnam, 1985a, 8.
9. Fowler, 2000, 102–104.
10. Putnam, 1985a, 13–19.

chus, in Book 10, the woman warrior Camilla as Penthesilea in Book 11. It will be more than just a second *Iliad*.

In fact, however, Virgil *doubles* the Antilochus and Memnon figures of this new Trojan War. He not only provides a second second Patroclus—that is, an Antilochus—in Pallas, to be slain by a Memnon-like Turnus. He proffers a second Antilochus—another second second Patroclus—in Lausus, slain by a Memnon-like Aeneas, and, in doing so, he constructs another chiasmus in the plotting of the *Aeneid*.

Eduard Fraenkel pointed out many years ago that the death of Lausus at the hands of Aeneas in Book 10 replays the death of Antilochus in the *Aithiopis*, where the youth has saved his father from the onslaught of Memnon.[11] In Pindar's retelling, an arrow of Paris has struck one of the horses of Nestor and disabled the old king's chariot. So an arrow of Paris kills a horse of Nestor in *Iliad* 8.81–86, who rears up in agony: the *Iliad* and *Aithiopis* episodes appear to be doubles of each other.[12] At Nestor's call of distress, Pindar goes on, Antilochus came forward to meet and be slain by Memnon: his death made Antilochus the heroic age's preeminent model of filial piety: "ὕπατος ἀμφὶ τοκεῦσιν ἔμμεν πρὸς ἀρετάν" ("foremost in virtuous behavior toward parents"; *Pyth.* 6.42).[13] Until, that is, Virgil's Aeneas, "*insignem pietate uirum*" (1.10), comes along.

Virgil divides and partly reverses the sequence of his model. Aeneas wounds Mezentius in the groin, and Lausus rushes to his father's aid (10.783–809). As we saw in the previous chapter, Aeneas threatens Lausus—your *pietas* deceives you, he says—and perhaps, just perhaps, gives the young warrior a chance to retreat (10.810–812). Lausus vaingloriously persists, the enraged Aeneas kills him, and now, at least now, as the verse pointedly designates him with the patronymic *Anchisiades* (10.822), he sees in Lausus the image of filial piety—"*et mentem patriae subiit pietatis imago*" (10.824), and he himself, naming himself as "*pius Aeneas*" (10.826), raises up Lausus's corpse and returns it to his Etruscan companions. Now Mezentius returns to battle, constrained by his wound to ride on his beloved steed Rhoebus. Aeneas's spear hits the horse between its temples, as Paris had wounded the horse of Nestor in the *Iliad* with an arrow to its forehead (*Il.* 8.83–86).[14] Rhoebus rears back, as that dying

11. Fraenkel, 1932; Manton 1962.
12. Janko, 1994, 378–379.
13. Pindar, 328.
14. And, as was observed in the last chapter, as Homer's Sarpedon fells with his spear Pedasos, the horse of Achilles' chariot on which Patroclus rides into battle against Sarpedon

horse of Nestor had done. Mezentius is entangled with the animal in its fall (10.892–894) and becomes prey to Aeneas. (In the much later *Posthomerica* of Quintus Smyrnaeus, which may nonetheless preserve the tradition of the *Aithiopis*, Memnon gallantly refuses to fight and spares ancient Nestor after killing his son [*Posthomerica* 2.309-338]—shades of Achilles and Priam in Book 24 of the *Iliad*. The more vigorous Mezentius appears to force Aeneas's hand.) Aeneas thus dispatches both the Antilochus figure Lausus and Mezentius, who, through his son's piety, plays out the role of Nestor. Mighty still, but slightly over the hill, Mezentius is already verging on being a Nestor figure. In this scenario, however, it is *Aeneas* who plays the part of Ethiopian Memnon. The *Aeneid* has already suggested as much, when Venus, asking Vulcan to forge the arms and shield of Aeneas, reminds the divine smithy that he had earlier made similar arms, at the requests not only of Thetis on behalf of her son Achilles, but also of Aurora, "*Tithonia ... coniunx*" (8.384), the mother of Memnon. It these arms of Memnon—"*nigri Memnonis arma*" (1.489)—on which the *Aeneid* has insisted when Aeneas looks at the sculptured temple walls at Carthage in Book 1 and when Dido mentions them again at the end of the book (1.751).[15] So the divinely armed Aeneas is cast not only as another Achilles but as a Memnon.[16]

But that role of Memnon, as I have argued above, has also been played by Turnus when he kills Pallas, the new beloved of Aeneas, in the other great set piece of battle earlier in Book 10. The narrator, in fact, twins Pallas and Lausus in age and beauty—"*nec multum discrepat aetas, / egregii forma*" (10.434–435)— yet announces that the ruler of Olympus would not let them fight face to face but reserved them each to fall beneath a greater warrior (10.436–438). Jupiter—or Virgil himself—in fact keeps them from meeting so that they can each act out the role of an Antilochus killed by a Memnon, Pallas by Turnus, Lausus by Aeneas. The same *Aithiopis* model thus holds together *both* of these two major battle episodes of Book 10. The effect is likewise to twin Turnus and Aeneas as Memnon figures. When Aeneas kills Turnus at the end of

---

(*Il.* 16.467). Virgil combines both models to tell two different stories, one in which Aeneas is for a moment like Sarpedon fighting a Patroclus in Mezentius, one in which Aeneas is a Memnon going after Mezentius, whose greater age than that of Aeneas now makes him a kind of Nestor figure.

15. Manton, 1962, 13–14.

16. In this light the seemingly formulaic opening line of Book 11, describing Aurora, the dawn, leaving the Ocean—"*Oceanum interea surgens Aurora reliquit*" (11.1; cf. 4.129)—may remind us of the Memnon-like role that Aeneas has just played at the end of the previous book.

the poem to avenge the death of Pallas as an Achilles slaying a Memnon, the poem's hero appears, in still another way, to kill his double. Aeneas punishes Turnus for doing much the same thing—mythologically it is the same thing—that he, Aeneas, has done to Lausus. Turnus, however, slays Pallas as a Memnon killing an Antilochus who is the beloved of Achilles; Aeneas slays Lausus as a Memnon killing an Antilochus who is the image of filial *pietas,* and *that* might appear a worse deed.[17]

These alternative ways of looking at the Memnon-Antilochus model return to color the close of the epic in Book 12. The defeated Turnus evokes the second of these perspectives. He pleads for his life in terms of *pietas*: his aged father, Daunus, Turnus says, might remind Aeneas of his own father—"*fuit et tibi talis / Anchises genitor*" (12.933–934)—and the scene, as Alessandro Barchiesi and Michael Putnam have shown, draws on Priam in *Iliad* 24 appealing to Achilles to remember *his* father, Peleus.[18] Aeneas famously hesitates and is slowly persuaded. But then the first perspective, triggered by the sight of Pallas's baldric, takes over. Readers have found good reasons why the oath-breaking Turnus has to die, deserves to die—Turnus himself says that he has it coming to him: "*equidem merui*" (12.931). But these are *not* the reasons that Aeneas kills him in the poem's last spasm of bloodshed. Following the evident mythic and poetic model controlling the scene, Aeneas becomes an Achilles taking vengeance on a Memnon for the killing of his erotically cherished Antilochus.[19] Private, sexual feeling—"*meorum ... Pallas ... Pallas*"

---

17. The issue of *pietas* is more muted, but present, in Turnus's duel with Pallas. Turnus first *impiously* taunts Pallas by wishing that Evander were there to be a spectator of his son's death—it was the unspeakable crime of Pyrrhus, Virgil's Priam had declared in Book 2, to slay his son Polites before Priam's eyes that marked Pyrrhus's degeneration from Achilles, who had restored to Priam the corpse of Hector in *Iliad* 24 (2.535–543). After he kills Pallas, however, Turnus freely sends the youth's body back to Evander—just as Aeneas will offer the slain body of Lausus to his Etruscan companions—in the guise of that good Achilles whom Priam had invoked. Virgil typically allows a mixed, double interpretation of Turnus's actions. Galinsky, 1981, in his criticism of Putnam, 1965, too sharply contrasts the behavior of Turnus and Aeneas in their respective killings of Pallas and Lausus in order to build up his case against Turnus; on the pairing of the two duels, see also Boyle, 1986, 98–99. The presence of the Memnon-Antilochus model behind *both* episodes lessens the distinctions and may even be unfavorable to the seemingly more pious and pitying Aeneas.

18. Putnam, 1981, 152–154; Barchiesi, 1984, 111–119 [Barchiesi, 2015, 86–91].

19. So Aeneas, the father of Rome, is also, the Achilles-Antilochus model would suggest, a lover of young men. It is an idea that criticism of the poem, prior to Putnam, 1985a, has been reluctant to acknowledge, and that, as much as the lack of a text of the *Aithiopis*, may have made

(12.947–948)—wins out over an appeal to piety, particularly the filial piety that is its hero's identifying quality, and morally unsettles the ending of the *Aeneid*.[20]

Memnon was a champion of Troy, as were Hector and Aeneas himself: Turnus ends up performing the parts of all three at the end of the poem, as the bulwark of Italian resistance to the now victorious Trojans and to their hero who has taken over the role of the top warrior Achilles. It is not a role that Aeneas has been used to playing. Even at Troy, he was the second mightiest Trojan warrior behind Hector. The most easily recognized literary model for the final duel of the poem between Aeneas and Turnus—what we might call the canonical model that Virgil follows at some length and detail—is the duel between Achilles and Hector in *Iliad* 22. Aeneas begins this sequence, however, *by pairing himself with Hector*—he has been so paired since his opening words in the *Aeneid* (1.99), and Diomedes has recently coupled them again in his speech to the Latin envoys (11.289–292). His kissing and taking leave of Ascanius to return to battle earlier in Book 12 repeats the famous scene of Hector's parting from Andromache and Astyanax in *Iliad* 6 (466f.). When Aeneas tells Ascanius to remember and be inspired not only by his own paternal example but by that of his uncle Hector as well, with the latter's name concluding the verse and the speech—"*et pater Aeneas et auunculus excitet Hector*" (12.440)—Virgil indicates the Homeric model for those who might miss it. Aeneas's words also invoke the words that Sophocles' Ajax—like Aeneas to Hector, the hero second to the greatest hero, Achilles, on his, the Greek side—speaks to *his* son (*Ajax* 545–551) before Ajax goes off to commit suicide.[21] There is a strong suggestion that Aeneas, beneath his confident words to Ascanius and against all the odds that the poem so far has stacked in his favor, may not expect to come out alive. He aspires to play gallant, if possibly doomed, Hector here, only to turn, five hundred lines later, into a victorious Achilles who mercilessly kills his Italian Hector, Turnus, at the end of the poem.

---

the model nearly invisible. Still, Aeneas hardly seems to have known Pallas long enough for a grand passion to form.

20. The distinction between private and public is unstable, however. Augustan ideology identified *pietas* with the duty to avenge the murder of Julius Caesar, so that the appeal to the father is double-edged. On the identification of Pallas with Julius Caesar, see Camps, 141–142; Quint, 1993, 75–79; Lowrie, 2005, 963–965.

21. Lyne, 1987, 9–12.

In a second model, discussed in chapter 1, this Aeneas-as-Achilles also faces in Turnus the stone-throwing *Aeneas* of *Iliad* 20 (284–290). You won't be snatched away from me—"*tune ... / eripiare mihi*" (12.947–948)—Aeneas says to Turnus as he is kindled with furies and terrible in wrath at the sight of Pallas's baldric; so Neptune recalls in Book 5 his having snatched Aeneas— "*rapui*" (5.810)—from the onslaught of Achilles at Troy. The dream specter Hector's first words to Aeneas as Troy was falling were "*nate dea, teque his ... eripe flammis*" (2.289)—snatch yourself from the flames and get out of town while you can, you son of a goddess—and three hundred lines later Venus, the goddess herself, repeats the message that the hero has failed to get: "*eripe nate, fugam*" (2.619). This Aeneas of the end of the epic chooses not to remember his own close calls at Troy—or perhaps he *does* remember them, and he gives Turnus no similar way out. When Aeneas, in still a third guise as Achilles, kills Turnus as the Greek hero had killed Ethiopian Memnon at Troy, he again switches roles: he has himself repeated the part of Memnon, fighting alongside Troy's defenders, when he killed the young, Antilochus-like Lausus two books earlier in Book 10.

Through the manipulation of these three models—the heroic duels of Achilles with Hector, Achilles with Aeneas, Achilles with Memnon—superimposed and spelling out the same logic, the *Aeneid* shows Aeneas replaying and now reversing the Trojan War, avenging the fates of Hector and Memnon and his own humiliating defeat and rescue at Troy. The disastrous Trojan past has been overcome as the victorious sword of Aeneas founds—"*condit*" (12.950)—a new historical order at the expense of his Italian foe who reflects that past back to him in a mirror image. Through the model of Antilochus, the second Patroclus, the *Aeneid* doubles down, as it were, on its own strategy of doubling the hero with his adversary and also of splitting the hero himself. Aeneas is an Achilles *and* a Memnon, an Achilles *and* a Hector, an Achilles *and* an ... Aeneas. The deliberately abrupt, shocking ending of the *Aeneid* concentrates and lays bare the strategies of doubling and chiasmic reversal that we have seen it exfoliate and work across its larger whole. Virgil's insistence on the reciprocity of war—particularly of internecine, *civil* war—would have it so. In its broad, "official," topical meaning, the new Roman order that Aeneas makes possible and that buries the past of Troy corresponds to the Augustan settlement that brought round after round of civil wars to an end— and with them the old republic with which those conflicts seemed to have become inseparable. Aeneas / Augustus sheds his old identity as Trojan / participant-in-republican-civil-war and sends it, laden on moaning, indignant

Turnus, to the underworld, over and done with. But complaining ghosts have a way of returning or of never having quite left. Aeneas kills a double of himself. Augustus had been part of the problem of which he promised to be the solution. That is where—Rome still a long way from being founded—Virgil leaves hero and *princeps* at the *Aeneid*'s end.

BIBLIOGRAPHY

Adorno, Theodor. 1984. *Aesthetic Theory*. Trans. C. Lenhardt. London and New York: Routledge & Kegan Paul.
Ahl, Frederick. 1970. *Lucan: An Introduction*. Ithaca: Cornell University Press.
Ahl, Frederick. 1989. "Homer, Vergil, and Complex Narrative Structures in Latin Epic: An Essay." *Illinois Classical Studies* 14:1–31.
Ameling, W. 1993. *Karthago*. Munich: C. H. Beck'sche Verlagsbuchhandlung.
Ameling, W. 2013. "Carthage," in P. F. Band and W. Scheidel, eds., *The Oxford Handbook of the State in the Ancient Near East and Mediterranean*, 161–182. Oxford University Press, Oxford.
Anderson, W. S. 1957. "Virgil's Second *Iliad*." *Transactions and Proceedings of the American Philological Association* 88:17–30.
Ando, Clifford. 2002. "Vergil's Italy: Ethnography and Politics in First-Century Rome," in David S. Leven and Damien P. Nelis, eds., *Clio and the Poets: Augustan Poetry and the Traditions of Ancient Historiography*, 123–142. Leiden: Brill.
Arrian. 1942. *The Anabasis of Alexander*. Trans. Edward J. Chinnock. In Godolphin, *The Greek Historians*, 2:402–620.
Ascoli, Albert Rusell. 2011. *A Local Habitation and a Name: Imagining Histories in the Italian Renaissance*. New York: Fordham University Press.
Athanassaki, Lucia, Richard P. Martin, and John F. Miller, eds. 2009. *Apolline Politics and Poetics: International Symposium*. Athens: European Cultural Centre of Delphi.
Auden, W. H. 1976. *Collected Poems*. Ed. Edward Mendelson. New York: Random House.
Austin, R. G. 1955. *P. Vergili Maronis Aeneidos Liber Quartus*. Oxford: Clarendon Press.
Austin, R. G. 1964. *P. Vergili Maronis Aeneidos Liber Secvndvs*. Oxford: Clarendon Press.
Bakker, Egbert J. 2013. *The Meaning of Meat and the Structure of the Odyssey*. Cambridge: Cambridge University Press.
Barchiesi, Alessandro. 1978. "Il lamento di Giuturna." *Materiali e discussioni per l'analisi dei testi classici* 1:99–121.
Barchiesi, Alessandro. 1984. *La traccia del modello: Effetti omerici nella narrazione virgiliana*. Pisa: Giardini.
Barchiesi, Alessandro. 1994. "Immobile Delos: Aeneid 3.73–98 and the Hymns of Catullus." *Classical Quarterly* N.S. 42: 438–443.
Barchiesi, Alessandro. 1996a. "Poetry, Praise, and Patronage: Simonides in Book 4 of Horace's *Odes*." *Classical Antiquity* 15:5–47.

Barchiesi, Alessandro. 1996b. "Simonides and Horace on the Death of Achilles." *Arethusa* 29:247–253.

Barchiesi, Alessandro. 1997 (1994). *The Poet and the Prince: Ovid and Augustan Discourse.* Berkeley: University of California Press.

Barchiesi, Alessandro. 1999 (1994). "Representations of Suffering and Interpretation in the *Aeneid*," in Hardie, 1999, 3:324–344; "Rappresentazioni del dolore e interpretazione nell'Eneide." *Antike und Abendland* 40 (1994): 109–124.

Barchiesi, Alessandro. 2005. "Learned Eyes: Poets, Viewers, Image Makers," in Galinsky, *Cambridge Companion*, 281–305.

Barchiesi, Alessandro. 2008. "*Bellum Italicum*: L'Unificazione dell'Italia nell'*Eneide*," in Gianpaolo Urso, ed., *Patria diversis gentibus una? unità, politica e identità etniche nell'Italia antica: atti del convegno internazionale, Cividale del Friuli, 20–22 settembre 2007.* Pisa: ETS.

Barchiesi, Alessandro. 2012. "Roma e l'Eneide: impero e cittadinanza," in Alberto Camerotto and Filippomaria Pontani, eds., *Classici Contro*, no. 1, 43–57. Milan: Mimesis.

Barchiesi, Alessandro. 2014. *Homeric Effects in Virgilian Narrative.* Trans. Ilaria Marchesi and Matt Fox. Princeton: Princeton University Press.

Barchiesi, Alessandro. 2017. "Colonial Readings in Virgilian Geopoetics: The Trojans at Buthrotum," in Rimmell and Asper, *Imagining Empire*, 151–165.

Bartsch, Shadi. 1998. "'Ars' and the Man: The Politics of Art in Virgil's *Aeneid*." *Classical Philology* 93:322–343.

Beard, Mary. 2007. *The Roman Triumph.* Cambridge, MA: Belknap Press.

Bellamy, Elizabeth J. 1992. *Translations of Power: Narcissism and the Unconscious in Epic History.* Ithaca: Cornell University Press.

Benjamin, Walter. 1969. *Illuminations.* Trans. Harry Zohn. New York: Schocken Books.

Bergemann, Johannes. 1998. *Die römische Kolonie von Butrint und die Romanisierung Griechenlands.* Munich: Pfeil.

Bettini, Maurizio. 1997. "Ghosts of Exile: Doubles and Nostalgia in Vergil's 'Parva Troia' ("*Aeneid*' 3.294ff.)." *Classical Antiquity* 16:8–33.

Bettini, Maurizio. 2005. "Un'identità 'troppo compiuta': Troiani, Latini, Romani, e Iulii nell'Eneide." *Materiali e discussioni per l'analisi dei testi classici* 55:77–102.

Binder, Gerhard. 1971. *Aeneas und Augustus: Interpretationen zum 8 Buch der Aeneis.* Meisenheim am Glan: Verlag Anton Hain.

Booth, Wayne C. 1974. *A Rhetoric of Irony.* Chicago: University of Chicago Press.

Bowie, A. M. 1990. "The Death of Priam: Allegory and History in the *Aeneid*." *The Classical Quarterly* 40:470–481.

Bowra, C. M. 1945. *From Virgil to Milton.* London: MacMillan.

Boyle, Anthony J. 1986. *The Chaonian Dove: Studies on the Eclogues, Georgics, and Aeneid of Virgil.* Leiden: Brill.

Boyle, Anthony J. 1993. "The Canonic Text: Virgil's *Aeneid*," in A. J. Boyle, ed., *Roman Epic*, 79–107. London: Routledge.

Boyle, Anthony J. 1999. "*Aeneid* 8: Images of Rome," in Perkell, *Reading Vergil's Aeneid*, 148–161.

Bremmer, Jan. 2009. "The Golden Bough: Orphic, Eleusinian, and Hellenistic-Jewish Sources of Virgil's Underworld in *Aeneid* VI." *Kernos* 22:183–208.

Buchheit, Vinzenz. 1963. *Vergil über die Sendung Roms: Untersuchungen zum Bellum Poenicum und zur Aeneis.* Gymnasium Heft 3. Heidelberg: Carl Winter.
Burgess, Jonathan. 2004. "Early Images of Achilles and Memnon." *Quaderni Urbinati di Cultura Classica.* N.S. 76:33–51.
Burke, Paul F. 1979. "Roman Rites for the Dead and *Aeneid* 6." *The Classical Journal* 74:220–228.
Cabanes, Pierre. 1976. *L'Epire de la mort de Pyrrhos à la conquête romaine.* Annales littéraires de l'université de Besançon, 186. Paris: Les Belles Lettres.
Cairns, Francis. 1989. *Virgil's Augustan Epic.* Cambridge: Cambridge University Press.
Camps, W. A. 1969. *An Introduction to Virgil's Aeneid.* London: Oxford University Press.
Casali, Sergio. 1995. "Aeneas and the Doors of the Temple of Apollo." *The Classical Journal* 91:1–9.
Casali, Sergio. 1999. "*Facta impia* (Virgil, *Aeneid* 4. 596–9)." *Classical Quarterly* 49:203–211.
Casali, Sergio. 2006. "The Making of the Shield: Inspiration and Repression in the *Aeneid*." *Greece & Rome* 53:185–204.
Casali, Sergio. 2007. "Killing the Father: Ennius, Naevius and Virgil's Julian Imperialism." In William Fitzgerald and Emily Gowers, eds., *Ennius Perennis: The Annals and Beyond.* Cambridge Classical Journal. Supplementary Volume 31, 103–128. Cambridge: Cambridge Philological Society.
Casali, Sergio. 2009. "The Theophany of Apollo in *Aeneid* 9: Augustanism and Self-Reflexivity," in Athanassaki et al., *Apolline Politics and Poetics*, 299–328.
Catullus. 1966. *Catullus, Tibullus, Pervigilium Veneris.* Trans. F. W. Cornish, J. P. Postgate, and J. W. Mackail. Loeb Classical Library. Cambridge, MA: Harvard University Press.
Cicero. 1970. *De Re Publica. De Legibus.* Trans. Clinton Walker Keyes. Loeb Classical Library. Cambridge, MA: Harvard University Press.
Cicero. 2000. *De Natura Deorum. Academica.* Trans. H. Rackham. Loeb Classical Library. Cambridge, MA: Harvard University Press.
Cicero. 2006. *Philippics.* Ed. and trans. Walter C. A. Ker. Loeb Classical Library. Cambridge, MA: Harvard University Press.
Cingano, Ettore. 2017. "Epic Fragments on Theseus: Hesiod, Cercops, and the *Theseis*," in Tomacz Derda, Jennifer Hilder, and Jan Kwapisz, eds., *Fragments, Holes, and Wholes: Reconstructing the Ancient World in Theory and Practice*, 309–332. The Journal of Juristic Papyrology, Supplement 30.
Clausen, Wendell. 1964. "An Interpretation of the *Aeneid*." *Harvard Studies in Classical Philology* 68:139–147.
Cole, Spencer. 2013. *Cicero and the Rise of Deification at Rome.* Cambridge: Cambridge University Press.
Cole, Thomas. 2008. *Ovidius Mythistoricus: Legendary Time in the Metamorphoses.* Frankfurt: Peter Lang.
Conington, John, and Henry Nettleship. 1883–98. *The Works of Virgil.* 3 vols. London: George Bell and Sons.
Conte, Gian Biagio. 1986. *The Rhetoric of Imitation: Genre and Poetic Memory in Virgil and Other Latin Poets.* Trans. Charles Segal. Ithaca and London: Cornell University Press.
Conte, Gian Biagio. 2007. *The Poetry of Pathos.* Ed. S. J. Harrison. Oxford: Oxford University Press.

Costa, Dennis. 2012. "'*incredibilis fama*': Some Remnants of Time in Virgilian Epic." *KronoScope* 12:7–15.

Dekel, Edan. 2012. *Virgil's Homeric Lens*. New York: Routledge.

Delvigo, Maria Luisa. 2005. "La rivelazione di Venere (Aen. 2, 589–623)." *Materiali e discussioni per l'analisi dei testi classici* 55:61–75.

Den Boer, Willem. 1969. "Theseus: The Growth of a Myth in History." *Greece and Rome* 16:1–13.

Deremetz, Alain. 1993. "Virgile et le labyrinthe du texte." *Uranie* 3:45–67.

Derrida, Jacques. 1967. *De la grammatologie*. Paris: Les éditions de Minuit.

Di Cesare, Mario A. 1974. *The Altar and the City*. New York: Columbia University Press.

Diodorus Siculus. 2000 [1939]. *The Library of History*. Trans. C. H. Oldfather. Volume 3. Loeb Classical Library. Cambridge, MA: Harvard University Press.

Doob, Penelope. 1990. *The Idea of the Labyrinth*. Ithaca: Cornell University Press.

Dorcey, Peter F. 1992. *The Cult of Silvanus: A Study in Roman Folk Religion*. Leiden: E. J. Brill.

Drew, D. L. 1927. *The Allegory of the Aeneid*. Oxford: Blackwell.

Duckworth, George E. 1962. *Structural Patterns and Proportions in Vergil's Aeneid: A Study in Mathematical Composition*. Ann Arbor: University of Michigan Press.

Dupont, Florence. 2011. *Rome, la ville sans origine*. Paris: Gallimard.

Eidinow, J. S. C. 2003. "Dido, Aeneas, and Iulus: Heirship and Obligation in *Aeneid* 4." *Classical Quarterly* 53:260–267.

Eliot, T. S. 1961 [1944]. "What Is a Classic?" in *On Poetry and Poets*. New York: The Noonday Press.

Ennius, 1985. *The Annals of Q. Ennius*. Ed. Otto Skutsch. Oxford: Clarendon Press.

Fantar, M'hamed Hassine. 1993. *Carthage: Approche d'une civilisation*. 2 vols. Tunis: Les Éditions de la Méditerranée.

Fantham, Elaine. 2006. "'*Dic si quid potes de Sexto Annali*': The Literary Legacy of Ennius's Pyrrhic War." *Arethusa* 39:549–568.

Feeney, D. C. 1984. "The Reconciliations of Juno." *Classical Quarterly* 34:179–194.

Feeney, D. C. 1986. "History and Revelation in Vergil's Underworld." *The Cambridge Classical Journal* 32:1–24.

Feeney, D. C. 1991. *The Gods in Epic*. Oxford: Clarendon Press.

Feeney, D. C. 1999. "Epic Violence, Epic Order: Killings, Catalogues, and the Role of the Reader in *Aeneid* 10," in Perkell, *Reading Vergil's Aeneid*, 178–194.

Feeney, D. C. 2016. *Beyond Greek: The Beginnings of Latin Literature*. Cambridge: Harvard University Press.

Feldherr, Andrew. 1997. "Putting Dido on the Map: Genre and Geography in Vergil's Underworld." *Arethusa* 32:85–122.

Feldherr, Andrew. 2014. "Viewing Myth and History on the Shield of Aeneas." *Classical Antiquity* 33:281–318.

Fitzgerald, William. 1984. "Aeneas, Daedalus, and the Labyrinth." *Arethusa* 17:51–65.

Fitzgerald, William, and Emily Gowers, eds. 2007. *Ennius Perennis: The Annals and Beyond*. Cambridge Classical Journal. Supplementary Volume 31. Cambridge: Cambridge Philological Society.

Fletcher, Frank. 1968. *Virgil Aeneid VI*. Oxford: Clarendon Press.

Fletcher, K. F. B. 2006. "Vergil's Italian Diomedes." *AJP* 127:219–259.
Fordyce, C. J. 1985 [1977]. *Virgil Aeneid VII–VIII*. London: Bristol Classical Press.
Fowler, Don. 1990. "Deviant Focalization in Virgil's *Aeneid*." *Proceedings of the Cambridge Philological Society* 36:42–63.
Fowler, Don. 2000. "Epic in the Middle of the Wood: *Mise en Abyme* in the Nisus and Euryalus Episode," in Alison Sharrock and Helen Morales, eds., *Intratextuality: Greek and Roman Textual Relations*, 80–114. Oxford: Oxford University Press.
Fowler, William Warde. 1917. *Aeneas at the Site of Rome: Observations on the Eighth Book of the Aeneid*. Oxford: B. H. Blackwell.
Fraenkel, Eduard. 1932. "Virgil und die Aithiopis." *Philologus* 87:242–248.
Fraenkel, Eduard. 1945. "Some Aspects of the Structure of *Aeneid* VII." *The Journal of Roman Studies* 35:1–14.
Fratantuono, Lee. 2007. *Madness Unchained: A Reading of Virgil's Aeneid*. Lanham, MD: Lexington Books.
Fratantuono, Lee, and Alden Smith. 2015. *Aeneid 5: Text, Translation and Commentary*. Leiden: Brill.
Freudenburg, Kirk. 2017. "Seeing Marcellus in Aeneid 6." *The Journal of Roman Studies* 107:116–139.
Galinsky, G. Karl. 1966. "The Hercules-Cacus Episode in *Aeneid* VIII." *American Journal of Philology* 87:18–51.
Galinsky, G. Karl. 1969. *Aeneas, Sicily, and Rome*. Princeton: Princeton University Press.
Galinsky, G. Karl. 1972. *The Herakles Theme: The Adaptations of the Hero in Literature from Homer to the Twentieth Century*. Totowa, NJ: Rowan and Littlefield.
Galinksy, G. Karl. 1981. "Vergil's Romanitas and His Adaptation of Greek Heroes." *Aufstieg und Niedergang der Römischen Welt* II.32.2:985–1010.
Galinsky, G. Karl. 1996. *Augustan Culture: An Interpretive Introduction*. Princeton: Princeton University Press.
Galinsky, G. Karl, ed. 2005. *The Cambridge Companion to the Age of Augustus*. Cambridge: Cambridge University Press.
García-Castañón, Santiago. 2001. "The Ruins of Rome Revisited: Translating Vitalis, Du Bellay, Szarzynski, and Quevedo." *Translation Review* 61:20–25.
Gärtner, Ursula. 2015. "Virgil and the Epic Cycle," in Marco Fantuzzi and Christos Tsagalis, eds., *The Greek Epic Cycle and Its Ancient Reception: A Companion*, 543–565. Cambridge: Cambridge University Press.
Gasché, Rodolphe. 1987. "Reading Chiasms: An Introduction." Preface to Andrezj Warminski, *Readings in Interpretation: Hölderlin, Hegel, Heidegger*, 9–26. Minneapolis: University of Minnesota Press.
Giardina, Andrea. 1997. *L'Italia romana: storie di un'identità incompiuta*. Bari: Laterza.
Giusti, Elena. 2017. "Virgil's Carthage: A Heterotopic Space of Empire," in Rimmell and Asper, *Imagining Empire*, 133–150.
Glenn, Justin. 1971. "Mezentius and Polyphemus." *American Journal of Philology* 92:129–155.
Godolphin, Francis R. B., ed. 1942. *The Greek Historians*. 2 vols. New York: Random House.
Goold, G. P. 1970. "Servius and the Helen Episode." *Harvard Studies in Classical Philology* 74: 101–168. Reprinted in Harrison, *Oxford Readings*, 60–126.

Goold, G. P. 1992. "The Voice of Virgil: The Pageant of Rome in *Aeneid 6*," in A. J. Woodman and J. G. F. Powell, eds., *Authors and Audience in Latin Literature*, 110–123. Cambridge: Cambridge University Press.
Gowers, Emily. 2011. "Trees and Family Trees in the Aeneid." *Classical Antiquity* 30:87–118.
Gransden, K. W. 1976. *Virgil: Aeneid Book VIII*. Cambridge: Cambridge University Press.
Gransden, K. W. 1984. *Virgil's Iliad: An Essay on Epic Narrative*. Cambridge: Cambridge University Press.
Gransden, K. W. 1991. *Virgil: Aeneid Book XI*. Cambridge: Cambridge University Press.
Greene, Thomas. 1963. *The Descent from Heaven*. New Haven: Yale University Press.
Grillo, Luca, 2010. "Leaving Troy and Creusa: Reflections on Aeneas's Flight." *The Classical Journal* 106:43–68.
Gurval, Robert Alan. 1995. *Aeneas and Actium: The Politics and Emotions of Civil War*. Ann Arbor: University of Michigan Press.
Hanson, John Arthur. 1982. "Vergil," in T. James Luce, ed., *Ancient Writers: Greece and Rome*, 2:669–701. New York: Scribners.
Hardie, Philip. 1986. *Virgil's "Aeneid": Cosmos and Imperium*. Oxford: Clarendon Press.
Hardie, Philip. 1992. "Augustan Poets and the Mutability of Rome," in Powell, *Roman Poetry and Propaganda*, 59–82.
Hardie, Philip. 1993. *The Epic Successors of Virgil*. Cambridge: Cambridge University Press.
Hardie, Philip. 1994. *Virgil, Aeneid Book IX*. Cambridge: Cambridge University Press.
Hardie, Philip. 2006. "Virgil's Ptolemaic Relations." *The Journal of Roman Studies* 96:25–41.
Hardie, Philip. 2012. *Rumour and Renown*. Cambridge: Cambridge University Press.
Hardie, Philip. 2013. "Dido and Lucretia." *Proceedings of the Virgil Society* 28:55–80.
Hardie, Philip. 2014. *The Last Trojan Hero: A Cultural History of Virgil's "Aeneid."* London: L. B. Tauris.
Hardie, Philip, ed. 1999 *Virgil: Critical Assessments of Classical Authors*. 4 vols. London and New York: Routledge.
Hardie, Philip, ed. 2009. *Paradox and the Marvellous in Augustan Literature and Culture*. Oxford: Oxford University Press.
Harrison, E. L. 1976. "Structure and Meaning in Vergil's *Aeneid*." *Papers of the Liverpool Latin Seminar 1976*, 101–112. Liverpool: Francis Cairns.
Harrison, E. L. 1984. "The *Aeneid* and Carthage," in Woodman and West, *Poetry and Politics*, 95–115.
Harrison, S. J. 1989. "Augustus, the Poets and the *Spolia Opima*." *Classical Quarterly* 39:408–414.
Harrison, S. J. 1991. *Vergil Aeneid 10*. Oxford: Clarendon Press.
Harrison, S. J., ed. 1990. *Oxford Readings in Vergil's Aeneid*. Oxford: Oxford University Press.
Harrison, T. W. 1967. "English Virgil: The *Aeneid* in the XVIII Century." *Philologia Pragensia* 10:1–11, 80–91.
Heinze, Richard. 1993 [1902]. *Virgil's Epic Technique*. Trans. Hazel and David Harvey and Fred Robertson. Berkeley: University of California Press.
Hejduk, Julia. 2009. "Jupiter's *Aeneid*: *Fama* and *Imperium*." *Classical Antiquity* 28, no. 2:279–327.
Heraclitus. 1962. *Heraclitus: Allégories d'Homère*. Ed. and trans. Félix Buffière. Paris: Les Belles Lettres.

Hershkowitz, Debra. 1998. *The Madness of Epic: Reading Insanity from Homer to Statius.* Oxford: Clarendon Press.
Hexter, Ralph. 1992. "Sidonian Dido," in Ralph Hexter and Daniel Selden, eds., *Innovations of Antiquity*, 332–384. New York and London: Routledge.
Hinds, Stephen. 1998. *Allusion and Intertext.* Cambridge: Cambridge University Press.
Holzberg, Niklas. 2006. *Vergil.* Munich: C. H. Beck.
Homer. 1930. *HomeriIlias.* Ed. Thomas W. Allen. 3 vols. Oxford: Clarendon.
Homer. 1951. *The Iliad of Homer.* Trans. Richmond Lattimore. Chicago: University of Chicago Press.
Horace. 1968. *Odes and Epodes.* Trans. C. E. Bennett. Loeb Classical Library. Cambridge, MA: Harvard University Press.
Horkheimer, Max, and Theodor W. Adorno. 1969 [1946]. *Dialectic of Enlightenment.* Trans. John Cumming. New York: Seabury Press.
Horsfall, Nicholas. 1971. "Numanus Remulus: Ethnography and Propaganda in *Aeneid* 9.598ff." *Latomus* 30:1108–1116.
Horsfall, Nicholas. 1973–74. "Dido in the Light of History." *Proceedings of the Virgil Society* 13:1–13. Reprinted in Harrison, *Oxford Readings*, 127–144.
Horsfall, Nicholas. 1986. "The Aeneas Legend and the *Aeneid.*" *Vergilius* 32:8–17.
Horsfall, Nicholas. 1995. *A Companion to the Study of Virgil.* Leiden: Brill.
Horsfall, Nicholas. 2000. *Virgil, Aeneid 7: A Commentary.* Leiden and Boston: Brill.
Horsfall, Nicholas. 2008. *Virgil, Aeneid 2: A Commentary.* Leiden: Brill.
Horsfall, Nicholas. 2013. "Poets and Poetry in Virgil's Underworld." *Vergilius* 59:23–28.
Hübner, Wolfgang. 1970. *Dirae im römischen Epos: Über das Verhältnis von Vogeldämonen und Prodigien.* Hildesheim: Georg Olms.
Hunter, Richard. 2006. *The Shadow of Callimachus: Studies in the Reception of Hellenistic Poetry at Rome.* Cambridge: Cambridge University Press.
James, Sharon L. 1995. "Establishing Rome with the Sword: *Condere* in the *Aeneid.*" *American Journal of Philology* 116:623–637.
Jameson, Fredric. 2009. *Valences of the Dialectic.* London: Verso.
Janko, Richard. 1994. *The Iliad: A Commentary. Volume IV: Books 13–16.* Cambridge: Cambridge University Press.
Jenkyns, Richard. 1998. *Virgil's Experience: Nature and History, Times, Names, and Places.* Oxford: Clarendon Press.
Johnson, W. R. 1976. *Darkness Visible: A Study of Vergil's "Aeneid."* Berkeley: University of California Press.
Johnson, W. R. 1999. "*Dis Aliter Visum*: Story-Telling and Theodicy in *Aeneid* 2," in Perkell, *Reading Vergil's Aeneid*, 50–63.
Jones, Prudence J. 2005. *Reading Rivers in Roman Literature and Culture.* Lanham, MD: Lexington Books.
Kenney, E. J. 1979. "Iudicium Transferendi: Virgil, *Aeneid* 2.469–505 and Its Antecedents," in Woodman and West, *Poetry and Politics*, 103–120.
Knauer, G. N. 1964. *Die Aeneis und Homer: Studien zur poetischen Technik Vergils mit Listen der Homerzitate in der Aeneis.* Göttingen: Vanderhoeck & Ruprecht.

Knauer, G. N. 1981. "Vergil and Homer." *Aufstieg und Niedergang der Römischen Welt* II.32.2: 872–918.

Knox, Bernard. 1950. "The Serpent and the Flame: The Imagery of the Second Book of the *Aeneid*." *American Journal of Philology* 71:379–400.

Kopff, E. Christian. 1981. "Virgil and the Cyclical Epics." *Aufstieg und Niedergang der Römischen Welt* II.32.2:919–947.

Kraus, Christina S. 1994. "'No Second Troy': Topoi and Refoundation in Livy, Book V." *Transactions of the American Philological Association* 124:267–289.

Kraus, Christina S., John Marincola, and Christopher Pelling, eds. 2010. *Ancient Historiography and Its Contexts: Studies in Honour of A. J. Woodman*. Oxford: Oxford University Press.

Labate, Mario. 2009. "In Search of the Lost Hercules: Strategies of the Fantastic in the *Aeneid*," in Hardie, *Paradox and the Marvellous*, 126–144.

Lactantius. 1964. *The Divine Institutes, Books I–VII*. Trans. Sister Mary Francis McDonald. Washington, D.C.: Catholic University of America Press.

Lancel, Serge. 1993. *Carthage: A History*. Trans. Antonia Nevill. Oxford: Blackwell.

Lange, Carsten Hjort. 2009. *Res Publica Constituta: Actium, Apollo and the Accomplishment of the Triumviral Assignment*. Leiden: Brill.

Lange, Carsten Hjort. 2016. *Triumphs in the Age of Civil War*. London: Bloomsbury.

La Penna, Antonio. 1988. "Brevi considerazioni sulla divinizzazione degli eroi e sul canone degli eroi divinizzai." In D. Porte and J.-P. Néraudau, eds., *Hommages à Henri Le Bonniec: Res Sacrae* (Collections Latomus 201), 2775–2787. Brussels: Éditions Latomus.

La Penna, Antonio. 2004. "Fasto e povertà nell'*Eneide*." *Maia* 56:225–248.

Lefèvre, Eckard. 1998. "Vergil as Republican (*Aen.* 6.815–835)," in Stahl, *Vergil's Aeneid* 101–118.

Lipking, Lawrence. 1981. *The Life of the Poet*. Chicago and London: University of Chicago Press.

Livy. 1922–59. *Livy*. Trans. B. O. Foster. 13 vols. Loeb Classical Library. London: William Heinemann.

Lowrie, Michèle. 2005. "Virgil and Founding Violence." *Cardozo Law Review* 27:945–976.

Lowrie, Michèle. 2009. *Writing, Performance, and Authority in Augustan Rome*. Oxford; Oxford University Press.

Lyne, R. O. A. M. 1987. *Further Voices in Vergil's "Aeneid."* Oxford: Clarendon Press.

Lyne, R. O. A. M. 1995. *Horace: Behind the Public Poetry*. New Haven: Yale University Press.

Mackenzie, Margery. 1964. "Who is Vergil's Aeneas? (A plea to let him be himself)." *Vergilius* 10: 1–6.

Manton, G. R. 1962. "Virgil and the Greek Epic: The Tragedy of Evander." *AUMLA* 17:5–17.

Marincola, John. 2010. "Eros and Empire: Virgil and the Historians on Civil War," in Kraus, Marincola, and Pelling, 184–204.

Martin, Charles. 1992. *Catullus*. New Haven: Yale University Press.

Martindale, Charles, ed. 1997. *The Cambridge Companion to Virgil*. Cambridge: Cambridge University Press.

Mazzocchini, Paolo. 2000. *Forme e significati della narrazione bellica nell'epos virgiliano*. Fasano: Schena editore.

McKay, Alexander G. 1998. "*Non enarrabile textum*? The Shield of Aeneas and the Triple Triumph of 29 BC (*Aeneid* 8.630–728)." in Stahl, *Vergil's Aeneid*, 199–221.

Miller, David Lee. 2003. *Dreams of the Burning Child*. Ithaca: Cornell University Press.
Miller, John F. 2011. *Apollo, Augustus, and the Poets*. Cambridge: Cambridge University Press.
Miller, John F. 2014. "Virgil's Salian Hymn to Hercules." *The Classical Journal* 109:439–463.
Morgan, Llewelyn. 1998. "Assimilation and Civil War: Hercules and Cacus (*Aen.* 8.158–267)," in Stahl, *Vergil's Aeneid*, 175–197.
Morgan, Llewelyn. 2005. "A Yoke Connecting Baskets: *Odes* 3.14, Hercules, and Italian Unity." *Classical Quarterly* 55:190–203.
Most, Glenn. 1992. "Il poeta nell'Ade: catabasi epica e teoria dell'epos tra Omero e Virgilio." *Studi italiani di filologia classica* LXXXV annata, terza serie, 10.1–2:1014–1026.
Murrin, Michael. 1980. *The Allegorical Epic: Essays in Its Rise and Fall*. Chicago and London: University of Chicago Press.
Murrin, Michael. 1994. *History and Warfare in Renaissance Epic*. Chicago and London: University of Chicago Press.
Mynors, R. A. B., ed. 1969. *P. Vergili Maronis Opera*. Oxford: Clarendon Press.
Nagy, Gregory. 1979. *The Best of the Achaeans: Concepts of the Hero in Archaic Greek Poetry*. Baltimore and London: Johns Hopkins University Press.
Nicolet, Claude. 1976. *Le métier de citoyen dans la Rome républicaine*. Paris: Gallimard.
Nicoll, W. S. M. 1988. "The Sacrifice of Palinurus." *The Classical Quarterly* N.S. 38:459–472.
Norden, Eduard. 1916. *P Vergilius Maro Aeneis Buch VI*. Leipzig: B. G. Teubner.
Ogilvie, R. M. 1965. *A Commentary on Livy, Books 1–5*. Oxford: Clarendon Press.
O'Hara, James J. 1990. *Death and the Optimistic Prophecy in Vergil's Aeneid*. Princeton: Princeton University Press.
O'Hara, James J. 2007. *Inconsistency in Roman Epic*. Cambridge: Cambridge University Press.
Oliensis, Ellen. 2004. "Sibylline Syllables: The Intratextual *Aeneid*." *The Cambridge Classical Journal* 50:29–45.
Oliensis, Ellen. 2009. *Freud's Rome*. Cambridge: Cambridge University Press.
Oram, William A., Einar Bjorvand, Ronald Bond, Thomas H. Cain, Alexander Dunlop, and Richard Schell, eds. 1989. *The Yale Edition of the Shorter Poems of Edmund Spenser*. New Haven and London: Yale University Press.
Otis, Brooks. 1964. *Virgil: A Study in Civilized Poetry*. Oxford: Clarendon Press.
Pandey, Nandini. 2018. "Blood beneath the Laurels: Pyrrhus, Apollo, and the Ethics of Augustan Victory." *Classical Philology* 113.
Parry, Adam. 1962. "The Two Voices of Virgil's *Aeneid*." *Arion* 2:66–80.
Perkell, Christine. 2002. "The Golden Age and Its Contradictions in the Poetry of Vergil." *Vergilius* 48:3–39.
Perkell, Christine, ed. 1999. *Reading Vergil's Aeneid: An Interpretative Guide*. Norman: University of Oklahoma Press.
Perret, Jacques. 1964. "Les compagnes de Didon aux enfers." *Revue des études latines* 42:347–361.
Philostratus. 1960. *Philostratus, Imagines; Callistratus, Descriptions*. Trans. Arthur Fairbanks. Loeb Classical Library. Cambridge, MA: Harvard University Press.
Philostratus. 2014. *Philostratus, Heroicus; Gymnasticus, Discourses 1 and 2*. Ed. and trans. Jeffrey Rusten and Jason König. Loeb Classical Library. Cambridge, MA: Harvard University Press.

Plutarch. 2014. *Lives*. Trans. Bernadotte Perrin. 11 vols. Loeb Classical Library. Cambridge, MA: Harvard University Press.

Pogorzelski, Randall J. 2009. "The 'Reassurance of Fratricide' in the *Aeneid*." *American Journal of Philology* 130:261–289.

Polybius. 2011. *The Histories*. Trans. W. R. Paton and revised by F. W. Walbank and C. Habicht. 6 vols. Loeb Classical Library. Cambridge, MA: Harvard University Press.

Pontani, Filippomaria. 2011. "Sogni, missioni e profezie: su *Aen.* VIII, 18–41." *Latomus* 70: 1000–1012.

Pöschl, Viktor. 1962 [1950]. *The Art of Vergil: Image and Symbol in the "Aeneid."* Trans. G. Seligson. Ann Arbor: University of Michigan Press.

Powell, Anton, ed. 1992. *Roman Poetry and Propaganda in the Age of Augustus*. London: Bristol Classical Press.

Propertius. 1933. *The Elegies of Propertius*. Ed. H. E. Butler and E. A. Barber. Oxford: Clarendon Press.

Purcell, Nicholas. 2005. "Romans in the Roman World," in Galinsky, *Cambridge Companion*, 85–105.

Putnam, Michael C. J. 1965. *The Poetry of the "Aeneid."* Ithaca and London: Cornell University Press.

Putnam, Michael C. J. 1980. "The Third Book of the *Aeneid*: From Homer to Rome." *Ramus* 9:1–21. Reprinted in Putnam, *Virgil's Aeneid*, 50–72.

Putnam, Michael C. J. 1981. "*Pius* Aeneas and the Metamorphosis of Lausus." *Arethusa* 14:139–156. Reprinted in Putnam, *Virgil's Aeneid*, 134–151.

Putnam, Michael C. J. 1985a. "Possessiveness, Sexuality, and Heroism in the *Aeneid*." *Vergilius* 31:1–21. Reprinted in Putnam, *Virgil's Aeneid*, 27–49.

Putnam, Michael C. J. 1985b. "Romulus *Tropaeophorus* (*Aeneid* 6.779–80)." *The Classical Quarterly* 35:237–240.

Putnam, Michael C. J. 1995. *Virgil's Aeneid: Interpretation and Influence*. Chapel Hill: University of North Carolina Press.

Putnam, Michael C. J. 1998. *Virgil's Epic Designs: Ekphrasis in the "Aeneid."* New Haven: Yale University Press.

Putnam, Michael C. J. 2011. *The Humanness of Heroes: Studies in the Conclusion of Virgil's Aeneid*. Amsterdam: Amsterdam University Press.

Quinn, Kenneth. 1968. *Virgil's Aeneid: A Critical Description*. Ann Arbor: University of Michigan Press.

Quint, David. 1983. *Origin and Originality in Renaissance Literature*. New Haven: Yale University Press.

Quint, David. 1993. *Epic and Empire*. Princeton: Princeton University Press.

Quintilian. 1966. *The "Institutio Oratoria" of Quintilian*. Ed. and trans. H. E. Butler. Loeb Classical Library. 4 vols. Cambridge, MA: Harvard University Press.

Reed, J. D. 2007. *Virgil's Gaze: Nation and Poetry in the Aeneid*. Princeton: Princeton University Press.

Rimmell, Victoria, and Markus Asper. 2017. *Imagining Empire: Political Space in Hellenistic and Roman Literature*. Heidelberg: Universitätsverlag Winter.

Rose, Charles Brian. 2014. *The Archaeology of Greek and Roman Troy*. New York: Cambridge University Press.

Rossi, Andreola. 2010. "*Ab urbe condita*: Roman History on the Shield of Aeneas," in Brian W. Breed, Cynthia Damon, and Andreola Rossi, eds., *Citizens of Discord: Rome and Its Civil Wars*, 145–156. Oxford: Oxford University Press.

Ryberg, Inez Scott. 1958. "Vergil's Golden Age." *Transactions and Proceedings of the American Philological Association* 89:112–131.

Sage, Michael. 2000. "Roman Visitors to Ilium in the Roman Imperial and Late Antique Period: The Symbolic Functions of a Landscape." *Studia Troica* 10:211–231.

Sallust. 1995. *Sallust*. Trans. J. C. Rolfe. Loeb Classical Library. Cambridge, MA: Harvard University Press.

Schein, Seth L. 1984. *The Mortal Hero: An Introduction to Homer's Iliad*. Berkeley: University of California Press.

Schiesaro, Alessandro. 2006. "Soothing Subversions." *Literary Imagination* 8, no. 3:497–511.

Schiesaro, Alessandro. 2008. "Furthest Voices in Virgil's Dido." *Studi italiani di filologia classica* 100:60–109 and 194–245.

Scobie, Alex. 1990. *Hitler's State Architecture: The Impact of Classical Antiquity*. University Park: Published for the College Art Association of America by the Pennsylvania State University Press.

Seem, Lauren Scancarelli. 1990. "The Limits of Chivalry: Tasso and the End of the *Aeneid*." *Comparative Literature* 42:116–125.

Servius Honoratus, Maurus. 1881. *In Vergilii carmina comentarii. Servii Grammatici qui feruntur in Vergilii carmina commentarii*. Ed. Georg Thilo and Hermann Hagen. 3 vols. Leipzig: B. G. Teubner.

Skard, Eiliv. 1965. "Die Heldenschau in Vergils Aeneis." *Symbolae Osloensis* 40:53–65.

Slatkin, Laura. 1991. *The Power of Thetis: Allusion and Interpretation in the Iliad*. Berkeley: University of California Press.

Smith, Alden. 2005. *The Primacy of Vision in Virgil's Aeneid*. Austin: University of Texas Press.

Spence, Sarah. 1999. "The Polyvalence of Pallas in the *Aeneid*." *Arethusa* 32:149–163.

Spence, Sarah. 2013. "Response to Horsfall: The Role of Discernment in *Aeneid* 6." *Vergilius* 59:29–35.

Stahl, Hans-Peter. 1998a. "Political Stop-overs on a Mythological Travel Route from Battling Harpies to the Battle of Actium, *Aeneid* 3.268–93," in Stahl, *Vergil's Aeneid*, 37–84.

Stahl, Hans-Peter, ed. 1998b. *Vergil's Aeneid: Augustan Epic and Political Context*. London: Duckworth.

Stanley, Keith. 1965. "Irony and Foreshadowing in *Aeneid* I, 462." *American Journal of Philology* 86:267–277.

Strazzulla, Maria José. 1990. *Il principato di Apollo: mito e propaganda nelle lastre "Campana" dal tempio di Apollo Palatino*. Rome: L'Erma di Bretschneider.

Sumi, Geoffrey S. 2005. *Ceremony and Power*. Ann Arbor: University of Michigan Press.

Syme, Ronald. 1939. *The Roman Revolution*. Oxford: Clarendon.

Tatum, J. 1984. "Allusion and Interpretation in *Aeneid* 6.440–76." *American Journal of Philology* 105:434–452.

Thomas, Richard. 1988. "Tree Violation and Ambivalence in Virgil." *Transactions of the American Philological Association* 118:261–273.
Thomas, Richard. 2001. *Virgil and the Augustan Reception*. Cambridge: Cambridge University Press.
Thome, Gabriele. 1979. *Gestalt und Funktion des Mezentius bei Vergil, mit einem Ausblick auf die Schlussszene der Aeneis*. Frankfurt am Main: Lang.
Toll, Katharine. 1991. "The *Aeneid* as an Epic of National Identity: *Italiam laeto socii clamore salutant*." *Helios* 18:3–14.
Toll, Katharine. 1997. "Making Roman-ness in the *Aeneid*." *Classical Antiquity* 16:34–56.
Traina, Alfonso. 1997. *Virgilio: l'utopia e la storia*. Turin: Loescher.
von Albrecht, Michael. 1999 [1965]. "The Art of Mirroring in Virgil's *Aeneid*," trans. H. Harvey, in Hardie, *Virgil*, 4:1–12.
Wallace-Hadrill, Andrew. 1983. *Suetonius, the Scholar and His Caesars*. London: Duckworth.
Weinstock, Stefan. 1971. *Divus Julius*. Oxford: Clarendon.
Welch, John W., ed. 1981. *Chiasmus in Antiquity: Structures, Analyses, Exegesis*. Hildesheim: Gerstenberg.
West, D. A. 1975–76. "*Cernere erat:* The Shield of Aeneas." *Proceedings of the Virgil Society* 15:1–7.
West, G. S. 1980. "Caeneus and Dido." *Transactions of the American Philological Association* 110:315–324.
Whitman, Cedric H. 1958. *Homer and the Heroic Tradition*. Cambridge, MA: Harvard University Press.
Whittington, Leah. 2016. *Renaissance Suppliants: Poetry, Antiquity, Reconciliation*. Oxford: Oxford University Press.
Williams, Gordon. 1983. *Technique and Ideas in the Aeneid*. New Haven and London: Yale University Press.
Williams, R. D. 1960. "The Reliefs on Dido's Temple (*Aeneid* 1.450–93)." *Classical Quarterly* N.S. 10:145–151. Reprinted in Harrison, *Oxford Readings*, 37–45.
Wofford, Susanne Lindgren. 1992. *The Choice of Achilles: The Ideology of Figure in the Epic*. Stanford: Stanford University Press.
Woodman, Tony, and David West, eds. 1984. *Poetry and Politics in the Age of Augustus*. Cambridge: Cambridge University Press.
Zanker, Paul. 1988. *The Power of Images in the Age of Augustus*. Trans. Alan Shapiro. Ann Arbor: University of Michigan Press.
Zarker, John W. 1967. "Aeneas and Theseus in *Aeneid* 6." *The Classical Journal* 62:220–226.
Zetzel, James E. G. 1996. "Natural Law and Poetic Justice: A Carneadean Debate in Cicero and Virgil." *Classical Philology* 91:297–319.
Zetzel, James E. G. 1989. "Romane Memento: Justice and Judgment in *Aeneid* 6." *Transactions of the American Philological Association* 119:263–284.
Zetzel, James E. G. 1997. "Rome and Its Traditions," in Martindale, *Cambridge Companion*, 188–203.
Ziolkowski, Jan M., and Michael C. J. Putnam, eds. 2008. *The Virgilian Tradition: The First Fifteen Hundred Years*. New Haven: Yale University Press.
Ziolkowski, Theodore. 1993. *Virgil and the Moderns*. Princeton: Princeton University Press, 1993.

INDEX

Achaemenides, 51–53
Achilles: Aeneas as, 13, 43, 170, 176, 189; and Aeneas in *Iliad*, 15–16, 33, 165–66, 189; all warriors as imitations of, 174; Antilochus as beloved of, *xv*, 180–82, 187; armor of, 43; burial of, 181; death of, 175; funeral of, 2; and Hector's death, 15, 25, 150, 156, 159–60, 168, 173–74, 176, 181, 184, 188; Mezentius as equivalent, 167–68; paired with Diomedes, 14–17, 176–77; primacy of, 188; Pyrrhus as, 43; sibyl of Cumae's prophecy of new, 174; Turnus as, 9, 13, 17, 22, 43, 174; as wounded lion, 16–17
Actium, battle of: Augustus as victor at, 57–59, 66, 110, 116, 135, 140; as defeat of foreign enemy rather a than civil war, *x*, 4, 26, 29, 39, 59–60, 66, 89, 104, 144; on the shield of Aeneas, 4, 26, 66, 79, 88–89, 99, 110, 114–15, 128, 132
adoption: and Augustus as heir of Julius Caesar, 3, 87–90, 98–100, 124
Adorno, Theodor, 26–27, 138–39
Aeacidae Pyrrhi (Virgil), 56–57
Aemilius Paullus, 58, 64
Aeneas: as Achilles, 13, 43, 170, 176, 189; as Achilles and Diomedes, 16–17, 176; *aristeia* of, 5–12, 162–64; and Ascanius, 188; and "correction" of Homer's *Iliad*, 32; deification of, 82n2; as divine offspring, 85–88, 86, 92–93, 136–37; and elevated perspective on fall of Troy, 37, 39–41, 44, 46, 50–51; and expectation of death, 18, 175–76, 188; and flight from Troy, 33–34; identification with Dido, 18; as innocent, 35; Juno's phantom made of mist, 166; and Lausus, *xv*, 157, 159, 169–70; marriage to Lavinia, 67, 75–76, 79–81, 91–92, 117, 120, 123–25, 177–78; as Memnon, 186–87; and Mezentius's death, 180; as narrator, 30–36, 51, 54; Pallas as beloved of, 124, 129, 180–84, 187–88; as Patroclus, 157; primacy of, 10, 156–57, 174, 179; as progenitor of Julian line, *viii*, 30–31, 62–63, 91–92, 178–79; as progenitor of Romulus and Rome, *xiii*, 63n45, 90–91; and Pyrrhus/Neoptolemus, 35–36, 41–48, 50–51, 60; rescued by gods in the *Iliad*, 15–16, 32–33, 164–65, 176–77, 189; and Sarpedon, *xv*, 157, 165–66, 175–79, 185n14; as treacherous, 33, 34; Troy's fall witnessed by, 37, 39–41, 44, 46, 50–51, 55; Turnus as mirror of, *x*, *xv*, 9, 18, 24, 133, 186–90; Venus's revelation to, 40, 44–45, 48–49
Aeneid (Virgil), events, scenes, and vignettes in sequence:
BOOK 1: storm scene, 18–21, 37–40; opening speech of Aeneas, 15–16, 75–77; statesman simile, 18–21; Jupiter's prophecy to Venus, 89; reliefs on temple of Juno at Carthage, 30–32, 184–185; supplicant Ilioneus, 52–53; Aeneas behind cloud, 71, 75; substitution of Cupid for Iulus, 76–77; song of Iopas, 184; Dido's questions to Aeneas, 14–15, 17, 186

BOOK 2: and Book 3, 54–55n29; Aeneas as narrator, 30–36, 51; suppliant Sinon, 51–52; Hector appears in dream to Aeneas, 33, 36–37, 188; Aeneas fights way to Priam's palace, 38–43; Aeneas cuts down tower, 40–41; Aeneas and Pyrrhus, 35, 41–51, 55–56, 60; Pyrrhus kills Priam and Polites, 34, 42–43; Venus points to gods destroying Troy, 44–47; treecutter simile, 47–51; omen of Iulus, 13–14, 36; Aeneas loses Creusa, 34, 36, 109

BOOK 3: and Book 2, 54–55n29; Aeneas suspends shield at Actium, 57; Buthrotum, 55–59, 61n43; gifts to Aeneas and Astyanax, 51–52; Polyphemus, 139

BOOK 4: Dido and Anna, 76; Fama, 67–68, 75; Iarbas, 69, 76, 100–101; suppliant Anna, 52–53; Dido and her pyre, 69, 71, 72–73; Dido's curse, 72; Dido and Phoenix, 75–77; Dido's difficult death, 75, 85

BOOK 5: deification of Anchises, 88, 110–111n57; Hercules and Eryx, 135–36; arrow of Achestes, 88n13; Lusus Troiae, 110–113

BOOK 6: Temple of Daedalus at Cumae, 84–85; Theseus, 84–85, 103–105; Icarus, 105; Sibyl's prophecy, 22, 43, 74, 123; Sibyl on sons of gods, 82–84, 86–87, 89; Misenus, xvii–xix; Dido and famous women, 60–62, 73–75, 101–102; Deiphobus and warriors, 60–62, 102; Tartarus, 101–103; Groves of the Blessed, 92–98; Anchises on transmigration of souls, 94–95; Anchises and parade of heroes, 60–66, 88–92, 98, 105, 106–107, 109; Silvius, 62–63, 89–91; Augustus, 62–63; Anchises addresses Julius Caesar, 63–64, 90–93; Marcellus, 105–113; Gates of Ivory, 27

BOOK 7: Latium in peace (?), 119–121; Allecto and Turnus, 22–23, 116; Silvia's stag, 92–119; death of Galaesus, 119, 141–142; Italian cities make arms, 116; catalogue of Italians, 141–142; Shield of Turnus, 117, 141; Camilla, 119, 173

BOOK 8: Tiber appears in dream to Aeneas, 125–126, 140, 147–148; Aeneas sails up the Tiber, 126–127; Evander and Pallas greet Aeneas, 124, 183; Hercules and Cacus, 130–139; Evander and Aeneas tour Pallanteum (future Rome), 67, 121, 148–149; Evander and Golden Age, 115; Vulcan and Venus, 136–138, 186; departure from Pallanteum, 128–130; Shield of Aeneas, 26, 88, 114, 116, 127–128, 132, 133–134, 140–141, 142–147

BOOK 9: Turnus and Tiber, 142; ships tranformed into nymphs, 151–55; Nisus and Euryalus, 17n18, 184; Iulus, Numanus Remulus, and Apollo, 120; Antiphates, bastard son of Sarpedon, 153–154; Pan-darus and Bitias, 152–55; Turnus inside Trojan camp, 140, 144; Cretheus, xviii–xix; Turnus borne up by Tiber, 142–143

BOOK 10: divine council, 157, 164, 178; Venus willing to sacrifice Aeneas, 178; defensive circle/crown around Iulus, 178–179, 179n30; brothers of Sarpedon, 155; Pallas and Aeneas shipboard, 183–184; tears of Hercules and Jupiter remembers Sarpedon, 156, 165; Turnus kills Pallas, 160–162, 186–187; *aristeia* of merciless Aeneas, 162–164, 170; Juno rescues Turnus, 164–167; Mezentius, Lausus and Aeneas, 167–173, 185–187

BOOK 11: Trophy of Mezentius, 165; mourning over Pallas, 183, 184; embassy to Diomedes, 16, 56, 154, 188; "Windy" Drances, 21; death of Camilla, 166, 173–174

BOOK 12: lion simile, 16–17; blush of Lavinia, 120; Eumedes, 153–154; Aeneas says farewell to Iulus, 188; double *aristeiai* of Aeneas and Turnus, 5–12; tree of Faunus, 127; reconciliation of Jupiter and Juno, 23–25, 80–81; descent of Dira,

INDEX

23–25; Juturna, 143;; duel of Aeneas and Turnus, 16–18, 189; Aeneas kills Turnus, 18, 25, 156, 187–190

Aeolides, and poet figure, *xviii–xix*

Aeolus, as lord of the winds, *xviii*; and storm, 15, 18–19, 35, 38

Aeolus, Trojan warrior: death of, 9–10; home of, 9–11

Agamemnon, 22, 33, 56, 61, 101–2

Agenor (Homer), 159, 166, 167n17

Ahl, Frederick, 34

Aithiopis, xv, 172; as model for Virgil, 180–87

Ajax, 39, 43, 61, 75, 188

Albula, Tiber as, 147–48

Alexander the Great, 55n30, 68n4; bridge built by, 145–46; and divine sonship, 98–100

Allecto, *xiv*; as figure of civil discord, 23n28; as Juno's emissary instigating war, 23–24, 92, 116, 119, 120, 131

Almo, 141–42

Aloides, 102

Amycus, 154

Anchises, *x–xi*, 14; and Achaemenides, 52, 54–55; and civil war, 92; Evander as beloved of, 129; funeral games for, 109–11; future Romans as descendants of, 90–92; as guide to underworld, *xiv*, 4, 27, 83n4, 84, 87, 90–92, 94, 99; as *imago*, 98; as Julius Caesar figure, 87–88, 90; and reincarnation, 94–95; and reversal of sibyl, 92–95

Andromache, 43n19, 51, 55

Andromache (Euripides), 51

Anna, 52–53, 72n11, 76

Annales (Ennius), 29, 56–57, 94n24, 109n56

anonymity, 93–94; of the dead, 42, 102–3, 177–78; of the prisoners of Tartarus, 102

Antilochus: as beloved of Achilles, 180–82, 187; as killed by Memnon and avenged by Achilles, *xv*, 187; Lausus and, 185–87; as model of filial piety, 181, 185, 187; Pallas and, 180–81, 183, 185; as second Patroclus, 181–83

Antiphates, bastard son of Sarpedon, 151, 153–55, 174

Antony, Mark, 3, 60; as both enemy and rival, 3–4, 29–30, 33–34, 55, 59, 60, 116, 117, 132; as descendant of Hercules, 133; on shield of Aeneas, 66; Turnus linked to, 144

Apollo: Aeneas saved by, 15, 159, 164, 166; Augustus and, 131–32, 134–35; and Camilla's death, 173; Cumaean temple of, 74, 84, 104; grudge against Troy, 32, 46; and Hector, 156, 158–61, 171; and Hercules' theft of tripod from Delphi, 134–35; imitation of Agenor by, 159, 166, 167n17; and Iulus, 91–92; and Patroclus's death, 156, 158–61, 171, 173; Temple on the Palatine to, 131–32, 134, 135

Apollonius Rhodius (*Argonautica*), 154

Araxes, 140, 143–47

Arcadians: disappearance of the, 123, 125; and the *Eclogues*, 115–22; and golden age, 121–22; and origin of Rome, 119, 121–22; *see also* Evander; Pallas

Argonautica (Apollonius Rhodius), 154

Ariadne, 73, 84–86, 101

aristeiai (battlefield exploits): of Aeneas, *xiv*, 162–64; of Aeneas and Turnus, 5–11; of Diomedes and Achilles (*Iliad*, Homer), 15, 17; of Pallas, 160–61; Virgil's chiastic structuring of, *xiv*, 5–11

armor: of Achilles, 17, 43; Aeneas's fire-spouting helmet, 133, 138; Chimera helmet of Turnus, 131; as disguise, 34, 39; and identity between Turnus and Aeneas, 131–33; of Memnon, 14–15; of Mezentius, 163, 186; of Neoptolemus, 43, 57; shifting symbolic valence of, 43–44; suspended by Aeneas at Actium, 57; as trophy, 57, 137, 161, 198; twin-plumed helmet of Augustus, 99; *see also* shield of Aeneas

Arruns, 173

Ascoli, Albert Russell, *xvi*n15

Astyanax, 55, 61n43

Athena, 24–25, 45; Allecto and Dira as substitutes for Homer's, *xiv*
Auden, W. H., 145
Augustus Caesar: as adopted son of Julius Caesar, 3, 87–90, 98–100, 124; Aeneas and mythic origin of, 30, 51, 63; Apollo and, 131–32, 134–35; deification of, 82, 82n2, 88–89, 97–101; as divine offspring, 82; and filial piety, 35n9; genealogy and dynastic legitimacy of, *xiii*, 4, 62–63, 82, 131, 131n33; Hercules as parallel to, 134–35; as new Romulus refounding Rome, 62–63, 91, 143; as patron of Virgil, 84; on shield of Aeneas, 79, 88, 99, 115, 133, 134; as victor at Actium, 57–59, 66, 110, 116, 135, 140; Virgil as propagandist for, *ix*, *xiv*, 59–60, 82–83, 99, 116

Barchiesi, Alessandro, 91n16, 154n7, 161–62, 187
battle sequence: as anticlimactic, 11–12; and blurring of identities, 156–57; comparison of events in *Aeneid* and *Iliad*, 157–60; as epitome of Virgil's use of chiasmus, 5–12; taunting of the defeated, 33, 158, 160, 163–64, 169–70, 171–72, 187n17
Beard, Mary, 99–100
bees, 93–95, 108
Bitias, 152–56, 179n30
bodies of the dead: as anonymous and lost, 177; divine removal of, 173, 176–77; heads as trophies, 7, 42–43; missing from battlefield, 176–77; the ransom of Hector, 23n27, 170; repatriation of, 176–77; spears pulled from, 157–59, 161, 167–68, 174; stepping on, 157, 158–59, 161–62, 167–68
Bowie, A. M., 60
Boyle, Anthony J., 136–37
bridges, 143–46
bronze, 114–15; in the name of Aeneas, 114; and Roman coinage, 114; and weapons of war, 114–15, 117 (*See also* shield of Aeneas)
brother warriors: Bitias and Pandarus, 152–56; civil war and, 151; Clarus and Thaemon, 7, 10, 155, 157, 178; doubling and interchangeability, 151, 155n8; Liger and Lucagus, 163, 170; as motif, 155n8; as versions of Sarpedon, 151, 154–59
Brutus, Decimus, 3
Brutus, L. Junius, 62, 63
Brutus, Marcus Junius, 3
Buchheit, Vinzenz, *x*
Buthrotum: and Aeneas's Actium inscription, 57–58; Aeneas's visit to, 56, 57; and connection between Pyrrhus and historical King Pyrrhus, 56; as Little Troy, 29, 43, 54n, 55; Roman colonization of, 58, 58n37; as underworld, 57–58, 61n43

Cacus: fire monster, 131, 133–34; and Hercules, 121, 130–35, 130–36, 138; Mezentius as second, 131–33, 139n48; and Polyphemus, 139; and primitivism or animality, 138; as son of Vulcan, 116, 131, 133, 136, 138
Caeneus/Caenis, 74, 77
Caesar, Augustus. *See* Augustus Caesar
Caesar, Julius. *See* Julius Caesar
Caesarion, 76–77, 125
Camilla: and armor of Chloreus, 129, 163; dart of, 119; death of, 166, 173–74; as Patroclus, 173–74; as Penthesilea, 184–85; as representative of young Italy, 173–74, 177; as Sarpedon, 173–74, 177
Campi Lugentes, 85, 101–2
Carthage: founding of, 67–69, 118; hospitality offered the Trojans, 81; national myth of, 67, 69; population and citizenship in, 76, 78–79, 81; Punic Wars, 54, 62, 69, 77–79, 106; Roman colonization of, 58–59; Rome's destruction of, 28, 31, 53, 54, 64–66, 77, 78–79; as Troy, 70; wealth of, 118–19; *see also* Dido
Casali, Sergio, 63n45, 80n24, 84–85, 91n17, 116
Cassander, 99n34, 100
Castor and Pollux, 99, 107
Catiline, 26, 144

Cato the Elder, 64, 122
Cato the Younger, 20, 144
cattle, 148–49; of Geryon, 121–22, 130–31, 135–36; Io upon the shield of Turnus, 116–17, 120, 141; Turnus and Aeneas as fighting bulls, 120–21
chiasmus: allusions and, 21–22; and blurring of identity, 156–57, 161–62; chiastic relationship between Books 1 & 12, 13–18; circularity and, 162, 178, 179n30; and collapse of dualisms, *xi–xii*; and conclusion of *Aeneid*, 189–90; *epanelepsis* and, *xix*n23; as figure of thought, 1–2; as framing device (*See* framing device, chiasmus as); and ideology in Virgil, *xiii*, 134, 178; and mirroring supplication scenes, 51–54; and ordering of parade of shades in underworld, 44, 62–65; reordering of events and thematic, 12–13; and reversal of position of Trojans and Greeks, 51–54; and reversals used by Virgil, 2, 4, 12–13, 21, 25, 38–40, 44, 51–52, 54, 106, 117, 123, 143, 177, 184; and "second thoughts" in the reader, *ix–xii*; Virgil's imitation and inversion of Homer, 12–13, 15–17, 21–22, 189; and Virgil's structure of battle in Book 10, 157–58; *see also* ring composition
Chloreus, 129, 163
Cicero, 3, 58n37, 94–95, 98–99, 144; and deification, 87n10; *De natura eorum*, 99–100; *De re publica*, 93–95; *Somnium Scipionis*, 94–95
civilization: chiasmus and reversal of perspective on, 122–25; fire and, 137–39; gleaming objects linked to, 125–26; gold linked to, 114–15, 123, 125–28; Greek culture and future Roman, 53–54; as human imposition upon nature, 83n4, 115, 122–23, 125–30, 140–41, 147–48; *vs.* primitivism, 130–33; *vs.* rusticity, xii, 115, 118, 123; as violent, 133, 138–39
civil wars, Roman: and adversaries as interchangeable, 12; all war as, 12; Augustus and end of, 189–90; disguised as foreign wars, *x*, 4, 26, 29–30, 39, 59–60, 65–66, 89, 104, 135, 144; as focus of last four books, 59; *Lusus Troiae* horse games linked to, 110, 112–13; and ordering of parade of shades in underworld, 62–63; as unresolved, 18–21, 189–90
Clarus and Thaemon, 10, 155, 157, 178–79
M. Claudius Marcellus (c. 268–208 BCE), 62
Clausen, Wendell, *x*
Cleopatra: defeated by Augustus at Actium, 57–59, 66, 110, 116, 135, 140; Dido linked to, 59, 72, 76–77, 79, 125; as foreign enemy in Rome's civil war, *xiv*, 4, 29–30, 59, 66, 135, 144; as Greek, 60; as monstrous, 132; as new Hannibal, 59–60; as new Pyrrhus, 54, 56–57, 59; on the shield of Aeneas, 144, 167
clouds or mist, 32–33, 39, 68, 71, 75, 164, 166, 173
Clytemnestra, 56, 101–2
colonization, Roman, 58–59; and extension of citizenship, 78–79, 81
combinatory imitation, 69, 150–51, 156–57, 166, 172–73, 186n14
Conte, Gian Biagio, *xi*
Coroebus, 34, 39
Cotta (Cicero), 99
Crete, 54n29, 56, 73, 84, 88n12, 105, 111
Cretheus, as self-portrait of the poet, *xviii–xix*
Creusa, 36; Aeneas and loss of, 34, 36, 109; as Eurydice, 109; the ghost of, 54n29, 124
Creusa as Eurydice, 109
Cumaean sibyl. *See* sibyl of Cumae
Cupid, sent by Venus to inflame Dido, 67, 70, 76, 125
Cybele: descendants of, 91, 93; offspring of, 112; and pines of Mount Ida, 151, 155

Daedalus, 74, 84–85, 95, 104, 105, 107
Dardanus, 8, 11, 12, 32, 96–97, 140, 164
Dares, 154

Darkness Visible (Johnson), x
death: Aeneas's expectation of, 18, 175–76, 188; and anonymity, 42, 102–3, 177–78; Dido's suicide, 18, 72–73, 77; as difficult birth, 77; as equalizer, 9; the grave as home or residence, 10–11; and loss of identity, 169; as personal annihilation, 108–9; poetic compulsion to bring back the dead, 107–9; progeny as return of the dead, 162–63; slavery as social, 162; *see also* bodies of the dead
deification: of Aeneas, 82n2; of Augustus, 82, 82n2, 88–89, 97–101; Cicero and, 87n10, 98; and doubleness, 88–89, 92, 97; as dynastic propaganda, *xiii*, 82–83, 92, 99; in *Eclogues*, 83; and fame, 82–83, 99, 101; in *Georgics*, 83n3; of Hercules, 97–99, 103–4; of Julius Caesar, 82, 87–88, 92–93, 98–99, 110; Jupiter as deified human, 100; poetry as alternative to, 83; of Romulus (Quirinus), 62, 82, 99, 109, 131n33; sibyl of Cumae on, 82–83, 93–94; skepticism and, 83, 99–101; as temporary or contingent, 104–5; Theseus as cult-god, 103–5
Deiphobus, *xviii*, 25n32, 60–61, 64–65, 101–2
De re publica (Cicero), 93–95
De rerum natura (Lucretius), 46n23, 87, 137
"De Roma" (Vitalis), 148
Derrida, Jacques, 107
Dido: and Aeneas in the underworld, 74–75; alternate story of, 68, 70, 75–76, 78; as Ariadne, 73, 84–85, 85–86, 101; and banquet scene, 28, 76–77, 183–84; Cleopatra linked to, 59, 72, 76–77, 79, 125; curses of, 53, 61, 90; and defense of Carthage, 69, 76; funeral pyre of, 14, 68, 69–70, 71–74, 77, 81, 120; and Hannibal, 58–59, 72, 77, 90; Iarbas and, 78n19; as lovestruck (enamored), 14, 52, 67, 69, 78, 81, 183–84; as loyal and chaste, 68–70, 74–75, 78; and masculine role, 74, 78n19; as monstrous, 72–74, 77–78; and motherhood or childbirth, 72–73, 76–77, 81, 125; as Penelope figure, 69; as phoenix (Phonissa), 75–78, 81; questions as framing device in Book 1, 14–15; as self-sacrificing, 69, 73, 74; Servius on, 68, 69; as shade in the underworld, 60–61, 73–75; and temple to Juno, 14–15, 30, 31, 68, 150, 184, 186; Turnus linked to, 16, 71; Virgil's rewriting of myth, 67–68, 70–75; *see also* Carthage
Diodorus Siculus, 101
Diomedes, 14–17, 56, 188; Aeneas as, 16–17, 176–77; and Aeneas in *Iliad*, 15; the horses of, 14–15; Latin attempts to enlist, 16, 56; and Nisus, 17n18; paired with Achilles, 14–17, 176–77; as stand in for Achilles, 14–15; Turnus as new, 5–12, 153–54; as wounded lion, 16–17
Diomedes (Homer), 164
Diores, 7, 10
Dira, *xiv, xvi,* 22, 23–25
divine offspring: and adoption, 87–88; Aeneas as, 85–88, 86, 87–88, 92–93, 136–37; Aeneas's shield as, 136–37; Alexander the Great as, 98–100; of Dardanus, 96–97; elevated to the stars, 85–86, 93; Iarbas as son of Ammon-Jupiter, 68n4, 100–101; and return from the underworld, 85; Romulus as son of Mars, 99; Sarpedon as son of Jupiter, 155–56, 161, 174
Dolon, 17nn18, 153–54
Donatus, *xvi–xvii*
doubleness, doubling: of Aeneas and Pyrrhus, 35–36, 41–48, 50–51; of Aeneas and Turnus, 8–12, 16–18, 141–43, 164–66, 185–90; and *Aithiopis* as model, 186–87; and collapse of distinctions, 169–70, 189; and deification, 88–89, 92, 97; of Diodo's story, 68, 70, 74–75, 78; doubles of doubles, 184–85; of genealogy of Rome and Julians, *xiii*, 61–62, 90–92, 177–79; generations as replicas, 151–52, 183; of Hercules shared by Augustus and Antony, 134–36; and interchangeability,

8–12, 150–51, 174; and moral ambiguity, 175; and multiple replicas of Sarpedon, 148, 157, 175, 177; names as signal of, 153–54; and reassignment of attributes, 161; similes and double distancing, 35–36; twins and, 4, 107, 125, 155; of Vigil's self-portraits, *xvii–xix*; and warrior brothers as motif, 155n8, 157

Drances, Turnus on, 21, 144

East-West binary, Actium as defeat of the East, 29, 39, 104

Eclogues (Virgil): *Georgics* contrasted with, 115–23; *First Eclogue*, 89, 144; *Fourth Eclogue*, 121; *Fifth Eclogue*, 83; *Ninth Eclogue, xix*; *Tenth Eclogue*, 121; and Arcadians in *Aeneid*, 115–22

Elysium: Anchises and, 88, 90, 92–93, 95; fame and immortality in, 103; the heavens and, 92–93, 96–97; poetry, memory, and residence in, *xiv*, 84, 95–96, 108–9

Ennius, 29, 56–57, 94n24, 109n56

Entellus, 135–36

*epanelepsis, xix*n23

Epicureanism, 99

Epirus, 56

Er, myth of, 94, 101

Erichaetes, 153, 162

Eriphyle, 74, 85n6

Eryx, 135–36

Euhemerus and Euhemerism, 83, 99–100; and Cassander, 99n34, 100; and Salmoneus, 101n38

Eumedes, 153–54

Euphorbus, 173

Euphrates, 140–43, 145

Europa, 120, 141

Eurus, 39–40

Euryalus, 17n18, 105n49, 184

Eurydice, 107–9

Evadne, 85

Evander, 116, 122, 129–30; Anchises as beloved of, 129, 136n40, 183–84; Hercules and, 132; as Nestor figure, 116, 136, 181, 183; poverty of, 121–22

Fama, 32n3, 67–68, 71, 75, 86–87; Mercury as inverse double of, 68n4

fame: deification as pinnacle of, 82–83; limits of, 94; names and, 83n3, 83n4; poetry and, 83; and the underworld, 95–103

farming: in the *Georgics*, 118–19, 120, 121, 123; of Italians contrasted with Arcadian herding, 122; weapons turned to tools for, 50, 119–20

Faunus, 119, 127

Feeny, Denis, 83n4, 94, 104n48

filial piety *(pietas)*, 35n9, 169–70, 185, 187–88

fire: and civilization, 137–38; Roman domestication of, 130–35, 137–39; serpents tongues and tongues of flame, 13–14, 36

Fraenkel, Eduard, 185

framing device, chiasmus as: in Book 1, 13–14, 17–18; in Book 8, 110, 140; in Book 9, 153–55; in Books 2 & 3, 51–54; in the *Iliad*, 2n1, 22–23; and rivers in Book 8, 140–43, 143–44; and structure of entire *Aeneid*, 4–5, 17–18, 22

fratricide, *xiii*, 4, 76–77, 125, 136

furor, x, 16, 23

Gaius Octavius. *See* Augustus Caesar

Galaesus, 118–19, 141–42

Galinsky, G. Karl, 135

gates: of Cumaean temple, 14, 74, 84, 104; of ivory and horn, 14, 27, 88n12

Gaul or the Gauls, 62, 79, 127–28, 139

genealogies: contradictory, *xiii*, 63, 90–91, 96; Dardanus as Italian, 12, 96, 140, 164; and divine offspring, 63, 68n4, 131; of Romulus, 63n45, 91, 99; *see also* Julian line

Georgics (Virgil): and Latins, xii, 115–22; bees in, 93–94, 108; deification as concern in, 83n3; and national ideology, 117–18; Orpheus in, 87n9, 107–8

gigantomachy, 19, 128, 138
gold: arms of, 114–17, 130 (*See also* shield of Aeneas); human civilization linked to, 114–15, 123, 127; as indistinguishable from bronze, 114–15, 129; Iulus as jewel set in, 179n30; Troy linked, 119, 129–30
Gowers, Emily, 35, 42–43, 112
Gransden, K. W, 131–32, 138, 173
Greeks: at Actium, 29–30, 57–60; Aeneas in armor of, 34, 39, 43; and Carthaginians, 51–54, 65; conquered by Rome, 28–31, 44, 51–65, 103–5, 144; as cultural dead end, 125; Roman appropriation of culture, 104–5, 123; Trojans playing Homeric roles of, 13, 16–18, 29–30, 150–51, 155–56, 177, 189–90; and the underworld, 60–61, 64–66, 100–105
green, as nature in opposition to the gold of civilization, 114–15, 122, 125–28

Hades. *See* underworld
Haemonides, 163
Halaesus, 160
Hammon, Jupiter as, 68n4, 100
Hannibal, 66, 77, 79; as avenger of Dido, 58–59; Cleopatra as new, 59–60
Hardie, Philip, *xi–xiii*, 19, 68n4, 128, 137n42, 144, 149n70, 152, 179n30
Harvard School, *x*
Hector, 36–37, 148; Achilles and death of, 15, 25, 150, 156, 159–60, 168, 173–74, 176, 181, 184; Aeneas and, 177, 188–89; Dido and role of, 71–72; funeral of, 2; ghost of, 33, 36–37, 54n29, 61n43, 189; ransoming and return of body, 23n27, 170, 172, 176–77, 187n17; Turnus linked to, 151, 161–62, 166–67, 172, 188
Heinze, Richard, 70
Helen of Troy, 37, 55, 61, 101; and judgment of Paris as cause of War, 44–45
Helenus: son of King Pyrrhus, 56; son of Priam, 43, 55, 56
Hercules: Aeneas and, 136–38; and Antaeus, 136; and Apollo and theft of tripod from

Delphi, 134–35; Augustus as parallel to, 116, 134–35; and Cacus, 121, 130–35, 138; deification of, 97–99, 103–4; doubling of, 97–98; and Eryx, 135–36; Jupiter's consolation of, 156, 158, 161, 164; lion skin as attribute of, 122, 130, 134; Nestor and, 136; Pallanteum and cult of, 114–16, 122, 132; Theseus freed by, 103; and the underworld, 85–86, 97
Hinds, Stephen, *xii*n10, 151
Hitler, Adolf, *x*
Homer: *Aeneid* as correction of, 32; *Iliad* as Virgil's model (*See* Iliad (Homer)); men as gods in, 48; *Osyssey* as Virgil's model (*See* Odyssey (Homer))
homosexual love, 124n19; of Achilles and Antilochus, 187; of Aeneas and Pallas, 124, 129, 180–84, 187–88; of Evander and Anchises, 129, 183–84; of Nisus and Euryalus, 184
Horace, 97, 109; on poetry and poets in *Odes*, 96–97, 109
Horatius Cocles, 143–44
Horkheimer, Max, 138–39
horses: of Aeneas, 17n18; of Diomedes, 14–15; Evander's gift of, 116, 129–30; the *Lusus Troiae* horse games, 109–13; of Nestor, 160, 172, 185; of Rhesus, 17n18; speeches to, 139n48, 160, 171, 172; Trojan horse ruse, 52

Iarbas, 68n4, 69, 76, 78n19, 100–101; divine sonship of, 68n4
Icarus, 14, 105, 107
ideology, 4; of Augustus, *x–xi*, *xiii*; chiasmus and presentation of, *xiii*, 134, 178; contradictions and Virgil's veiled criticisms of, *x–xi*, *xiii*; as contradictory, 92; dynastic, 178; ideological biases in the poem, *ix–x*; and narrator's elevated position, 51; and reinterpretation of history, 4, 28–29, 30, 51, 57–58, 91n17; and reversal of official myth, 134; Virgil and denaturalization of, 140–41; Virgil's

Georgics and national, 117–18; *see also* propaganda

Idomeneus, 56

Iliad (Homer): Aeneas in, 16, 32–36, 96–97, 150, 162–64, 169–70, 175–77; *Aeneid* and inversions or reversals of, 13, 22–25, 71–72, 152–53, 165, 167–68, 175, 189–90; chiasmus and the, 2n1, 22; divine intervention in, 32–33, 164–66, 175–76; and role exchange, 13, 16–17, 22, 150–51, 153–54, 160–69, 171, 173–75; Sarpedon in, *xv*, 154–56, 160–62, 169, 171, 173–75; sequence of battle in *Aeneid* 10 mapped against, 157–60; *Teichoscopia* in, 37; and Virgil's combinatory imitation, 69, 150–51, 156–57, 166, 172–73, 186n14; as Virgil's model, *xiv–xvi*, 12–13, 17n18, 22, 53, 61n43, 70, 97, 102, 150–51, 157–60

Ilioneus, 52

Iliou persis, 30

Inachus, 116, 120, 141, 144

Institution Oratoria (Quintilian), 1

Io, 119; on the shield of Turnus, 116–17, 120, 141

Iris, 71, 77, 85

Italians, Latins, and Rutulians: claims to the land, 127, 141–43; as equivalents of Trojans, 157; and the *Georgics*, 115–22; Trojans as, 79–81, 177

Italy, bull (*uitulus*) as symbol of, 117

Iulus, Ascanius: as Aeneas's son, 33–34, 36, 61n43, 91, 170; chiasmus and defensive "ring" around, 178–79; and fire as divine omen, 36, 133; as jewel set in gold, 179n30; and the *Lusus Troiae* horse games, 110–11; and Pallas, 124, 178–79; as progenitor of Julian line, 32, 36, 62–63, 89, 91–92, 178–79; Romulus as descendant of, 63n45, 125; and stag of Silvia, 92

Ixion, 102

Johnson, W. R, *x–xii*

Julian line: Aeneas as progenitor of, 30–31, 62–63, 91–92; Anchises as progenitor of, 32, 44; fertility and continuity of, 112; Iulus as progenitor of, 32, 36, 62–63, 89, 91–92, 178–79; survival and triumph of, 44, 178–79

Julius Caesar, 63, 66; and Anchises, 87–88, 90; assassination of, 3, 35n9, 87; and comet or Julian star, 87–88, 104; deification of, 82, 87–88, 92–93, 98–99, 110

Juno: Carthage favored and doomed by, 80; Dido's temple to, 14–15, 30, 31, 68, 77, 150, 184, 186; as divine irrational violence, 20–21, 24, 45; and Io, 120; as Juno Lucina, 77; pact with Jupiter, 23–25, 80–81, 123, 166, 177–78; and pity for Dido, 77, 85; rescue of Turnus by, 33, 158–59, 164–67; and storm sent to trouble Aeneas, 15, 18–20, 35, 38, 47–48

Jupiter: complaint of Iarbus to, 100–101; and consolation of Hercules, 156, 158, 161, 164; and deification of Augustus, 88–89, 92–93, 97–98, 101; and the Dirae, *xi*, 23–24; as Hammon, 68n4; and justice for the dead, 86–87, 103; Mercury as messenger for, 58, 67–68, 101; pact with Juno, 23–25, 80–81, 123, 166, 177–78; prophecy to Venus, 16, 26, 49, 85, 88–89, 92–93, 98, 109; as Roman power, 104; Sarpedon as son of, 155–56, 161, 174

justice: as arbitrary, 102; Jupiter and judgment of the dead, 86–87, 102–5; poetic, 84, 103

Juturna, 5, 11, 33, 143

Kebriones, 158, 163–64

Knox, Bernard, 13–14, 36

Kopff, E. Christian, 183

L. Aemilius Scipio, 64

labyrinths, 74, 84–85, 95, 98, 105–12, 111–12

Laocoon, 13

Laodamia, 85

Laomedon, 32

La Penna, Antonio, 99

Latins. *See* Italians, Latins, and Rutulians

Latinus, 4, 119, 121

Lausus: Antilochus as model for, *xv*, 180, 181, 185; cast as Patrocles, 157; cast as Sarpedon, 157, 160–61; and events of battle in Book 10, 157–60; and fatherly grief of Mezentius, 139n48, 159, 171, 174, 178, 185–86; filial piety and, 169–70, 185–86; killed by Aeneas, *xv*, 157, 159, 169–70, 185–87; as representative of young Italy, 177

Lavinia, 5; as courted by Turnus, 79, 144; Dido and, 79–81, 124; as wife of Aeneas and progenitrix of Rome, 5, 67, 75–76, 79–81, 91–92, 117, 120, 123–25, 177–78

Lethe, river of, and forgetting, 94–96

Liger, 153, 158, 162–63, 170

lions: Aeneas and lionskin, 130; Diomedes and Achilles in *Iliad* as wounded, 16–17; Evander and the skins of beasts, 122, 129–30; and Furor of war, 16–17; Hector and Patroclus as, 17, 158, 161; in *Iliad*, 16–17; lion skin as attribute of Hercules, 122, 130, 134; lion skin as gift to Salius, 130n29; Turnus as wounded, 16–17, 158, 161–62

Livy, 58, 63n45, 147; on human agency in Rome's history, 49–50; on intermarriage and Rome's expansion, 79–80

love: Aeneas's shield as product of lovemaking between Venus and Vulcan, 136–38, 183; Dido's, 14, 52, 67, 69, 78, 81, 183–84; homosexual, 120, 124, 129, 180–84, 187–88; as madness, 69, 72–74, 78, 90, 108, 120, 187–88

Lucagus, 158, 163, 170

Lucretia, 69

Lucretius: as influence on Virgil, 46n23, 87n9, 94–95, 137; Mars in *De rerum natura*, 137

Lusus Troiae (horse games), 109–13

Lycaon, 153–54, 162–63, 170

Lyne, R. O. A. M., 133

Macedonian Wars, 54, 58

Magus, 158, 162–63, 170

Manton, G. R., 180n1, 183

Marcellus, M. Claudius (42–23 BCE), 14, 84, 92n18, 105–13

Mars, 49n25, 91, 99, 115, 137

Medea, 72n10

Memnon the Ethiopian: Aeneas and Turnus as, 184–87; armor of, 14–15, 186

memory: geographical names as only trace of forgotten kings, 147–48; Lethe and forgetting, 94–96; poetry as vessel of, *xiv*, 96–97, 108–9; Tartarus and erasure of, 101–2

Menoetes, 7, 9, 10

Mercury, 58, 67–68, 101; Fama as inverse double of, 68n4

Meriones, 158, 163

Messapus, 153, 162

Metamorphoses (Ovid), 89–90, 136, 144, 151–52

Mezentius: as Achilles, 167–68; Aeneas as adversary and killer of, 91n17, 156, 163, 167, 171–72, 178, 180; arms of, 163; burial plea of, 160, 172; as impious, 171, 175; Lausus's death and fatherly grief of, 139n48, 159, 171, 174, 178, 185–86; as monstrous tyrant and second Cacus, 131–33, 139n48; as Nestor figure, 171, 185–86; as Patroclus, 157, 171–72; as Sarpedon, 157; speech to horse, 139n48, 159

Minos, as judge in underworld, 74, 84, 103–4

Minos, tyrant of Crete, 104

mirroring: of elements in Books 2 & 3, 54; of Trojans and Greeks, 42–44, 46, 52–53; *see also* doubleness, doubling

Misenus, as self-portrait of the poet, *xvii–xviii*

Mnestheus, 8, 11, 179n30

morality: and admission to Elysium, 95–96; and behavior during battle, 162–63, 175; filial piety as Aeneas's identifying quality, 187–88; moral contrasts, 132, 134; moral distinctions among characters, 174–75; and Rome's dominance, 49; *see also* piety, filial piety

INDEX 213

Morgan, Llewellyn, 133
Moschus, 120, 141
Most, Glenn, 97
Musaeus, 96

names: Aeneas and reluctance to name the enemy, 176; anonymity of the dead, 42, 102–3, 177–78; conventions of assigning Greek names to Trojans, 53; Dido as Elissa, 68; fame and, 83n3; of forgotten kings, 147–48; imposed on nature by civilization, 83n4, 140–41, 147–48; and replicas of characters, 153–54; *see also* anonymity
narrative structure of *Aeneid:* as bifurcated, 12–13, 59, 90, 123; chiasmus and, 4–5, 12–17, 23–25, 59, 122–25; death of Marcellus as supplement, 64, 84, 92n18, 107; four elements and organization of, 117; positioning of Greek Books (2&3) between Carthaginian (1&4), 54, 59
Natural Questions (Seneca), 143
nature: contrasted with intentional destruction by the gods, 49–50; divine personification of, 37–39, 46; fall of Troy as natural disaster, 37–38; geographical names as human invention, 140–41; as green world in opposition to gold of civilization, 114–15, 122–23, 125–30; interplay of natural, divine, and human actors, 35–38, 40, 42, 45–50, 127; rivers, 140–49; and timelessness, 144–45
Nausicaa (Homer), Dido and, 69
negative capability, 2–3
Neoptolemus, 43; *see also* Pyrrhus
Neptune: and fall of Troy, 45, 46–47; intervention and rescue of Aeneas in *Iliad,* 15; and pacifying statesman, 18–21; as Poseidon in Homer, 32–33, 46; sacrifices demanded by, 14; trident as attribute of, 20–21, 40, 43, 46
Nestor: in *Aithiopis,* 183, 185; Evander as modeled on, 116, 136, 181, 183; and family distroyed by Hercules, 136; horse of, 160, 172, 185; Mezentius as, 171, 185–86; in Ovid's *Metamorphoses,* 136; and paternal grief over death of Antilochus, *xv,* 136, 172n21, 180n1, 181, 183
New Criticism, *x*
Nile, 140–42
Nisus, 17n18, 105n49, 130n29, 184
Notus, 38–40, 46
Numa, 91
Numanus Remulus, 91, 119–20
nymphs, transformed from ships, 151–55

Octavia, 106, 109
Octavian. *See* Augustus Caesar
Odes (Horace), 96–97, 109
Odyssey (Homer): Achilles' tomb and conclusion of, 181; *Aithiopis* and, 182; Antilochus in, 181–82; Athena in, xii, 24–25; and bifurcated structure of *Aeneid,* 12–13, 21, 43, 183; and chiastic structure of the *Aeneid,* 12–13, 21–22, 43n19; deification and doubling of Herakles in, 96–97; Polyphemus in, 69, 72, 139; Pyrrhus in, 61; and the suffering of the victor, 31–32; tears wept by Odysseus and Aeneas, 31; underworld in, 61, 75, 84, 85n6, 97–98, 101–2, 181; as Virgil's model, 12–13, 21–22, 25, 31, 43–44, 61, 69, 71–72, 75, 84, 85n6, 97, 101–2, 112, 122, 152n3, 181
Omphale, 135
Orestes, 55–56, 61n43
Orodes, 159, 167–68, 170
Orontes, 178n27
Orpheus, 85, 87n9, 107–9
Ovid, 89–90, 136, 144–45, 151–52

Palamedes, 34
Palinurus, 14, 178n27
Pallanteum: departure from, 128–30; as future Rome, 67, 122, 126, 147–48; Hercules cult and, 114–15, 114–16, 132
Pallas: Aeneas and revenge for death of, 9, 25, 125, 129, 156, 162–63, 169–70, 180–84,

Pallas (*continued*)
186–89; Antilochus and, 180–81, 183, 185; *aristeia* of, 160; Camilla as double for, 173; death as central to Book 10, 160–62; departure from Pallanteum, 128–29; and disappearance of the Arcadians, 123, 125; Evander's gifts to, 129; Hercules weeps for, 97, 157n9, 158, 161, 164–65, 174; Homeric models for, 168; and Iulus, 178–79; as Julius Caesar, 188n20; killed and despoiled by Turnus, 161–62, 170, 184, 187, 189; Lausus and, *xv*, 160, 169, 181, 186, 187; linked to lovestruck Dido, 183–84; and Patroclus, 156, 158, 160–62, 178–79, 183; as representative of young Italy, 177; and Sarpedon, 155–58, 160–62, 178–79

Pallas Athena. *See* Athena

Pan, 121

Pandarus, 152–56, 179n30

Panthus, 33–34, 36

Paris, 44–45, 160, 165, 172, 185; and death of Achilles, 175

Parry, Adam, *x*

Pasiphae, 73–74

Patroclus: Antilochus as second, 181–82; Apollo and death of, 156, 158–61, 171, 173; Camilla as, 173; and Hector, 157–62, 160–61, 163, 168, 173, 181, 184; and Hector as lions, 158, 161; in *Iliad*, 182; as lion, 158, 161; Mezentius as, 171–72; multiple characters cast as, 148, 157; in *Odyssey*, 181; and Pallas, 156, 158, 160–62, 178–79; in Pindar, *Pythia 6*, 181; and Sarpedon's death, 151, 156

Pedasos, 160, 172, 185n14

Peisistratos, 181

Penelope (Homer), 69

Penthesilea, 184–85

Perithous, 102

Perseus of Macedon, 58

Phaedra, 73, 85n6

Philippic (Cicero), 4

Philip V. of Macedon, 58

Phillips, Jane E., 77

Phlegyas, 102–3

piety: Aeneas and, 169–70, 187; as alibi for Augustus' revenge, 35n9, 188n20; filial piety (*pietas*), 35n9, 55, 169–70, 185, 187–88; the hubris of Salmoneus, *xviii*, 100–101; impiety and punishment in Tartarus, 100–101; impiety of Mezentius, 171; skepticism and, 99–100; and Turnus, 187

Pilumnus, 142

Pindar, 181, 185

Plato, 22, 94, 101, 108

Plutarch, 20, 103–4, 134–35

poetry: and compulsion to bring back the dead, 108–9; Cretheus and Misenus as figures of Virgil, *xvii–xix*; as *eidolon / imago*, 97; Elysium and remembrance in, *xiv*, 84, 95–96, 108–9; in Horace's *Odes*, 96–97, 109; and ideology, 25–27, 50–51, 70, 92, 103–5, 140–41, 145, 178, 189–90; Misenus as self-portrait of Virgil, *xvii–xviii*; and political power, 84, 103–5; and timelessness, 145; as vessel of memory, *xiv*, 84, 96–97, 108–9

Polites, killed by Pyrrhus, 34, 42, 44, 55, 112, 187n17

Polybius, 78–79, 98

Polydeuces, 154

Polyphemus, 52, 53, 69, 72, 139, 160

Polyphemus, and Cacus, 139

Pompey the Great, 42, 44, 63, 66, 109

Po river, 96

Pöschl, Vikor, 19–20

Poseidon (Homer): Aeneas saved by, 32–33; grudge against Troy, 46; *see also* Neptune

Posthomerica (Quintus Smyrnaeus), 186

Priam: beheaded by Pyrrhus, 42–43; as cursed, 32; death and transfer of power to the Aenean line, 30, 32–33, 35–36, 44, 112

Priam, son of Polites, grandson of Priam, 112–13

Procris, 74, 85n6

pronouns, and chiastic reversal, 7–8, 10–11

propaganda, 51; Aeneas's shield as, 4, 116; Anchises and, 92, 99; critical readings and *Aeneid* as, *xiii*, *xiv*; deification as dynastic, 82–83, 92, 99; and depiction of civil wars as foreign war, 59–60, 65–66; and Hercules and Cacus story, 131–32; Propertius and, 59; and treatment of Marcellus, 106–7; Virgil's *Aeneid* as, *ix*, *xiv*, 4, 82–83, 99, 116, 131–32, 135, 189–90

Propertius, Sextus, 59, 77

Publius Sulpicius, 58

Puglia, settlement in, 56

Punic Wars, 54, 62, 69, 77–79, 106

Putnam, Michael, *x*, 52–53, 115n2, 143–44, 187

Pyrrhus: armor of, 57; and beheading of Priam, 42–43; death of, 55–56; linked to King of Epirus, 54–60, 65; as "new Ptolemy," 44n21, 60; as next Achilles, 43; prominent role played by, 54–55; as son of Achilles, 36

Pyrrhus, King of Epirus, 56–58, 60, 65, 66

Pythia 6 (Pindar), 181

Quintilian, on chiasmus (*antimetabole*), 1–3

Quintilius, 109

Quintus Smyrnaeus, 186

Quirinus. *See* Romulus

Remus, *xiii*, 4, 118, 125

Republic (Plato), 94

Rhadamanthus, 74, 84

Rhoebus, 139n48, 160, 171–72, 185–86

ring composition, 2, 13, 26, 60–66, 142–43, 157, 167, 178–79; and organization of parade of shades, 65

rivers: bridges as affront to, 143–44, 146–47; as chiastic framing device, 143–44; Juturna as goddess of, 143; Lethe in the underworld, 94–96; and relationship of civilization to nature, 140–47; as subject to kings, 147; as subject to Rome, 142–45; Tiber, 140; upon the shield of Aeneas, 140

Rome: Aeneas and, 66; as ascendant over Greeks and the East, 30–31, 54, 58, 66; and Buthrotum, 58; and Carthage, 28, 31, 53, 54, 58–59, 64–66, 77, 78–79; as eternal, 112, 147–49; extension of citizenship to Italian allies, 79; and fall of Troy, 30–31; founding of (*See* Rome, founding of); Greek culture and, 53; and opposition to monarchy, Caesarism, 20, 144; Pallanteum as future site of, 67, 122, 126, 147–48; transience of, 147–49

Rome, founding of: Aeneas and, 67, 190; Arcadians and origin of Rome, 119, 121–22; Augustus and "refounding," 62–63, 91, 143; Mars and, 49n25, 91, 115; Romulus and, 62, 66–67, 91; she-wolf and, 115, 137n42; Trojans and, 13

Romulus: contradictory genealogies of, 63n45, 91, 99; deification of (Quirinus), 62, 82, 99, 109, 131n33; and founding of Rome, 62, 66–67, 91; Remus killed by, 4, 125; as shade in the underworld, 62, 105; Theseus and, 103–4

The Ruines of Rome (Spenser), 148

Rutulians. *See* Italians, Latins, and Rutulians

sacrifice, logic of, 178n27

Salius and Salii, 130n29

Salmoneus: and Euhemerus, 101n88; punishment in Tarturus, *xviii*, 101–2, 105; as skeptic, 101

Sarpedon: Aeneas as double for, *xv*, 157, 165–66, 175–78, 185n14; and Aeneas as expendable, *xv*, 177–79; Antiphates, son of, 151, 155; brothers of, 10, 151, 155, 157, 177–79; Camilla as, 156, 173–74; death of, 151, 156; as designated victim, *xv*, 150, 165, 178; and doubling and interchangeable replicas of, 148, 150–51, 157, 175, 177; and Lausus, 158, 160; and Mezentious, 159–60, 169; multiple characters cast as, 148, 157, 175, 177; and Pallas, 155–58, 160–62, 178–79; and Patroclus, 151, 156,

Sarpedon (*continued*)
174; as son of Jupiter, 155–56, 161, 174; trees and warriors of Ida linked to, 154–55; and Turnus, 151, 157, 178–79; and Virgil's chiastic structure, 180

Scipio, Aemilius Paullus, 64–65, 94–95

"Secondary Epic" (Auden), 145

Seneca, 73, 143

Serestus, 163

serpents, 13–14, 36

Servius, 25, 42, 89, 109, 145–46; on the Araxes, 145–46; on Dido, 69, 77

shades or ghosts: Dido, 60–61, 73–75; Hector's appearance to Aeneas, 36–37, 61n43; parade of shades, 27, 62–63, 65, 84, 87, 94, 109; and poetic representation, 97–98

shield of Aeneas, 116; and Aeneas as Memnon figure, 186; Antony on, 66; Augustus on, 79, 88, 99, 115, 133, 134; battle of Actium as depicted upon, 4, 26, 66, 79, 88–89, 99, 110, 114–15, 128, 132; battle of Actium on, 4, 66, 132; Cleopatra, 79; as divine offspring, 136–37; "future" Roman history represented upon, 27, 79, 110, 114, 136–37, 141, 145; Gate of Ivory and, 27; rivers upon, 140–42; *vs.* shield of Turnus, 117; and the sow of portent, 125–26; Venus and gift of, 115–16, 127, 129, 132; Vulcan and creation of, *xiv*, 4, 26, 67, 114, 116, 128, 132–33, 137–38, 139, 174, 186; as weapon, 115–16, 130, 137–38; as work of art similar to the *Aeneid* itself, 4

ships, 126

sibyl of Cumae, 1, 9, 13, 23, 43, 82–86; Anchises' account as reversal of, 92–95; chiasmus and, 83–84; as guide to the underworld, 98n29, 100–103; and the prisoners of Tartarus, 102; and prophecy of a new Achilles, 9, 22, 43, 123, 174; on the underworld, 1, 9, 13, 84–89

Silvius Postumus: and Iulus, 92; as progenitor of Rome, 62, 63n45, 80n24, 81, 91–92, 125

similes: and chiasmus, 4, 9, 16–21, 50–51, 116; Virgil's exploitation of Homer's, 152, 154–55, 161–62; *see also specific figures e.g.* lions

Sinon, 34, 51–52; and Achaemenides, 54–55; and defamation of Aeneas, 34; as suppliant, 51–53; as treacherous, 51–52

Sisyphus, 102

Skutsch, Otto, 56–57

Social Wars, 79

Somnium Scipionis (Cicero), 94–95

Sophocles, 188

sorrows of empire, 31–32

soul, concepts of, 22; transmigration and, 83, 93–94

Spence, Sarah, 24

Spenser, Edmund, 148

stag of Silvia, 92, 116, 119

stars: Aeneas to be raised to, 110; comet or Julian star, 87, 88, 89, 129, 133; divine sonship and placement among, 85–86; linked to human souls, 93–94; Pallas as morning star, 129

statesman, 18–21

storms: in Book 1:, 18–21, 38–40, 46; *see also* winds

Suetonius, *xvi*, 110, 113

Sulla, 110

suppliants: chiasmus and mirroring, 51–54; Dido and the Carthaginians as, 53; Greeks as, 28, 51–53; Italians as, 153–54; Lycaon, 153–54, 158–59, 162–63, 170; and reversals of role, 54; Sinon as false, 51–53; Trojans as, 52–53; Turnus, *x*, 23, 125, 180

Sychaeus, 69, 118–19

Symposium (Plato), 181

Tantalus, 102

Tarquin, King, 26, 91, 143

Tarquitus, 153, 162

Tartarus: fame and, 82, 102, 103; impiety, 100–101; models for Virgil's, 101–2; Salmoneus in, *xviii*, 100–101; Theseus in, 74, 84, 85–86, 101, 103, 105, 107; and the

unnamed and unremembered dead, 101–2
taunting of the defeated, 33, 158, 160, 163–64, 169–70, 171–72, 187n17
Thaemon and Clarus, 10, 155, 157, 177–78
Theseus: Aeneus as, 85–86, 104; and Ariadne, 73, 84–85; as criminal trapped in Tartarus, 74, 84, 85–86, 101, 103–5, 107; as cult-god, 103–5; as divine offspring, 86, 90, 104–5; as epic subject, 103–4; as founder king, 104; as freed by Hercules, 103; as victim of cultural politics, 104–5
Thrace, 54n29
Thybris, 140, 147
Tiberinus, 125, 140, 141
Tiberius, 110, 113
Tiberius (Suetonius), 110
Tiber river: as Abula, 141, 147–48; as link between Books 7, 8, & 9:, 141–42
transience of Rome, 147–49
trees: fallen or cut down, 49–50, 126–27; men cut down like, 152–54; pines transformed to ships and nymphs, 151–53; similes of, 37, 39–40, 47–50, 154n7; as symbol of family, 48; tree of dreams in the underworld, 88, 98; Troy as falling, 40–41, 47–51
Trojan horse, 52
Trojans, 35; as culturally Greek, 53; and founding of Rome, 13; and Italians, 157n9; playing Greek Homeric roles, 13, 16–18, 29–30, 150–51, 155–56, 177, 189–90
Troy, fall of: Aeneas as witness to, 44, 46, 50–51; as cursed by the gods, 32; and end of Roman Republic, 29, 30, 44; human responsibility for, 38, 49–50; and internal divisions in, 29, 33, 34, 44; as result of divine actions, 45–46, 45–49, 48–49, 80–81; Rome's ascendance as dependent upon, 30–31
Turnus: as Achilles, 9, 13, 17, 22, 43, 174; Allecto as Juno's emissary instigating war, 21–25, 92, 116, 119, 120, 131; Antony linked to, 144; arms and shield of, 116; cattle images and, 116–17, 120–21, 141; Chimera-helmet of, 133; death of, 16–18, 120–21, 189–90; Dido linked to, 16, 71; as Diomedes, 5–18, 153–54; and Dira, 23–25; Hector linked to, 151, 161–62, 166–67, 172, 188; Juno's protection of, 33, 117, 158–59, 164–67; and Lavinia, 5, 120, 144; as lion, 16–17, 158, 161–62; as Memnon, 184–88; as mirror of Aeneas, *x, xv,* 9, 18, 24, 133, 186–90, 187, 188, 189–90; Pallas killed and despoiled by, 161–62, 170, 184, 187, 189; as Patroclus, 157, 161; piety of, 142; as representative of young Italy, 177; and Sarpedon, 151, 157, 178–79; as suppliant, *x,* 23, 125, 180; and Tiber river, 142–43

Ufens, 141
Ulysses, Odysseus, 21, 30, 43–44, 51–52, 56, 69, 97, 101
underworld: Anchises as guide, 44, 60; Campi Lugentes in, 101–2; Cumaean sibyl on difficulty of return from, *xiv,* 1, 83–84; Deiphobus in, 60–61; Dido in, 60–61; as dream sequence, 88n12, 98; few and many in, 86, 91, 93, 95; as hall of fame and memory, 82, 95–96; in Homer's *Odyssey,* 61, 82, 84, 97, 101–2, 181; justice in the, 74, 87, 103–5; as labyrinth, 74, 84–85, 95, 98, 105–12; parade of shades in, 27, 62–63, 65, 84, 87, 94, 109; as place of fame, 82–84, 95–98, 103–5; as place of forgetting, 82, 102; and poetic compulsion to bring back the dead, 107–9; poetic justice and, 84; and shades as *eidola* (images), 97; and transmigration souls, 83, 93–94; *see also* Elysium

Venus: Aeneas's shield as gift from, 115–16, 127, 129, 132; appearance to Aeneas, 50–51, 189; and Dido's passion, 67–68, 74; and instigation of Trojan war, 45; interventions on behalf of Aeneas, 15, 44–48, 71, 127; and judgment of Paris as cause of war, 44–45, 165; Julius Caesar as

Venus (*continued*)
   descendant of, 110–11; as mother of Aeneas, 92–93, 136–37; prophecy of Jupiter to, 49, 85, 92–93, 98; Temple of Venus Genetrix, 110–11n57; and Vulcan, 136–37

Vita (Donatus), *xvi–xvii*

Vitalis, Janus, 148

Volcens, 184

Vulcan: and Aetnean cyclopes, 139; Cacus as son of, 116, 131, 133, 136, 138; as creator of Aeneas's shield and arms, *xiv*, 4, 26, 67, 114, 116, 128, 132–33, 137–38, 139, 174, 186; as fire god, 136–38; lovemaking of Venus and, 136–38, 183

war: and animality, 121; and binary oppositions, 2; civil (*See* civil wars, Roman); and civilization as violent, 139; as context for criticism of the *Aeneid*, *x*; Dido's curse of continual, 58–59; as equalizer, 175; as harvest of trees, 49–50; human motives for, 38–39, 47, 49–50; Italians as warlike farmers, 118–19; as natural disaster, 37–41; reciprocity of, 2–12, 18, 29–30, 42–44, 48–49, 55, 59–60, 66, 133–34, 135, 146, 150–51, 155–79, 189; and wealth, 118–19, 144

weapons: bronze and, 114–15, 117 (*See also* shield of Aeneas); transformed to and from peaceful tools, 50, 119–20; *see also* armor; shield of Aeneas

weeping and tears: of Aeneas at images of fall of Troy, 30, 31; and Aeneas's love for Dido, 72, 75; of Hercules, 97, 156, 157n9, 161, 164–65, 174; of Juno, 165; of Odysseus (Homer), 31

winds: Aeolus, as lord of, *xviii*, 15, 18–19, 35, 38; calmed by Neptune, 18–21; Eurus, 39–40, 46; Notus, 38–40, 46; war as storm, 39–40; Zephyrus, 39–40, 46

wolves, 38–39; on the shield of Aeneas, 115

Xerxes, 145–46

A NOTE ON THE TYPE

This book has been composed in Arno, an Old-style serif typeface in the classic Venetian tradition, designed by Robert Slimbach at Adobe.